Everyday Stalinism

Everyday Stalinism

Ordinary Life in Extraordinary Times:
Soviet Russia in the 1930s

Sheila Fitzpatrick

New York   Oxford
OXFORD UNIVERSITY PRESS
1999

Oxford University Press

Oxford New York
Athens Auckland Bangkok Bogotá
Buenos Aires Calcutta Cape Town Dar es Salaam
Delhi Florence Hong Kong Istanbul Karachi
Kuala Lumpur Madras Madrid Melbourne
Mexico City Mumbai Nairobi Paris Singapore
Taipei Tokyo Toronto Warsaw

and associated companies in
Berlin Ibadan

Library of Congress Cataloging-in-Publication Data
Fitzpatrick, Sheila
Everyday Stalinism : ordinary life in extraordinary times.
Soviet Russia in the 1930s / Sheila Fitzpatrick.
p. cm. Includes bibliographical references
and index.
ISBN 0–19–505000–2
1. Soviet Union—Social conditions.
2. Soviet Union—History—1925–1953.
3. City and town life—Soviet Union.
4. Communism—Soviet Union.
I. Title.
HN523.F57 1999 306'.0947—dc21 98–15421

1 3 5 7 9 8 6 4 2
Printed in the United States of America
on acid-free paper

C

To My Students

C

Contents

Acknowledgments

This book has been a long time in the making—almost twenty years, if one goes back to its first incarnation; ten years in its present form. Over that period, I acquired intellectual debts to so many people that I cannot list them all. Those whom I acknowledge here made a direct contribution in the final stages of the project.

Jörg Baberowski, Dietrich Beyrau, Terry Martin, and Yuri Slezkine were kind enough to read the whole manuscript and make detailed comments that were extremely helpful. To Yuri I owe an additional debt for answering all my e-mails about Russian linguistic usage and esoteric aspects of Soviet culture. In the sphere of politics and police matters, J. Arch Getty generously played a similar role. James Andrews, Stephen Bittner, Jonathan Bone, and Joshua Sanborn aided me as research assistants at various times. Michael Danos read the whole manuscript in all its drafts and made useful editorial suggestions as well as helping to shape my thinking about the topic. Thanks are also due to two fine editors at Oxford University Press: Nancy Lane, an old friend, without whose tireless prodding and cajoling over many years the book might never have been written, and Thomas LeBien, whose support and good advice made the final stages of the project easier.

It is a particular pleasure to acknowledge my debt to a remarkable cohort of students at the University of Chicago who wrote or are writing Ph.D. dissertations dealing with aspects of the 1930s: Golfo Alexopoulos, Jonathan Bone, Michael David, James Harris, Julie Hessler, Matthew Lenoe, Terry Martin, John McCannon, Matthew Payne, and Kiril Tomoff. I have learnt a great deal from their work and from working with them; and it is in recognition of this exceptionally stimulating and happy collaboration that I dedicate this book to past and present students. I have also benefited from working with other current and former members of the Chicago Russian Studies Workshop, notably Stephen Bittner, Christopher Burton, Julie Gilmour, Nicholas Glossop, Charles Hachten, Steven Harris, Jane Ormrod, Emily Pyle, Steven Richmond, and Joshua Sanborn, as well as my much-valued colleagues, Richard Hellie and Ronald Suny.

Other young scholars whose recent work on the 1930s has been particularly useful to me include Sarah Davies, Jochen Hellbeck, Oleg Khlevniuk, Stephen Kotkin, and Vadim Volkov.

I thank the John Simon Guggenheim Foundation, the John D. and Catherine T. MacArthur Foundation, IREX, the National Council for Soviet and East European Research, and the University of Texas at Austin for support at various stages of the project. Equally heartfelt gratitude goes to the University of Chicago for providing the best of all possible environments for scholarship.

EXPLANATORY NOTE

To make it easier for the reader, I have used familiar anglicizations of names of well-known figures like Trotsky, Tukhachevsky, Lunacharsky, Gorky, Vyshinsky, Zinoviev, Mikoyan, and Tolstoy. Given names like Natalia, Maria, and Evgenia are rendered without the extra "i" that a strict transliteration requires. For other names I have followed the standard transliteration model set by the Library of Congress, except that in the text I have not used diacritical marks for proper names and place names.

Since this is a social history, I saw no reason to burden the reader with a proliferation of undecipherable institutional names and acronyms in the text. Where necessary, elucidation about institutional provenance is given in the footnotes. I have referred throughout to "Ministries" and "Ministers" in place of the "People's Commissariats" and "People's Commissars" that are strictly correct for this period. In my text, "province" or "region" stands for the Russian *oblast'* and *krai*, and "district" for *raion*.

Everyday Stalinism

Introduction

This book is about the everyday life of ordinary people, "little men" as opposed to the great. But the life these ordinary people lived was not, in their own understanding and probably ours, a normal life. For those who live in extraordinary times, normal life becomes a luxury. The upheavals and hardships of the 1930s disrupted normalcy, making it something Soviet citizens strove for but generally failed to achieve. This book is an exploration of the everyday and the extraordinary in Stalin's Russia and how they interacted. It describes the ways in which Soviet citizens tried to live ordinary lives in the extraordinary circumstances of Stalinism. It presents a portrait of an emerging social species, *Homo Sovieticus*, for which Stalinism was the native habitat.[1]

There are many theories about how to write the history of everyday life. Some understand the "everyday" to mean primarily the sphere of private life, embracing questions of family, home, upbringing of children, leisure, friendship, and sociability. Others look primarily at worklife and the behaviors and attitudes generated at the workplace. Scholars of everyday life under totalitarian regimes often focus on active or passive resistance to the regime, while a number of studies of peasant life focus on "everyday resistance," meaning the mundane and apparently everyday ways in which people in a dependent position express their resentment at their masters.[2] This book shares with many recent studies of everyday life a focus on practice—that is, the forms of behavior and strategies of survival and advancement that people develop to cope with particular social and political situations.[3] But the book was not written to illustrate any general theory of the everyday. Its subject is extraordinary everydayness.

The times were extraordinary because of the revolution of 1917 and the upheavals, no less deracinating and disruptive, that accompanied the regime's turn to rapid industrialization and collectivization of agriculture at the end of the 1920s. These were times of massive social dislocation, when millions of people changed their occupations and places of residence. Old hierarchies were overturned, old values and habits discredited. The new values, including condemnation of religion as "superstition," were puzzling and unacceptable to most of the older generation, although the young often embraced them with fervor. It was declared to be a heroic age of struggle to destroy the old world and create a new world and a new man. The regime, committed to social, cultural, and economic transformation, rammed through radical changes regardless of the human cost, and despised those who wanted to rest from the revolutionary struggle. Savage punishments, worse than anything known under the old regime, were inflicted on "enemies" and sometimes randomly on the population. Large numbers of people found themselves stigmatized as "social aliens" in the new society.

All these circumstances were part of the reason Soviet citizens felt they were not living normal lives. But when they made this complaint, they usually had, in addition, something specific in mind. The most extraordinary aspect of Soviet urban life, from the perspective of those living it, was the sudden disappearance of goods from the stores at the beginning of the 1930s and the beginning of an era of chronic shortages. Everything, particularly the basics of food, clothing, shoes, and housing, was in short supply. This had to do with the move from a market economy to one based on centralized state planning at the end of the 1920s. But famine was also a cause of urban food shortages in the early 1930s, and for some time ordinary people, as well as political leaders, hoped that the shortages were temporary. Gradually, however, scarcity began to look less like a temporary phenomenon than something permanent and systemic. Indeed, this was to be a society built on shortages, with all the hardship, discomfort, inconvenience, and waste of citizens' time associated with them. The *Homo Sovieticus* emerging in the 1930s was a species whose most highly developed skills involved the hunting and gathering of scarce goods in an urban environment.

This is a book about life in urban Russia in the heyday of Stalinism. It is about crowded communal apartments, abandoned wives and husbands who failed to pay child support, shortages of food and clothing, and endless queuing. It is about popular grumbling at these conditions, and how the government reacted to it. It is about the webs of bureaucratic red tape that often turned everyday life into a nightmare, and about the ways that ordinary citizens tried to circumvent them, primarily patronage and the ubiquitous system of personal connections known as *blat*. It is about what it meant to be privileged in Stalinist society, as well as what it meant to be one of the millions of social outcasts. It is about the police surveillance that was endemic to this society, and the epidemics of terror like the Great Purges that periodically cast it into turmoil.

For *Homo Sovieticus*, the state was a central and ubiquitous presence. In the first place, it was the formal distributor of goods and the near-monopolistic producer of them, so that even the black market dealt largely in state products and relied heavily on state connections. In the second place, all urban citizens worked for the state, whether they were workers or typists or teachers or shop assistants: there were virtually no alternative employers. In the third place, the state was a tireless regulator of life, issuing and demanding an endless stream of documents and permits without which the simplest operations of daily life were impossible. As everybody including the leaders admitted, the Soviet bureaucracy, recently greatly expanded to cope with its new range of tasks and thus full of inexperienced and unqualified officials, was slow, cumbersome, inefficient, and often corrupt. Law and legal process were held in low regard, and the actions of officialdom, from top to bottom, were marked by arbitrariness and favoritism. Citizens felt themselves at the mercy of officials and the regime; they speculated endlessly about the people "up there" and what new surprises they might have in store for the population, but felt powerless to influence them. Even the jokes that Soviet citizens loved to tell, despite the danger of being caught in "anti-Soviet conversation," were typically not about sex or mothers-in-law or even ethnicity but about bureaucrats, the Communist Party, and the secret police.

The pervasiveness of the state in urban Russia of the 1930s has led me to define the "everyday" for the purposes of this book in terms of everyday interactions that in some way involved the state. In the Soviet context, such a definition largely excludes topics like friendship, love, and some aspects of leisure and private sociability. But the definition can scarcely be seen as narrow, since it includes such diverse topics as shopping, traveling, celebrating, telling jokes, finding an apartment, getting an education, securing a job, advancing in one's career, cultivating patrons and connections, marrying and rearing children, writing complaints and denunciations, voting, and trying to steer clear of the secret police.

The term "Stalinism" in the title needs some explanation. Stalinism often connotes an ideology and/or a political system. I use it here as a shorthand for the complex of institutions, structures, and rituals that made up the habitat of *Homo Sovieticus* in the Stalin era. Communist Party rule, Marxist–Leninist ideology, rampant bureaucracy, leader cults, state control over production and distribution, social engineering, affirmative action on behalf of workers, stigmatization of "class enemies," police surveillance, terror, and the various informal, personalistic arrangements whereby people at every level sought to protect themselves and obtain scarce goods, were all part of the Stalinist habitat. While some of this was already in existence in the 1920s, it was the 1930s that saw the establishment of the distinctive Stalinist habitat, much of which survived into the post-Stalin era right up to Gorbachev's *perestroika* in the 1980s. In my usage, Stalinist and Soviet are overlapping concepts, the former representing both a maximalist version of the latter and its defining moment.

MILESTONES

Our story has a clear starting point: the transformation of everyday life in Russia that occurred at the end of the 1920s and beginning of the 1930s following the abandonment of the relatively moderate and gradualist New Economic Policy (NEP) and the adoption of collectivization and the First Five-Year Plan.

The term "Stalin's revolution" has been used for this transition, and that conveys well its violent, destructive, and utopian character. But this revolution was largely the result of state initiative, not popular movements, and it did not result in a change of political leadership. The point of the revolution, in Stalin's eyes, was to lay the economic foundations for socialism by rooting out private enterprise and using state planning to promote rapid economic development.

In the towns, private trade and private businesses were closed down. The state took over distribution as part of a new system of centralized state economic planning that was vastly ambitious but poorly thought out. Planning was seen in heroic terms as the conquest of hitherto uncontrollable economic forces. The planning process had an immediate objective, which was to carry out rapid industrialization, particularly in underdeveloped regions of the country, according to the First Five-Year Plan (1929–32). That involved massive investment in heavy industry, skimping in the area of consumer goods, and substantial involuntary sacrifice of living standards by the general population to pay for it all.

It had been the leaders' hope that the peasantry could be made to pay most of the costs of industrialization; the collectivization of peasant agriculture that accompanied the First Five-Year Plan was intended to achieve this effect by forcing peasants to accept low state prices for their goods. But that hope was disappointed, and the urban population ended up bearing a considerable part of the burden. Collectivization turned out to be a very costly project. Several million "kulaks" (prosperous peasants regarded as exploiters) were expropriated and deported to distant parts of the country. Millions more fled to the cities. The results were food shortages, rationing, and overcrowding in the towns and, in 1932–33, famine in most of the major grain-growing regions of the country. Although famine was a temporary condition, shortages of food and all kinds of consumer goods were not. Marxists had expected that socialism would bring abundance. Under Soviet conditions, however, socialism and scarcity turned out to be inextricably linked.

In politics, social relations, and culture, the First Five-Year Plan period was also a watershed. Stalin and his supporters defeated the last open opposition within the Soviet Communist movement, the Left Opposition, expelling its leaders from the party at the end of 1927. A more tentative Right Opposition was defeated without an open contest a few years later. Stalin emerged from this not only as the party's undisputed leader but also as the object of an orchestrated cult that can be dated from the celebrations of his fiftieth birthday in 1929. The secret police expanded mightily to handle the kulak deportations and other punitive operations, and these years also saw the return of the old Tsarist practice of administrative exile and the establishment of Gulag's labor camp empire.

Isolationism was a hallmark of the First Five-Year Plan period. This was a throwback to the Civil War of 1918–20, in which the young Soviet state had been isolated both by the hostility of all the major Western powers and its own intransigence. During NEP, despite the state monopoly on external trade on which Lenin insisted, cultural and economic contacts with the outside world revived in a limited way, and there was a fair amount of traffic across the Soviet Union's frontiers. A major war scare in 1927 changed the climate, and soon after the government decided to put the country on a "pre-mobilization" footing, where it remained throughout the 1930s. From this time on, Soviet frontiers were largely closed to traffic, both human and goods, and the Soviet Union declared its intention of achieving "economic autarchy." In the short term, this move had the beneficial, if accidental, effect of cutting the Soviet Union off from the Great Depression. In the long term, however, it set the stage for a retreat into suspicious, parochial isolation that was in some ways reminiscent of Muscovite Russia in the sixteenth century.[4]

Increased suspicion of foreign enemies at this period was matched by a sharp rise in hostility to "class enemies" at home: kulaks, priests, members of the prerevolutionary nobility, former capitalists, and others whose social class made them, in the Communists' view, natural opponents of the Soviet state. But stigmatization of class enemies already had its history. The 1918 Constitution of the Russian Republic deprived various categories of "non-toilers"—former exploiters—of the vote, and these disfranchised people were also subject to a wide range of civil disabilities such as exclusion from higher education and extra taxation. Despite party leaders' efforts during NEP not to "fan the flames of class war," rank-and-file Communists always favored policies that strongly discriminated against "former people," members of the old privileged classes, and in favor of workers, the new "dictator class." These instincts were given free rein in the First Five-Year Plan period.

Another feature of this period was a tumultuous "cultural revolution" in which members of the prerevolutionary intelligentsia, known as "bourgeois specialists," were a prime target of Communist attack. During NEP, Lenin and other leaders had insisted on the state's need for the specialists' expertise, even though recommending that they be supervised closely by Communists. But this changed dramatically in the spring of 1928, when a group of engineers from the Shakhty region of the Donbass was charged with "wrecking" (meaning intentionally damaging the Soviet economy) and treasonous contacts with foreign capitalists and intelligence services. The Shakhty trial, the first of a series of such show trials, heralded a wave of arrests among engineers and, to a lesser extent, other professions.[5]

Cultural revolution had an "affirmative action" component as well. Announcing the urgent need for the Soviet Union to acquire its own "workers' and peasants' intelligentsia" to replace the "bourgeois intelligentsia" inherited from the old regime, Stalin initiated a major program for sending workers, peasants, and young Communists to higher education, particularly engineering school, so that they could prepare for leadership in the new society. The intense drive to "proletarianize" the intelligentsia lasted only a few years, but made a lasting impact. Its beneficiaries collectively achieved extraordinarily rapid promotion during the Great Purges. Not only were they a core group within professions like engineering, they also constituted a remarkably long-lasting political elite—the "Brezhnev generation"—whose tenure in power started in the immediate prewar years and continued for almost half a century.

But it was not only future Brezhnevs who were climbing the ladder at this time. Many of the semiliterate low-level bureaucrats whose ineptness and self-satisfaction were regularly criticized in *Pravda* and lampooned in the humorous journal *Krokodil* were affirmative-action beneficiaries too. The whole Soviet bureaucracy was full of inexperienced people without proper training for their jobs. In some branches like state trade it was not only individual officials but whole institutions that were undergoing a high-pressure process of learning on the job.

The ranks of labor, like those of management, were full of raw recruits. During the First Five-Year Plan period alone, more than ten million peasants moved to towns and became wage earners. The massive migration produced a housing crisis of mammoth proportions. Like other kinds of scarcity, this one turned out to be a permanent feature of Soviet life, with families jammed for decades in tiny single rooms in communal apartments with shared kitchens and (if such existed) bathrooms. During the famine, as the flood of migrants to the cities grew unmanageable, the state introduced internal passports for the first time since the revolution and set up a system of urban residence permits. Both were administered by the OGPU (secret police, precursor to the NKVD), which brought a new dimension of control over citizens' movements that complicated life enormously for many people.

In 1935, Stalin announced that "Life has become better, life has become more cheerful." This marked a relaxation that some saw, over-optimistically, as a partial return to the spirit of NEP. None of the major substantive policy initiatives of the First Five-Year Plan period, like collectivization and the outlawing of urban private enterprise and trade, were reversed, but there was some tinkering at the margins and a softening of rhetoric. Rationing was lifted (prematurely, in the opinion of some workers who could not pay the new "commercial" prices). The "bourgeois intelligentsia" was rehabilitated, emerging warily to a position of privilege in a society where material rewards were increasingly differentiated. The new "Stalin" Constitution of the Soviet Union of 1936 promised a dazzling array of civil rights to Soviet citizens, including freedom of assembly and freedom of speech, but failed to deliver them.

Life was easier during the "three good years," 1934–36, than it had been during the First Five-Year Plan. But this is not saying much, given that what immediately preceded these years was famine and industrial crisis. The first of the "good" years was shadowed by the recent famine, and the third, 1936, produced so poor a harvest that there were long breadlines in the towns and panicky rumors about a new famine. In popular memory, indeed, the only really good year of the 1930s in Russia seems to have been 1937—ironically, the first year of the Great Purges—when the harvest was the best in the decade and there was plenty of food in the stores.

Politically, too, there were problems. At the end of 1934, just before the lifting of rationing and promulgation of the "Life has become better" slogan, the Leningrad party leader Sergei Kirov was assassinated in Leningrad. This was the single most shocking political incident of the decade, comparable in American history to the assassination of President John Kennedy in 1963. Although no conspiracy has ever been proven and the murder may well have been the act of a single, disgruntled man, many people believed (and continue to believe) that this was the result of a conspiracy. Stalin pointed the finger at the former Left Oppositionist leaders, Lev Kamenev and Grigorii Zinoviev, who were tried twice for complicity, receiving the death sentence at the second trial in August 1936. Others have pointed the finger at Stalin.

Terror—meaning extralegal state violence against groups and randomly chosen citizens—was so frequently used that it must be regarded as a systemic characteristic of Stalinism in the 1930s. Kulaks, priests, Nepmen (the term for private businessmen used during NEP), and "bourgeois specialists" were the chosen victims at the beginning of the decade, and "former people" were targetted after Kirov's death. But the most spectacular episode of terror was undoubtedly the Great Purges of 1937–38, which are discussed in detail in the last chapter. Quantitatively, the scope of this terror was not too different from that waged against kulaks during "dekulakization." [6] What made its impact greater, at least as far as the urban population was concerned, was that the elites, including the Communist elite, suffered disproportionately. Despite the elite focus, however, there was also an important random element in this terror. Anybody could be exposed as an "enemy of the people"; the enemies, like witches in earlier ages, bore no reliable external marks.

The fear of external enemies that had characterized the Soviet Union throughout the 1920s and 1930s, including periods where no significant threat was visible to outside observers, was part of the dynamics of the Great Purges, especially in the purge of Marshal Tukhachevsky and other military leaders (accused of being German spies) and the confessions of the accused in the show trials of 1937 and 1938 that their anti-Soviet activities were carried out in cooperation with foreign intelligence services, notably the German and the Japanese.

As an older cohort of Communist leaders and administrators was being destroyed in the Great Purges, a generation of new men, many of them beneficiaries of the affirmative-action programs earlier in the decade, was coming to the fore. Whatever the merits of the new men in the long term,[7] in the late 1930s they were inexperienced newcomers struggling to restore an economy and administrative system that had been badly damaged by the Great Purges. War, long feared, was now truly imminent, but the Red Army was in disarray, not only because of purge losses but also because it was in the process of rapid expansion and conversion to a standing army.[8]

A policy shift of the late 1930s that deserves attention because of its impact on everyday life was the tightening of labor discipline by the laws of 1938 and 1940 introducing stricter punishments for absenteeism and lateness to work. Although there was already a fairly tough labor discipline law on the books from 1932, it was honored in the breach rather than the observance. The new laws were more stringent, that of 1940 mandating dismissal and imposing criminal penalties for any worker or employee who was 20 minutes late for work. Given the unreliability of public transport, not to mention that of Soviet clocks and watches, this put every employed person at risk and aroused great resentment in the urban population. As far as ordinary wage-earners were concerned, the negative impact of the labor laws was probably much stronger than that of the Great Purges, or indeed of anything since the acute food shortages and sharp drop in the standard of living at the beginning of the decade.

STORIES

People understand and remember their lives in terms of stories. These stories make sense out of the scattered data of ordinary life, providing a context, imposing a pattern that shows where one has come from and where one is going. In theory, the possible range of stories is as large as the human imagination, but in practice it is much smaller. Most people internalize stories that are common property in a given society at a particular time. The purpose of this section is to introduce the reader to some of the "common property" stories through which Soviet citizens understood their individual and collective lives.

In the Soviet Union in the 1930s, the regime had a keen interest in shaping such stories. This was the function of agitation and propaganda, a basic branch of Communist Party activity. For the purposes of this book, however, where the stories came from is less important than what they said about the past, present, and future, and the connections between them. One of the stories that was most widely disseminated in the 1930s may be called "The Radiant Future," after Aleksandr Zinoviev's book of that name.[9] In this story, the present was the time when the future, socialism, was being built. For the time being, there must be sacrifice and hardship. The rewards would come later.

According to the "Radiant Future" story, Soviet people could be confident that there *would* be rewards because of their knowledge of historical laws, derived from Marx. In the October Revolution of 1917, the proletariat, headed by the Bolsheviks, had overthrown the exploiting capitalists, whose concentration of wealth in a few hands had left the majority to poverty and deprivation. Socialism was the predetermined outcome of proletarian revolution. This prediction was visibly being fulfilled in the 1930s as the industrialization drive and the elimination of small capitalist enterprise laid the economic foundations of socialism. By abolishing exploitation and privilege and increasing production and productivity, socialism would necessarily bring abundance and raise the living standards of all. Hence, a radiant future was assured.

This knowledge about the future had implications for the understanding of the present. A person who did not know the story might look at Soviet life and see only hardship and misery, not understanding that temporary sacrifices must be made in order to build socialism. Writers and artists were urged to cultivate a sense of "socialist realism"—seeing life as it was becoming, rather than life as it was—rather than a literal or "naturalistic" realism. But socialist realism was a Stalinist *mentalité*, not just an artistic style. Ordinary citizens also developed the ability to see things as they were becoming and ought to be, rather than as they were. An empty ditch was a canal in the making; a vacant lot where old houses or a church had been torn down, littered with rubbish and weeds, was a future park.[10]

In its crudest forms, "socialist realism" was hard to distinguish from outright deception—the creation of "Potemkin villages" where nothing lay behind the facade. During the famine, for example, the press depicted collective farms as happy and prosperous, with merry peasants gathering around laden tables in the evening hours to dance and sing to the accordion.[11]

Another story, propagated by the regime but accepted by many citizens, may be called "Out of Backwardness." In this story, which showed the present in relationship to the past rather than the future, the Soviet Union was overcoming the legacy of backwardness inherited from Tsarist Russia. Backwardness, according to a Soviet dictionary definition of 1938, was "a deficiency of development," whose use was illustrated by the sentence: "The Great October Socialist revolution liquidated the age-old backwardness of our country."[12] But that was an optimistic formulation: "liquidation of backwardness" was very much an ongoing project in the 1930s.

Imperial Russia's backwardness (as understood in the 1930s) had many dimensions. Economically, it was a late industrializer whose predominantly peasant agriculture was technically primitive. Militarily, it had suffered humiliating defeats in the Crimean War of the 1850s, the Russo-Japanese War of 1904–5, and the First World War. Socially, its citizens still belonged to legal estates, as in Western Europe in the Middle Ages, and peasants had been enserfed until 1861. Culturally, the literacy and education level of the population was low by comparison with Western Europe. The Soviet Union, accordingly, was overcoming backwardness by industrializing and modernizing peasant agriculture. Military modernization rested on the foundations of industrialization, in particular the buildup of defense industry. The country was striving energetically toward universal literacy and universal seven-year schooling. Its citizens, no longer classified by estate, were guaranteed equal rights by the 1936 Constitution.

In the "Out of Backwardness" story, the contrast of "then" and "now" was very important. *Then* workers' and peasants' children had no chance of an education; *now* they could become engineers. *Then* peasants had been exploited by gentry landlords; *now* the landlords were gone and they held the land collectively. *Then* workers had been abused by their masters; *now* workers themselves were masters. *Then* the people had been deceived by priests and lulled by the opiate of religion; *now* their eyes had been opened to science and enlightenment.

While backwardness was a problem for the Soviet Union as a whole, some people were obviously more backward than others. The Soviet Union was a multiethnic state, but the "friendship of peoples" that linked its different ethnic groups was often represented in terms of an elder brother, Soviet Russia, leading and teaching younger siblings. The Muslim peoples of Soviet Central Asia and the reindeer-herding "small peoples" of the north, regarded as the most backward in the Union, were the archetypal beneficiaries of the Soviet civilizing mission, which tapped veins of idealism that were Russian as well as Communist.[13] But ethnicity was not the only determinant of backwardness. Peasants were backward compared to town-dwellers. Women were backward, generally speaking, compared to men. The Soviet civilizing mission was raising the cultural level of all these backward groups.

The last of the stories that informed Soviet thinking may be entitled, in the words of a popular song, "If Tomorrow Brings War." This possibility was never far from the minds of ordinary people and political leaders alike in the 1930s. The fear of war was based on experience as well as ideology. The experiences were the war with Japan in 1904–5, the First World War (interrupted by revolution in Russia, thus lacking a sense of closure in popular memory), and the Civil War, in which numerous foreign powers had intervened on the White side. Ideologically, the premise was that the capitalist nations that encircled the Soviet Union could never be reconciled to the existence of the world's first and only socialist state. Capitalism and socialism represented radically opposing principles that could not coexist. The capitalists would try to overthrow the Soviet Union militarily as soon as a good opportunity presented itself, just as they had done in the Civil War.

War, then, was a likely if not inevitable outcome, the ultimate test of the strength of Soviet society and the commitment of its citizens. The present, in this picture, became a breathing space "before the new struggle with capitalism begins."[14] Whether the Soviet Union survived that "last, decisive battle" (in the words of *The International*, known to every Soviet schoolchild) would depend on how much socialism had been built—measuring socialism in the most concrete way possible as numbers of new blast furnaces, tractor and tank factories, hydroelectric dams, and kilometers of railroad track.

The war motif was constantly elaborated in the press, which provided detailed surveys of the international situation, with particular emphasis on the Nazi regime in Germany, the Japanese in Manchuria, the possibility of a Fascist takeover in France, and the Spanish Civil War as a site of confrontation between "democratic" and "reactionary" forces. State policies were predicated on the danger of war. The point of the rapid industrialization program, Stalin underlined, was that without it the country would be vulnerable to its enemies and would "go under" within ten years. The purpose of the Great Purges, as described by propagandists at the time, was to rid the country of traitors, hirelings of the Soviet Union's enemies, who would betray it in time of war. Popular attention was equally engaged: in a society that lived on rumor, the most frequent rumors of all concerned war and its likely consequences.

A NOTE ON CLASS

So far, class—in the Marxist sense of social groups linked by shared consciousness and relationship to the means of production—has received almost no discussion. This may seem strange, since after all this was a regime that described itself as a "dictatorship of the proletariat" and espoused a Marxist ideology based on class. The terminology of class was omnipresent—"kulaks," "bourgeois specialists," "class enemies," "class war." Moreover, whole generations of Soviet scholars have used class as the basic framework of analysis. In Soviet usage, the term for everyday life, *byt*, rarely appeared without a class modifier: working-class life, peasant life, nomadic life, and so on. Even the classic work on Soviet everyday life, written by American scholars in a non-Marxist framework, used the standard class units of Soviet prewar statistics: workers, peasants, and intelligentsia.[15] Why, then, am I being so reckless as to ignore class as a basic unit of analysis in this book?

One reason is pragmatic: I am interested in the experiences and practices that were common to the urban population as a whole, not just parts of it. (This is why work, a part of everyday life that varies greatly from one occupational group to another, is not a central topic in this study.[16]) But there are other reasons to be wary of class as an objective category in Soviet life.

In the first place, the "great proletarian revolution" of October had the paradoxical effect of declassing Soviet society, at least in the short run. The old privileged classes were expropriated. Millions of other citizens were uprooted and lost their social moorings. Even the industrial working class, the Bolsheviks' pride and joy, fell apart during the Civil War as workers returned to their native villages or went away to serve in the Red Army.[17] The interval of NEP allowed the working class to re-form, and other social structures also started to solidify. But then came the upheavals of the First Five-Year Plan and collectivization, uprooting millions once again, "liquidating" whole classes, prompting an enormous influx of peasants into the urban labor force as well as considerable upward mobility from the old working class. This was in effect a second declassing, only a decade after the first one.

In the second place, the Bolsheviks' attachment to the idea of class, and the political uses they made of it, corrupted it as a sociological category. For the Bolsheviks, proletarians were allies and members of the bourgeoisie were enemies. The new regime introduced systematic discrimination on the basis of class in all sorts of contexts important for everyday life: education, justice, housing, rations, and so on. Even the right to vote was reserved for those who came from the "toiling" classes. A young worker had privileged access to higher education, Communist Party membership, and a host of other benefits, while the son of a noble or a priest suffered corresponding disadvantages and restrictions. What this meant, of course, was that people from "bad" social backgrounds had a strong incentive to hide their class and try to pass as proletarians or poor peasants.[18]

To complicate matters further, the party defined itself as "the vanguard of the proletariat." That meant that the concepts of "proletarian" and "Bolshevik" ("Communist")[19] became hopelessly entangled. "Proletarian" soon became a term denoting political loyalty and ideological correctness rather than social position. "Bourgeois" and "petty-bourgeois," similarly, became catch-all terms implying political unreliability and ideological deviation.

Of course, class was important in Soviet society. But it was not important in the ways one might expect, for example, as a basis for social and political organization or collective action. Trade unions, the main form of workers' class organization, were emasculated during the First Five-Year Plan, when they effectively lost the right to defend labor interests against management. Their main role in the 1930s was to administer benefits like pensions, sick leave, and vacations for their members. Other kinds of voluntary association withered, were closed down, or came under tight state control at the same period.

The main way class was significant in Soviet society was as a state classificatory system determining the rights and obligations of different groups of citizens. By stressing class, in another paradox, the regime had managed to engineer something like a de facto reversion to the old and despised estate system, where your rights and privileges depended on whether you were legally classified as a noble, a merchant, a member of the clerical estate, or a peasant. In the Soviet context, "class" (social position) was an attribute that defined one's relationship to the state. A citizen's social position was entered in his passport, along with his nationality, age, and sex, just as social estate had been written in passports in Tsarist times. Peasants (kolkhozniks) belonged to a Stalinist "estate" that was not entitled to passports—although, in contrast to urban "estates," its members had the right to trade at the kolkhoz markets. Members of the new "service nobility" enjoyed a variety of privileges including access to closed stores, dachas, and use of chauffeur-driven government cars.[20]

Relations between classes were comparatively unimportant in Stalinist society. What mattered was the relationship to the state—in particular, the state as an allocator of goods in a economy of chronic scarcity. This brings us to a final paradox about class in Stalinist society. In Marxist theory, it is the relationship to the means of production that is crucial: there is a class of owners, a class of hired hands who own nothing but their labor, and so on. In the Soviet context, however, the state owned the means of production. Depending on one's interpretation, that could either mean that everyone had become an owner or that everyone had joined a proletariat exploited by the owner-state. But it certainly meant that production no longer served as a meaningful basis of class structure in Soviet urban society. In fact, the meaningful social hierarchies of the 1930s were based not on production but consumption.[21] "Class" status in the real world was a matter of having greater or lesser access to goods, which in turn was largely a function of the degree of entitlement to privilege that the state allowed.

A word of warning about the scope of this book: its subject is everyday life in Russia, not the Soviet Union, and the time period with which it deals is the 1930s, not the whole of the Stalin era. While I believe the patterns described here will often be found in non-Russian regions and republics of the Soviet Union, there will also be significant variations. A similar caveat may be made about the postwar period. Patterns of everyday life persisted—indeed, were to persist in many ways until the end of the Soviet Union—but the Second World War also brought significant changes, so that the experience of the 1930s cannot simply be extrapolated into the 1940s and 1950s. Finally, it should be noted that this is a study of urban life, not rural. The latter is treated in my book *Stalin's Peasants* (1994).

1

"The Party Is Always Right"

Few histories of everyday life start with a chapter on government and bureaucracy. But it is one of the peculiarities of our subject that the state can never be kept out, try though we may. Soviet citizens attempting to live ordinary lives were continually running up against the state[1] in one of its multifarious aspects. Their lives were tossed around by Communist policies; their tempers were tried on a daily basis by incompetent and arbitrary officials, clerks, and salespeople, all working for the state. This was the omnipresent context of Soviet everyday life; there was no way to live without it. Thus, our story begins with an overview of the Stalinist regime and its institutions and practices, particularly the Communist Party's style of rule and mentalité.

At the end of the 1920s, the conventional starting point for the Stalin period, the Soviet regime had been in power for not much more than a decade. Its leaders still thought of themselves as revolutionaries, and they behaved like revolutionaries too. They meant to transform and modernize Russian society, a process they described as "building socialism." Since they believed that this revolutionary transformation was in the long-term interests of the people, they were willing to force it through, even when, as with collectivization, a majority of the relevant population clearly opposed it. They explained popular resistance as a result of the backwardness, prejudices, and fears of the unenlightened masses. The Communists' sense of mission and intellectual superiority was far too great to allow them to be swayed by mere majority opinion. In this, they were like all other revolutionaries, for what revolutionary worth his salt has ever conceded that "the people's will" is something different from the mission he has undertaken to carry out on the people's behalf?

"Backwardness" was a very important word in the Soviet Communist lexicon: it stood for everything that belonged to old Russia and needed to be changed in the name of progress and culture. Religion, a form of superstitition, was backward. Peasant farming was backward. Small-scale private trade was backward, not to mention petty-bourgeois, another favorite term of opprobrium. It was the Communists' task to turn backward, agrarian, petty-bourgeois Russia into a socialist, urbanized, industrialized giant with modern technology and a literate workforce.

For all the party's dedication to the idea of modernization, however, Soviet Communist rule in the 1930s was definitely acquiring some neotraditional features that few would have predicted in 1917. One obvious example was the evolution of the party's "proletarian" dictatorship into something close to personal autocratic rule by Stalin exercised through the Communist Party and the secret police. Unlike the Nazis, Soviet Communists had no Leader principle, but they did increasingly have a Leader practice. Some of what Khrushchev would later call Stalin's "cult of personality" reflected the contemporary style of self-presentation of the Fascist dictators, Mussolini and Hitler, but in other respects the cult—or the Russian public's reception of it—had more in common with the Russian tradition of the "little-father Tsar" than with anything in modern Western Europe. The image of Stalin, "father of peoples," was acquiring a distinctly paternalist cast in the 1930s.

The paternalism was not limited to Stalin. Regional party officials lower in the hierarchy practiced it too, receiving and responding to many humble petitions from their obedient subjects who appealed, often in astonishingly traditional terms, to their fatherly benevolence. The official rhetoric increasingly emphasized the state's protective function with respect to its weaker and less-developed citizens: women, children, peasants, and members of "backward" ethnic groups.

REVOLUTIONARY WARRIORS

The party was by self-conception a vanguard. In terms of Marxist theory, this meant a vanguard of the proletariat, the class of industrial workers in whose name the party had established its revolutionary dictatorship in October 1917. But the significance of the concept went far beyond class. It was the framework in which Communists thought about and justified their mission of leadership in Russian society. By the 1930s, as the old concept of revolutionary mission was increasingly acquiring overtones of civilizing mission, the party came to see itself not only as a political vanguard but also as a cultural one. This, of course, was not very convincing to the old Russian intelligentsia, many of whom regarded the Bolsheviks as unschooled barbarians; but the party's claim to cultural superiority seems to have been accepted as reasonable by much of the rest of the population. The "cultural vanguard" concept received a further boost in 1936, when Stalin appropriated the term "intelligentsia" as a designation for the new Soviet elite, of which Communist administrators formed a major part.[2]

An important aspect of the party's claim to cultural vanguard status was its possession of esoteric knowledge, namely Marxist-Leninist ideology. Knowledge of the basics of historical and dialectical materialism was a prerequisite for all Communists. What this meant in practice was a grasp of Marx's theory of historical development, which showed that the driving power of history was class struggle; that capitalism throughout the world must ultimately succumb to proletarian revolution, as it had done in Russia in 1917; and that in the course of time the revolutionary proletarian dictatorship would lead the society to socialism. To outsiders, the boiled-down Marxism of Soviet political literacy courses might look simplistic, almost catechismic. To insiders, it was a "scientific" worldview that enabled its possessors to rid themselves and others of all kinds of prejudice and superstition—and incidentally master an aggressive debating style characterized by generous use of sarcasm about the motives and putative "class essence" of opponents. Smugness and tautology, along with polemical vigor, were among the most notable characteristics of Soviet Marxism.

Party membership and education, preferably combined, were the main routes to advancement in Soviet Russia. This meant that party membership was a desirable, even necessary qualification for the ambitious; as a result the party spent a great deal of effort trying to differentiate between those who were ambitious in a good sense, meaning that they were prepared to take the responsibilities of leadership, and "careerists," who only wanted the privileges. Throughout the 1920s and 1930s, admission to the party was not lightly gained, especially by white-collar office workers and professionals. For most of this period, the party's enrollment rules strongly favored those with worker or poor peasant background, as did college admissions procedures. In addition, many would-be Communists failed to make it through the complicated admissions procedure, involving letters of reference, investigations of social background, examination in political literacy, and so on. The same was true of the Komsomol, and many "true believers" fretted because of their inability to join. As the French historian Nicolas Werth notes, "The difficult admissions procedure reinforced . . . the deep sentiment of belonging to a world of the elect, of being part of those who walk in the direction of History."[3]

Of course there were important changes in the membership of the party in the course of the 1930s. The ideal at the beginning of the Stalin period was a *proletarian* party: factory workers were encouraged to join, while office workers and professionals found the way blocked. The big enrollment of workers from the bench and peasants of the First Five-Year Plan period swelled the ranks but also introduced a lot of ballast. The party suspended admissions in 1933, and the first in a series of party "cleansings" was held the the same year. The party suffered substantial membership loss during the Great Purges; at the same time, some young Communists found themselves propelled up the ladder at dizzying speeds to fill the jobs of those who had been removed as "enemies of the people." When admissions were renewed in the last years of the decade, the old proletarian emphasis had largely disappeared and stress was put on getting "the best people" in Soviet society, which in practice meant that it became much easier for white-collar professionals to enter.

We may also note another important change. From the beginning of the 1930s, organized opposition and open debate no longer existed in the Communist Party. Leaders of the Left Opposition were expelled from the party at the end of 1927, and this sufficiently intimidated the "Right Opposition" of 1928–29 that it never really organized at all. After that, there were only a few embryonic underground "opposition" groups, dealt with harshly by the OGPU. Although some prominent former Oppositionists recanted and were briefly reinstated in high positions in the early 1930s, it was well understood by all former Oppositionists that even social meetings between them were likely to be interpreted as "anti-Soviet discussions" and provoke fresh punishment.

Internal party discussion and debate were correspondingly constricted. In the 1920s, the party had had its own intellectual centers, notably the Communist Academy and the Institutes of Red Professors, institutions where Marxism was taken seriously and debated at a relatively high intellectual level.[4] Leading politicians like Bukharin and Stalin had personal followings among the young Communist intellectuals, whose militancy and radicalism were well in evidence during the Cultural Revolution. By the middle of the 1930s, however, the Cultural Revolution was over, many of its leaders discredited, and the Communist Academy closed down. This was almost the end of serious intellectual-political debate within a Marxist framework in the Soviet Union. The intense interest and involvement with which many Communists and Komsomol members had followed high politics and policy debates in the 1920s were no more; it had become dangerous to be too interested in politics and political theory.

"An army of revolutionary warriors," was how Politburo member Lazar Kaganovich described the party at the XVII Party Congress of 1934. This notion was dear to Communists, many of whom still carried a gun, looked back on the Civil War with nostalgia, and, like Stalin, continued to wear a version of military dress, with field jacket and boots. It was a party of urban men with a strong macho ethos: words like "struggle," "fight," and "attack" were constantly on the lips of its members. Throughout the 1930s, Communists lived with the expectation, justified or not, of foreign attack.[5]

In Stalin's view, the danger in which the Soviet Union stood required a special kind of assertive confidence in dealing with the outside world. Commenting to Molotov on the draft of a public statement on international affairs in 1933, he wrote: "It came out well. The confident, contemptuousness tone with respect to the 'great' powers, the belief in our own strength, the delicate but plain spitting in the pot of the swaggering 'great powers'—very good. Let them eat it." [6]

Stalin, thinking in terms of great power relations, was not greatly interested in the prospect of international revolution in the 1930s. But it was otherwise for a whole generation of the young who grew up in the 1920s and 1930s, for whom world revolution was something inspiring, urgently desired, and, as Lev Kopelev's memoir suggests, integrally linked with dreams of modernity and access to a wider world:

> The world revolution was absolutely necessary so that justice would triumph, all those incarcerated in bourgeois prisons would be set free, those starving in India and China would be fed, the lands taken from the Germans and the Danzig "corridor" would be returned and our Bessarabia would be taken back from Rumania. . . . But also so that afterward there would be no borders, no capitalists and no fascists at all. And so that Moscow, Kharkov and Kiev would become just as enormous, just as well built, as Berlin, Hamburg, New York, so that we would have skyscrapers, streets full of automobiles and bicycles, so that all the workers and peasants would go walking in fine clothes, wearing hats and watches. . . . And so that airplanes and dirigibles would go flying everywhere. [7]

For Communists of Kopelev's generation, education was extremely important: to acquire an education was not just a path to personal success but also an obligation that one owed the party. Communists must be "constantly learning, especially from the masses," the Reichstag-fire hero Georgii Dimitrov told an audience at the Institute of Red Professors. [8] In the real world, however, studying in school was more important than learning from the masses. A network of party schools provided Communist administrators with a mixture of general and political education; in addition, many Communists were "mobilized" to attend college to study engineering, especially during the First Five-Year Plan. (Khrushchev, Brezhnev, and Kosygin all had this experience in the early 1930s.) It was a party member's duty to "work on himself" and raise his cultural level, even if he was not involved in a formal education program.

At the lower levels of the party, one of the touchstones of a good Communist was having rid oneself of the superstition of religion. Conversely, one of the most common ideological offenses for a party member was to have allowed his wife or other female relative to remain a believer, to christen their children, attend church, or keep icons in the house. Party members were frequently cross-examined on this score, as in this dialogue reported from a local party cell meeting:

Did you baptise your children?

The last one to be baptised in my family was my daughter in 1926.

At what date did you break with religion.

In 1923.

It seems that there are still icons in your house.

Yes, that's because my mother-in-law doesn't want me to take them down! [9]

Discipline and unity were high on the list of party values. They were spoken about in almost mystical terms even in the 1920s: as early as 1924, the speech in which Trotsky conceded defeat in the leadership struggle included the words "The party is always right" and "One cannot be right against the party." One of the defendants in the Great Purge trials noted in his final plea that "the shameful example of my fall shows that the slightest rift with the Party, the slightest insincerity towards the Party, the slightest hesitation with regard to the leadership, with regard to the Central Committee, is enough to land you in the camp of counterrevolution." [10] The requirements of democratic centralism meant that every Communist was bound to obey unswervingly any decision of the party's highest organs. The old qualification that unswerving obedience was required once a decision had been reached lost its force as the pre-decision stage of public party discussion disappeared.

There existed a formal scale of punishments for Communists who violated party discipline, starting with a warning and proceeding through various levels of rebuke to expulsion, which meant exclusion from public life and deprivation of privileges like access to special stores and health clinics.[11] In practice, however, the scale of punishments went higher. Already in the late 1920s, members of the Left Opposition were sent into administrative exile in distant parts of the Soviet Union, and Trotsky was actually deported from the Soviet Union. During the Great Purges a few years later, execution of disgraced party members as "enemies of the people" became commonplace.

Vigilance—an attitude of watchful suspicion—was an important part of Communist *mentalité*. According to Dimitrov, a good Communist must "continually manifest the greatest vigilance in relation to the enemies and spies that secretly penetrate into our ranks." A Communist who was not ceaselessly vigilant, that is, endlessly suspicious of his fellow citizens and even fellow party members, was failing in his duty to the party and falling into "Rightism." Enemies were everywhere; and, most dangerous of all, these enemies were often disguised. A Communist must always stand ready to "unmask" hidden enemies and show their "true face." [12]

Like freemasons, Communists had many rituals. They were brothers and their brotherhood was in some sense secret. Their status as Communists was related to their mastery of esoteric language. They had symbols they cherished, like the Red flag, and a history, including a martyrology, that every Communist had to know. They had a body of sacred texts, comprising the works of Marx, Engels, Lenin, and Stalin, and were required to study new additions to the corpus like Stalin's latest speeches and important Politburo resolutions. There was an atmosphere of mystery in the party's oblique forms of communication, only fully comprehensible to the initiated, and its Aesopian language practices. To be expelled from the party meant to be outcast from this community, cut off from the common purpose: in Bukharin's words at his trial, "isolated from everybody, an enemy of the people, in an inhuman position, completely isolated from everything that constitutes the essence of life." [13] "Don't push me to despair," wrote one Communist threatened with expulsion in less extreme circumstances, adding this pathetic postscript:

Now spring is coming, the May day holiday. People will be happy to be alive, cheerful, but as for me, I will be weeping in my soul. Can everything be collapsing this way? Is it possible that I could have become the enemy of the party which has formed me? No, it is a mistake.[14]

One of the key rituals through which vigilance was exercised was the "small-p" purge or cleansing,[15] a periodic review of party membership to weed out undesirables. In the Cultural Revolution period, similar purges were conducted in all government offices as well, bringing excitement into the workaday bureaucratic routine. The proceedings would begin with an autobiographical statement by the person under review, followed by interrogation by the purge commission and members of the audience. The questions could deal with any aspect of his political or personal life.

What was he doing before 1917 and during the October Revolution? Was he at the front? Was he ever arrested before the revolution? Did he have any disagreements with the party? Does he drink? . . . What does he think about Bukharin and the right deviation, about the kulak, the Five-Year Plan, the events in China? . . . Is it true that he has a private automobile and a pretty wife who was an actress? . . . Did he get married in church? Did he baptize his son? . . . Whom did his sister marry? [16]

In her memoirs, Elena Bonner, later wife of the dissident Andrei Sakharov, describes her childhood memories of a purge of the offices of the Communist International, probably in 1933. Her stepfather Gevork Alikhanov worked for the Comintern, and the purge meetings were held in the evenings after work over a period of weeks in the "Red Corner" of the Hotel Luxe, where the Alikhanov/Bonner family and other Comintern officials lived. Elena and other Comintern children hid behind the curtains and eavesdropped.

You could see that they were nervous. . . . They asked about people's wives and sometimes about their children. It turned out that some people beat their wives and drank a lot of vodka. Batanya [Elena's formidable grandmother] would have said that decent people don't ask such questions. Sometimes the one being purged said that he wouldn't beat his wife anymore or drink anymore. And a lot of them said about their work that they "wouldn't do it anymore" and that "they understood everything."

It reminded young Elena of being called into the teachers' room at school for a dressing-down and having to say you were sorry. "But these people were more nervous than you were with the teacher. Some of them were practically crying. It was unpleasant watching them." [17]

There was a confessional as well as an intimidatory quality to these purge rituals, and when simple people went through them they often got sidetracked out of the political and social realm into personal confessions and revelations. But it was a special kind of confessional ritual: one in which there was no absolution. "Going through the purge" meant confessing your sins endlessly, especially membership of oppositions and bad social origin, but there was no provision in the ritual for being relieved of the burden. You "recognized your errors," you apologized, and, if lucky, you were sent away with a warning. But the errors were still there next time, for by the 1930s the party was no longer interested in your "subjective" attitude to your sins, but only in the existence of a record of past sins in your file.[18]

Show trials, which also often featured public confessions, were organized for a broader audience. The show trial may be defined as a public theatrical performance in the form of a trial, didactic in purpose, intended not to establish the guilt of the accused but rather to demonstrate the heinousness of the person's crimes. As an entertainment-cum-agitational genre, it went back to the Civil War period, when extemporized theater of all kinds was very popular, and arose as a result of local initiative. In its early years, it often took the form of a theatricalized trial of a symbolic figure ("the kulak," "the wife-beater"), though real-life offenders, persons accused of hooliganism or absenteeism from work, were also sometimes "prosecuted" in show trials as a local disciplinary measure. These early trials did not result in real sentences.

A pioneering centrally organized show trial of former political opponents of the Bolsheviks (Right Socialist Revolutionaries) was held in 1923. But it was not until the Cultural Revolution of the late 1920s that show trials, featuring elaborately planned "scenarios" and intensive media coverage aimed at a national audience, became an important agitational tool of the Central Committee. In the Shakhty trial (1928) and the "Industrial Party" trial (1930), engineers and other "bourgeois specialists" were accused of sabotage and counterrevolutionary conspiracy in association with foreign powers.[19] All confessed their guilt, providing circumstantial detail of their extraordinary (and in general totally fictitious) crimes, and all received sentences of death or substantial periods of imprisonment. Much the same pattern was followed in the better-known "Moscow trials" of the Great Purges period—the Zinoviev–Kamenev trial of 1936, the Piatakov trial of 1937, and the Bukharin trial of 1938—except that in the Moscow trials the defendants were not bourgeois specialists but top-ranking Communist leaders.

Whether Stalin and other Communist leaders believed in a literal sense in the conspiracies described in the show trials is a hard question to answer. In his secret correspondence with officials about the trials of the early 1930s, Stalin wrote as if he *did* believe—yet at the same time these letters could be read as coded instructions about what kind of scenario should be written. For the party leadership, as Terry Martin writes, the accusations made at the trials probably represented psychological rather than literal truth. But the leaders hoped ordinary people would take them literally; indeed, workers' responses to the Shakhty trial, which included calls for still harsher punishment of the defendants, suggest that this was often the case.[20]

Conspiracy

In 1926, a former Cheka man confided in Victor Serge, an old revolutionary, his secret knowledge of a monstrous plot. As Serge related their conversation,

> The secret is that everything has been betrayed. From the years when Lenin was alive, treason has wormed its way into the Central Committee. He knows the names, he has the proofs. . . . At the peril of his life, he is submitting his analysis of the gigantic crime, studied over years, to the Central Committee. He

whispers the names of foreigners, of the most powerful capitalists, and of yet others which have an occult significance for him. . . . I follow his chain of reasoning with the secret uneasiness that one feels in the presence of some lunatic logician. . . . But in all that he says, he is driven by one basic idea which is not the idea of a madman: "We did not create the Revolution to come to this." [21]

This man may have been crazy, but the way of thinking was characteristic of Communists. Their work was being undermined by a conspiracy of people inside and outside the Soviet Union whose hatred of the revolution was absolute. The Cheka man thought the center of the plot was the current party leadership, a position only marginally different from the one Stalin and Ezhov were to take in the Great Purges. For the rest, he was totally typical in his super-suspiciousness. Foreign capitalists were in league with hostile forces within the country. The conspirators were hidden; only the most diligent efforts could unmask them. Finally, and perhaps most important, these conspirators, with their ingrained hatred of the Soviet Union, were *making everything go wrong*. There must be a conspiracy, because otherwise the fact that the revolution was not turning out as planned was inexplicable. *Someone must be to blame.*[22]

The Soviet regime was adept at creating its own enemies, whom it then suspected of conspiracy against the state. It did so first by declaring that all members of certain social classes and estates—primarily former nobles, members of the bourgeoisie, priests, and kulaks—were by definition "class enemies," resentful of their loss of privilege and likely to engage in counterrevolutionary conspiracy to recover them. The next step, taken at the end of the 1920s, was the "liquidation as a class" of certain categories of class enemies, notably kulaks and, to a lesser extent, Nepmen and priests. This meant that the victims were expropriated, deprived of the possibility of continuing their previous way of earning a living, and often arrested and exiled. Unfortunately this did not reduce the danger of conspiracy against the state but probably only increased it. For, as Stalin (wise after the fact?) realized, a member of an enemy class did not become any better disposed to Soviet power after his class was liquidated. On the contrary, he was likely to be full of anger and resentment. The person who had been dekulakized was a more desperate, intransigent enemy than the kulak. Moreover, he had very likely fled to the cities and disguised himself, assuming a more acceptable identity as a worker. He had become a *hidden* enemy, hence more dangerous as a potential conspirator.[23]

Enemies were not the only conspirators in the Soviet world. Remarkably, the old prerevolutionary self-designation of the party as "conspiratorial" remained in use (albeit secret use) into the 1930s, and Communists were regularly urged in internal party documents to observe "conspiracy" and "conspiratorialness," that is, to maintain secrecy about party affairs.[24] In the old days, conspiracy had been a necessity of the fight against the Tsarist regime; under postrevolutionary conditions, the awkward question "conspiracy against whom?" hung in the air. "The Soviet people" was one possible answer, though it is implausible that Communists or any other rulers should perceive themselves as engaged in a malevolent conspiracy against the nation;

"the encircling capitalist world" was another. But perhaps the best way of understanding the Communists' attachment to conspiracy is to see the party, in their eyes, as a kind of freemasonry, whose ability to act for good in the world depended on protecting its inner life from the hostile scrutiny of outsiders.

An increasing number of party affairs were being handled in secrecy from the beginning of the 1930s. In the late 1920s, a procedure was introduced whereby Politburo and Central Committee documents were sent out to local party branches with strict limitations on the persons allowed to read them and the requirement to return them within a few days (at the end of 1938, even this stopped). Minutes of the Central Control Commission were similarly restricted: it was "absolutely forbidden" for them to be shown to persons not on the approved list to read them, or to be copied or cited in public; and the minutes had to be returned. A Communist who violated the secrecy rules, even in a speech to a factory meeting full of presumed class allies, could be accused of "betraying the party to the working class." [25]

Secrecy was invading government as well as party practice. Among the topics classified as "top secret" or "secret" in internal government and party communications were military and mobilization plans, including defense industry construction; export of precious metals; important inventions; OGPU reports on the mood of the population and other matters; prosecutions under article 58 of the Criminal Code, which dealt with crimes against the state; and administrative exile, deportation, and special settlements. Strikes and workers' protests were also classified topics, though at the lower level of "not for publication." Reports on cases of plague, cholera, typhus, and other infectious diseases were classified as well. [26]

One reason secrecy had become so important, we may assume, is that the Communist rulers were doing things they were ashamed of, or at least thought that outsiders would have difficulty understanding. In the early years of the revolution, the Bolsheviks had made a point of *not* being ashamed of their practice of terror, which they claimed to be a necessary and even constructive part of revolution: in his radical days, circa 1920, the later Rightist Nikolai Bukharin described it as "a method of creating communist mankind out of the human materials of the capitalist epoch," and another enthusiast called it "a source of great moral encouragement." [27] Nevertheless, the Bolsheviks' handling of public relations after the suppression of the Kronstadt sailors' revolt in 1921 suggests that they were ashamed and deeply embarrassed by this event; and the collectivization struggle and its aftermath of famine produced similar reactions from the regime. The old defiant, unapologetic stance about violence by the revolutionary state was replaced by evasion, euphemism, and denial. By 1933, a secret Politburo order was in force forbidding newspapers to report executions without special clearance. [28]

It is true that in the mid 1930s the secret police was greatly publicized in certain connections and its leaders acclaimed as heroes. The NKVD's big projects, like the building of White Sea Canal, were acclaimed for "reforging" the convicts who worked on them, its officers were honored and decorated, and its border guards were held up as exemplars for Soviet youth. At the end of

1937, the NKVD's twentieth anniversary was celebrated with fanfare, and the Kazakh bard Dzhambul hailed its leader, Nikolai Ezhov, as "a flame, burning the serpents' nests," and a "bullet for all scorpions and serpents." [29] But the presumably massive growth in the security agency and its network of informers in the course of the 1930s was (and remains) a state secret; and the NKVD's more mundane activities like surveillance, arrest, and interrogation were usually treated as a dirty secret and kept under wraps. It was standard practice for a person released after arrest or interrogation to be required to sign an agreement not to speak of what had happened to him.

STALIN'S SIGNALS

In principle, the Soviet Communist Party had no leader. It had only a Central Committee, elected by its periodic national congresses of delegates from local party organizations, and three standing bureaus of the Central Committee elected in the same way: the Politburo, a group of seven to twelve members in charge of political and policy matters, and the Orgburo and Secretariat, both of which dealt with organizational and personnel questions. In the mid 1920s, however, in the course of the undeclared succession struggle that raged after Lenin's death, Stalin had used his position as party secretary to stack local organizations and congresses with his supporters.[30] In the 1930s, Stalin was still general secretary of the party, as he had been from 1922 and would be until 1952, but he no longer spent the time with personnel files and appointments that had characterized his rise to power. He was now acknowledged as the party's supreme leader, its *vozhd'*. Although he retained his previous demeanor as a simple and accessible man (not flashy and arrogant like his main rival for power, Trotsky), his humility had a special character: when he modestly and unobtrusively entered the hall at a party congress now, the whole audience rose to its feet to give him a standing ovation. Although Stalin at times deprecated his cult, he also tolerated and perhaps covertly encouraged it.[31]

For Communists of the old guard, the Stalin cult was probably something of an embarrassment. Yet in their eyes too, he was becoming a charismatic leader, though of a somewhat different kind than for the broad public. Stalin's public image in the 1930s, like the Tsars' before him, was that of a quasi-sacred leader, font of justice and mercy, and benevolent protector of the weak; he was often photographed smiling paternally on shy peasant women and children. To the party elite, in contrast, Stalin was known as "the boss," whose main characteristics were sharpness and shrewdness of mind, decisiveness, the capacity for hard work, and dislike for fancy rhetoric and other kinds of personal flamboyance. His associates also knew him to have an excellent memory for slights and a penchant and formidable talent for political intrigue.[32]

In the Politburo, the convention of an assembly of equals was maintained. Stalin usually chaired, but he tended to sit quietly smoking his pipe and let others have their say first. (This underlined his lack of pretension, but it also gave Stalin the advantage of having others show their hands before he did.)

Arguments occurred in the Politburo, even heated ones in which the volatile Georgian Sergo Ordzhonikidze would lose his temper. There were also sharp factional disputes between Politburo members based on their institutional affiliations: Ordzhonikidze, for example, would speak for the cause of heavy industry, Klim Voroshilov for the armed forces, Sergei Kirov for Leningrad. But very rarely were there arguments in which a Politburo member knowingly set himself at odds with Stalin.[33]

"The Politburo is a fiction," one insider said in the early 1930s. What he meant was that the formal Politburo meetings—large-scale affairs attended not only by Politburo members but also by Central Committee members, representatives of many government agencies, and selected journalists—were not where the real business got done. Serious business was handled by a smaller group selected by Stalin who met privately in an apartment or in Stalin's office in the Kremlin. At any given moment, the group might include individuals who were not formally Politburo members. It also routinely excluded some Politburo members who were in disfavor or regarded as lightweights, like Mikhail Kalinin.[34]

There was an inner circle in the Politburo, but even its members had to be wary of Stalin's disapproval. Viacheslav Molotov, the leadership's no. 2 man for most of the 1930s and Stalin's close associate, put up with the arrest of several of his trusted assistants during the Great Purges; in 1939, his wife, Polina Zhemchuzhina, was dismissed from her position as Minister of Fisheries on the grounds that she had "involuntarily facilitated" the activity of "spies" in her milieu. Threats to family members became a favored technique of Stalin's for keeping his associates under control. Ordzhonikidze's brother was arrested in 1936 on suspicion of anti-Soviet activities. Kalinin's wife was arrested as an enemy of the people while he continued to serve as President of the Soviet Union; the same was to happen after the war to Molotov's wife. Mikhail Kaganovich, former head of the Soviet defence industry and brother of Lazar, a Politburo member who remained one of Stalin's closest associates, was arrested and shot at the end of the 1930s. It is indicative of the distance that separated Stalin from even his closest Politburo colleagues and the intensity of fear in the purge years that of these four political heavyweights (Molotov, Kalinin, Ordzhonikidze, and Kaganovich), only Ordzhonikidze seems to have protested vigorously to Stalin and unqualifiedly asserted his brother's innocence.[35]

This is only one example of Stalin's characteristic way of keeping his associates off-balance. Insight into this aspect of the man is provided by a letter he wrote his wife, Nadezhda Allilueva, when he was on vacation in 1930. She had asked him with some irritation why he had given her one date for his return from the South and his colleagues another. He replied that he had given her the correct date—but "I put about that rumor that I could return only at the end of October via Poskrebyshev [Stalin's secretary], *as a conspiratorial measure*.[36]

No Politburo member could be sure that he would not fall out of favor with Stalin, as Bukharin had done at the end of the 1920s and then, even more disastrously, in 1936. When this happened, the news did not come directly from Stalin but through various signs of slipping influence and clout: exclusion from inner-circle meetings, derogatory comments appearing in *Pravda* or *Izvestiia*, or rejection of routine patronage interventions on behalf of clients and subordinates. The result was that the fallen leader found himself stigmatized and outcast by his erstwhile colleagues, almost all of whom followed the unwritten rule that a disgraced person should not be acknowledged or greeted in public.[37]

The obliqueness of Stalin's communications of favor and disfavor in high politics was matched by a similar lack of explicitness in policy formulation. This may seem strange, since Stalin's regime was notoriously insistent on obedience to central directives, and how can one obey when one has not clearly been told what to do? The fact is, however, that important policy changes were often "signalled" rather than communicated in the form of a clear and detailed directive. A signal might be given in a speech or article by Stalin or an editorial or review in *Pravda* or via a show trial or the disgrace of a prominent official associated with particular policies. What all these signals had in common was that they indicated a shift of policy in a particular area without spelling out exactly what the new policy entailed or how it should be implemented.

The collectivization drive in the winter of 1929–30 is a case in point. In contrast to previous major Russian agrarian reforms, such as the 1861 emancipation of the serfs or the Stolypin reforms of the early twentieth century, no detailed instructions about how to collectivize were ever issued, and local officials who asked for such instructions were rebuked. The signal for a radical shift in policy toward the countryside was given in Stalin's speech to the Communist Academy in December 1929, although it offered no specific guidance on collectivization other than the instruction that kulaks were to be "liquidated as a class." The closest thing to an explicit public policy statement on collectivization was Stalin's letter "Dizzy with success" published in *Pravda* on March 1, 1930—but this appeared only after two disastrous months of all-out collectivization and constituted a repudiation of much of what had been done without precise instructions by local officials.

A less momentous example was Stalin's letter to the editors of a journal of party history, *Proletarskaia revoliutsiia*, in 1931, endlessly cited as a major policy pronouncement for the cultural field. Written in a passionate polemical style, its general message seemed to be that Communist intellectuals, inclined to hair-splitting and faction-fighting, needed to clean up their act, but what that meant concretely, except in the specific and apparently trivial case with which the letter dealt, was obscure. Its practical policy meanings were constructed only after the fact, as each cultural institution held long, painful meetings "drawing organizational conclusions from comrade Stalin's letter," that is, deciding whom to discipline and punish.[38]

There are various ways of explaining this surprising reticence. In the first place, Stalin's regime was a great generator of mystification, consciously or unconsciously treating mystery as an enhancer and sanctifier of power. It was the aura of mystery and secrecy settling over the Kremlin in the 1930s that perhaps more than anything else set Stalin's style of rule apart from Lenin's. In the second place, the regime operated with a primitive administrative machinery that responded to only a few simple commands, such as "stop," "go," "faster," "slow down," which could adequately be conveyed by signals. Moreover, the regime itself had a low degree of legislative competence: on the occasions when the government did try to issue detailed policy instructions, its decrees and orders usually had to be repeatedly clarified and expanded before the message was satisfactorily communicated.[39]

There were also political advantages, at least from Stalin's Byzantine perspective. In the event that a new policy went wrong, as in the case of collectivization, signals could be more easily repudiated and reinterpreted than explicit policy statements Signals were ambiguous, which was useful if there was a lack of leadership consensus behind a policy, if a new policy violated existing Soviet law, or if its nature was such that the regime did not want foreigners to understand it. All three of these last factors were at play, for example, in the case of policy toward the church in 1929–30. Soviet law and administrative practice through most of the 1920s extended tolerance, at least of a limited sort, to religion and forbade the arbitrary closing or destruction of functioning churches. A substantial group of "soft-line" Communist leaders, mainly working in government rather than party agencies, strongly supported these policies, as of course did international opinion. But in 1929, with the onset of the Cultural Revolution and an upsurge of radical militancy in the party and Komsomol, a powerful "hard line" in favor of mass closing of churches and arrests of priests became dominant and evidently won Stalin's approval. Secret "hard-line" instructions were issued to local party organizations but not published.[40] When the anti-religious drive inflamed the anger of the rural population, not to mention that of the Pope and other Western church spokesmen, the regime was able to back off from a policy that it had never publicly endorsed anyway.

In cases like these, ambiguity and secrecy may have had political advantages, but they also had enormous practical disadvantages. In the church case, for example, Soviet officials in charge of religious affairs asked plaintively how they were to explain the actions of local authorities to church representatives when the formal law was actually on the churches' side. They pointed out in vain that an instruction allowing former priests to register at labor exchanges (giving them the right to employment) was unlikely to have a beneficial effect as long as it remained secret and hence unknown to labor-exchange officers.[41]

The combination of ambiguous policy signals and the cult of secrecy could produce absurd results, as when certain categories of officials could not be informed of relevant instructions because the instructions were secret. In one blatant example, the theater censorship and the Ministry of Enlightenment, headed by A. V. Lunacharsky, spent weeks arguing at cross purposes about Mikhail Bulgakov's controversial play *Day of the Turbins*, despite the fact that the Politburo had instructed the Ministry that the play could be staged, because "this decree was secret, known to only key officials in the administration of art, and Lunacharsky was not at liberty to divulge it." [42] A few years later, after Stalin had expressed strong views on cultural policy in a private letter that had circulated widely, if unofficially, on the grapevine, Lunacharsky begged him to allow publication of the letter *so that people would know what the party line on art actually was*.[43]

Some of Stalin's cultural signals were even more minimalist, involving telephone calls to writers or other cultural figures whose content was then instantly broadcast on the Moscow and Leningrad intelligentsia grapevine. A case in point was his unexpected telephone call to Bulgakov in 1930 in response to Bulgakov's letter complaining of mistreatment by theater and censorship officials. The overt message of the call was one of encouragement to Bulgakov. By extension, the "signal" to the non-Communist intelligentsia was that it was not Stalin who harrassed them but only lower-level officials and militants who did not understand Stalin's policy.

This case is particularly interesting because the security police (GPU, at this date) monitored the effectiveness of the signal. In his report on the impact of Stalin's call, a GPU agent noted that the literary and artistic intelligentsia had been enormously impressed. "It's as if a dam had burst and everyone around saw the true face of comrade Stalin." People speak of Stalin's simplicity and accessibility. They "talk of him warmly and with love, retelling in various versions the legendary history with Bulgakov's letter." They say that Stalin is not to blame for the bad things that happen:

> He follows the right line, but around him are scoundrels. These scoundrels persecuted Bulgakov, one of the most talented Soviet writers. Various literary rascals were making a career out of persecution of Bulgakov, and now Stalin has given them a slap in the face.[44]

The signals with Stalin's personal signature usually pointed in the direction of greater relaxation and tolerance, not increased repression. This was surely not because Stalin inclined to the "soft line," but rather because he preferred to avoid too close an association with hard-line policies that were likely to be unpopular with domestic and foreign opinion. His signals often involved a "good Tsar" message: "the Tsar is benevolent; it is the wicked boyars who are responsible for all the injustice." Sometimes this ploy seems to have worked, but in other cases the message evoked popular skepticism. When Stalin deplored the excesses of local officials during collectivization in a letter, "Dizzy with success," published in *Pravda* in 1930, the initial response in the villages was often favorable. After the famine, however, Stalin's "good Tsar" ploy no longer worked in the countryside, and was even mocked by its intended audience.[45]

BUREAUCRATS AND BOSSES

Nobody was more critical of Soviet bureaucracy than the Soviet leaders. Stalin's attack on collectivization officials was part of a whole genre of high-level criticisms of bureaucracy, and "bureaucracy" was always a deeply pejorative word in the Soviet lexicon. It was the revolutionary dream to communicate directly with the population without intermediaries, to follow the spirit of the revolution, not the dead letter of the law. In the early years, this meant that

Communist leaders were highly suspicious of the influence of Tsarist hold-overs in the state administration and felt more comfortable using the suppos-edly less bureaucratic party apparatus to carry out their will. By the mid 1930s, the concern about Tsarist holdovers had waned, but bureaucrats were still routinely pilloried at "self-criticism" meetings at enterprises and in the Soviet press. Members of the public were encouraged to send letters to higher au-thorities detailing cases of abuse of power by officials in their districts. The fact that these guilty officials were now usually Communists was irrelevant: the party leaders had little confidence in their own bureaucratic cadres, and constantly bemoaned their lack of education, common sense, and a work ethic.

The stupidity, rudeness, inefficiency, and venality of Soviet bureaucrats constituted the main satirical targets of the Soviet humorous journal, *Krokodil.* Its stories and cartoons illustrated the various methods by which of-ficials secured scarce goods and luxuries for themselves and their acquain-tances and denied them to the rest of the population.[46] They showed officials absent from their workplaces, slacking off when present, refusing desperate citizens' pleas for the precious "papers" that were necessary for even the sim-plest operations in Soviet life, like buying a railroad ticket. An eloquent *Krokodil* cartoon, headed "Bureaucrat on the trapeze," shows two circus art-ists in performance. One of them, representing the hapless citizen, has just launched himself into the air from his trapeze. The other, representing the bu-reaucrat, is supposed to catch him, but in fact sits smugly on his own trapeze holding a sign saying "Come back tomorrow." [47]

The problems were compounded by the fact that "Stalin's revolution" at the beginning of the 1930s had greatly expanded the functions and responsi-bilities of Soviet bureaucracy. Private trade had been abolished; hence a new state trade bureaucracy had to be created almost from scratch, not to mention new bureaucracies to administer the rationing system and set up public dining rooms to feed people in compensation for the deficiencies of state trade. Col-lectivized agriculture required an expanded bureaucracy for agricultural pro-curements and kolkhoz supervision. Services ranging from tailoring to shoe-repair were now in state or cooperative hands, a distinction without a real difference. The First Five-Year Plan industrialization drive expanded the state's industrial bureaucracy, while the repression that accompanied it ex-panded its secret police. Internal passports and urban registration permits, in-troduced in 1932, added more layers of bureaucracy to everyday life, as did the requirement that personnel departments of all state agencies maintain ex-tensive personal dossiers on their employees.

These new bureaucrats carrying out new tasks were inexperienced by defi-nition; they were also usually poorly educated and inefficient. They could not count on the support of the regime, whose record of repudiating and punish-ing its servitors was formidable even before the Great Purges.[48] They were feared, resented, envied, and despised by ordinary citizens, who frequently denounced them to higher authorities. Yet for all this disapproval, bureau-cracy flourished. In his own little world, the bureaucrat was king.

"Little Stalins"

Stalin was not the only Soviet leader with a cult. As a young British scholar has recently pointed out, he was not even the only leader to whom the exalted word "*vozhd'*," a term often seen as comparable to the Nazi "Führer," was applied.[49] It was not just that Stalin was acquiring the aura of a charismatic leader, but that leadership itself was acquiring that aura. Newspapers wrote of "our leaders" (*nashi vozhdi*) in the plural, referring to the Politburo. Some Politburo members like Ordzhonikidze, the popular industrial leader, Molotov, head of the Soviet government, and, for a few years, Nikolai Ezhov, head of the NKVD, were celebrated in terms almost as extravagant as Stalin. In 1936, a diarist noted that on revolutionary holidays "the portraits of party leaders are now displayed the same way icons used to be: a round portrait framed and attached to a pole . . . just like what people used to do before on church holidays."[50]

Tsaritsyn on the Volga became Stalingrad in Stalin's honor, Iuzovka in the Donbass became Stalino. But other leaders, living and dead, were similarly honored by having cities or regions named after them. The city of Vladikavkaz became Ordzhonikidze; Samara became Kuibyshev, Perm became Molotov, and Lugansk became Voroshilovgrad, not to mention some ill-fated name changes that later had to be reversed (e.g., Trotsk, Zinovevsk, and Rykovo). In addition, it was the custom to name enterprises and collective farms in honor of party leaders, like the Kaganovich Metro in Moscow. Ordzhonikidze, Kaganovich, and even the future "wrecker" Iurii Piatakov (Ordzhonikidze's deputy) all surpassed Stalin in the number of industrial enterprises renamed in their honor in 1935. Streets were also renamed after political leaders and prominent cultural figures, with Moscow's main street, Tverskaia, becoming Gorky Street (for the writer Maxim Gorky), Miasnitskaia becoming Kirov Street, and Bolshaia Lubianka becoming Dzerzhinsky Street. In the provinces, the same kind of naming and name-changing went on in honor of regional party leaders.[51]

On occasion, Stalin or someone else would point out that this was all becoming a bit excessive. Stalin, for example, rejected the suggestion that Moscow be renamed Stalinodar in his honor. When the practice of glorification of leaders was criticized, however, it was most often in connection with the disgrace of the political leader in question or with a general critique of "little Stalins" out in the provinces. When large numbers of provincial party leaders were disgraced during the Great Purges, their local "cults of personality" were prime objects of criticism. A typical comment from that era, directed at the head of a regional railroad, noted that "toadyism and servility flourish on the railroad. Comrade Bazeev encourages flatterers. It's already standard on the railroad that whenever comrade Bazeev shows up anywhere, he is met with stormy applause and even shouts of 'Hurrah.'"[52]

Sometimes local personality cults were attributed to the backwardness of the population and "leaderism" was treated as an ethnic disease. This was the approach that the head of a regional party organization took in his mild criticism of a subordinate who was top party official in the national region of Chuvashia:

> Not long ago comrade Petrov—secretary of the Chuvash party committee—thanked our regional committee . . . from the heart for saving him from the disease of leaderism. You know that comrade Petrov is a modest man, a good Bolshevik, a good worker, popular in his organization. But in Chuvashiia they began to look on comrade Petrov as they do on Kalmykov in Kabardino-Balkariia, as they do on other national leaders who[se status is] also exaggerated. In Chuvashiia some comrades thought: why shouldn't comrade Petrov be Kalmykov? And when such an atmosphere is created, you don't have to wait long for executants. They began to write poems and addresses, and invented the "six conditions of comrade Petrov" (laughter). Petrov at first frowned and said "What is this for?," but then more or less got used to it.[53]

Eugenia Ginzburg gives a vivid description of the metamorphosis of the Kazan party leader, Mikhail Razumov, an Old Bolshevik of impeccable proletarian origins, with whom her husband worked closely in the pre-purge years. In 1930, Razumov "still lived in one room in my father-in-law's flat, and sliced a sausage for his dinner with a penknife on a piece of newspaper." By 1933, he was being hailed locally as "the foremost worker in Tartary," and when the region received the Order of Lenin for success in collectivization, "[Razumov's] portrait was carried triumphantly through the town and enterprising artists copied it in any medium from oats to lentils for exhibition at agricultural shows."[54]

Of course, there was more to being a Communist leader than having your portrait carried through town. Communist leaders projected themselves as tough guys, an image that generally corresponded with reality. They cultivated a peremptory style of command, barking orders, demanding instant obedience and no backchat, and insisting on the Soviet version of the bottom line, which was to meet plan targets at all costs. Consultation or lengthy deliberation was a sign of weakness; a leader must be decisive.

At its worst, this kind of managerial style involved a great deal of bullying, bluster, and cursing. "He is very crude in dealing with rank-and-file Communists. Shouting is his only form of communication with people," wrote a critic of one party official in Iaroslavl. He "likes to show off his talents to bystanders," shouting and throwing people out of his office for no good reason, ran another complaint, directed against a department head in the Leningrad city party committee. "A cloud of cursing hangs in the air of the department. Not for nothing does the head of the department not want to hire women for clerical work."[55]

The idealized leader of the 1930s, modeled on the real-life industrial managers, heroes of the Five-Year Plans, who built and ran Soviet metallurgical and machine-building plants, was anything but an office type. He was out in the mud at the construction site, hard on himself and everyone else, ruthless if need be, tireless, and practical. A manager's task was to get more out of people than they thought they had to give, using exhortation, intimidation, threats, arrests, or whatever it took. A lot of work was carried out in "campaign" style, that is, in short, hectic bursts of concentrated attention to particular tasks, not through routine, incremental activity. This made life at the factory resemble life at the front, justifying another military metaphor—"storming." Storming was what took place in the frantic days at the end of each month as each enterprise tried to fulfil its monthly plan. The best Soviet managers were risk-takers; indeed, they had to break rules and take risks to do their jobs, for regular channels and legal methods would not provide them with the parts and raw materials they needed to achieve plan targets.[56]

Among the top party leaders, Sergo Ordzhonikidze and Lazar Kaganovich best exemplified the hard-driving, can-do style as heads of heavy industry and the railroads, respectively. Ordzhonikidze was "a typical administrator of the Stalinist type, energetic, coarse, and tough," a Russian historian writes. "He had completely mastered only one method of leadership—pressure on subordinates, keeping a constant eye on his 'property,' and promoting managers who were capable of guaranteeing success locally by the same means." From those who worked for him, Ordzhonikidze expected dedication, results, and loyalty. But he also offered protection, intervening energetically on behalf of "his people" when they got into trouble with the party, the secret police, or other control agencies. (After Ordzhonikidze died, probably by his own hand, at the start of the Great Purges, Stalin noted that this unquestioning loyalty to subordinates and strong commitment to his role as a patron was one of his defects.)[57]

The practice of patronage, however, was characteristic not only of Ordzhonikidze but of all Soviet leaders, starting with Stalin and going down to local level. They all tried to have "their own" people working for them—people who were personally loyal, associated their interests with their boss's, relied on him as a patron, and so on. As the political scientist Ken Jowitt suggests, the Soviet system of rule was personalistic and "patrimonial," meaning that an institution was like a fiefdom, its status and power inseparable from that of the man in charge. Bosses of this type acted as patrons for a stable of political clients, subordinates, and associates from whom they expected loyalty and offered protection in exchange. With his "family" around him, the local boss could hope to keep local challenges or criticism of his rule to a minimum. He could also hope that, with the "family" controlling information flow, local problems and shortfalls would be successfully concealed from the probing eyes of the center.[58]

These functions of local mutual-protection circles were well understood in the center. As Stalin complained at a Central Committee plenary meeting early in 1937, regional party leaders were choosing their subordinates on personalistic, not objective, grounds—because they were "acquaintances, friends, from the same part of the country, personally devoted, masters at flattering their bosses." Local elites form self-protective "families," whose members "try to live in peace, not to offend each other, and not to wash their dirty linen in public, praise each other and from time to time send the center empty and nauseating reports about their successes." When a local boss was transferred, he would seek to take a retinue or "tail" of his most trusted subordinates and specialists along with him. In his speech to the Central Committee, Stalin described this practice as pointless, a "petty-bourgeois philistine" approach to personnel matters, but in a draft of the speech he noted its political rationale: "What does it mean to drag after you a whole group of pals?. . . It means that you received a certain independence from local organizations [presumably meaning secret police and control agencies] and, if you like, a certain independence from the Central Committee." [59]

Stalin's characterization is borne out by this picture, drawn from local NKVD archives, of how one regional "family" in the Urals secured the loyalty of its members and defended its interests.

> The clique employed a range of tactics to ensure its control, mostly in the nature of unsubtle positive and negative reinforcements. The positive reinforcements were largely financial. The members of the clique and "especially important members of the [regional] Party aktiv" were ensured an excellent standard of living in exchange for their loyalty. They received large apartments, dachas, special access to consumer goods and food supplies and large supplements to their salaries . . . Negative reinforcements were the flip side of the graft coin. Those who made trouble for the members of the clique were removed from their posts, thereby losing all the attendant privileges. The Party purges of the [mid]1930s . . . were favoured means of removing untrusted colleagues. It was generally not difficult to find some element from an enemy's past and use it to get him purged. . . . Once the offending parties had been removed, those who replaced them were carefully chosen, known friends of the clique. They were coopted, rather than elected by an obkom plenum as had been the practice in the 1920s and early 1930s. [60]

"Petty tutelage" was the contemporary Soviet term for administrative micromanagement, in particular the bureaucratic desire to control even the minutiae of everyday life. This had a long history in Russia, going back at least as far as Peter the Great, with his famous instructions to the nobility on how to dress and comport themselves in public. Eighteenth-century serf-owners sometimes dressed their serfs in uniforms, drilled them, and prescribed detailed rules for their conduct. In the reign of Alexander I, General Arakcheev's military colonies, where peasant soldiers had to conform to set standards of hygiene and propriety, were models of the same kind of administrative practice. [61]

Nineteenth-century Russian literature provides many similar examples, notably in the works of Nikolai Gogol and Mikhail Saltykov-Shchedrin, whose *History of a Town* (1869–70) presents a series of satirical portraits of officials who arrive in the provinces with detailed and totally unrealistic blueprints for universal betterment. Critics of Soviet "petty tutelage" often cited Chekhov's character Prishibeev, a retired NCO, "who had grown accustomed to giving orders in the barracks and still conducted himself in the same bossy way in retirement," going round the village "ordering people not to sing songs and not to light candles" on the grounds that there was no law that specifically allowed these activities. [62]

One of *Krokodil's* examples of petty tutelage was the order—apparently genuine—issued by the director of a starch factory about shaving and haircutting.

> In view of the opening of a hairdresser's at the plant it is categorically forbidden to perform haircutting and shaving privately. I instruct the Commendant of the plant, Botarev, and the medical assistant Chikin to keep an eye on this and if he discovers anyone shaving at home to make out a charge and turn the matter over to the court for criminal prosecution and the exaction of a fine. (Signed) Director Kaplan.[63]

Nadezhda Mandelstam provides another example of this bureaucratic style in her description of a kolkhoz chairman she encountered in the mid 1930s.

> Three days before we met him Dorokhov had issued an order that every house in the village must display two pots of flowers on the windowsill. He issued orders like this in a constant stream, and they were all couched in the language of the first years of the Revolution. He went around to a dozen houses with us to check whether his instructions had been complied with. He set enormous store by this measure, since he believed that flowers imbibe the moisture and thus help "against the rheumatism." The village women explained to him that they had nothing against flowers, but that one couldn't get pots for love or money, and that in any case three days was not enough time to grow burdock or nettles, never mind flowers. Dorokhov was furious, and only our presence restrained him from meting out punishment on the spot.[64]

Dorokhov's aims were cultural and utopian, and he punished people by beating them with his fists. But other micromanagers had a different aim and mode of punishment: their objective was to create misdemeanors that provided the pretext for levying fines, and these fines often went directly into their pockets. Peasants complained frequently about such practices on the part of district officials and kolkhoz chairmen. It was alleged that in a district in the Voronezh region, one rural soviet chairman imposed fines on kolkhoz members totalling 60,000 rubles in 1935 and 1936: "He imposed the fines on any pretext and at his own discretion—for not showing up for work, for not attending literacy classes, for 'impolite language,' for not having dogs tied up . . . Kolkhoznik M. A. Gorshkov was fined 25 roubles for the fact that 'in his hut the floors were not washed.'"[65]

A Stalingrad city ordinance of 1938 forbade people to travel on the streetcar in dirty clothes on pain of a 100-ruble fine. The investigator who reported this noted that "when I asked why that point was included, I received the answer that in this way we are pushing man into a cultured attitude to himself." In Astrakhan, a man received a 100-ruble fine for wearing a hat. By order of the central Ministry for Communal Economy, only singing birds could be kept in cages in apartments and it was forbidden to store food in the urban Russian's basic "refrigerator" of the period—the space between the outer and inner window.[66]

The passion of local authorities for micro-management of the everyday life of the population received particular critical attention at the end of the 1930s, although whether this was because it got worse during the Great Purges is hard to determine. In May 1938, a national meeting of regional public prosecutors deplored the tendency of district and city soviets to issue compulsory ordinances on trivial matters. As the Belorussian prosecutor told the meeting, to hilarity from the floor:

> Turov district soviet published a compulsory resolution in which it forbade old people and young children from lighting matches under pain of administrative penalty (100 ruble fine) as an anti-fire measure.
> *Vyshinsky:* Even in the kitchen.
> *Voices from the floor:* It's out of Gogol's *Inspector General.*
> The Rechitsa city soviet published a compulsory resolution which said that all houseowners and heads of institutions were obligated to build new asphalt pavements and to paint their houses. Moreover it even established the color of the paint, for example, bright green on Soviet Street, bright yellow on Lenin Street, blue on Cooperative Street, and dark green for all the rest. For violation of that resolution there was a fine of 100 rubles.[67]

A GIRL WITH CHARACTER

The *aktiv*, the collective noun from which the term "activist" is derived, was a kind of ginger group in all kinds of Soviet settings. Party and Komsomol members were activists almost by definition. In trade unions, factories, offices, universities, and other workplaces and associations, the membership was divided into an activist minority, whose function was "to call to action, rouse to greater efforts," and the rest, who were the objects of activization. It was to be expected that party and Komsomol members would be activists in any institution or association to which they belonged. But there was room for "non-party activists" as well—people with energy or ambition who were willing to work with the party people.[68]

The main categories of activists, apart from Communists, were Komsomol members (from the Communist youth movement), Stakhanovites (workers and peasants honored for outstanding production), worker and peasant correspondents who served as stringers for newspapers, and members of the wives' volunteer movement. To be an activist was, in the first place, to be a volunteer who helped party and soviet bureaucracies to carry out tasks such as enrolling pupils in school, collecting state procurements quotas from the collective farms, or improving labor discipline in factories. This aspect of activism was naturally highly unpopular with the non-activist population, which often regarded the activists with the same disfavor as schoolchildren regard teachers' pets.

But activists also had other functions. Komsomol activists from the towns, proud of their militancy, were prominent in the collectivization and anti-religious drives of the early 1930s, armed and outfitted in a quasi-military uniform of "knickers, botinki [boots], stockings, semi-military tunic, belt, and a sam-brown belt (worn diagonally across the chest from shoulder to hip)." [69] Throughout the decade, they considered it their special task to keep watch on bureaucracy and expose official abuses, "regardless of who committed them." These were the aspects of activism that were exciting and appealing to many young people. The watchdog-on-bureaucracy function also had

some legitimacy with a broader population, insofar as the activists were representing a public interest in attacking unpopular bureaucrats. The paradox of
activism in the 1930s was that it involved supporting the regime yet simulta-
neously criticizing its executants.

The critical aspect was personified by Katia, a humble state farm activist in
the Soviet Far East whose problems with her boss are the starting point for the
story of a popular musical of the late 1930s, *A Girl with Character*.

> On the screen appears a bright-haired girl. She is delivering an angry speech un-
> masking her boss, the director of a state grain farm, before a noisy, jeering audi-
> ence of his sycophantic followers. Such is the viewer's first acquaintance with the
> heroine of the film. . . Katia Ivanova. With Katia, we are indignant with the bu-
> reaucrat Meshkov and wait impatiently for [his crimes] to be exposed.[70]

Since district officials are hand in glove with Meshkov, Katia's complaints
are brushed aside. But this "girl with character" will not accept defeat. Full of
high spirits and youthful daring, she makes the long journey to Moscow to
find justice. For her, activism means *challenging authority*—but she challenges
it with the confidence that in the Kremlin, at the highest level, such behavior is
applauded and expected of young Soviet patriots.

Stories like Katia's figure prominently in memoirs of former activists, especially Komsomol members, of this generation. For a number of the young refugees and defectors interviewed in Munich shortly after the war, the most
memorable aspect of their lives in the Komsomol was the struggle against the
corruption and obscurantism of local officials. One respondent, who had
been a teacher and Komsomol activist in a village in Kazakhstan, remembered
fighting the cliques who "dominated kolkhoz leadership and squandered kolkhoz property"; he found allies in the political department of the local
Machine-Tractor Station, a control agency reporting to the center, whose
"implacable attitude" toward local wrongdoing won his admiration.[71]

Another respondent was a Kirgiz who had been posted to a distant region
of the republic, was horrified by the backwardness and corruption he encountered there, and became an activist. "The only people who tried to fight ignorance were teachers who had come from the North and the local Komsomol
leaders." Later, this man became a muckraking journalist, Soviet-style, and exposed a local boss's mistreatment of his wives and children. This prompted his
conservative Kirgiz father to accuse him of having chosen the "low trade" of
informer, but he saw himself in a more heroic guise: "My Komsomol, journal-
istic conscience would not allow me to condone evil." [72]

One of the younger Munich respondents, born in 1921 in the central Russian province of Tver, grew up venerating the Komsomol members from the
city who "literally took over the village" during collectivization, wearing
smart military-style uniforms and carrying guns. "They were fighters who had
declared war on rural backwardness and ignorance." He told the story of how
these activists attacked and ousted the secretary of the rural soviet, a petty bureaucrat who was "the living incarnation of an official of Gogol's day [and]
forced people to come three or four times to the soviet for the simplest matter." This respondent saw the Komsomol in a very different light from later

postwar generations, for whom its iconoclastic and militant spirit was scarcely even a memory. The Komsomol's function, he told the Munich interviewers, was "combatting every shortcoming in the life of the country without regard for the higher-ups, proclaiming boldly the demands and claims of youth." [73]

The "demands and claims of youth" were very important in forming the activist spirit of the prewar years. Another Munich respondent tried to explain why, as a young person growing up in this period (born in 1914), he had supported Soviet power and wanted to be an activist.

> In spite of material difficulties, such as the constant food shortage which was particularly acute at the time, neither I nor the young people around me had any anti-Soviet feelings. We simply found in the heroic tension involved in the building of a new world an excuse for all the difficulties . . . The atmosphere of undaunted struggle in a common cause—the completion of the factory—engaged our imagination, roused our enthusiasm, and drew us into a sort of front-line world where difficulties were overlooked or forgotten.

Activism, as this respondent perceived it, was strongly correlated with youth.

> Of course, it was only we, the younger generation, who accepted reality in this way. Our parents were full of muted but deep discontent. The arguments of our elders, however, had little effect upon us, being, as they were, wholly concerned with material things, while we found in the official justification of all these difficulties a superficial idealism which had considerable appeal to the young.[74]

For some, youth activism seemed the only thing that could save the revolution. A slightly older Munich respondent (born in 1904) described the convictions that had drawn him into activism, starting in the 1920s.

> It . . . was not a desire for honors or rewards that caused me to do without sleep and to devote all my energy to the Party and the Komsomol. . . . I saw that the older generation, worn out after the years of the war and the postwar chaos, were no longer in a position to withstand the difficulties involved in the construction of socialism. I thus came to the conclusion that success in transforming the country depended entirely on the physical exertions and the will of people like myself.[75]

Activists expected to encounter difficulties and dangers. One source of danger was local bosses, incensed by activists' criticisms and interference. Peasant correspondents who criticized kolkhoz and village soviet chairmen were particularly vulnerable because of their physical isolation. One activist schoolteacher in a Siberian village described her struggle against corrupt local bosses:

> I write about various things to the district prosecutor, I write to the district committee of the Communist Party, to the district newspaper, but if you knew how passively those district organizations react, and the wreckers take advantage of that. And how they hate me, some of those big-mouths who have power locally as members of the rural soviet and the board, they take revenge on me in any way they can, they starve me out. . . . But I will not yield my "position." They won't get me by starving me out.[76]

People who disliked the regime and considered activists its surrogates were another source of danger. Even members of the Young Pioneers, the Komsomol's junior branch for ten to fourteen-year olds, might be targetted for attack. In the Rossosh district of central Russia, a stronghold of religious sectarianism and monarchism, Pioneers were subject to regular harassment by religious believers who "call the Pioneer tie 'the devil's noose' and consider that it is a sin to wear it." In 1935, a group of adult believers ambushed some Young Pioneers as they were coming back from the Pioneer club at midnight.

> The sectarians dressed all in white, fell on the Pioneers, drove them into the ravine and didn't let them out for more than half an hour. Arepev [the sectarians' leader] seized Pioneer K. I. Loboda and tore off his clothes and threw stones at the others and broke the head of one of them. As they threw stones, the sectarians shouted: "Little idolatrous devils, I'll show you how to wear a tie." [77]

In the Urals, the worker activist Grigorii Bykov, an aspiring writer, was murdered by local youths with kulak connections after he contributed to a history of the local factory that unmasked class enemies there. Such incidents, frequently reported in the press, made all activists feel that they were living lives of bravery and danger, even when their actual circumstances were quite humdrum, and the story of Pavlik Morozov, the martyred Young Pioneer, had a similar impact.[78]

Activists were supporters of the regime. Some undoubtedly became activists out of ambition, for their support could well be rewarded by honors and promotion. That was why activists were often seen as the regime's protégés, favored and privileged. But in their own self-image they were fighters, people who put their lives on the line in the real-life struggle for socialism. They were militant opponents of "backwardness," which primarily meant religion, subordination of women, and other traditional practices. They were opponents of "bureaucracy," meaning that they were often locked in conflict with local officials. Moscow in principle approved of such struggles. In practice, however, the activists could not rely on Moscow's protection if local officials retaliated, so their perception of their activism as risky and brave was not without foundation.

ঌ ঌ ঌ

The Communists saw themselves as a vanguard, leading the masses to socialism. This mobilizing, exhortatory, educative role was the one they understood best and found most congenial. It gave them a sense of cultural as well as political superiority that outsiders often found difficult to understand. Like the notion of benign conspiracy, the vanguard concept was rooted in the party's prerevolutionary past. When applied to a different situation, that of a regime in power, it was inadequate in several ways. In the first place, the ruling vanguard found that the masses did not always want to follow where it led. Leadership lost some of its glamor in real life: it was less like an officer heroically leading his men in the charge than a tugboat pulling a dead weight into harbor. Sometimes, to make the troops move at all, the officers had to get behind them with guns drawn and drive them forward.

In the second place, this vanguard, mobilizing concept of leadership was little help when it come to the everyday running of the country. That required administration; but since Communists despised bureaucracy and were impatient with law and routine procedures, their relationship with their own administrative apparatus was ambivalent. Bureaucracy, to them, was at best a necessary evil. But it was an evil that kept growing as the state's powers and control aspirations expanded. Once the state had become a virtual monopolist of urban production and distribution, allocation of consumer goods became one of its most important functions, and certainly the one that was of most direct concern to the urban population. Up to the end of the 1920s, the Communists' main interest in this sphere had been redistribution, taking goods and benefits from those who had been privileged under the old regime and giving them to those who had been exploited. Now, as Stalin's revolution ushered in an era of scarcity, distribution itself became a central bureaucratic task and the dominant preoccupation of the party leaders.

2

Hard Times

Ivy Litvinov, wife of future Foreign Minister Maxim Litvinov, made a perceptive comment not long after her arrival in Russia in the hard times at the end of the Civil War. She had supposed, she wrote to a friend in England, that in revolutionary Russia "ideas" would be everything and that "things" would hardly count "because everyone would have what they wanted without superfluities." But "when I walked about the streets of Moscow peering into ground-floor windows I saw the *things* of Moscow huggermuggering in all the corners and realized that they had never been so important." [1] That insight is crucial for understanding everyday Soviet life in the 1930s. *Things* mattered enormously in the Soviet Union in the 1930s for the simple reason that they were so hard to get.

The new importance of things and their distribution was reflected in everyday language. In the 1930s, people no longer talked about "buying" something, but about "getting hold of" it. The phrase "hard to get hold of" was in constant use; a newly popular term for all the things that were hard to get hold of was "deficit goods." People went round with string bags in their pockets, known as "just in case" bags, on the off chance they were able to get hold of some deficit goods. If they saw a queue, they quickly joined it, inquiring what goods were on offer after securing a place. The way to formulate this question was not "What are they selling?" but "What are they giving out?" But public access to goods through regular distribution channels was so unreliable that a whole vocabulary sprung up to describe the alternatives. It might be possible to get the goods informally or under the counter ("on the left") if one had "acquaintances and connections" or "pull" with the right people.[2]

The 1930s was a decade of enormous privation and hardship for the Soviet people, much worse than the 1920s. Famine hit all the major grain-growing regions in 1932–33, and in addition bad harvests caused major disruptions in the food supply in 1936 and 1939. Towns were swamped with new arrivals from the villages, housing was drastically overcrowded, and the rationing system was close to collapse. For the greater part of the urban population, life revolved around the endless struggle to get the basics necessary for survival— food, clothing, shelter.

The new era was ushered in by the closing down of the urban private sector at the end of the 1920s and the onset of collectivization. An American engineer, returning to Moscow in June 1930, after some months absence, described the dramatic impact of the new economic policies:

> On the streets all the shops seemed to have disappeared. Gone was the open market. Gone were the nepmen [private businessmen of the NEP period]. The government stores had showy, empty boxes and other window-dressing. But the interior was devoid of goods.[3]

Living standards dropped sharply at the beginning of the Stalin period in both town and countryside. The famine of 1932–33 took at least three to four million lives and affected the birth rate for several years. Although the state's policy was designed to shield the urban population and let peasants take the brunt, the urban population suffered too: mortality went up, natality down, and per capita urban consumption of meat and lard in 1932 was less than a third of what it had been in 1928.[4]

In 1933, the worst year of the decade, the average married worker in Moscow consumed less than half the amount of bread and flour that his counterpart in Petersburg had consumed at the beginning of the twentieth century and under two-thirds the amount of sugar. His diet included virtually no fats, very little milk and fruit, and a mere fifth of the meat and fish consumed at the turn of the century.[5] The situation improved somewhat in 1935, but a bad harvest in 1936 brought new problems: near famine conditions in parts of the countryside, peasant flight from the collective farms, and urban breadlines in the spring and summer of 1937. The best harvest of the prewar Stalin period, long remembered by the population, was in the fall of 1937. But the last prewar years brought renewed shortages and another drop in living standards.[6]

Over this same period, the Soviet urban population grew at record rates, causing extraordinary housing shortages, overloading of all services, and discomfort of all kinds. Fifteen million people were added to the urban population in the years 1926–33, an increase of almost 60 percent, and by 1939, another 16 million had been added. Moscow's population jumped from 2 million to 3.6 million, Leningrad's rose nearly as steeply. The population of Sverdlovsk, an industrial city in the Urals, rose from under 150,000 to close to half a million, and the growth rates in Stalingrad, Novosibirsk, and other provincial industrial centers was almost as spectacular. Towns like Magnitogorsk, a new metallurgical center in the southern Urals, and Karaganda, a new mining center with a large convict population, climbed from zero population in 1926 to well over 100,000 in 1939.[7] Industrial construction, not housing, was the top priority in the Five-Year Plans of the 1930s. Most of the new urban residents found themselves living in dormitories, barracks, or even mudhuts. Even the infamous communal apartment, the *kommunalka*, with one family per room and no privacy, was almost luxurious by comparison.

SHORTAGES

With the transition to a centrally planned economy at the end of the 1920s, goods shortages became endemic in the Soviet economy. With hindsight, we can see the shortages as partly structural, a product of an economic system with "soft" budgetary constraints where all producers had an incentive to hoard supplies.[8] But few people thought of them that way in the 1930s; scarcity was perceived as a temporary problem, particularly in the first years of the decade, part of the general belt-tightening and sacrifice required by the industrialization drive. Indeed, the shortages of these years, in contrast to those of the post-Stalin period, really were caused as much by underproduction of consumer goods as systemic distribution problems. Under the First Five-Year Plan (1929–32), heavy industry was the top priority and consumer goods took a poor second place. Communists also attributed food shortages to "hoarding" by kulaks and, when the kulaks had gone, to intentional anti-Soviet sabotage in the production and distribution chain. Even if shortages could be rationalized, however, they could not be disregarded. They were already a central fact of economic and everyday life.

When food shortages and bread lines first appeared in 1929–30, the population was alarmed and indignant. To quote *Pravda*'s summary of readers' letters, prepared in August 1930 for the benefit of the party leaders:

> What are people discontented about? In the first place, that the worker is hungry, he has no fats, the bread is ersatz which is impossible to eat. . . . It's a common thing that the wife of a worker stands the whole day in line, her husband comes home from work, and dinner is not prepared, and everyone curses Soviet power. In the lines there is noise, shouting and fights, curses at the expense of Soviet power.[9]

There was worse to come. Famine took hold in the Ukrainian countryside in the winter of 1931. Although there were no reports of famine in the newspapers, news spread quickly by word of mouth; in Kiev, Kharkov, and other cities, despite the authorities' efforts to restrict rail travel and entry into the towns, its effects were visible. The next year, 1932–33, famine spread to the major grain-growing areas of central Russia as well as the North Caucasus and Kazakhstan. The news blackout continued, and in December 1932 internal passports were introduced in an effort to control the flight of hungry peasants to the cities. Bread shortages continued episodically after the famine crisis passed. Even in good years, breadlines in various cities and regions were sufficiently alarming enough to be included on the Politburo's agenda.

The most serious and widespread recurrence of bread lines occurred in the winter and spring of 1936–37, after the harvest failure of 1936. In the Voronezh region, urban bread shortages were reported as early as November, reportedly caused by peasants coming into towns to buy bread because there was no grain in the villages. People were waiting in line for bread from 2AM in Western Siberia that winter, and a local diarist recorded huge lines in his small town, with pushing and shoving and hysterical outbursts. From Vologda, a wife wrote her husband: "Mama and I stood from 4 in the morning and didn't even get any black bread because they didn't bring any at all to the store and that happened in almost all the stores of the town." From Penza, a mother wrote to her daughter: "There is an awful panic with bread here. Thousands of peasants are sleeping outside the bread stores, they came into Penza for bread from 200 kilometers away, it's just indescribable horror. . . . It went below freezing and seven people froze to death taking bread home. They smashed the glass in the store, broke the door." In the villages, it was even worse. "We stand in line for bread from 12 o'clock at night, and they only give one kilogram, even if you're dying of hunger," a woman wrote to her husband from a Iaroslavl kolkhoz. "We go hungry for two days. . . . All the kolokhozniks are queuing for bread and there are awful scenes—people push, many people have been injured. Send us something, or we will die of hunger." [10]

Bread shortages appeared again throughout the country in 1939–40. "Iosif Vissarionovich," wrote a housewife from the Volga to Stalin, "something just awful has started. For bread, you have to go at two o'clock at night and stand until six in the morning to get two kilograms of ryebread." A worker from the Urals wrote that to get bread in his town you had to stand in line from 1 or 2 o'clock at night, sometimes earlier, and wait for almost 12 hours. In Alma-Ata in 1940, there were reports that "the most enormous lines stand around whole days and even nights at bread stores and kiosks. Often, going past these lines, one can hear shouts, noise, squabbling, tears, and sometimes fights." [11]

Bread was not the only thing in short supply. The situation was no better with other basic foodstuffs like meat, milk, butter, and vegetables, not to mention necessities like salt, soap, kerosene, and matches. Fish disappeared too, even from regions with substantial fishing industries. "Why there is no fish . . . I can't imagine," wrote one indignant citizen to Anastas Mikoyan, head of the Food Ministry, in 1940. "We have seas, and they are still the same as before, but then you could have as much [fish] as you wanted of whatever kind, and now I have even forgotten what it looks like." [12]

Even vodka was hard to come by in the early 1930s. This was partly the result of a short-lived temperance movement that resulted in dry laws in various
towns and industrial settlements. The temperance movement was doomed,
however, because of the more powerful imperatives of revenue generation for
industrialization. In a note to Molotov written in September 1930, Stalin
stressed the need to increase vodka production to pay for military expansion
in view of the imminent danger of Polish attack. Within a few years, state
vodka production had expanded to supply as much as a fifth of total state revenue; by the middle of the decade, vodka had become the most important
commodity in state commercial stores.[13]

Clothing, shoes, and all kinds of consumer goods were in even shorter supply than basic foodstuffs, often being completely unobtainable. This reflected
both the state's production priorities, which were strongly weighted in favor
of heavy industry, and the disastrous results of the destruction of artisan and
craft industries at the beginning of the decade. In the 1920s, artisans and
craftsmen had been either the sole or the dominant producers of many necessary everyday items: pottery, baskets, samovars, sheepskin coats, and hats, to
name only a few. All these goods become essentially unobtainable at the beginning of the 1930s, while in public cafeterias, spoons, forks, plates, and
bowls were in such short supply that workers had to queue up for them as well
as for their food; knives were usually unobtainable. Throughout the decade, it
was all but impossible to get such ordinary necessities as basins, oil-lamps, and
kettles because it was now forbidden to use nonferrous metals to manufacture
consumer goods.[14]

The poor quality of the few goods available was a subject of constant complaint. Clothes were sloppily cut and sewn, and there were many reports of
gross defects like missing sleeves in those on sale in state stores. Handles fell
off pots, matches refused to strike, and foreign objects were baked into bread
made from adulterated flour. It was impossible to get clothes, shoes, and
household items repaired, to find a locksmith to replace a lock, or a painter to
paint a wall. To compound the difficulties for ordinary citizens, even those
with the appropriate skills were usually unable to obtain the raw materials to
make or fix things themselves. It was no longer possible to buy paint, nails,
boards, or anything similar for home repairs from the retail trade network;
they had to be stolen from state enterprises or construction sites if they were
to be obtained at all. Nor was it usually possible even to buy thread, needles,
buttons, or other similar items. The sale of flax, hemp, yarn, and linen to the
population was prohibited because these materials were all in such short
supply.[15]

The situation was only slightly improved by a law of March 27, 1936, that
re-legalized the individual practice of such trades as shoe-repair, cabinetmak-
ing, carpentry, dressmaking, hairdressing, laundering, locksmith work, pho-
tography, plumbing, tailoring, and upholstery. Individual craftsmen were
allowed one apprentice, but they could only make goods when customers ordered them, not for general sale. Customers had to provide their own materials (e.g., buttons and thread as well as cloth for a suit to be made by a private

tailor). Other forms of artisan activity, including almost all those involved with food, remained prohibited. Baking, sausage-making, and other food-related trades were excluded from the sphere of legitimate individual-artisan activity, although peasants were still permitted to sell homemade pies at designated locations.[16]

Shoes were one of the the worst problems for consumers. In addition to the catastrophes that had hit all small-scale consumer production, shoe production was affected by acute leather shortages—the result of mass slaughter of farm animals during collectivization. As a result, the government forbade *any* artisan production of shoes in 1931, making the consumer totally dependent on the shoes produced in inadequate quantities by state industry, which were often of such poor quality that they fell apart at first wearing. Every Russian who lived through the 1930s has horror stories about shoes: trying to buy them, trying to get them repaired, patching them up at home, losing a shoe or having it stolen (as in Mikhail Zoshchenko's famous story "The Galosh"), and so on. Children's shoes were even more of a problem than adults': in Iaroslavl as the new school year began in 1935, not one single pair of children's shoes was to be had in the stores.[17]

On more than one occasion the Politburo resolved that something really must be done about the supply and distribution of consumer goods. But even Stalin's personal interest in the problem failed to produce results.[18] At the end of the 1930s, just as at the beginning, acute shortages of clothing, shoes, and textiles were reported: there were queues of up 6,000 people in Leningrad, and the NKVD reported that one shoe store in central Leningrad was attracting such long lines that movement along the street was disrupted and store windows had been shattered by the crowds. In Kiev, a citizen complained that thousands of people were standing in line all night outside clothing stores. In the morning, the police was escorting customers into the store in batches of five to ten people, "arms linked (so that nobody can jump the queue) . . . like convicts."[19]

Once there were shortages, there had to be scapegoats. Supply Minister Anastas Mikoyan wrote to the OGPU in the early 1930s suggesting there must be "wrecking" in the distribution chain: "We send out a lot, but the goods don't arrive." The OGPU obligingly came up with a list of "counterrevolutionary organizations" that were baking mice into bread and mixing screws in salad. A Moscow gang of former kulaks allegedly "threw rubbish, nails, wire and broken glass into the food" in 1933 so as to cripple workers who ate it. There was more scapegoating of "wreckers" after the 1936–37 bread shortages: in Smolensk and Boguchar, for example, officials were accused of creating artificial shortages of bread and sugar; in Ivanovo, they were accused of poisoning the workers' bread; and in Kazan the breadlines were blamed on rumors spread by counterrevolutionaries.[20] When the next round of acute shortages hit, in the winter of 1939–40, such accusations came from the public rather than from the government, as concerned citizens wrote in to the political leaders urging them to find and punish the "wreckers" who were responsible.[21]

Housing

Despite the extraordinary growth in the Soviet urban population in the 1930s, residential housing construction was almost as neglected as the manufacture of consumer goods. It was not until the Khrushchev period that anything was done to alleviate the tremendous overcrowding that had characterized Soviet urban living for over a quarter of a century. Meanwhile, people lived in communal apartments, usually one family to a room, and in dormitories and barracks. A small, highly privileged group had separate apartments. A larger group made their homes in corridors and "corners" in other people's apartments: those in corridors and hallways usually had beds, but corner-dwellers slept on the floor in a corner of the kitchen or other public space.

Most urban residential buildings had become the property of the state after the revolution, and municipal soviets had charge of this housing stock.[22] The housing authorities determined how much space apartment dwellers were entitled to, and these space norms—the notorious "square meters"—were engraved on every big-city-dweller's heart. In Moscow, average living space was 5.5 square meters per capita in 1930, dropping down to just over 4 square meters in 1940. In new and rapidly industrializing towns the situation was even worse than in Moscow: Magnitogorsk and Irkutsk both had under 4 square meters, and in Krasnoiarsk the per capita norm in 1933 was a mere 3.4 square meters.[23]

Municipal housing authorities had the right to evict existing residents—for example, those they regarded as "class enemies"—and move new residents into already occupied apartments. The latter practice, known euphemistically as "consolidation," was one of the main bourgeois nightmares of the 1920s and early 1930s. It meant that a family apartment could suddenly, by municipal fiat, become a multifamily or communal apartment whose new inhabitants, usually lowerclass, were unknown and frequently uncongenial to the original residents. Once such a blow struck, there was virtually no escape. The original family could not move because of the housing shortage and the absence of a private rental market.

From the end of 1932, when internal passports and urban registration were reintroduced, residents of big cities were required to have residence permits, issued by a department of the security police. In individual apartment houses, superintendents and cooperative boards had the obligation of registering the residents. As under the old regime, superintendents and yardmen, whose basic function was to keep the building and courtyard clean, had a regular relationship with the police, keeping an eye on residents and acting as informers.[24]

All sorts of housing scams were practiced in Moscow and other big cities: fictive marriages and divorces, registration of nonrelated persons as relatives, the renting out of "beds and corners" at exorbitant prices (up to 50 percent of monthly wages). It was reported in 1933 that "conversion of coalsheds, warehouses, cellars, and substairway spaces [into housing] has become a mass phenomenon in Moscow." The shortage of housing meant that divorced couples often remained in the same apartment for want of anywhere to move to. This was the case with the Lebedevs, whose attachment to their luxurious apartment of almost 22 square meters in central Moscow led them to continue cohabitation, together with their eight-year-old son, for six years after their divorce, even though relations were so bad that they were regularly taken to court for beating each other. Sometimes physical violence went even further. In the Crimean city of Simferopol the authorities discovered the decomposing corpse of a woman in the apartment of the Dikhov family. She turned out to be their aunt, whom they had murdered to gain possession of her apartment.[25]

So acute was the housing crisis in Moscow and Leningrad that even the best connections and official status often failed to secure a separate apartment. Politicians and government offices were deluged by citizens' pleas and complaints about inadequate housing. A thirty-six-year-old Leningrad worker who had been living for five years in a corridor wrote to Molotov begging for "a room or a little apartment where I can build a personal life," that was "as necessary to me as air." The children of a Moscow family of six begged for rescue from their accommodation in a windowless cubbyhole under the staircase totalling 6 square meters, that is, 1 square meter per capita.[26]

Communal apartments with one family per room were the standard form of housing in Russian cities in the Stalin era.

> The room had no running water; sheets or curtains marked off subareas where two or three generations slept and sat; food dangled out of winter windows in sacks. Shared sinks, toilets, washtubs, and cooking facilites (usually nothing more than Primus . . . burners and cold water taps) lay either in a no-man's land between the dwelling rooms or down an unheated, laundry-festooned hallway.[27]

The term "communal" has an ideological ring, summoning up a image of collective socialist living. But the reality was very different, and even in theory there was little attempt to develop an elaborate ideological justification. True, in the Civil War years, when municipal soviets first started "consolidating" apartments, one of the motives was to equalize living standards of workers and the bourgeoisie; Communists often took pleasure in observing the dismay of respectable bourgeois families forced to let scruffy proletarians live in their apartments. For a brief period during the Cultural Revolution at the late 1920s and early 1930s, radical architects favored communal apartments for ideological reasons and built new workers' housing with shared kitchens and bathrooms. In Magnitogorsk, for example, the first permanent residential buildings were built on a plan that not only obliged families to share bathrooms and toilets but also initially provided no kitchens—on the assumption that everyone would be eating in public cafeterias.[28] Except in new industrial cities like Magnitogorsk, however, most communal apartments of the 1930s were converted from old single-family apartments, not newly built, and the main reason for conversion was practical: housing shortage.

In reality, by most accounts, communal apartments were far from encouraging of communal attitudes and practices among residents; in fact, they tended to do the opposite. Private property, including the pots, pans, and plates that had to be stored in the kitchen, a public area, was jealously guarded by each individual family. Demarcation lines were strictly laid down. Envy and covetousness flourished in the closed world of the *kommunalka*, where space and family size were often mismatched and families with large rooms were often deeply resented by families with small ones. Out of these resentments came many denunciations and lawsuits whose objective was to increase the denouncer's or plaintiff's living space at the expense of a neighbor.

One such long-running feud was described in a complaint from a Moscow teacher whose husband was serving an eight-year sentence for counterrevolutionary agitation. The family (parents and two sons) had lived for almost two decades in a large room—42 square meters—in a communal apartment in Moscow. "For all these years our room has been the apple of discord for all residents of our apartment," the teacher wrote. Hostile neighbors harassed them in various ways, including writing denunciations to various local authorities. The result was that the family was successively disfranchised, refused passports, and finally, after the father's arrest, evicted.[29]

Life in a communal apartment, side by side with people of different backgrounds and classes who were strangers sharing facilities and the responsibility of keeping them clean, without privacy and under constant surveillance by neighbors, was extremely stressful for most people. No wonder the satirist Mikhail Zoshchenko, in a famous story about a communal apartment, called its inhabitants "nervous people." A catalogue of the awful possibilities of life in the communal apartment appeared in a government circular of 1935 condemning "hooligan behavior" in apartments, including "organizing regular drinking parties accompanied by noise, quarrels, and cursing in the apartment; the infliction of beatings (in particular of women and children); insults, threats to get even by use of one's official or party position; immoral conduct; national [i.e., ethnic] persecution; personal insults; carrying out of various mean tricks (throwing other people's things out of the kitchen and other places of communal use, spoiling food prepared by other residents, damaging property and produce, and so on)."[30]

"Each apartment had its mad person, just as each apartment had its drunkard or drunkards, its trouble-maker or trouble-makers, its informer, and so on," said one veteran of communal apartment life. Persecution mania was the most common form of madness: for example, "a woman neighbor would become convinced that others were putting bits of glass in her soap, that they wanted to poison her."[31] The conditions of communal living clearly exacerbated mental illness and created nightmarish conditions for both the sufferers and their neighbors. In one case, a woman named Bogdanova, 52 years old and single, living in a good-sized room of 20 square meters in a communal apartment in Leningrad, maintained a feud with her neighbors that lasted many years and involved innumerable denunciations and lawsuits. Bogdanova said her neighbors were kulaks, embezzlers, and profiteers. The neighbors said she was crazy, which this was also the opinion of the NKVD, called in to sort the quarrel out, and the doctors. Despite this conclusion, the authorities decided that it was impossible to evict Bogdanova because she refused to accept placement in another apartment and her "extremely nervous condition" meant that she could not be moved by force.[32]

Against the horror stories must be put the recollections of a minority whose neighbors in communal apartments were mutually supportive and came to constitute a kind of extended family. An example was the communal apartment in Moscow, where neighbors were friendly and helpful to each other, left their doors unlocked during the day, and turned a blind eye when the wife of an "enemy of the people" moved in illegally with her young son to share her sister's room.[33] Most of the positive recollections of communal apartments, including this one, are of childhood: children, with less developed private-property instincts than their parents, often liked having other children to play with and found it interesting to observe so many varieties of adult behavior.

In the new industrial towns, a peculiarity of the housing situation—and indeed of urban services in general—was that housing and other services were provided by enterprises rather than by local soviets, as was otherwise standard. Thus, the "company town," with the plant controlling all facilities as well as providing employment, became a feature of Soviet life. In Magnitogorsk, 82 percent of living space was owned by the city's main industrial plant, the Magnitogorsk Metallurgical Complex. Even in Moscow, company-built housing became common in the 1930s.[34]

This housing usually took the form of barracks or dormitories. At one big new industrial site in Siberia at the beginning of the 1930s, 95 percent of the workers were living in barracks. In Magnitogorsk in 1938, only 47 percent of all housing was in barracks—but an additional 18 percent consisted of mud huts, built over dugouts out of sod, thatch, and scraps of metal by the inhabitants themselves.[35] One-story barracks, consisting either of large rooms with many iron beds in rows or divided into small rooms, were the basic housing for unmarried workers in new industrial cities and common on the outskirts of old ones; married workers with families sometimes had to live in them too, despite the absence of privacy. Dormitories were the standard housing for students and also common for young unmarried blue- and white-collar workers.

John Scott describes a relatively decent barracks in Magnitogorsk—a low wooden structure, whitewashed, "whose double walls were lined with straw. The tarpaper roof leaked in spring. There were thirty rooms in the barrack. The inhabitants of each had made a little brick or iron stove so that as long as there was wood or coal the rooms could be kept warm. The low corridor was illuminated by one small electric light bulb." A room for two people "was about six feet by ten and had one small window, which was pasted around with newspaper to keep the cold out. There was a small table, a little brick stove, and one three-legged stool. The two iron bedsteads were rickety and narrow. There were no springs, just thick planks put across the iron frame." The barracks had no bathroom and probably no running water. "There had been a kitchen, but now a family was living in it so that everybody did his cooking on his own stove."[36]

As a foreigner, albeit a worker, Scott was put in barracks that were better than the norm. Magnitogorsk was full of barracks, all "one-story structures that stretched in rows as far as they eye could see and had no individual or distinguishing features. 'You'd come home, searching and searching,' explained one bemused barracks resident, 'but all the barracks were identical and you couldn't find yours.'" The barracks in such new towns were usually divided into large common areas furnished with "cots for sleep, a stove for heating, a table in the middle, often even no tables and chairs," as was reported of Kuznetsk in Siberia. Usually men and women were in separate barracks, or at least separate large common rooms. The largest barracks, built for 100 people, were often occupied by 200 or more, with the beds used in shifts. Such overcrowding was not uncommon. One barracks in Moscow, owned by a big electrical plant, housed 550 men and women in 1932: "At two square meters per tenant, the space was so tight that 50 slept on the floor and some used the straw-mattress beds in shifts." [37]

Dormitories for students and wage earners followed the same general pattern as barracks: large rooms (separate for men and women) sparsely furnished with iron beds and nightstands with a single hanging bulb in the center for light. Even in an elite Moscow plant like "Serp i Molot," 60 percent of the production workers lived in dormitories of one kind or another in 1937. An investigation of workers' dormitories in Novosibirsk in 1938 found some in parlous condition. Two-story wooden dormitories for construction workers lacked electricity or any form of light, and the construction company did not supply heating fuel or kerosene. The inhabitants included single women, whom the report recommended should be moved out forthwith, since the lifestyle in the dormitory was "degenerate (drinking etc)." Conditions were better elsewhere, however. Women workers, mainly Komsomol members, were living in relatively comfort in a dormitory furnished with beds, tables, and chairs, and with electric light, albeit no running water.[38]

The miserable condition of barracks and dormitory life aroused concern, and in the second half of the 1930s, there was a campaign to improve it. Activists from the wives' volunteer movement added curtains and other amenities. Enterprises were instructed to divide up the big rooms in dormitories and barracks so that families living there could have some privacy. The Urals Machine-building Plant in Sverdlovsk reported in 1935 that it had already converted almost all its big barracks into small separate rooms; a year later the Stalino Metallurgical Plant reported that all the 247 workers' families living in "general rooms" in the barracks were about to get individual rooms. In Magnitogorsk, the conversion process was almost completed by 1938. But the era of barracks living was not so quickly outlived, even in Moscow, let alone the new industrial towns of the Urals and Siberia. Despite a Moscow ordinance of 1934 forbidding further construction of barracks in the city, 225 new barracks were added in 1938 to the 5,000 already in use.[39]

MISERIES OF URBAN LIFE

Urban life in the Soviet Union in the 1930s was a mess. In the old cities, urban services such as public transport, roads, and power and water supply were all overwhelmed by sudden population growth, heightened industrial demand, and tight budgets. The new industrial towns were even worse off, since services there were starting from zero. "The physical aspect of the cities is dreadful," wrote an American engineer working in the Soviet Union in the early 1930s. "Stench, filth, dilapidation batter the sense at every turn." [40]

Moscow was the showcase city of the Soviet Union. The construction of the first lines of the Moscow Metro, complete with escalators and murals in its palatial underground stations, was one of the country's proudest achievements; even Stalin, with friends, took a midnight ride when it opened in the early 1930s.[41] Moscow had trams, trolley buses, and buses. More than two-thirds of its inhabitants were connected to sewage systems and had running water even at the beginning of the decade; by the end, it was close to three-quarters. To be sure, most of them lived in houses without bathrooms and had to take their baths once a week or so at public bathhouses—but at least the city was relatively well supplied with bathhouses, in contrast to many others.[42]

Outside Moscow, life quickly became grimmer. Even the province surrounding Moscow was poorly supplied with basic services: Liubertsy, a district center in the Moscow region, had not a single bathhouse for its population of 65,000 people, while in Orekhovo-Zuevo a model workers' settlement with nurseries, a club, and a dispensary still lacked street lighting and running water. In Voronezh, similarly, new apartment buildings for workers were being built without running water or sewage connections as late as 1937. In the cities of Siberia, the majority of the population lacked running water, sewage, and central heating. With a population approaching half a million, Stalingrad still had no sewage system in 1938. Novosibirsk, with limited sewage and water systems in 1929, had only three bathhouses for a population of over 150,000.[43]

Dnepropetrovsk, a booming and well-established industrial city in the Ukraine with a population of close to 400,000, situated in the midst of fertile agricultural land, had no sewage system as of 1933, and its workers' settlements lacked paved streets, public transport, electric light, and running water. Water was rationed and sold for 1 ruble a bucket in the barracks. The whole city was short of power—in the winter, almost all the street lights on the main street had to be turned off—even though the big Dnieper hydroelectric project was next door. In 1933, the party secretary sent a desperate appeal to the center asking for funds for urban improvement, pointing out that the public health situation had seriously deteriorated: malaria was rampant, with 26,000 cases registered that summer as against 10,000 the year before.[44]

The new industrial towns had even fewer amenities. Top officials of Leninsk city soviet in Siberia painted a gloomy picture of their town in a begging letter to a senior Siberian official.

> With a population of 80,000 . . . Leninsk-Kuznetsk is extremely backward in the area of culture and urban amenities. . . . Out of 80 kilometers of city streets, only one street is paved and that not completely. Because of the absence of proper roads, crossings, footpaths etc, the mud reaches such proportions in spring and

autumn that workers have great difficulty getting to work and back home, and classes are interrupted in the schools. Street lighting is also substandard. Only the center is lighted for a distance of 3 kilometers, the rest of the city, not to speak of the outskirts, is in darkness.[45]

Magnitogorsk, the paradigmatic new industrial town, in many respects a showplace, had only one paved road of 15 kilometers and little street lighting. "Most of the city [was] served by outdoor cesspits (*iamy*), whose contents were emptied into cisterns hauled away by trucks"; even the comparatively elite Kirov district did not have a proper sewage system for many years. The city's water supply was contaminated by industrial effluents. Most of Magnitogorsk's workers lived in settlements on the outskirts of town consisting of "makeshift housing along a single dirt road, . . . covered by huge puddles of filthy water, piles of garbage and numerous open outdoor toilets."[46]

Residents and visitors to Moscow and Leningrad have left vivid descriptions of its streetcars and their incredible overcrowding. There were strict rules that passengers must enter the car through the rear door and exit at the front, requiring a constant forward-squirming motion by the passengers. Often, the crush made it impossible for passengers to get out when they reached their stop. Schedules were erratic: sometimes streetcars simply failed to run; in Leningrad there were sightings of "wild streetcars" (i.e., unscheduled cars with unauthorized drivers and conductors), cruising along the tracks and illegally collecting passengers and pocketing their fares.[47]

In provincial towns, where paved roads were still a comparative rarity at the end of the decade, public transport services of any kind were minimal. Stalingrad in 1938 had a streetcar system with 67 kilometers of track, but no buses. Pskov, with a population of 60,000, had no streetcar system and no paved roads in 1939: its entire municipal transport consisted of two buses. Penza also lacked a streetcar system before the Second World War, although one had been planned as far back as 1912; its municipal transport in 1940 consisted of twenty one buses. Magnitogorsk acquired a short streetcar route in 1935, but at the end of the decade it still had only eight buses, used by the major employers "to circle the city and round up and drop off their workers, regardless of where they lived."[48]

It was dangerous to walk the streets in many Soviet cities in the 1930s. The new industrial towns and the workers' settlements in old ones were the most perilous. Here drink, the congregation of restless single men, inadequate policing, bad living conditions, and unpaved and unlighted streets all contributed to a lawless, frontier atmosphere. Robberies, murders, drunken fights, and random attacks on passersby were common. Ethnic conflicts often occurred at worksites and barracks with an ethnically mixed labor force. The authorities attributed the problems to peasant workers newly arrived from the countryside, "often with dark pasts or déclassés elements."[49]

The Soviet word for disruptive and anti-social public behavior was "hooliganism." This was a term with a complex history and shifting definition, associated in the 1920s and early 1930s with disruptive, disrespectful, and anti-social behavior, often by young men. The flavor was caught in the catalogue of "hooligan" acts listed in a law journal in 1934: insults, fistfights, breaking of windows, shooting off guns in the streets, challenging passersby, breaking up cultural events in the club and smashing plates in the cafeteria, disturbing residents' sleep with fights and noise late at night.[50]

The upsurge of hooliganism in the first half of the 1930s became a matter of public concern. In Orel, hooligans so terrorized the population that workers stopped going to work; in Omsk, "workers of the evening shift were obliged to remain at the plant and spend the night so as not to risk being beaten and stripped." In Nadezhdinsk in the Urals, citizens

> have been literally terrorized by hooliganism not only at night but even in the daytime. Hooliganism took the form of pointless accosting, shooting on the street, hurling insults, fisticuffs, breaking of windows, and so on. Hooligans go in whole gangs to the club, breaking up cultural events, going into the cafeteria and snatching plates from waiters, and so on. [They] go into the workers' dormitory, making a pointless noise there and sometimes fighting, interfering with the workers' sleep.[51]

Parks were frequently sites of hooliganism. At one factory settlement on the upper Volga with a population of 7,000, the park and club were described as hooligan territory.

> At the entrance to the park and in the park itself you can buy wine of all kind in any quantity. It is not surprising that drunkenness and hooliganism have assumed great dimensions in the settlement. The hooligans for the most part remain unpunished and get more and more brazen. Not long ago they inflicted knife wounds on comrade Davydov, head of production in the chemical plant, and killed chauffeur Suvoreva and other citizens.

Hooligans disrupted the triumphant opening of the Khabarovsk Park of Culture and Rest. The park was poorly lit, and as soon as darkness fell, "the hooligans began 'doing the rounds.'. . . [They] bumped women unceremoniously from behind, knocked off their hats, used foul language, and started fights on the dance floor and in the alleys."[52]

Trains and railway stations were other places where crime flourished. Gangs of robbers preyed on passengers in suburban and intercity trains in the Leningrad region: they were described as "bandits," a tougher term than "hooligan," and received the death sentence. Railway stations were always thronged with people—recent arrivals with nowhere to stay, would-be travelers trying to get tickets, black marketeers, pickpockets, and the like. A station in the Leningrad region was described in the mid 1930s as "more like a flophouse than a decent station"; "suspicious people live for three or four days in the waiting room, drunks are often lying about, speculators trade in cigarettes, various dubious types flit to and fro. In the buffet there is continual drunkenness and unbelievable filth." At the Novosibirsk railway station, the only way to get a ticket was to buy it on the black market from a gang headed by "the professor": "middle height, nickname 'Ivan Ivanovich,' in a white straw hat with a pipe in his mouth."[53]

SHOPPING AS A SURVIVAL SKILL

With the outlawing of private enterprise at the end of the 1920s, the state became the main and often the only legal distributor of goods. All large social goods like housing, medical care, higher education, and vacations were distributed by state agencies.[54] The citizen obtained them by making an application to the relevant bureaucracy. This bureaucracy would weigh the claims according to various criteria, including the citizen's social class: proletarians had highest priority, disenfranchised "class aliens" lowest. Almost always, there were long waiting lists because the relevant good was in short supply. After the citizen's name came to the top of the list, he or she was supposed to be allocated an apartment of the appropriate size or assigned a vacation place. Apartments and resort places did not come free, but the charges were low. For most of these large social goods, no legal private market existed.[55]

In the sphere of trade—that is, the distribution of food, clothing, and other consumer goods—the situation was a little more complicated. The state was not the only legal distributor, since from 1932 peasants were allowed to sell produce in kolkhoz markets. Moreover, the existence of high-priced "commercial" stores provided a quasi-market element, even though they were stateowned. Nevertheless, in this sphere, too, the state had become a near-monopolistic distributor.

It is scarcely surprising that the new distribution system malfunctioned, given the magnitude of the task of replacing private trade and the fact that it was accomplished in haste, without prior planning, and at a time of general crisis and upheaval. But the scale of the malfunctioning and its impact on the everyday life of urban citizens were remarkable. This was a policy disaster whose dimensions and long-term consequences were exceeded only by those of collectivization. Town-dwellers, to be sure, did not usually starve as a result of the new trade structure, nor were they liable to be arrested and deported, as happened to peasants during collectivization. Nevertheless, the conditions of urban life worsened suddenly and drastically at the end of the 1920s, and the attendant suffering and discomfort of the population were enormous. Although the situation improved somewhat in the mid 1930s, distribution of consumer goods remained a major problem in the Soviet economy for the next half century.

While Soviet political leaders held certain assumptions about trade, notably that the profit-driven capitalist market was evil and the resale of goods for more than the purchase price constituted a crime ("speculation"), they gave little advance thought to what "socialist trade" might mean. They had no notion that their system would generate chronic scarcity, as the Hungarian economist Janos Kornai has argued that it did; on the contrary, they expected that it would soon generate abundance. Similarly, they had no notion that creating a state monopoly on distribution would mean conferring on the state bureaucracy a central allocative function that was to have immense implications for the relationship of state and society as well as for social stratification. As Marxists, the Soviet leaders thought it was production that mattered, not distribution. Many retained an instinctive feeling that trade, even state trade, was a dirty business—and the formal and informal distribution systems that emerged in the 1930s only confirmed that opinion.[56]

Initially, the main aspects of the new trade system were rationing and so-called "closed distribution." Rationing meant distributing limited quantities of goods on presentation of ration cards along with money payment. Closed distribution meant that goods were distributed at the workplace through closed stores to which only employees or persons on the list were admitted. In a longer perspective, it can be seen that this was the beginning of a system of hierarchically differentiated access to consumer goods that became a permanent feature of Soviet trade and a stratifier of Soviet society.

Both rationing and closed distribution were improvisations in the face of economic crisis, not policies adopted for ideological reasons. True, some enthusiastic Marxist theorists revived the old Civil War arguments that rationing was precisely the form of distribution that was appropriate to socialism. The party leaders, however, had little sympathy for this line of reasoning. They felt rationing was something to be ashamed of, an indication of state poverty and economic crisis. When rationing reappeared at the end of the 1920s, it was a product of local initiative, not a central policy decision. When bread rationing was abolished at the beginning of 1935, it was presented to the public as a major step toward socialism and the good life, even though in fact it meant a fall in real wages and many low-paid workers resented the change. In the closed councils of the Politburo, Stalin was particularly insistent on the importance of abolishing rationing.[57]

Despite the leaders' lack of enthusiasm for rationing, it was so frequently practiced that it may be regarded as the default option of Stalinist distribution. Rationing was introduced in Russia during the First World War and continued through the Civil War. It was officially in force again from 1929 to 1935 and from 1941 to 1947—in total, almost half the Stalin period. Even in nonrationing periods, local authorities were likely to impose rationing locally, without central approval, whenever supply problems got out of hand. In the late 1930s, both rationing and closed distribution crept back into widespread use as a result of the unsanctioned initiative of local authorities. When goods were really scarce, rationing seemed to them—and often to the local population—the easiest way of handling the problem. Closed distribution appealed to local officials and elites, but not the rest of the population, because it guaranteed their own privileged access to scarce goods.

Rationing was primarily an urban phenomenon, introduced spontaneously in 1928–29 in Soviet cities, starting with Odessa and other Ukrainian centers, as a response to supply problems caused by grain procurements problems. It applied to all major food items and was later extended to most common manufactured items like coats and shoes.[58]

As in the Civil War, rationing in the First Five-Year Plan period was explicitly socially discriminatory, with industrial workers in the highest category, and the lowest category—traders, including former traders who had changed their occupation within the past year, priests, beer-hall owners, and other social aliens—debarred from the possession of ration books altogether.[59] This was the same principle of "proletarian preference" that was applied in other contexts (e.g., educational admissions and allocation of housing) as part of the Soviet affirmative action policies. In practice, however, the distribution of goods under rationing followed more complex patterns. In the first place, "proletarian preference" was undermined when various white-collar categories like professors and engineers acquired equal priority with workers. In the second place, the level of total state provisioning, hence of rations, varied greatly according to the priority accorded different regions, bureaucracies, industries, and enterprises.[60]

The most important factor subverting the "proletarian preference" principle, however, was closed distribution. Closed distribution was the distribution of rationed goods at the workplace through closed stores and cafeterias accessible only to registered workers at that enterprise.[61] It developed along with the rationing system, coexisting with the "open distribution" network of state stores accessible to the public as a whole, and in the course of the First Five-Year Plan came to embrace industrial workers, railwaymen, timber workers, state farm personnel, office workers in state agencies and many other categories—a total of about 40,000 stores at the beginning of 1932, constituting almost a third of all retail outlets in urban areas. The concentration of supply at the workplace was increased by the expansion of enterprise cafeterias, where workers had their hot meal of the day. Their number grew fivefold during the First Five-Year Plan, reaching over 30,000. By July 1933, two-thirds of the population of Moscow and 58 percent of the population of Leningrad were served by them.[62]

Closed distribution was meant to protect the working population from the worst consequences of shortages and link rations to employment. But it also quickly developed another function (described in more detail in Chapter 4), which was to provide privileged supply for certain categories of privileged people. Special closed distributors were established for various elite categories of officials and professionals, supplying them with much higher-quality goods than were available in the normal closed stores and enterprise cafeterias. Foreigners working in the Soviet Union had their own closed distribution system, known as Insnab.[63]

Closed distribution was officially abolished in 1935. Six months later, however, inspectors of the Ministry of Internal Trade noticed that "some shops were reserving goods for special groups of buyers, creating various forms of closed provisioning." Although Trade Minister Izrail Veitser categorically forbade it, the practice continued because it was advantageous to local elites, providing them with privileged access to goods. As shortages once again became acute at the end of the decade, closed distribution points multiplied. For example, when big breadlines reappeared in Kustanai, Alma-Ata, and other provincial towns at the end of 1939, local authorities established closed stores to which only those "on the list" were admitted. There were closed snackbars for employees in institutions and enterprises all over the country.[64]

State and cooperative stores in the 1930s, both during and after rationing, tended to have low prices and long lines, and were constantly running out of goods. But other options were available if you had the money. The legal alternatives were kolkhoz markets, Torgsin shops, and state "commercial" stores.

Kolkhoz markets were successors to the peasant markets that had existed in Russian towns for centuries. Although tolerated in the NEP period, markets like Moscow's Sukharevka acquired a very unsavory reputation, and during the First Five-Year Plan many were closed down by local authorities. In May 1932, however, the legality of their existence was recognized in a central government decree regulating their functioning. This decree was prompted by the urgent need to increase the flow of produce from countryside to town, which was threatening to dry up. One of its peculiarities was that it restored the right to trade to peasants and rural craftsmen, but not to anyone else. Any urban citizen who engaged in trade was labeled a "speculator," and local authorities were sternly instructed "not to allow the opening of stores and booths by private traders and in every way to root out resellers and speculators trying to make a profit at the expense of workers and peasants." [65]

In practice, Soviet authorities never succeeded in keeping "resellers and speculators" out of the kolkhoz markets, which became a major locus of black-market activity and shady dealings of all kinds. Altogether the battle against "speculation" was never-ending, the authorities became quite tolerant of urban citizens coming in to hawk secondhand clothes and other personal possessions, or even to sell small quantities of new (bought or handmade) goods. The markets, in fact, became "oases of private trade" in the Soviet economy.[66]

Kolkhoz market prices, which were not set by the state but allowed to float, were always higher than prices in ordinary state stores and sometimes even higher than those in the commercial stores discussed below. In Moscow markets in 1932, the going price for meat was 10 to 11 rubles a kilo, as against 2 rubles in ordinary state stores, while the going market price for potatoes was 1 ruble a kilo, compared to 18 kopecks.[67] Although the differential went down in the mid 1930s, it remained significant and was always liable to rise again when supplies ran short. For most ordinary wage earners, the kolkhoz market was too expensive to be used, except on special occasions.

Equally anomalous, though short-lived, were the Torgsin stores, which from 1930 to 1936 sold scarce goods for foreign currency, gold, silver, and other valuables. Forerunners of the later Soviet hard-currency stores, the Torgsin stores differed from them in being open to any member of the public with the appropriate currency. Their purpose was simple: to expand Soviet hard currency reserves so that the country could import more equipment for the industrialization drive. Torgsin prices were not high (both Soviet "commercial" prices and prices at the kolkhoz market were higher), but for Soviet citizens, Torgsin was a very costly place to shop because you had to sacrifice the remnants of the family silver or your grandfather's gold watch, or even your own wedding ring. Some of the central Torgsin stores, especially the one on Gorky Street in Moscow that took over from the famous Eliseev grocery store, were luxuriously appointed and lavishly stocked. In the famine years, a shocked foreign journalist reported, "People [stood] outside there in wistful groups looking at tempting pyramids of fruit; at boots and fur coats tastefully displayed; at butter and white bread and other delicacies that are for them unobtainable." [68]

"Commercial" stores originally meant state stores selling goods for high prices outside the rationing system. They emerged as a recognized institution at the end of 1929, initially selling clothes and cotton and woolen cloth, but the range of goods soon expanded to include luxury food items like smoked fish and caviar as well as more mundane goods like vodka, cigarettes, and basic foods. In the rationing period, commercial prices were usually twice to four times as high as those charged for purchases with ration cards. In 1931, for example, shoes that cost 11 to 12 rubles in ordinary stores (if you could find them!) cost 30 to 40 rubles in commercial stores; trousers priced at 9 rubles in ordinary stores cost 17 rubles. Cheese was almost double the ordinary price in commercial stores, while sugar was more than eight times the price. In 1932, commercial stores accounted for a tenth of all retail turnover. By 1934, after a substantial lowering of the differential between commercial and ordinary prices, their share had risen to a quarter. [69]

With the abolition of rationing in 1935, the network of commercial stores expanded. Model department stores opened in many cities, along with specialized stores selling manufactured goods of higher quality and for higher prices than ordinary state stores. The new Trade Minister, Izrail Veitser, put forward a philosophy of "Soviet free trade," which meant emphasizing customer choice and competition between stores within a state-trade framework. There undoubtedly was a great improvement in the trade system in the third quarter of the 1930s, associated in large part with a substantial increase in state investment, which was three times as great during the Second Five-Year Plan (1933–37) as it had been during the First. [70]

But the improvement was greatest for the better-off segments of the urban population. While the differential between commercial and ordinary state prices was further reduced, this was achieved as much by raising the ordinary prices as by lowering commercial ones. Whereas at the beginning of the 1930s, acute shortages constituted the main burden on citizens at all levels of society, from the middle of the decade, complaints that real wages were too low and goods consequently out of reach were heard almost as frequently, particularly from low-income groups. "I can't afford to buy food in the commercial shops, everything is expensive, and so you walk and wander around like a deathly shade, and get very thin and weak," wrote one worker to the Leningrad authorities in 1935. When basic state prices for clothing and other manufactured goods doubled in January 1939, the biggest one-time rise of the decade, the Leningrad NKVD reported enormous grumbling in the city, with many complaints that privileged people were indifferent to the plight of ordinary citizens and that Molotov had deceived the people by promising that prices would not rise again. [71]

"Speculation"

As we have already seen, it was extraordinarily difficult to obtain goods of any kind, from shoes to apartments, via the state's formal bureaucratic distribution channels. In the first place, there were simply not enough goods to go round. In the second place, the bureaucracies that distributed them did so extremely inefficiently and corruptly. State stores had long lines and often empty shelves. The housing waiting lists of local authorities were so long, and the informal methods of circumventing them so prevalent, that virtually nobody ever reached the top unaided.

What this meant was that informal distribution—that is, distribution that bypassed the formal bureaucratic system—was immensely important. There was a thriving "second economy" in the Soviet Union throughout the Stalin period (though the term itself is of later vintage); it had existed as long as the "first" economy and could in fact be regarded as a continuation of the private sector of the 1920s, despite the switch from barely tolerated legality to illegality. Like the NEP private sector, the Stalinist second economy essentially distributed goods produced and owned by the state, with privately produced goods in a distinctly secondary role. Goods leaked out of every state production and distribution unit at every stage from the factory assembly line to the rural cooperative store. Anyone who worked at any level of the trade system was likely to be involved in some way, which meant that this type of employment, while bringing a higher than average standard of living, was also seen as shady and lacked social status.

As Joseph Berliner and other economists have pointed out, the Stalinist first economy could not have functioned without the second economy, since industry relied on more or less illegal procurement practices to get the necessary raw materials and equipment, and industrial enterprises employed a whole army of second-economy procurements agents or "pushers" for this purpose.[72] What was true of industry was also true, *a fortiori*, of ordinary citizens. Buying food or clothing from speculators and getting an apartment, railway ticket, or pass to a vacation resort by "pull" was a part of everyone's everyday life, although some people were more frequent and adept users of the second economy than others.

The Soviet authorities applied the blanket term "speculation" to any buying of goods for resale at a higher price and treated it as a crime. This aspect of Soviet mentalité could be attributed to Marxism (though few Marxists outside Russia ever had such a vehement and categorical objection to trade), but it also seems to have had Russian popular roots.[73] Certainly both speculation and its moral condemnation proved extremely durable in Soviet Russia.

Who were the "speculators"? They ranged from big-time criminal operators with lavish life styles and connections in many cities to poverty-stricken old women who bought sausage or stockings at the store in the morning and then resold them outside at a small profit a few hours later. Some speculators had been engaged in legal trade in earlier times: for example, a man named Zhidovetskii, sentenced to an eight-year prison term for speculation in 1935, bought up lengths of woolen cloth in Moscow and took them to Kiev for re-sale. Others, like Timofei Drobot, sentenced to five years for speculation in the Volga region in 1937, were former peasants uprooted by dekulakization living a marginal, hand-to-mouth existence.[74]

Among the cases of big-time speculation reported in the press, one of the largest and most complex involved a group of speculators, described as former kulaks and private traders, who set up a sizable trade in bay leaves, soda, pepper, tea, and coffee, utilizing contacts and outlets in a series of Volga and Urals cities as well as Moscow and Leningrad. One of the men was carrying 70,000 rubles at the time of his arrest, another was said to have made a total of over 1.5 million rubles from the operation. Nazhmudin Shamsudinov and Magomet Magomadov, artisans from Dagestan, were not in the same league as the bay-leaf gang, but they had almost 18,000 rubles on them when they were arrested for disorderly conduct in a restaurant in the Chechen capital, Groznyi, and had just mailed another 7,000 rubles home.[75]

Many provincial speculators acquired goods simply by taking the train to better-supplied Moscow and Leningrad and buying them in the stores. A group of twenty-two speculators prosecuted in Voronezh in 1936 used this method, setting up a legal dressmaking workshop as cover for the goods thus obtained, which at the time of their arrest included 1,677 meters of cloth and forty-four dresses, as well as two bicycles, many pairs of shoes, gramophone records, and some rubber glue.[76]

The best large-scale operations, however, had more effective methods of obtaining goods from state stores than purchasing them like ordinary customers. Big-time operators often had "connections" with store managers or warehouse personnel (or were themselves store managers) and systematically collected goods at the back door. Store managers and other trading personnel might also be directly involved, like the commercial director of a Leningrad clothing store who was prosecuted for heading a speculation ring that got its goods directly from the store's warehouse. In this clothing store, however, the commercial director was not the only one involved in speculation. One of the salesmen and the head of the store's fire department, for instance, had made deals with professional speculators to give advance warning when goods were coming into the store and let them in without queuing, charging 40 to 50 rubles a time.[77]

Such cases underline the point made in a three-part cartoon in *Krokodil* entitled "The Magician." The first drawing shows a store open and full of goods, the second shows it locked for the night, and the third shows it the next day—open and empty. "Before your eyes I locked the store for the night," says the magician. "In the morning I open it. Allez-houp! . . . The store is completely empty." This trick, the caption explained, was "nothing fantastic: just exceptional dexterity and a great deal of swindling [on the part of store employees]."[78]

Everybody in jobs connected with trade was popularly presumed to have some connection with the second economy or at least to abuse his or her preferential access to goods. *Krokodil* reflected this in many jokes: for example, the cartoon in which a mother says to her daughter, "It doesn't matter, darling, whether you marry a party member or a non-party man, just as long as he works in a closed store," or the one in which an employee in a cooperative store is shown looking in confusion at a consignment of shirts: "What should I do? How to distribute them? I received twelve shirts, but there are only eight people in my family." [79] Not surprisingly, prosecutions of cooperative employees for speculation were frequent.

Another occupation often associated with speculation was that of train conductor. For example, a conductor on the Stalino railroad in the Donbass bought shoes and manufactured goods of various kinds in Moscow, Kiev, and Kharkov and resold them along the run. Another conductor "would pick up cloth in the provinces from people who were employed in textile factories. He also took trains to Shepetovka which was close to the frontier and he obtained goods, which were smuggled across the Russo-Polish frontier." Bathhouse personnel were also known as likely speculators, as were chauffeurs (who could use the state cars they drove to go out to collective farms and pick up produce for sale in the town). Many small-scale speculators were housewives who stood in line at state stores and bought up goods like textiles and clothing for resale at the market or to neighbors. For example, one Ostroumova, a housewife was described as a regular speculator in cloth. She would only buy 3 to 4 meters at a time, but on her arrest 400 meters were found stored in a trunk in her apartment. [80]

Apartments were often venues for reselling goods. [81] Neighbors would know that a certain person (usually a woman) was likely to have a certain kind of good, or could acquire it, and would drop in in the evening to look at what she had. As with many other "second economy" transactions, this one was likely to be regarded in a quite different light by the participants, who saw it as an act of friendship, and the state, which saw it as a crime. Other popular venues were railway stations and stores, where hawkers outside would peddle the goods bought earlier within.

But probably the most important of all sites of speculation was the kolkhoz market. All sorts of things were traded there, illegally or semilegally: agricultural produce bought from peasants by middlemen, manufactured goods stolen or bought from state stores, secondhand clothing, even ration cards and forged passports. While it was legal for peasants to sell their own produce at the market, it was not legal for other people to do it for them, though this was often more convenient for the peasants than to spend the whole day at the market. A Dnepropetrovsk report described the process as follows:

> Often on the road to the bazaar kolkhozniks meet a middleman. "What are you bringing?" "Cucumbers." A price is named and the cucumbers, collected from the kolkhozniks' individual private plots, are bought by the middleman wholesale and are sold at the market for a higher price. Many middlemen are known, but they often find themselves under the protection of the officials who collect bazaar taxes. [82]

It was not supposed to be legal for any private individual to sell manufactured goods at the kolkhoz market, with the exception of rural craftsmen selling their produce. The rule was extremely difficult to enforce, however, partly because state manufacturers used the markets as a venue to sell their products to peasants. This was intended to encourage peasants to bring their agricultural produce to market, but it also provided speculators with the opportunity to buy up manufactured goods and resell them at a higher price. In Moscow in 1936, speculators in the Iaroslavl and Dubinin markets, "both Muscovites and outsiders," were reported to be selling rubber slippers, galoshes, and shoes, as well as ready-made dresses and gramophone records.[83]

CONTACTS AND CONNECTIONS

In 1940, Petr Gattsuk, a concerned citizen from Novgorod, wrote to Andrei Vyshinsky, deputy chairman of the Council of Ministers, deploring the phenomenon of *blat*, which may be roughly rendered in English as "pull."

> The word *blat* has appeared in the lexicon of the Russian language. I cannot literally translate that for you, since perhaps it comes from some kind of foreign word. But still in Russian I understand it well and can give an exact literal translation. In translation into the Russian language the word *blat* means swindling, cheating, stealing, speculation, slipshod practices, and so on. And what does it mean if we meet the expression: "I have *blat*"[?] It means that I have a close connection with a swindler, speculator, thief, cheat, toady, and similar.

The citizen without *blat*, Gattsuk argued, was effectively disfranchised.

> Not to have *blat*, that's the same thing as having no civil rights, the same as being deprived of all rights. . . . Come with a request, and they will all be deaf, blind, and dumb. If you need . . . to buy something in a shop—you need *blat*. If it's difficult or impossible for a passenger to get a railroad ticket, then it is simple and easy *po blatu*. If you live without an apartment, don't ever go to the housing administration, to the procurator's, but better to use just a little *blat* and you will at once get your apartment.[84]

Blat undermined planned distribution in the socialist economy and was "alien and hostile to our society," Gattsuk concluded. Unfortunately at the moment it was not punishable by law. Gattsuk recommended that it be made a criminal offense with its own specific penalties. (Vyshinsky, a lawyer by training, or someone in his office, underlined this passage.)

Gattsuk was not alone in thinking that without *blat*, Soviet life was impossible. "The key-word, the most important word in the language, was *blat*," wrote the British journalist Edward Crankshaw of the late Stalin period.

> It was impossible, without the necessary blat, to get a railway ticket from Kiev to Kharkov, to find accommodation in Moscow or Leningrad, to purchase a new valve for a wireless set, to find a man to mend a hole in the roof, to obtain an interview with a Government official. . . . For many years [*blat*] was the *only* way to get what was needed.[85]

Nor was Gattsuk unusual in treating *blat* as a pathology, something fundamentally deviant and alien to Russian society. In 1935, the authoritative Soviet dictionary identified the word "*blat*" as "thieves' jargon" for crime or theft, adding that the new colloquial vulgarism "*po blatu*" meant "by illegal means." [86] Respondents in the postwar Harvard refugee interview project, distancing themselves as much as possible from both the word and the practice, described *blat* as "a coarse Soviet term," "a word that arose from the people and will never get into literature," and "a word that is derived from an abnormal way of life," and apologized for using it ("Excuse me, but I will have to use some Soviet jargon. . . ."). *Blat* was much the same thing as bribery, said some; *blat* was the same thing as protection or patronage. Euphemisms for *blat* abounded: "blat means acquaintanceship"; "blat . . . in polite society was called 'letter z' for 'znakomye'" (acquaintances); *blat* was the same as "*Zis*," an acronym for acquaintanceship and connections (*znakomstvo i sviazi*).[87]

Blat may be defined as a system of reciprocal relationships involving goods and favors that, in contrast to patronage relations, entail equals and are nonhierarchical. As the participants perceive these relationships, their basis was friendship, even if money sometimes changed hands. Thus, from the participants' standpoint, the Russian proverb "One hand washes the other," which is the equivalent of our "You scratch my back, I'll scratch yours," is a rather crude parody of the genuine personal regard and good feeling associated with *blat* transactions. A better representation (from the participants' standpoint) is another proverb reported by one of the Harvard Project respondents: "As they say in the Soviet Union: 'One must have not 100 rubles but 100 friends.'" [88]

In the Harvard Project, only a minority of respondents wanted to talk at length about their own *blat* dealings,[89] but those who did always used the language of friendship and stressed the human element in *blat* relations. "Friends" were very important in the Soviet Union, said one woman who clearly had extensive *blat* relations, because they "help" one another. Answering a hypothetical question about what she would have done if she had a problem, she painted a picture of a warmly mutually supportive network of family, friends, and neighbors: "My relatives . . . had friends who could have helped me. . . . One . . . was the head of a big trust. He often helped and if he needed help in turn, he would also come. He was our neighbor. . . . One relative was a chief engineer in a factory. He could always help people if he was asked." [90]

A former engineer who became essentially a *blat* professional as procurements agent for a sugar trust used the word "friend" constantly: "I make friends easy and in Russia, without friends, you cannot do a thing. I had some important Communists as my friends. One of them advised me to go to Moscow where he had a friends (sic) who was just made head of the construction of new sugar plants. . . . I went to talk to him and, over the almighty glass of vodka, we became friends." It was not only his bosses he made friends with, but also the supply officials out in the provinces with whom he dealt: "I asked the manager to have dinner with me and filled him with vodka. We became good friends. . . . This ability of mine to make friends and get the necessary supplies was greatly appreciated by my boss." [91]

Drinking was very important as part of the male *blat* relationship. For the respondent quoted above, drinking and the establishment of friendship were inseparably linked; moreover, the drinking was clearly at least sometimes re-

lated to conversation "from the heart," as in his first conversation with his future boss in the sugar trust, who felt out of his depth in his job and confided
that "only a couple of years ago, he did not even know what sugar was made
of." True, this respondent sometimes treated the drinking in more instrumen-
tal terms: "usually it works," he noted in passing after describing one
vodka-and-friendship session. Other respondents did the same, saying that
the way to get something or solve a problem was to take a bottle of vodka to
someone who could help. But the vodka was not just a gift, it had to be drunk
together before the deal was cut—hence the term "sharing a bottle" applied
to *blat* transactions.[92]

Some people were *blat* professionals. You could solve a problem, one Harvard respondent, said, if you were acquainted with some "professional
'blatniks'," "persons who have contacts with higher persons and know the Soviet system. They know who can be bribed or presented with a gift, and what
this gift should be." Another kind of *blat* professionalism is portrayed in a
story about a procurements trip (based on the real-life experiences of a Pol-
ish-Jewish wartime exile in Kazakhstan) that offers pen pictures of a whole series of *blat* professionals in the industrial sphere, all agreeable and generous
personalities, who in the author's summation were "members[..] of an elusive
underground network of people whose jobs provided them with the opportunity to exchange favours with the other members."[93]

Blat professionals were the subject of a humorous verse by the popular poet
Vasilii Lebedev-Kumach published in *Krokodil* in 1933 under the punning title "*Blat*-book." The "*blat*-book" was the notebook in which you kept all the
telephone numbers and addresses of your *blat* connections, plus cryptic notations: "Peter's buddy (sanatorium)," "Sergei (records, gramophone)," "Nik.
Nik. (about grub)." This "secret code" told you how to get expert help ("Just
call—and in a minute you have 'Nik. Nik.' He will get you everything you
need"). The only problem, the poem concluded, was that contact with these
shady characters might land you at the public prosecutor's under interrogation.[94]

The category of *blat* professional would include the procurements agent
for the sugar trust who has been quoted several times. Like many others, he
enjoyed his work: "I was happy in my job. It paid well, there was plenty of
blat, I traveled throughout the Soviet Unions—the per diems and traveling allowances came in handy—and besides I had the satisfaction of achievements,
as I succeeded where others were failing." Pleasure in work was also characteristic of *blat* virtuosi, those nonprofessionals for whom *blat* was an avocation.
One such virtuoso was an unusual character: an exile from Leningrad who
worked as a kolkhoz bookkeeper, he was a jack of all trades (skilled at carpentry and box- and barrel-making) but also considered himself a member of the
intelligentsia. In the summer, he took in paying guests in his house, and developed particularly friendly relations with the director of a big Leningrad garage, with whom he went hunting as well as maintaining regular *blat* relations
(wood from the forest was exchanged for flour and sugar from the city). "My
father was esteemed," his son remembered. "He worked well, and besides

this, he could do very many things. He helped many people and he loved to arrange blat and knew how to do it."[95]

But *blat* was not only the prerogative of *blat* professionals and virtuosi. Some of the Harvard Project respondents thought it was restricted to people of some substance: "You know, nobody would help a poor man. He has nothing to offer. Blat usually means that you have to do something for somebody in return." But those who made such statements, disclaiming personal connections with *blat* on the grounds that they were too insignificant to practice it, often related what were essentially *blat* episodes in their own lives (getting a job or a promotion through personal connection) in other parts of the interview.[96] From these and other data, it seems that the principle of reciprocity could be quite widely interpreted: if someone liked you sufficiently, that might be the basis for a *blat* relationship.

The *blat* dealings that the Harvard respondents reported in their own lives (usually not calling them *blat*) had a multitude of purposes: for example, to get residence papers or false identity documents; to get a better work assignment; to get the materials to build a dacha. Large numbers of reported *blat* transactions had to do with acquiring clothes and shoes ("I . . . had a friend who worked in a warehouse and I got clothing through her," "I knew someone working at a shoe factory, a friend of my wife's; and thus I managed to get shoes cheaply, and of good quality"). One respondent, whose father worked in a cooperative store, reported that his family's *blat* connections were so extensive that "we always had everything. The suits were expensive, although you could get some at government [i.e., state, low] prices. We only had to stand in line for shoes, because we had no friends working in shoe stores."[97]

Blat was a surprisingly frequent theme in *Krokodil*, whose cartoons on the topic dealt with university admissions, medical certificates, and obtaining places in good vacation resorts and restaurants. "How come, friend, you are so often ill?" "I know a doctor," reads the caption of one cartoon. Another shows a guest and a doctor talking on the balcony of a posh resort hotel: "I have been on holiday here for a month and I still haven't once seen the director," says the guest. "Do you really not know him? Then how did you get a room in the hotel?"[98]

One of *Krokodil*'s cartoons captured the way in which Soviet informal distribution mechanisms tended to convert every formal bureaucratic transaction into a personal one. Headed "A Good Upbringing," it shows a store manager talking politely to a customer, while the check-out clerk and another woman look on. "He's a courteous man, our store manager," says the check-out clerk. "When he sells cloth, he calls all the customers by name and patronymic." "Does he really know all the customers?" "Of course. If he doesn't know someone, he doesn't sell to them."[99]

∾ ∾ ∾

Personal connections took the edge off the harsh circumstances of Soviet life, at least for some people. They also subverted the meaning of Stalin's great economic restructuring, creating a second economy based on personal contacts and patronage parallel to the first, socialist, economy based on principles of state ownership and central planning. Because of the acute shortage of goods, this second economy was probably more important in ordinary people's lives than the private sector had ever been during NEP, paradoxical as this may seem.

Even for the best-connected citizens, however, discomfort had become the inescapable norm of Soviet life. Citizens spent long hours standing in queues for bread and other basics. Traveling to and from work was an ordeal, especially as many people were struggling with shopping baskets on jam-packed and rickety buses and streetcars in the big cities or walking through unpaved streets that were piled with snow in winter and seas of mud in autumn and spring in the provinces. Many of the small comforts of life like neighborhood cafes and small shops, had vanished with the end of NEP; under the new centralized state trading system, it was often necessary to travel into the center of town to get your shoes mended. At home, life in the communal apartments and barracks was miserably overcrowded and uncomfortable and often poisoned by quarrels with neighbors. An additional source of discomfort and exasperation was the "continuous work week," which abolished the Sunday holiday and often meant that family members had different days off.[100]

All these discomforts, shortages, and inconveniences were surely transitional phenomena—or were they? As the 1930s progressed, and particularly as living standards declined again at the end of the decade, many people must have started to wonder. Still, the trajectory of the mid-1930s was upward, and the later downturn could be attributed to the imminent threat of war. And there was a vision of a socialist future of abundance (the subject of the next chapter) to set against the privations of the present. In the words of one Harvard Project respondent, "I thought that all the difficulties were connected with the sacrifices which were necessary for the building of socialism and that after a socialist society was constructed, life would be better."[101]

3

Palaces on Monday

An Eastern juggler . . .
Planted plum pips on Sunday,
Which came up palaces on Monday.
Nursery rhyme.[1]

This was an age of utopianism. Political leaders had utopian visions, and so did many citizens, especially the younger generation. The spirit is hard to capture in an age of skepticism, since utopianism, like revolution, is so unreasonable. How could anyone have seriously believed in a radiant future, totally different from the miserable past and the chaotic present? The problem of understanding is all the greater because of the distance between the utopian vision and Soviet reality. It is tempting to dismiss the vision as simply deception and camouflage, especially since the utopian rhetoric actually did serve those purposes, among others, for the Soviet regime. But the vision cannot be dismissed in a study of everyday Stalinism. Not only was it a part of Stalinism, and an important one at that, but it was also a part of everyone's everyday experience in the 1930s. A Soviet citizen might believe or disbelieve in a radiant future, but could not be ignorant that one was promised.[2]

The utopian vision of the 1930s was of a human and natural world transformed through industrialization and modern technology. This transformation was called "building socialism," but the vision had very little specificity when it came to social relations and structures. Reading through the journal Maxim Gorky founded to publicize Soviet transformative feats, *Our Achievements*, the vision comes across as an almost imperial one, focused on mastery of geographical space and the natural environment and a civilizing mission toward the backward inhabitants of the Soviet Union. "Broad is my native land," says the famous first line of the Soviet national anthem. This was not just a description or a boast, but an assertion of a core value—bigness.[3]

Look at the map of Russia, Lenin once said. "North of Vologda, southwest of Orenburg and Omsk, and north of Tomsk stretch boundless spaces in which dozens of large cultured states could fit. And in all these spaces what reigns is patriarchalism, semi-barbarity, and real barbarity." Were he alive now, an editorialist of the early 1930s wrote, Lenin might look at the map of the Soviet Union and see a different picture. "North of Vologda we have built a mighty industry for extracting agricultural fertilizer, we have built the new city of Khibinogorsk. East of Moscow, in the ancient merchant city of Nizhny Novgorod, we have put up a giant auto works. South of Saratov we have constructed the powerful Stalingrad tractor plant " and so on in an exhaustive catalogue of Soviet industrial construction.[4]

Modern industry was the key to this transformation. "The time has come to take all the riches of the country into our hands," the editorialist proclaimed. "The time has come to construct our fatherland anew with the hands of machines . . . to dress the whole country, from Archangel to Tashkent and from Leningrad to Vladivostok in the iron armor of industrial giants, . . . to weave the whole country into a network of electrical powerlines." [5] Only by bringing modern industry to these boundless spaces could their inhabitants be rescued from the colonialist oppression of Tsarist days and offered de facto, as opposed to mere de jure, equality with the Russian heartland.[6]

Gorky's journal was read by a relatively limited public, partly, he claimed, because the paper shortage limited its print run (even *Our Achievements* sometimes had to mention *Our Defects*). But a very broad public knew the popular songs that delivered the same message. "We are taming space and time," boasted "March of the Happy-Go-Lucky Guys," "We are the young masters of the earth." Another popular song—also, appropriately, a march, with the title "Ever Higher"—proclaimed "We were born to make fairy tales come true." [7]

BUILDING A NEW WORLD

We shall build our world, a new world.
The International (Russian text)[8]

The generation that grew up in the 1930s took these words to heart. Most memoirs about the period, including many written in emigration, recall the idealism and optimism of the young, their belief that they were participants in a historic process of transformation, their enthusiasm for what was called "the building of socialism," the sense of adventure they brought to it, and their willingness (at least rhetorical) to go off as pioneers to distant construction sites like Magnitogorsk and Komsomolsk on the Amur. Terror was not a part of this picture. Aleksei Adzhubei, son-in-law of Soviet leader Nikita Khrushchev and editor of *Izvestiia*, was a schoolboy in 1937. He recalled:

> The only thing that existed for us that year was Spain, the fight with the Fascists. Spanish caps—blue with red edging on the visor—came into fashion, and also big berets, which we tilted at a rakish angle. . . . For boys and girls of that time, the world divided only into "Whites" and "Reds." It didn't even come into our heads to think which side we should be on. It was that red world in which the Polar explorers, the Cheliushkinites [rescuers of a team stranded in the Arctic in 1934], [and] the Papaninites [Ivan Papanin's record-breaking aviation team] lived and accomplished their heroic feats.[9]

Another facet of the time was caught by Raisa Orlova, a contemporary of Adzhubei's with a very different life path of dissidence and emigration in the post-Stalin period. Remembering her youth in the 1930s, she wrote:

> I had an unshakable faith that my existence between these old walls [in an apartment on Gorky Street] was merely a preparation for life. Life, properly speaking, would begin in a new and sparkling white house. There I would do exercises in the morning, there the ideal order would exist, there all my heroic achievements would commence.
>
> The majority of my contemporaries ... shared the same kind of rough, provisional, slapdash way of life. Faster, faster toward the great goal, and there everything would begin in a genuine sense.
>
> It was both possible and necessary to alter everything: the streets, the houses, the cities, the social order, human souls. And it was not all that difficult: first the unselfish enthusiasts would outline the plan on paper; then they would tear down the old (saying all the while, "You can't make an omelette without breaking eggs!"); then the ground would be cleared of the rubble and the edifice of the socialist phalanx would be erected in the space that had been cleared.[10]

This was the age of the great "General Plan for the Reconstruction of Moscow" that was supposed to set a pattern for urban planning throughout the country and provide a model of the socialist capital for foreigners and Soviet citizens to marvel at. Plans, blueprints, and models were everywhere: the 1931 film *Chabarda!* by the Georgian filmmaker Mikhail Chiaureli dwelt lovingly on an elaborate model of a future city, accompanied by appropriate commentary ("Here there will be a school!"). The first line of the Moscow Metro came into operation in the mid 1930s, and its chandeliers, deep escalators, and spacious stations astonished the citizenry. New monumental buildings appeared: the Moscow Hotel, with its planned 1,200 rooms in a prime location near Red Square, was like "a fairy-tale palace" to one awed provincial.[11]

Palaces were in the spirit of the age. There were palaces of culture, palaces of sport, and palaces of labor, usually large, lavishly decorated, and imposing buildings to match their names. One of the most ambitious projects of Moscow's General Plan was the towering Palace of Soviets, topped by a statue of Lenin, that was to have been built on the site of the Christ the Savior cathedral, which was demolished in the early 1930s. This Palace was never actually built because of groundwater problems, giving rise to many rumors that the devil's work had been duly punished, but its image was more familiar than most actual buildings. In Aleksandr Medvedkin's film *New Moscow* (1939), the (unbuilt) Palace of Soviets has been superimposed as part of the background of real Moscow street scenes—a triumph of the socialist-realist perspective in which future and present are indistinguishable.[12]

The General Plan called for a widening of Gorky Street (formerly Tverskaia) and the creation of a set of uniform facades, decorated in the "Stalinist baroque" manner, of the buildings on either side. The building on Tverskaia where the young Orlova lived narrowly escaped destruction. Nearby, as one Muscovite recorded in his diary, an "unheard of thing" happened: "the enormous House of the Moscow Soviet [the Governor's House in Tsarist times] was moved backward 14 meters" to allow for the widening of Gorky Street; moreover, the building itself was also expanded, acquiring two new storys and two extra columns on its classical facade.[13]

Behind the new world, however, lay the old one. Its deficiencies, particularly its economic and cultural backwardness, were keenly felt and had to be overcome before the Soviet Union could achieve its aim of "catching up and overtaking" the capitalist West. "Socialism cannot be built in this country," Lenin had said, "so long as that terrible, centuries-old gulf still separates that small part of it that is industrialized and civilized from the part that is uncivilized, patriarchal, and oppressed for centuries through slavery and colonial exploitation."[14]

Great changes took place in the 1930s. At the end of the 1920s, less than one-fifth of the population was urban. This figure would rise to one-third by the end of the 1930s. The total wage- and salary-earning workforce in the late 1920s stood at 11 million, out of a population of around 150 million. This figure would triple in the course of a decade. Eleven million was also the figure for children in school in the late 1920s, of whom 3 million were in secondary schools. A decade later, there were 30 million children in school, 18 million of them in secondary schools. Only 57 percent of the total Soviet population aged 9 to 49 was literate according to the 1926 census, although illiteracy was concentrated in Russia's rural regions and the Central Asian republics, and the Soviet urban literacy rate stood at 81 percent. In 1939, the same proportion (81 percent) of the *whole* Soviet population was literate.[15]

These were some of the achievements that Gorky's journal and others trumpeted. It was indeed an age of achievement, but it was also an age of extraordinary boosterism, boasting, and exaggeration of what had been achieved. Statistical handbooks were published, often in foreign languages as well as Russian, to document these achievements. (Data that failed to do this were excluded.) The Soviet press boasted of new hydroelectric projects and blast furnaces ("the biggest in the world!"), of modern technology in industry and agriculture, of aviators who broke long-distance records and polar explorers who survived the hazards of the Arctic North, of the setting up of kindergartens and the emancipation of women, of literacy schools and the number of Russian peasant grandmothers and Kazakh erstwhile nomads who had been taught in them, of violinists and chess players who won international competitions—in short, of anything and everything that supported the claim that the

Soviet Union was catching up and overtaking the West. Its publicists solicited and disseminated congratulatory comments from any famous foreigner who could be persuaded to visit the country. A permanent Agricultural Exhibition (later renamed the Exhibition of Economic Achievements) opened in Moscow in 1939, offering a sort of Soviet World's Fair and attracting 20,000 to 30,000 visitors a day.[16]

This barrage of self-congratulation was aimed at both the foreign audience and the domestic one. But the Soviet Union continued to feel beleaguered, trapped in the hostile encirclement of capitalist powers. It was necessary to catch up and overtake the West so as not to be destroyed by it. Russia's backwardness vis-à-vis the West was her Archilles' heel; if it was not overcome in ten years, Stalin said in 1931, "we will go under." [17]

The fear of war was ever-present in the Soviet Union throughout 1930s; it was the shadow that dimmed the prospect of the radiant future. The popular song "If Tomorrow Brings War" dealt explicitly with this threat, but the same motif occurred again and again in Soviet popular culture in a variety of contexts: "If our enemy decides to start a battle. . . . Then we'll . . . leap to defend our motherland" ("March of the Happy-Go-Lucky Guys"), "When the time comes to beat the enemy / Beat them back from every border!" ("The Sportsmen's March"). Even the song "Life's Getting Better," based on Stalin's canonical text, included a mention of the war threat ("Know, Voroshilov, we're all standing guard / We won't give the enemy even a yard").[18] The spirit of readiness and even willingness to fight was captured in a photograph of Young Pioneers practicing at the shooting range published in the journal *Our Achievements*. The caption read: "Everyone remembers the Stalinist words: 'We don't want the territory of others, but . . . .' And at that 'but' each one grips his weapon more tightly." [19]

HEROES

When our country commands that we be heroes,
Then anyone can become a hero.
"March of the Happy-Go-Lucky Guys" (1934)[20]

This is an age of heroism, the song claims, in which even ordinary people become heroes. The First Five-Year Plan inaugurated the heroic age, launching the country on a make-or-break effort to transform itself. A heroic age called forth heroic personalities and feats, and gloried in them. In Maxim Gorky's Nietzschean formulation, Soviet man was becoming Man with a capital letter ("Superman" for Nietzsche). Free from the burden of serf consciousness inculcated through past exploitation and deprivation, the contemporary hero— "man of the new humanity"—is "big, daring, strong." He pits the force of human will against the forces of nature in a "grandiose and tragic" struggle. His mission is not only to understand the world but also to master it.[21]

The word "hero" was ubiquitous in the 1930s, used for record-breaking aviators and polar explorers, border guards, Stakhanovites, and all kinds of Heroes of Labor. Political leaders might also be described as heroes performing heroic feats: in poems by folk bards, Voroshilov was "a fantastic knight" on his steed, Stalin "the hero Joseph-Our-Light Vissarionovich." The Soviet hero was often described as a bogatyr, using the old word for the hero of Russian folk epics, and ascribed the same qualities of daring, defiance, and high spirits.[22]

The quintessential "bogatyrs" of the 1930s were the polar explorers, who dared to pit their strength against the elements in the most hostile natural conditions, and aviators, who literally launched themselves off the face of the earth to perform their heroic feats. Arctic enthusiasm started when the Cheliushkin expedition, led by Otto Schmidt, set off to explore the northern sea route in the Arctic in 1933 and was caught in ice floes. The subsequent rescue operation by Soviet aviators went on for weeks and received enormous publicity. Even children in remote villages heard about it and were carried away by the drama. On their return, the explorers and their rescuers were feted, embraced by Stalin and other Politburo members, and declared "Heroes of the Soviet Union." Despite the current moratorium on party admissions, four of the aviators involved in the rescue were accepted as members of the Communist Party by special decision of the party's Central Committee. Otto Schmidt, a bearded giant of 6 ft 6 in, became a particular favorite of caricaturists, one of whom portrayed him as a latter-day Peter the Great striding across the Russian landscape.[23]

The Cheliushkin publicity set the pattern for the rest of the 1930s, with record-breaking aviators dominating the headlines, and children all over the Soviet Union dreaming of becoming aviators. The names of Soviet record-breaking aviators—Ivan Papanin, Valerii Chkalov, Mikhail Babushkin, Georgii Baidukov, and the rest—were known to everybody in the Soviet Union (at least everyone who read the newspapers). They were dubbed "Stalin's eagles" and "Stalin's bogatyrs," and Stalin and other party members did their best to cash in on their popularity. When the aviators set off on their latest record-breaking flights, Politburo members would be on hand to see them off; when they returned in triumph, Stalin and his colleagues were at the airport to embrace them. Stalin was represented as a father to the aviators, some of whom actually called him "father." When, as happened on a number of occasions, aviators perished in the course of a record-breaking attempt, the Politburo led the nation in mourning. After Babushkin's airplane N-212 crashed in 1938, killing all on board, there was a state funeral, on Politburo orders, and the urn with the pilots' ashes was displayed in a hall on Red Square so that the public could pay its last respects.[24]

The press, monitored and encouraged by the party leadership, did a great deal to make the aviators and polar explorers into celebrities. Nevertheless, the popular response is unmistakable: these men received huge amounts of fan mail and were lionized on appearances throughout the country. As a Muscovite recorded in his diary, "Today they met the heroes of the flight across the North Pole—Chkalov, Baidukov, and Beliakov. The platforms and square were crowded with people. They greeted the heroes very stormily. The whole of Tverskaia Street was also crowded. Their cars, driving to the Kremlin, drove along a living corridor."[25] Folk ballads celebrated "Beard-to-the-Knees"

(Otto Schmidt) and the Cheliushkin rescue with particular affection and mourned the heroic deaths of aviators like Chkalov and Polina Osipenko.[26]

Films and plays about these national heroes appeared in abundance. The Cheliushkin expedition was celebrated in the film *Seven of the Brave* (1936) and also was the subject of a play by one of the participants in the expedition, Sergei Semenov, *We Won't Give In*, focusing on the theme of collective heroism in the face of a hostile environment.[27] A whole string of films about aviators appeared, starting with *Aviators* (1935) and including *The Fatherland Calls* (1936), *Tales of Aviation Heroes* (*Wings*) (1938), *Brother of a Hero* (1940), and *Valerii Chkalov* (1941). The last, released in the States under the title *Wings of Victory*, was based on an idea from the late Chkalov's co-pilot, Baidukov.[28] Increasingly, the aviator films became celebrations of Soviet military aviation, emphasizing the pilots' role as defenders of the native land.

When asked about their heroes, Soviet adolescents named three "generic" hero types—aviators, polar explorers, and border guards—as well as individual heroes. Similarly, when young auto workers were asked about their life plans in 1937, many said they wanted to be aviators (including military pilots) or serve in the border guards. The individual heroes chosen by the first group ranged from party and military leaders (Stalin, Voroshilov, Semen Budennyi) and Civil War heroes (Chapaev and Shchors, both the subjects of popular films of the period) to aviators (Chkalov), explorers (the Norwegian explorer of the North, Friedrich Nansen), scientists (Konstantin Tsiolkovskii, a rocket pioneer who publicized the idea of space travel), Stakhanovite workers, chess players, and footballers from the Dinamo club.[29]

Pavlik Morozov, the legendary young Pioneer who denounced his father to the authorities as a hoarder of grain and was subsequently murdered by angry relatives,[30] was another name on this 1937 list of heroes of Soviet youth. Pavlik, an odious figure to Russian intellectuals in the waning years of the Soviet Union, was a real hero to many young people in the 1930s, symbolizing youthful bravery, self-sacrifice, and willingness to challenge unjust authority at the local level, whether parental or that of other adults.[31]

An exploration of the same issue was offered in *The Squealer*, a play written for Natalia Sats' Moscow Children's Theater in the mid 1930s. As described in the Children's Theater publicity materials, *The Squealer*'s emotional pivot was very similar to that of the American film *On the Waterfront* a decade or so later, whose subject is the agonizing decision of one man to inform on the gang (including his friends and relatives) that is terrorizing the docks.[32] In both cases, informing is represented as the more difficult, even heroic choice, because it involves resisting the pressure of local opinion in favor of a broader and more abstract notion of collective good:

> Here are a lot of youngsters in a shoe-making shop, learning a trade [runs the description of *The Squealer*]. A short while ago they were "besprizorni," homeless, errant waifs. Some of them have taken to their work, learned to like it. Others are recalcitrant. There are cases of theft in the shop. His pals won't say who the thief is. Squeal? Not on your life! They think better of themselves than that. But are they doing the right thing in spoiling the whole aim and purpose of their shoemaking shop?[33]

The "little man" as hero was a favorite motif. The heroes of Gorky's *Stories about Heroes* (1931) were rank-and-filers—rural teachers, worker correspondents, worker inventors, reading-room organizers, activists of all kinds. The newspapers ran many stories on the extraordinary achievements of ordinary people, whose photographs, serious or smiling, looked out from the front page. Factory and kolkhoz "shockworkers" were the heroic "little people" of the early 1930s. Then, in the mid 1930s, the Stakhanovite movement gave new dimensions to the celebration of ordinary people. Stakhanovites—named for the record-breaking Donbass coalminer, Aleksei Stakhanov—were supposed to be not only record-breakers but also rationalizers of production. The movement started in industry, but soon Stakhanovites, both male and female, were emerging in the kolkhoz and even in such unlikely arenas as Soviet trade.[34]

The most visible Stakhanovites became members of a new social status group that might be called "ordinary celebrities." [35] These were ordinary people—workers, kolkhozniks, saleswomen, teachers, or whatever—who suddenly became national media heroes and heroines. In theory, they were selected because of their achievements, but in practice patronage from a local party secretary or journalist often played a large role.[36] Stakhanovites' photographs were published in the newspapers; journalists interviewed them about their achievements and opinions; they were selected as delegates to conferences of Stakhanovites, and learned to make public speeches; some of the lucky ones even met Stalin and were photographed with him.

Stakhanovites and other "ordinary celebrities" were living examples that little people mattered in the Soviet Union, that even the most humble and ordinary person had a chance of becoming famous for a day. "I became a hero along with the people," wrote the Stakhanovite tractor-driver Pasha Angelina modestly.[37] However, the representative function was only part of it. Stakhanovites were also celebrated for their *individual* achievements and encouraged to show their individuality and leadership potential. To become a famous Stakhanovite was to acquire a self whose worth turned out to be far greater than anyone had dreamed:

> I . . . am an old Donbass worker; I used to work as a winch operator in the mine. *Who knew me then? Who saw me then?* But now a lot of people know me, not only in the Donbass, but also beyond its borders.[38]

In theory, Stakhanovism functioned on the "celebrity for a day" principle. In practice, however, some of the most successful Stakhanovites, like Stakhanov himself or Pasha Angelina, became full-time and essentially permanent celebrities, being elected deputies of the Supreme Soviet, writing books about their experiences, going to state banquets, and losing contact with their original work and social milieu. Some of these high-profile Stakhanovites, especially the women, seem to have established quite close personal relations with Soviet leaders and journalists from the top echelons, way beyond the reach of their original patrons.[39] Even Stalin seems to have had a genuine liking for some of the most celebrated Stakhanovites like the Ukrainian Maria

Demchenko and Pasha Angelina; most of his best and most "human" photographs of this period were taken in the company of such people.

In return, the Stakhanovites were untiring and devoted contributors to the Stalin cult. Describing her joy at seeing Stalin for the first time at a Stakhanovite conference in the Kremlin, Pasha Angelina wrote, "It was as if I was carried into a new, fairytale world. No, not 'as if.' Before me had really opened a new world of happiness and reason, and it was the great Stalin who led me into that world." Her description of the reactions of an old peasant woman beside her was even more vivid. Silver hair glistening (she had thrown back her kerchief), eyes bright with ecstasy, she quietly whispered to herself: "Our dear one, our Stalin! . . . A deep bow to you from our whole village, from our children, grandchildren and great grandchildren. . . . Oy, dear people, [there is] my darling! Look at our sun, our happiness!"[40]

THE REMAKING OF MAN

"Comrades, I am forty-five years old, but I have been alive for only eighteen years," a veteran worker told a Stakhanovite congress in 1935. The image of the 1917 revolution as a second birth was common in Soviet rhetoric. Sometimes a man or woman was "born anew" by the revolution, sometimes by a later event like collectivization. There were also specific conversion experiences that carried individuals from the old life to the new. *Krokodil* published a tongue-in-cheek cartoon in which parachute-jumping, a popular sport in the mid 1930s, served that purpose. The cartoon shows a traditional snowy village scene, with peasants in horsedrawn sleds, and a church with a bell tower—but the tower is now being used for parachute jumps. The caption reads: "In that church I was christened twice, the first time when I was a baby, the second time quite recently, when I received my aerial baptism there."[41]

It was work, however, not parachute-jumping, that usually allowed men to be remade. Work under Soviet conditions was regarded as a transformative experience because it was collective and imbued with a sense of purpose. Under the old regime, work had been an exhausting, soul-destroying chore; under socialism, it was the thing that filled life with meaning. As one man wrote to Maxim Gorky about his work at a new construction site, "It turned out that I, a disfranchised person, a man with a grievance, understood here, among these ill-matched people of a single spirit, how great is the pleasure of getting to know life and taking part in its reconstruction."[42]

The idea that men could be remade was very important in the Soviet worldview. It was associated, in the first place, with the belief that crime was a social disease, the result of a harmful environment. This was conventional wisdom in Soviet criminology in the 1920s and early 1930s, although its hold ultimately waned as it became more difficult to attribute all criminal behavior to problems of the transition or "survivals" from the past. More broadly, the idea of human remaking was part of the whole notion of transformation that was at the heart of the Soviet project. As Bukharin put it, "plasticity of the organism [is] the silent theoretical premise of our course of action," for without it, why would anyone bother to make a revolution? "If we were to take the point of view that racial and national characteristics were so great that it would take thousands of years to change them, then, naturally, all our work would be absurd."[43]

The theme of man's remaking was popular in all sorts of contexts in the 1930s. But most popular of all were stories of the remaking or "reforging" of criminals and juvenile delinquents through labor and membership of a work collective. The press was full of such reclamation stories, particularly in the first half of the decade, and they were intensively publicicized for a foreign as well as domestic audience. As far as the domestic audience is concerned, however, these stories cannot be dismissed as mere propaganda, for they obviously caught the public imagination to an unusual degree. Even in the Gulag labor camps, where the reforging theme was strongly emphasized, it seems to have had some genuine inspirational impact.[44]

The conversion tales that were so popular in the 1920s and 1930s had the dual appeal of adventure stories, like the bandit tales that were popular in Russia before the revolution, and psychological dramas in which an unhappy, isolated, individual finally finds happiness in membership of the collective. Typically, the protagonist was some kind of social outcast in his old life —a habitual criminal, a juvenile delinquent, or even a child of deported kulaks making a new life in exile. A new Soviet man emerges in these stories by sloughing off the dirt and corruption of the old life, just as in a reclamation myth from another culture Charles Kingsley's waterbaby sloughs off the sooty skin he has acquired in his miserable life as a chimney sweep.[45]

One of the classic Soviet works on the remaking of man was *The White Sea Canal*, a famous (or infamous) collective project whose participants included Maxim Gorky and an array of literary stars that included the satirist Mikhail Zoshchenko. The book was based on a visit the writers made in 1933 to the White Sea Canal construction project, which was run by the OGPU and used convict labor. Drawing on interviews with convicts and camp management, as well as written sources like the camp newspaper, *Reforging*, the writers described the process whereby convicts were remade into good Soviet citizens. This was clearly a propaganda project: the visit could not have occurred except as the result of a high-level political decision, the book was dedicated to the Seventeenth Party Congress, and it was swiftly translated into English and achieved wide circulation via the Left Book Club and other "fellow-traveling" outlets. Nonetheless, the book is not without literary interest, and there are some gripping stories in it.[46]

One of the most interesting is the story of Anna Iankovskaia, a former professional thief with a long arrest record who was sent to the White Sea Canal camp in 1932. As Anna related, she was at first skeptical of the NKVD's promise that the prisoners would be reeducated, not punished. She found the physical work intolerably hard and initially refused to work. One of the camp educators, herself a former inmate, then had a four-hour talk with her about their lives that brought Anna to tears. This was the crucial conversion moment—the discovery that here, for the first time, she mattered as an individual. After this, Anna could start working and begin her new life.[47]

Another story deals with a different category of convict, a bourgeois engineer convicted of wrecking and sabotage, that is, a political prisoner of the type charged in the Shakhty show trial in 1928. His name is Magnitov. In Katerina Clark's paraphrase,

> The authors relate how, after Magnitov began to labor on the canal, he developed a quicker pulse and faster thought processes and nervous reactions. "He begins to take on the new tempo, to adjust his reason to it, his will and his breathing." Once changed so radically, the engineer had trouble associating his former self with its present version. The authors reported: "Engineer Magnitov thinks of the old engineer Magnitov, and for him that person is already alien. Magnitov calls that person 'him.'"[48]

The remaking of juvenile delinquents was a particularly appealing dramatic theme. Homeless children, congregating in cities and railroad stations and forming gangs with their own argot and survival skills, had been a feature of the Soviet landscape since the Civil War. Their numbers diminished somewhat in the course of the 1920s, but increased again in the wake of collectivization and famine. Orphanages, known euphemistically as "children's homes," were set up to get them off the streets and prepare them for adult life, but the path of reclamation was often rocky. Some delinquents were sent to labor colonies run by the OGPU, a number of which had idealistic and dedicated directors and teachers. The film, *Road to Life* (1931)—one of the first sound films made in the Soviet Union—was based on a real-life OGPU colony for juvenile delinquents not far from Moscow, and used children from the commune as actors. As in the later American film *Blackboard Jungle*, the main agent of the children's reclamation in the film is a charismatic teacher.[49]

A literary work on a similar theme was *Pedagogical Poem* by Anton Makarenko. Makarenko, who started his career running colonies for delinquents under OGPU auspices and achieved a literary career in the mid 1930s under Maxim Gorky's patronage, based his book on his own experiences as an educator. In *Pedagogical Poem*, the typical conversion process involves a delinquent youth who comes to the colony unwillingly and at first defies its rules, but is then brought by collective pressure to repudiate his old life and become a real member of the community. There is a charismatic leader in Makarenko's story, the fictional representation of Makarenko, but he stays in the background. It is the collective that struggles with its black sheep and ultimately achieves their conversion.[50]

The reclamation theme appeared often in newspapers of the 1930s. An example was the story of the rehabilitation of a long-time criminal, Sergei Ivanov, whose conversion was described in an *Izvestiia* article as an agonizing personal struggle—"a complex and tormenting process of internal remaking and return to life." Ivanov was a pickpocket whose life had been an endless alternation of prison and a sordid round of drinking, drugs, prostitution, and violence. While he was in prison in the mid 1920s, his wife was murdered by one of his criminal associates and his daughter sent to an orphanage. Some years later, Ivanov landed in an NKVD labor commune in the Urals and his moral rebirth began. Like engineer Magnitov, "breaking forever with the past, a man renewed, he had already become another person." With the encouragement of the collective, he searched for and ultimately found his lost daughter.[51]

Izvestiia also ran an admiring profile of Matvei Pogrebinskii, creator of the NKVD's Bolshevo labor commune, a reclamation project for habitual thieves that had neither guards nor fences and was a standard stop on the itinerary of foreign visitors in the 1930s. The focus of this story was on Pogrebinskii's stubborn struggle for the soul of each individual former criminal. Winning conversion was no easy matter, even for so experienced an educator as Pogrebinskii. It often took three years intensive work before a former criminal was ready to make the ultimate break with his old milieu and recognize that his primary loyalties were not with them but the broader Soviet community.[52]

The reclamation of criminals took a remarkable form early in 1937, thanks to the initiative of Lev Sheinin, an intriguing figure who combined a day job as a high-ranking investigator in the State Procuracy, deputy to Andrei Vyshinsky, with an avocation as a writer and journalist. Sheinin published an article in *Izvestiia* called "Giving Themselves Up" in which he claimed that criminals of all types, from pickpockets to murderers, were appearing more and more often at militia offices to confess their crimes and give themselves up. He cited two letters recently received by the State Procuracy, both from habitual criminals who repented of their crimes. One of these letters was from a thief named Ivan Frolov, a repeat offender who had come to despise his past life and asked to be sent to work anywhere in the country, "so as to be useful to Soviet society." In his *Izvestiia* article, Sheinin called on Frolov to appear at the State Prosecutor's office and discuss the disposition of his case. Would he come? "I know that he will come," Sheinin concluded. "He will come because our life is seething around him, new human relations are emerging ever more confidently. And that is stronger than fear of possible punishment, stronger than habits and survivals of the past. Stronger than anything." [53]

The next day, more than a dozen habitual criminals—colorful characters with names like Cockroach, Pigeon, and Count Kostia—showed up at the Procuracy asking for Sheinin. They announced their wish to abandon their old lives and asked for help starting new ones. Late in the evening, the meeting was reconvened in the *Izvestiia* offices, this time with State Procurator Vyshinsky present. He promised that none would be prosecuted and all would be given work and the documents necessary for a new life. Count Kostia, the unofficial leader of the group, whose specialty was high-class robbery in the international sleeping cars of long-distance trains, accepted this guarantee on behalf of his comrades. Cockroach and Pigeon drafted an appeal to all criminals still living a life of crime, urging them to "understand that the Soviet Union is extending its proletarian hand to us and wants to pull us out of the rubbish pit," "throw away doubt and suspicion," and follow their example.[54]

"These people sincerely want a new life," Vyshinsky told *Izvestiia* a few days later, "they are literally thirsting for it." More criminals appeared in militia and procuracy offices in Leningrad and in the provinces to give themselves up and ask for work and documents. The flow in Moscow continued too.

Some of the criminals had special work requirements. For example, a swindler (by current profession) showed up at Sheinin's door reciting a monologue from *Othello* to support his request to be sent to retrain as an actor. ("He was sent to the Arts Committee," Sheinin reported. "They tested him there and found that he really has a lot of talent. He was admitted to the State Theater Institute.") After a few weeks, the first contingent of repentant criminals departed from Moscow in various directions to begin their new lives. They were seen off by Count Kostia, who turned out to be a skilled topographer as well as conman and had accordingly been seconded to a new expedition to the Arctic. The subsequent fate of the reformed thieves is unknown, but one report has it that Count Kostia, at any rate, prospered for several years.[55]

The reality behind these reclamation stories, like their outcomes, was undoubtedly more complicated than anything that found its way into print. All the same, it was probably true that in real life a criminal past, particularly on the part of a juvenile, was not an irredeemable stain on one's record. To have been one of the homeless children of the 1920s, taken into a Soviet children's home and then taught a trade, was certainly no obstacle to success; on the contrary, such experiences appear quite frequently in the biographies of men on their way up in the late 1930s.[56]

In one respect, however, the rhetoric of reforging was grossly misleading. It stated that anyone, no matter what his or her past, was redeemable, even those like engineer Magnitov whose crimes were political. But that was simply not true, as we will see in a later chapter. Taints of social origin could not be overcome, and neither could political sins in the strict sense, like having belonged to the Opposition. Even Makarenko, the great propagandist of human reclamation, included a character who turned out to be unredeemable ("not a conscious wrecker but some sort of vermin by nature") in a work written during the Great Purges.[57] Of course, one could say, with Bukharin, that if people could be vermin by nature, that made the whole revolutionary project absurd. But Makarenko had grasped the spirit of the age. People tainted by social origin or political history were, in practice, almost invariably disqualified as objects of reclamation. To be eligible for reforging, you had to have committed real crimes.

MASTERING CULTURE

Culture was something that had to be mastered, like virgin lands and foreign technology. But what *was* culture? In the 1920s, there had been heated arguments among Communist intellectuals on this question. Some stressed the essential class nature of culture, and therefore wanted to destroy "bourgeois" culture and develop a new "proletarian" culture. Others, including Lenin and Lunacharsky thought that culture had a meaning beyond class, and moreover that Russia had too little of it. The "proletarian" side achieved brief dominance in the years of Cultural Revolution but was then discredited. That left the alternative view, that culture was something immensely valuable and beyond class, in the ascendant. But it also left a tacit agreement that the meaning of culture was something that should not be probed too deeply. Culture, like obscenity, was something you knew when you saw it. Tautologically, it was the complex of behaviors, attitudes, and knowledge that "cultured" people had, and "backward" people lacked. Its positive value, like its nature, was self-evident.[58]

In practice, we can distinguish several levels of the culture that people throughout the Soviet Union were busy mastering. The first was the culture of basic hygiene—washing with soap, tooth-cleaning, not spitting on the floor—and elementary literacy, which was still lacking among a substantial part of the Soviet population. Here, the Soviet civilizing mission was construed in very similar terms to that of other European nations among backward native peoples, although it should be noted that in the Soviet case the "backward elements" included Russian peasants. The second, emphasizing such things as table manners, behavior in public places, treatment of women, and basic knowledge of Comunist ideology, was the level of culture required of any town-dweller. The third, part of what had once been called "bourgeois" or "petty-bourgeois" culture, was the culture of propriety, involving good manners, correct speech, neat and appropriate dress, and some appreciation of the high culture of literature, music, and ballet. This was the level of culture implicitly expected of the managerial class, members of the new Soviet elite.

Newspapers and journals carried regular accounts of successes in mastering the first level of culture, though as reports of reality these should not always be taken too literally. In 1934, for example, a "cultural expedition" to Chuvashia—really a combination education-and-propaganda jaunt in which teachers and doctors as well as journalists and photographers took part—came back with wondrous news about the kolkhozniks' conversion to culture in the form of towels, soap, handkerchiefs, and toothbrushes. Until quite recently, people used soap only on big holidays; now 87 percent of kolkhoznik households used soap, while 55 percent of kolkhozniks had individual towels. In the past, bathing was a rarity; now the great majority of kolkhoznik families took baths at least once every two weeks. In the past, "a handkerchief was a wedding present, something to be worn on holidays"; now a quarter of the kolkhozniks had handkerchiefs. In one village, one in every ten households even possessed eau de cologne.[59]

A different kind of report came from the far North, where the hunters and reindeer herders of the "small peoples" proved very resistant to Russian elementary cultural norms. "Why are you Russians trying to prevent us from living our way?" a Khanty woman asked a young Russian student who was among the Soviet "missionaries" to the North. "Why do you take our children to school and teach them to forget and to destroy the Khanty ways?" When the native children were taken to Russian boarding schools, they put up their own resistance to becoming cultured. As one historian reports, they "boycotted certain foods, refused to solve math problems with fictitious characters, secretly communicated with the spirits, suffered from depression and continued to 'spit on the floor, behind the stove and under the bed'." [60]

At the second level, appropriate for an urban working-class context, major markers of culture were sleeping on sheets, wearing underwear, eating with knife and fork, washing hands before meals, reading the newspaper, not beating your wife and children, and not getting so drunk you missed work. That these conventions were still often flouted is evident in the pages of *Krokodil*. One cartoon shows two diners in a public cafeteria (where, it will be remembered, there had often been acute shortages of cutlery and crockery in earlier years). The caption reads: "It's nice that knives and forks have appeared in our cafeteria. Now you don't need to wash your hands." [61]

At this level, culture required that children slept separately, not with their parents, and had their own towels and toothbrushes and a separate corner of the apartment in which to do their homework. [62] This was not easy to achieve in a crowded communal apartment, still less a barracks, so those working-class families who did so were justly proud. One wife of a Stakhanovite worker, Zinovieva, related her cultural achievements under questioning by local political leaders at a conference:

ZINOVIEVA: ... I have two daughters in secondary school. One is an "A" student, the other a "B" student. I dress them neatly. I received a prize from the school for bringing them up well and for keeping their room clean and cozy.

KHOROSHKO: Do they have a room of their own?

ZINOVIEVA: Yes, and separate beds, too.

IVANOV: Do they brush their teeth?

ZINOVIEVA: They brush their teeth; they have their own towels, skates, skis—they have everything.

IVANOV: Do they live better than you used to live?

ZINOVIEVA: You bet—nobody humiliates them; nobody beats them up. [63]

Culture at the second level involved what Stephen Kotkin has called "speaking Bolshevik," that is, learning the mores and rituals of the Soviet workplace, the rules of meetings, and the public language of newspapers. A cultured person not only did not spit on the floor, he also knew how to make a speech and propose a motion at a meeting, understood concepts like "class struggle" and "socialist competition," and was informed about the international situation. [64]

This aspect of being cultured—the development of what the Bolsheviks called "consciousness"—was expressed in various ways. At its least political, it involved learning the urban poise described by one young woman worker:

I have changed a lot since I joined the Komsomol; I have become more mature. Before, I used to be very quiet, but now when I go back to the village, I can hear the boys say, "Marusia Rogacheva has become really mature. Moscow has taught her a lot. She used to be afraid to say a word." [65]

More political variants were the Stakhanovite Aleksandr Busygin's close, line-by-line reading of the new Stalinist text, *The Short Course on the History of the Communist Party of the Soviet Union*, which makes "you feel that you are learning the Bolshevik way of thinking," and the decision of one of Marusia's fellow workers, Praskovia Komarova, to improve herself by joining the party.

Since she became an activist, Praskovia wrote, "I understood that the Party was the vanguard of the working class. I thought to myself: 'Why should I be backward?' and in 1931 my husband and I joined the Party together." [66]

Stakhanovites had a special relationship to the acquisition of culture, for in this field, as well as production, they were expected to be exemplary. If their mastery of reading and writing was weak, it was their obligation to improve. They must "work on themselves," as Busygin did with his *Short Course* reading. If they skimped this duty, their wives should bring them up to scratch: one Stakhanovite wife described how she shamed her husband into going to literacy classes by telling him that it was expected of him as a trade-union organizer; another, whose husband read only with difficulty and unwillingly, managed to interest him in further education by reading aloud to him Nikolai Ostrovsky's inspirational autobiographical novel, *How the Steel Was Tempered*. Stakhanovite spouses should "[go] to theater and concerts together and borrow . . . books from the public library." [67]

Members of the new elite—many of them recently upwardly mobile from the working class and peasantry—had to acquire the same cultural skills as the second level, but under more pressure. A worker who mastered *War and Peace* as well as the *Short Course* was a high achiever, deserving praise; the wife of a manager who was ignorant of Pushkin and had never seen *Swan Lake* was an embarrassment. Reading the nineteenth-century classics of Russian literature, keeping up with the news and the contemporary cultural scene, going to the theater, having your children learn the piano—this was all part of the culture expected of people in managerial and professional jobs.

The managerial stratum had to meet higher demands in some respects. From the mid 1930s, they were expected to dress in a way that distinguished them from blue-collar workers at the plant. "The white collar and the clean shirt are necessary work tools for the fulfilment of production plans and the quality of products," Ordzhonikidze instructed his managers and engineers in heavy industry. He also told them to shave regularly, and ordered factories to provide extra mirrors so that personnel could monitor their appearance.[68] Apart from observing these marks of status, managers also needed to acquire organizational skills, which should be applied not only in the workplace but in their own lives. A newly appointed shop head at a ball-bearings plant described how he coped with his demanding job. He started the day with gymnastics at 6.15. After an eleven-hour workday, he arrived home in the evening early enough for cultural recreation: visits to the theater and cinema, drives in the car. He made a point of keeping up with technical literature in his field as well as with belles-lêttres. The secret was his methodical nature and ability to stick to a routine.[69]

Women had different cultural imperatives than men at this level, since with the exception of the small (but prized) group of women who were themselves managers and professionals, most were full-time housewives. Their responsibility was to create a "cultured" home environment in which the breadwinner could relax when he came from his demanding job. "Culture" in this context implied propriety and good household organization, as well as comfort and tastefulness. Home life should run to schedule; apartments should be appointed with "snow-white" curtains, spotless tablecloths, and lampshades shedding "soft light." Women, in view of their responsibility for household purchases, should also be discerning consumers, knowledgeable about where to acquire goods and connoisseurs of quality.[70]

Elite wives should use the skills acquired in a domestic context to make life outside the home more cultured. This was the central task of the wives' movement (discussed in Chapter 6), whose functions had much in common with "bourgeois" philanthropy. The wives took on the task of beautifying public space.

> Women's hands have sewn tens of thousands of table napkins, runners, rugs, curtains, lampshades, which are adorning Red Army barracks. They lovingly equipped the quarters of submariners. Carnations and asters have crowded out weeds and nettles in Trans-Baikal. . . . Wives of the commanders of the Amur river fleet dug 68,000 flowerbeds and planted 70,000 trees.[71]

Cultural requirements at the third level included knowledge of how to dress for formal public occasions, conduct oneself at polite parties, and entertain guests. For one outside observer, an uneducated Jewish watchmaker, it was forms of sociability that most clearly distinguished "the intelligentsia," by which he meant broadly the upper class, from the lower classes. "The intelligentsia is educated, it is cultured, it gives parties," he said. "The peasants and the workers don't have dances, they don't have parties, they don't have anything cultured." This man specifically included Communists in the category of cultured people. "The Party man is more advanced and more cultured because the Party educates him. A Party man might ask permission before taking a cigarette whereas a non-Party man will grab one without asking permission." [72]

Alas, there was still a lot of grabbing, cursing, spitting, and other uncultured behavior in Soviet society, even in the top echelon. "How cultured [our boss] Ivan Stepanovich has become!" runs the caption of a *Krokodil* cartoon appropriately titled "Good tone." "Now when he curses people out he uses only the polite form." A cartoon with the same title published a few months later shows a man in a suit, evidently a parvenu, with a smartly coiffed woman sitting in a cafe. As they rise to go, it is revealed that his chair and the table on his side are covered with cigarette butts. Aspiring to culture, but not quite making it, the man smugly informs his companion that he "was not brought up to throw butts on the floor." [73]

Changing Names

The cultured person needed a cultured name. What that meant changed over time. Exotic, revolutionary names were much in fashion in the 1920s: Elektron, Edison, Barrikada, Iskra (for the Bolsheviks' prerevolutionary newspaper, *The Spark*), Kim (the Russian acronym for "Communist Youth International"), and the like. In the 1930s, such names became less popular, with the exception of a few Lenin derivatives like Vladlen (*Vlad*imir *Len*in) and the graceful Ninel. A few people called their daughters Stalina or Stalinka. But this was not very common, and there was no boom in the name Iosif (Stalin's first name) for boys.[74]

Name changes had to be registered with ZAGS, the office of births, deaths, and marriages; and for a few years the newspaper *Izvestiia* regularly carried lists of such changes. Looking at them, we find that, as always, some people were abandoning undignified or embarrassing last names, often choosing a literary or scientific name to replace them—Svinin to Nekrasov, Kobylin to Pushkin, Kopeikin to Fizmatov (derived from "physics and mathematics"). Ethnic name changes were less common. In contrast to the late Tsarist period, not many people were dropping foreign names in the mid 1930s (a few even acquired them), and changes of a non-Russian name, for example, a Tatar one, to Russian were also infrequent. Jews were the exception, for many Jewish names redolent of the pale were being dropped in favor of Russian names: Izrail to Leonid, Sarra to Raisa, Mendel and Moisei to Mikhail, Avram to Arkadii. During the Great Purges, some people changed their last names because they were the same as notorious "enemies of the people" and thus dangerous. A Bukharina was one who changed her name in 1938, a Trotskaya (female form of Trotsky) another.[75]

But by far the most common name changes in the mid 1930s were changes from old-fashioned rural names to modern, urban "cultured" ones. What exactly gave "culture" to a name is hard to define, though a large number of the most favored names had also been popular with the Russian nobility in the previous century and thus figure prominently in literary classics like Tolstoy's novels. It is easier to discern the principle that made names unattractive: it was a general aura of "backwardness" or a particular association with the non-noble estates of Imperial Russia: peasants, merchants and townsmen, and clergy. (The dropping of Jewish names may often have been similarly motivated.)

Men were abandoning "peasant" names like Kuzma, Nikita, Frol, Makar, Tit, and Foma, as well as names connected with the clergy like Tikhon, Varfolomei, Mefodii, and Mitrofan. In their place, they were assuming modern, cultured identities with names like Konstantin, Anatolii, Gennadii, Viktor, Vladimir, Aleksandr, Nikolai, Iurii, Valentin, Sergei, and Mikhail. Women, for their part, were repudiating names like Praskovia, Agafia, Fekla, Matrena, and Marfa and becoming Liudmilas, Galinas, Natalias, Ninas, and Svetlanas.

Some local officials and media reportedly encouraged people to "shake the dust off [their] feet" and, in the cause of modernity, get rid of "old peasant names." But the modernizing name changes look more like products of the Zeitgeist than of directives from the Kremlin. The Central Committee's propaganda chief considered it vulgar and trivial to encourage people to drop old-fashioned names.[76] Yet for many people, it was clearly an important part of a transition from village to town, or from an older, estate-based, tradition-bound identity to modern citizenship.

Changing Places

I can imagine how astonished "Madame Matilda" would be if she knew that I, the apprentice—the thin little milliner Zhenka—had become Evgenia Fedorovna, technical director.

Like Chekhov's Vanka Zhukova, I was apprenticed to Matilda: I put on the samovar, swept the floor, ran round delivering to customers . . . "Madame Matilda," who was really Matrena Antonovna, held me in a grip of iron and often beat me.

And now I am technical director of a big sewing factory.[77]

Evgenia Fedorovna's success story was a common one in the 1930s, and so was her pride in it. This was an age of opportunity for energetic and ambitious people, particularly those with good working-class or peasant social origins. In the first place, the economy was expanding rapidly and generating ever more managerial and professional jobs. In the second place, it was government policy to "promote" young workers and peasants into higher education and elite occupations, especially during the intensive "affirmative action" program of the First Five-Year Plan. The result was a whole cohort of upwardly-mobile engineers, managers, and party officials who felt they were "the young masters" of the Soviet Union and were ready to thank Stalin and the revolution for their opportunities.[78]

The "log cabin to White House" myth, familiar from American legend, was equally popular in the Soviet Union. In film, its classic representation was *Member of the Government* (1939), tracing the life path of a woman who rose from being a simple peasant to kolkhoz chairman, Stakhanovite, local soviet deputy, and finally member of the Supreme Soviet, the national parliament. A. L. Kapustina, a real-life woman with a biography similar to that of the film's heroine, expressed a common Soviet belief when she confidently explained that this was possible only in the Soviet Union.

On November 7th, I was in our Leningrad region for the holiday. On the tribune I met some foreign workers and talked to them through a translator. I told them that . . . I, in the past a simple, downtrodden, rural woman, am a member of the Soviet government. They were . . . astonished. . . . Yes, comrades, for them it is a miracle, because over there it would be impossible.[79]

To be sure, Kapustina's position as "member of the government" was essentially an ornamental one, conferring prestige and privilege but no political or administrative power. But there were people, and not few of them, whose ascent had landed them in power in a more substantive sense. Leonid Brezhnev and most of his long-lived Politburo of the 1970s and 1980s were affirmative-action beneficiaries of the 1930s, most of them from working-class backgrounds; so was Brezhnev's predecessor, Nikita Khrushchev. Even Mikhail Gorbachev belonged to this upwardly mobile category, although he was of the postwar generation and came from the peasantry.[80]

The careers of the "Brezhnev generation" were helped not only by the affirmative-action programs of the First Five-Year Plan but also by the Great

Purges of 1937–38, which removed a whole stratum of top officials and party leaders. A few examples will serve as illustration. Georgii Aleksandrov, born in 1909, was the son of a worker who died when he was ten. He was briefly on the streets as a homeless child before being taken into an orphanage and trained as a metalworker. He joined the party at the age of eighteen, and a few years later was sent off to Moscow University. By the age of twenty-nine, he had defended his Ph.D. and become a professor of history of philosophy; in the 1940s, he was head of the agitation and propaganda department of the Central Committee. Sergei Kaftanov, one of Aleksandrov's colleagues in the Central Committee apparat of the 1940s and First Deputy Minister for Culture in the 1950s, worked in a mine as an adolescent and made his way to the Mendeleev Chemical Institute via the Komsomol and trade school.[81]

Two who rose into top industrial positions in the late 1930s were Roman Belan, of Zaporozhe Steel, and Viktor Lvov, of the Leningrad Putilov works. Lvov, born in 1900 in a cooper's family, was orphaned early and as a child worked as an agricultural laborer. During the revolution, he joined the Red Guards and then the Red Army, ending up as a commander of border troops before being chosen as one of an elite group of affirmative-action beneficiaries (the "party thousanders") and sent to college to study engineering. Belan, the son of poor peasants, joined the Komsomol in his village at the age of thirteen and fought in the Civil War. When the war ended, he was sent to the rabfak (workers' preparatory school) of the Kiev Polytechnic Institute, from which he graduated as a metallurgical engineer in 1931.[82]

These flashy success stories were just the tip of the iceberg. All over the Soviet Union, at every level, people were changing their social status—peasants moving to town and becoming industrial workers, workers moving into technical jobs or becoming party officials, former school teachers becoming university professors. Everywhere there was a shortage of qualified people to take the jobs; everywhere there was inexperience, incompetence, and turnover of personnel. The Stakhanov movement turned out to be a major vehicle of upward mobility, though this was scarcely its intended purpose. Stakhanovites like Aleksei Stakhanov himself, Aleksandr Busygin, Maria Demchenko, Pasha Angelina, and others claimed their reward after a few years of super-productivity in the factory or state farm and moved on to college, becoming engineers, industrial managers, and agronomists.[83]

Upward mobility was so much a part of Soviet life that the standard personnel questionnaires filled in by trade-union members included the following cryptic entry (Question 8): "Year of moving out of production or quitting agriculture." This was shorthand for two questions, easily deciphered by Soviet citizens of the period and applicable in one or the other case to a large proportion of them. The first question meant "If you moved out of blue-collar work into a white-collar occupation, when did that happen?" The second asked the same question with regard to peasant movement from the village into urban employment.[84]

Of course upward mobility was not necessarily a success story. Some promotees pleaded to be released from jobs they were unable to handle—for example, the thirty-one-year-old former shepherd promoted to district soviet chairman in 1937, who was driven frantic by the tensions of the purge period and the mockery of his constituents. Others clung on, but their mistakes on the job brought misfortune not only to themselves but to all around them.[85] It was possible to plummet even more rapidly than to ascend, and this could mean a prison term or, during the Great Purges, twenty years in Gulag. For this reason, some people thought it more prudent *not* to respond to the siren song of upward mobility.

Although in some cases "promotion" meant being sent to study and then going on to a higher-level job, in many cases it was the reverse. The expansion of part-time schools and courses of all kinds was extraordinary. Every year, huge numbers of adults attended courses to become literate or improve their reading and writing, learn the basic skills of a trade, raise their qualifications in their job, and pass the "technical minimum" examination, to prepare themselves for technical school or college. Even kolkhozniks vied for the privilege of being sent off to the district center for a month's course in animal husbandry or accountancy or to learn to drive a tractor. There were special networks of party schools to give Communist officials a mixture of general education and ideological training; "industrial academies" like the one attended by Khrushchev, provided select members of the same group with engineering training (albeit at a slightly lower level than normal engineering schools). Industrial managers and Stakhanovite workers who were too busy to go to courses were assigned tutors who came to their homes in the evening to work with them.

Evgenia Fedorovna, the milliner-turned-technical director, was one of many promotees who had risen without formal education but was now anxious to acquire it. "I have travelled a long road from the illiterate Zhenka to a cultured Soviet woman," she wrote. "And I am stubbornly studying at home even now. But that is not enough. I want to graduate from technical college." [86] That sentiment—"I want to study"—was repeated constantly again by everyone from managers to housewives. In a survey taken in 1937, almost half the young workers of both sexes at the Stalin Auto Plant questioned stated that "continuing my education" was their main short-term personal goal, and more than one in eight of the whole group was planning to go to college in the next two or three years.[87]

"In Moscow I had a burning desire to study," recalls a woman of peasant origins uprooted by collectivization. "Where or what wasn't important; I wanted to study." From the story she tells, this was not because she had any clearly formulated ambition or intellectual interests, but because she perceived that education was the ticket to a decent life: "We had a saying at work: 'Without that piece of paper [the diploma] you are an insect; with it, a human being.' My lack of higher education prevented me from getting decent wages." [88]

Even in their spare time, after work and after class, Soviet citizens were busy improving their minds. Every visitor to the Soviet Union in the 1930s commented on the passionate love of reading and zest for learning of the Soviet

population. The Pushkin jubilee in 1937 became a national celebration, and
large editions of nineteenth-century Russian literary classics were published.
The popular weekly magazine *Ogonek* ran a regular feature in 1936 called
"Are you a cultured person?" that allowed readers to test their general knowledge. Among the things a cultured Soviet person should know were the
names of five plays by Shakespeare, five makes of Soviet automobile, four
rivers in Africa, three types of warplanes, seven Stakhanovites, two representatives of Utopian social thought, two poems by Heinrich Heine, and two Soviet icebreakers.[89]

Pasha Angelina, the Stakhanovite, was one of those who not only went to
college but, as is evident from her writing, acquired a general knowledge that
would have enabled her to do quite well on the *Ogonek* quizzes. By the 1940s,
evidently as a result of her reading of the magazines *America* and *The British
Ally* in the war years, she had learned enough about the outside world to
know (unlike many of her contemporaries) that upward mobility was not only
a Soviet phenomenon.

> In these foreign magazines one frequently finds descriptions of "dizzying ca-
> reers" and "exceptional" biographies. I remember, for instance, an enthusiastic
> account of the life of one important man who, in the words of the magazine,
> "came from the people." He used to be a simple newspaper boy, but then made
> a lot of money, became the owner of many newspapers, and received the title of
> lord.

So, Angelina asked herself, what was the difference beteen Lord
Beaverbrook's brilliant career and her own? The answer she gives encapsulates
a crucial element in the mentalité of the times, particularly that of the
affirmative-action cohort—the conviction that in the Soviet Union upward
mobility neither meant separation from the people nor implied the existence
of an hierarchical social structure in which some were more privileged than
others. What was unique about the Soviet case, according to Angelina, was
that "my rise is not exceptional. For if that gentleman, as the magazine rightly
puts it, 'rose from the people,' I rose together with the people." [90]

4

The Magic Tablecloth

One facet of "making fairy tales come true" was particularly dear to Soviet citizens: the promise that socialism would bring abundance. This was literally an excursion into the world of Russian fairy tales, whose furniture included a Magic Tablecloth[1] that, when laid, produced an extravagant array of food and drink of its own accord. Perhaps the hope of future abundance made the scarcity of the present easier to bear. In the mid 1930s, in any case, food, drink, and consumer goods came to be celebrated with a fervor that even Madison Avenue might have envied.

For the time being, products were still scarce and of poor quality. But the Magic Tablecloth had already been laid on some tables. Communist officials and parts of the intelligentsia were the main beneficiaries; Trotsky, the old revolutionary leader now in foreign exile, saw this emergence of a new privileged class as part of Stalin's betrayal of the revolution.[2] Domestically, however, the message was more complicated. For it was not only officials and members of the intelligentsia who had access to Magic Tablecloths, but also

Stakhanovites—ordinary people whose outstanding achievements had earned them rewards. In Soviet conceptualization, it was society's vanguard, not its elite, that had first access to scarce goods and services. What the vanguard had today, the rest of society could expect tomorrow.

IMAGES OF ABUNDANCE

"Life has become better, comrades; life has become more cheerful."
Stalin, 1935[3]

This phrase, endlessly reiterated in Soviet propaganda, was one of the favorite slogans of the 1930s. It was carried on placards at Soviet demonstrations, run as a banner headline in newspapers to mark the New Year, displayed in parks and labor camps, quoted in speeches, celebrated in song by the Red Army choir—and sometimes angrily mimicked by those whose lives had not become better.[4] The change of Soviet orientation that it celebrates, labeled "the Great Retreat" by an American sociologist, was inaugurated at the beginning of 1935, when the lifting of bread rationing was the occasion for a propaganda campaign celebrating the end of privation and the coming of plenty.[5]

The new orientation meant several things. First, at the simplest level, it was a promise that there would be more goods in the stores. This involved a more fundamental shift away from the anti-consumerist approach of earlier years toward a new (and, in Marxist terms, surprising) appreciation of commodities. Second, it meant a move away from the ascetic puritanism characteristic of the Cultural Revolution toward a new tolerance of people enjoying themselves. All kinds of leisure-time activities for the masses were now encouraged: carnivals, parks of culture and rest, masquerades, dancing, even jazz. For the elite too, there were new privileges and possibilities.

The lip-smacking public celebration of commodities in the mid 1930s was virtually a consumer-goods pornography. Food and drink were the primary objects. Here is a newspaper's description of the goodies available at the newly opened commercial grocery store (formerly Eliseev's, and most recently a Torgsin store) on Gorky Street.

> In the grocery department, there are 38 types of sausage, including 20 new types that have not been sold anywhere before. This department will also sell three types of cheese—Camembert, Brie and Limburg—made for the store by special order. In the confectionery department there are 200 types of candies and pastries. . . . The bread department has up to 50 kinds of bread . . . Meat is kept in refrigerated glass cases. In the fish department, there are tanks with live carp, mirror carp, bream, and pike. When the customers choose their fish, they are scooped out of the tank with the aid of nets.[6]

Anastas Mikoyan, the party leader in charge of provisioning throughout the 1930s, contributed a lot to this trend. Certain goods, such as ice cream and frankfurters, particularly aroused his enthusiasm. These were new products, or products made with new technology, that Mikoyan was trying to introduce to the mass urban consumer. He used the imagery of pleasure and plenty, but also that of modernity. Frankfurters, a kind of sausage new to Russians, derived from the German model, had once been "a sign of bourgeois abundance and well-being," according to Mikoyan. Now they were available to the masses. Since they were mass-produced on machines, they were superior to foods produced in the old-fashioned way by hand. Mikoyan was also an enthusiast for ice cream, "very tasty and nutritious," especially as mass-produced with machine technology in the United States. This too had once been a bourgeois luxury item, eaten only on holidays, but it would now be available to Soviet citizens on a daily basis. The latest ice-cream-making machines were imported, and exotic varieties were soon on sale: even in the provinces one could buy chocolate Eskimo, Pompa (not further identified), cream, cherry, and raspberry.[7]

Mikoyan's patronage also extended to beverages, especially up-scale ones. "What kind of happy life can we have if there's not enough good beer and good liqueurs?" he asked. It was a scandal that the Soviet Union was so far behind Europe in wine-growing and viniculture; even Romania was ahead. "Champagne is a symbol of material well-being, a symbol of prosperity." In the West, only the capitalist bourgeoisie could enjoy it. In the Soviet Union, it was now within the reach of many, if not all: "Comrade Stalin said that the Stakhanovites now earn a lot of money, engineers and other toilers earn a lot." To satisfy their rising demands, Soviet production must be sharply increased, Mikoyan concluded.[8]

New products were often advertised in the press, despite the general curtailment of newspaper advertisements at the end of the 1920s. These advertisements were not so much intended to sell goods—generally the products they touted were unavailable in the stores—as to educate the public. Knowledge of consumer goods, like good taste, was part of the culture expected of Soviet citizens, especially women, who were the acknowledged experts in the consumer field. It was a function of Soviet "cultured trade" to make this knowledge available through advertisements, instruction of customers by sales personnel in stores, customers' conferences, and exhibitions.[9] The trade exhibitions organized in major cities of the Soviet Union displayed goods never available to the ordinary consumer, like washing machines, cameras, and automobiles. ("That's all very well," said one disgruntled consumer after viewing an exhibition, "but [the goods] aren't in the stores and you won't find them.")[10]

The didactic function of advertisement was evident in the advertisements for ketchup, another of Mikoyan's new food products based on an American model. "Do you know what ketchup is?" was the lead sentence in one advertisement. Another explained that "In America a bottle of KETCHUP stands on every restaurant table and in the pantry of every housewife. KETCHUP is the best, sharp, aromatic relish for meat, fish, vegetables and other dishes." "Ask for KETCHUP from the factories of Chief Canned Goods Trust in the stores of Union Canned Goods Distribution syndicate and other food stores," the copy concluded in a burst of wild optimism (or perhaps simply imitating American copywriting conventions).[11]

Another product that was given great play in the of educational advertising of the 1930s was eau de cologne. "Eau de cologne has firmly entered the life of Soviet woman," pronounced a popular illustrated weekly in a special feature on perfume in 1936. "Hairdressers of the Soviet Union require tens of thousands of vials of eau de cologne every day." An accompanying photograph showed a hairdresser spraying generous quantities of eau de cologne on a client's hair.[12] Rather surprisingly, contraceptives were also advertised, although in real life they were almost impossible to obtain.[13]

Clothing and textiles received almost as much loving attention as food and drink. "Moscow is dressing well," was the heading of an article allegedly by a tailor published in the labor newspaper in 1934.

> Comparing the May Day celebrations, one may assert that never before was Moscow so well dressed as this year! Rarely, rarely could one meet a person in the first days of May whose suit would not have been suitable for a wedding or an evening party. A stiff starched collar was a normal thing in the columns of worker demonstrators [in the May Day march]. The women wore good suits made out of Boston cloth, cheviot, and fine broadcloth, elegant and well-sewn dresses out of silk or wool.[14]

Communist leaders were doing their bit to popularize the image of the well-dressed man by partially abandoning the military style of dress preferred in the 1920s in favor of civilian suits. One account gives Molotov credit for the change, another accords primacy to the Komsomol leader Aleksandr Kosarev, who "one day declared a new slogan: 'Work productively, rest culturally.' After that he always wore European clothes." Clearly, however, it was a collective project of the party leadership. A front-page photograph in the newspapers in the summer of 1935 showed Politburo members at a physical-culture parade nattily dressed in matching white, lightweight jackets.[15]

Communist women, still normally affecting a sober style of dress as close to men's as possible in the early 1930s, were encouraged to make similar adjustments. One Bolshevik woman of the Old Guard, invited to Moscow for a Kremlin banquet on International Women's Day sometime in the mid 1930s, recalled the last-minute instructions

> that all our activists of the women's movement should appear at the banquet not in severe English suits, with sweater and tie, but looking like women and dressed accordingly. Our activists ran around Moscow as if they had been stung, putting themselves into order as instructed by Stalin.[16]

The change in mores was spelled out clearly in the story of Kostia Zaitsev, a coal-hewer and Komsomol activist in the south. Back in the NEP period, Zaitsev had bought a silk jacket with blue satin lapels from an old aristocrat and wore it on an evening stroll in the steppe. For this, he had received a sharp rebuke from the Komsomol cell for bourgeois degeneracy. Now, in 1934, he was not only wearing a jacket and tie, but was also the possessor of "a couple of excellent suits, an expensive watch, a hunting rifle, a bicycle, a camera, [and] a radio." He had acquired a Turkish rug for the floor of his room and painted the walls and ceiling. He had an "elegant bookstand" holding "dozens of books." All this was not bourgeois degeneracy, it was culture, part of Zaitsev's self-improvement process. "Zaitsev is studying to become an engineer." [17]

Entertainment

"Red Russia becomes rose-colored," reported the *Baltimore Sun's* Moscow correspondent toward the end of 1938.[18] Luxury items like silk stockings, long considered "bourgeois," were back in vogue in elite circles. Tennis had become fashionable; jazz and foxtrots were all the rage. The party maximum on salaries had been abolished. This was *la vie en rose*, Soviet style. To some people, it looked like embourgeoisement or "a second NEP."

One of the signs of the times was the revival of Moscow restaurant life in 1934. This followed a four-year hiatus during which restaurants had been open only to foreigners, payment was in hard currency, and the OGPU regarded any Soviet citizens who went there with deep suspicion. Now, all those who could afford it could go to the Metropole Hotel, where "wonderful live starlets swam in a pool right in the centre of the restaurant hall," and hear jazz by Antonin Ziegler's Czech group, or to the National to hear the Soviet jazzmen Aleksandr Tsfasman and Leonid Utesov, or to the Prague Hotel on the Arbat where gypsy singers and dancers performed. The restaurants were patronized particularly by theater people and other "new elite" members, and their prices were, of course, out of reach of ordinary citizens. Their existence was no secret, however. The Prague advertised its "first-class" cuisine ("Blinzes, pies, and pelmeni every day. Assortment of wines"), its gypsy singers, and "dancing with lighting effects" in Moscow's evening newspaper.[19]

But it was not only elite members who profited from the relaxation of mores and encouragement of leisure culture of the mid 1930s. Sound film was the new mass cultural medium, and the second half of the 1930s was the great age of Soviet musical comedy. Cheerful and fast-moving entertainment movies like *Happy-Go-Lucky Guys* (1934), *Circus* (1936), *Volga-Volga* (1938), and *Radiant Path* (1940), with catchy music in a jazzy idiom, achieved great popularity. There were even ambitious plans, never realized, to build a "Soviet Hollywood" in the South. Dancing was also in fashion, for the masses as well as the elite. Dancing schools sprang up like mushrooms in the towns, and a young working-class woman describing her cultural development mentioned that not only was she going to literacy classes, but she and her Stakhanovite husband were learning to dance.[20]

The New Year's holiday—complete with fir tree and Grandfather Frost, the Russian equivalent of Father Christmas—returned in this period, after some years of banishment. New Year's was celebrated extravagantly in 1936, according to newspaper reports. "Never was there such gaiety," was the heading of a report from Leningrad:

> Finely dressed male and female workers and children gathered in the decorated and illuminated houses of culture, clubs and schools . . . The luxurious halls of the Aleksandrovskii palace in Detskoe selo [formerly Tsarskoe selo] were opened for the first time for a noisy ball, where leading workers and engineers of

the Red Triangle plant were the hosts. With games, dances, fireworks, riding on the snow in a troika with bells, the Detskoe selo park was never so lively. The music played until dawn.[21]

The new leisure culture included long-distance car races (a central feature in Ilf and Petrov's humorous novel *The Little Golden Calf*), as well as long-distance bicycle and motorcycle races: in 1934, a sound documentary film on the "heroic autorace" from Moscow to Kara-Kum and back showed how participants (and camera crew) survived six and a half days in a "waterless desert." [22] The popularity of football as a spectator sport soared in the 1930s, mainly without explicit official encouragement but with the benefit of a new modern stadium in Moscow's Luzhniki district and generous funding of teams from the trade unions, secret police, and the Army.[23] Airshows were also very popular.

In the realm of amateur sport, the most publicized activities were parachute-jumping and gymnastics. Parachute-jumping turned up everywhere: in displays at airshows by professionals, in the paramilitary training conducted under the "Ready for Labor and Defence" program, in photographs and cartoons in newspapers and magazines, on the vitas of Stakhanovites, and in recreational parachute-jumping towers set up in parks of culture and rest. No doubt this sport symbolized Soviet daring and mastery of the air (or, to put it another way, the Soviet propensity, popular and governmental, for risk-taking). Gymnastics, known as physical culture, was highly visible because it lent itself to mass demonstrations, held in the summer on Red Square and elsewhere, as well as providing photographers and painters with a rare opportunity for depicting the human body. "Physcultura—hurrah-hurrah!," sang the sportsmen in the popular "Sportsman's March." [24]

"Parks of culture and rest," recently opened in many cities across the Soviet Union, were intended to offer a new kind of cultured leisure to the masses. They were parks with attractions, rides, dance-floors, pavilions, and kiosks. The prototype was Gorky Park in Moscow, planned and directed by an American, Betty Glan. For the opening of the park's winter season in 1935, a banner proclaiming Stalin's slogan "Life has become better, life has become more cheerful" was hung across the gates, and more than 10,000 people arrived in the first three hours. Every foreign visitor who went to Russia visited Gorky Park and left a description of it, variously emphasizing the entertainment aspect, like Ferris wheels, bowling alleys, dance-floors, and cinemas, and the educational aspect of newspaper readings, agitational corners, and so on. (Almost everyone mentioned the parachute jump.[25])

A report of Gorky Park on May Day in a Soviet newspaper stuck to the basics—food and drink.

> It is hard to describe how Moscow enjoyed itself in these joyous days of the May Day celebrations. . . . We have to talk about the garden of plenty behind the Manège building, this garden where sausages and Wurst were growing on the trees . . . where a mug of foaming beer was accompanied by delicious Poltava sausages, by pink ham, melting Swiss cheese and marble white bacon. . . . Walking across this square one could get a giant appetite.[26]

Summer became carnival time under the new dispensation. Still popular, though less prominent than in the mid to late 1920s, were the parades lampooning various enemies of the revolution and Soviet state. For the eighteenth anniversary of the revolution, 3,000 eighteen-year-olds from some of Moscow's biggest industrial plants participated in a "carnival of happy youth" parade, with each district taking a separate theme and organizing its own decoration. The Sokolniki Komsomol branch invited the famous caricaturists, the Kukriniksy, to design their display, which ridiculed everything that belonged to the past. Gods, angels, and saints headed the cavalcade, followed by Adam and Eve. Monks, capitalists, and the Romanov court followed in separate trucks, and "walking self-importantly" behind were ostriches, donkeys, and bears representing "generals, counts, and so on." [27]

For the first nighttime carnival, held in Gorky Park in July 1935 to celebrate Constitution Day, costumes and masks were obligatory, with a carnival parade and cash prizes for the best. Newspaper reports did not neglect the romantic possibilities of the mask, while also describing the variety of costumes worn: Pushkin's Onegin and Tatiana, Charlie Chaplin, Gorky's Mother, eighteenth-century marquesses, toreadors, Mark Anthony, and so on. Laughter was much emphasized: as *Krokodil* reported, carnival slogans proposed by "individual enthusiasts" included "He who does not laugh, does not eat," and "Make fun of those who fall behind!" [28]

Despite elements of spontaneity and similarity with earlier forms of popular celebration, the carnivals of the mid 1930s were carefully scripted and staged by leading artistic figures, and the intention to invent tradition was quite explicit: "This carnival merriment must enter the tradition of the Soviet Union like the colorful national celebrations of France and Italy." [29] Press descriptions, as well as the recollections of some foreign visitors, stress the excitement and gaiety of the crowds during carnival. Others were less sure. "There is no doubt that they 'take their pleasure sadly,'" noted an Australian visitor to Gorky Park. "Among the many thousands there we saw scarcely a smile, though we assumed that they were enjoying themselves." [30]

PRIVILEGE

In the future, there would be abundance; for the present, there was scarcity. The worst period of scarcity, during the First Five-Year Plan, naturally prompted the regime to make special arrangements to feed its own, just as it had done, though less systematically, during the Civil War. Communist officials became in the literal sense a privileged class in the Soviet Union.

But Communists were not the only people with privilege. A less predictable beneficiary was the intelligentsia, or at least key segments of it. This too could be traced back to the Civil War period, when at Maxim Gorky's urging special rations were established for members of the Academy of Sciences and others regarded as cultural treasures. In material terms, the intelligentsia was a relatively privileged group in the 1920s. But its privileged status in the 1930s had a different flavor. Not only was it more conspicuous, but it followed the period of Cultural Revolution, when "bourgeois specialists" had been roughly

handled. The turnaround in the first half of the 1930s was dramatic; it was evident, an emigré journal commented, that the political leaders had a new approach to the intelligentsia: "They are courting and coaxing and bribing it. It
is needed." [31]

Engineers were among the first groups of the intelligentsia to receive special privileges—understandably, given their essential contribution to the industrialization drive. More surprising was the honoring of writers, composers,
architects, painters, theater people, and other members of "the creative intelligentsia." The effusive honoring of writers in connection with the First Congress of Soviet Writers in 1934 established the new tone, which combined
conspicuous deference to high culture with an implicit reminder to intellectuals of their obligation to serve the Soviet cause. [32]

While the press was normally silent about the privileges of Communist officials, intelligentsia privileges were often proudly announced. Perhaps this was
a strategy to deflect possible popular resentment of privilege away from Communists. Although it does not appear to have had that result, [33] it did imprint
on popular imagination the notion that some members of the creative intelligentsia were the most fabulously privileged people in the Soviet Union. According to a rumor that every Soviet citizen seemed to know, the novelist
Aleksei Tolstoy (an aristocrat by birth), Maxim Gorky, the aviation engineer
A. P. Tupolev, the jazz man Leonid Utesov, and the popular-song composer
Isaac Dunaevsky were all millionaires whom the Soviet regime allowed to have
bottomless bank accounts. [34]

Privilege in Stalin's Russia had more to do with access—the ability to obtain goods, services, apartments, and so on—than it did with ownership. The
key factor in the emergence of an institutionalized hierarchy of access in the
1930s was scarcity, particularly the structures generated by extreme scarcity at
the beginning of the decade. This critical period not only saw the reintroduction of rationing, which had its own internal differentiation, but also of various forms of "closed distribution" of goods to those in special categories. The
reason for this was not ideological (the ideology of the period tended to be
egalitarian and militant) but practical: there was simply not enough to go
round.

Food privileges took a number of forms: special rations, special elite closed
stores, and special cafeterias at the workplace. Starting in the late 1920s,
senior party and government officials received special rations. The system was
internally differentiated, and Elena Bonner remembers that her parents—
Communists in senior jobs, her stepfather with the Comintern, her mother
with the Moscow Party Committee—were on different rungs of the ladder:

> Papa's [food parcel] was delivered to the house, twice a month or more, but I
> don't know whether we paid for it. It had butter, cheese, candies and canned
> goods. There were also special parcels for the holidays, with caviar, smoked and
> cured fish, chocolate, and also cheese and butter. You had to pick up Mama's
> parcels—not far away, on Petrovka. The dining room of the Moscow Party
> Committee was on the corner of Takhmanovsky Alley, and once a week they
> gave out the parcels. I often went for ours, and you had to pay. It contained but-
> ter and other items, but it was much less fancy than Papa's. [35]

"Academic" rations for the intelligentsia returned at about the same time, with members of the Academy of Sciences the first beneficiaries. Writers came next, being allocated 400 "academic rations" in 1932; and later an additional 200 rations were allocated to artists.[36]

The special stores for the elite were known by the acronym GORT in the first half of the 1930s. Access to them was reserved for a privileged group that included administrators working in central government, party, industrial, trade-union, planning, and publishing agencies, as well as economists, engineers, and other experts working for state agencies. These stores stocked basic foods, "luxuries" like sausage, eggs, and dried fruit, clothing, shoes, and other vital goods such as soap. Elena Bonner remembered her family buying stainless-steel cutlery there, the first she had ever seen. The GPU had its own special stores for its employees (as did the Red Army), and the GPU's Moscow store was renowned as "the best in the whole Soviet Union." [37]

The network of special stores extended into the provinces, although the quality of even elite provisioning was usually worse there than in the capitals. Engineers and managers at major industrial enterprises and new construction sites were provisioned by a special network of closed stores: in 1932, there were said to be 700 closed distributors for engineers and managers throughout the country.[38] Outside of industry and other special networks like the military and the OGPU, provincial and district officials had their own closed stores, accessible to all those above a certain rank. Officials of rural soviets were too junior to have access, even when there was a closed store in the locality, and one of them complained bitterly about this discrimination in a letter to Kalinin.

> I was in GORT, they'd brought in box-calf boots for 40 rubles a pair and I asked them to let me have one pair, but no they wouldn't, after all they were 40 rubles. That's appropriate for the party aktiv, . . . regardless of the fact that the party activists all have a pair of boots and some have even two pairs. . . . But they refused me, who hasn't got any footwear, and [only] allowed me to take rubber boots selling for 45 rubles.[39]

This complaint points up one of the strangest features of Soviet closed distribution, that goods in the special store were priced *lower* than in ordinary stores. As a general rule, the harder it was to get access to a store, the lower the prices of its goods.

Because of the food shortages and distribution problems, most people took their main meal at work in a cafeteria in the first half of the 1930s. Some form of differentiation within the cafeteria framework was common, and in large institutions the hierarchy (expressed in the quantity and quality of the meal and also the room in which it was eaten) was quite complex. Some factories had one dining room for upper management, a second for middle management, and a third for high-achieving workers (shockworkers), in addition to the cafeteria for ordinary workers and employees. In other cases, shockworkers ate with the rest of the workers but were issued extra ration cards so that they could get a double or triple helping. Foreigners who encountered these arrangements were often disconcerted or even outraged. "Probably nowhere, save for the Eastern countries, would it be possible for the range of classes to be publicly displayed so blatantly as it was in Russia," the Finnish Communist Arvo Tuominen commented after describing the dining hierarchies of the early 1930s. When Tuominen, who was working in the Comintern, tried to eat with his assistants in the Comintern cafeteria, "it was not considered seemly. The reproachful glances in themselves said: your place is not here, go to your own caste!" [40]

In an earlier chapter, we have already noted the tendency of local officials to maintain closed distributors for themselves even when the center decreed this was no longer necessary. If there was no closed distributor, officials (and their wives) often informally enforced special-access rules on goods that came into local stores for general distribution. For example, a local store in the Western province received a consignment of textiles for shipping to the villages—but the next morning the local party committee asked the store manager to set aside 1,000 meters of cloth for officials who "do not have time to stand in line." The same process was at work in the Far East, where an aggrieved local resident reported that "for the May Day holiday they brought wine into the cooperative store. Sinner that I am, I asked for half a liter, but they refused, no you can't have it, that's for the party aktiv." The "nomenclatura first" convention was so strong that a district health department in Siberia advertised that the local pharmacy received a shipment of a particular medicament "to protect responsible workers [i.e., officials] . . . from the bites of malaria mosquitos." [41]

Officials also unofficially enjoyed the prerogative of charging their own entertainment to the state in various ways. This prerogative was periodically denounced, however, as in this regional newspaper attack from 1937:

> Wine flowed in a river [at the banquest for district leaders]. Some, like for example the head of the municipal economy department, Koniushenko, drank themselves into unconsciousness. That banquet cost the state 2,300 rubles, which the chairman of the district soviet executive committee obliged the financial department to pay the grocery store.

Earlier in the year, according to the same report, the district soviet chairman had held a banquet at his apartment, charging the food and drink served to the school construction budget. [42]

The elites also had privileges involving other kinds of scarce goods, such as housing, dachas, and vacation resorts. In the 1920s, little was done to build special accommodations for the elite, and top party and government leaders were placed rather haphazardly in apartments in the Kremlin or hotels like the National, the Metropole, and the Hotel Luxe. Then in 1928 construction began on the first apartment house built specifically for high officials, Government House (immortalized by Iurii Trifonov in his novel of the Great Purges, *House on the Embankment*), which was located across the river facing the Christ the Savior Cathedral and diagonally opposite the Kremlin. This building had 506 spacious, furnished flats, all with telephones and constant hot water, along with many amenities. [43]

New elite housing was also provided in the first half of the 1930s by turning existing buildings into cooperatives for the use of personnel in various government agencies like the Central Committee, the OGPU, the Red Army, the Ministry of Foreign Affairs, and the Ministry of Heavy Industry. The Writers' Union also got its cooperative building in a central location, as did scientists, composers, artists, and aircraft designers; engineers had their own housing cooperatives in various central locations. The Moscow Arts Theater got a house just off Gorky Street for its actors, while Bolshoi Theater personnel occupied most of the apartments at 25 Gorky Street. The Vakhtangov Theater, wealthy and blessed with powerful patrons, managed to build two well-appointed five-story houses in Moscow out of theater profits. Certain intelligentsia professions were recognized as having special professional needs that entitled them to a larger living space (measured in square meters) than ordinary citizens, a hotly contested privilege. From 1933, scientists and writers received this privilege, which was extended to artists and sculptors two years later.[44]

A special building plan for apartment blocks for engineers was launched in the early 1930s. According to a plan adopted in 1932, over 10,000 apartments for engineers and other specialists were to be built over a two-year period in sixty seven cities; Moscow's allocation was ten new apartment houses with a total of 3,000 apartments. In Magnitogorsk, engineers and managers did particularly well because they inherited housing originally built for foreign specialists in the suburb of Berezki. These were not apartments but separate two-story houses with their own gardens—an almost unimaginable luxury in the Soviet Union of these years.[45]

Although some of the elite apartments were luxurious, many were modest in terms of size and amenities. Moreover, there were nowhere near enough of them to go round, especially in the capitals, and many people whose jobs and credentials qualified them as elite members remained in communal apartments. Even for those in substandard housing, however, it was normal to have a servant. The convention was that this was permissible if the wife worked. "We had a servant—even two when my daughter was small," a factory buyer told Harvard Project interviewers. "They are cheap but hard to get. I would go to a kolkhoz and select a girl—every girl is anxious to leave the hard life in a kolkhoz and move to the city—and then I would have to talk to the kolkhoz chief. He, of course, hates to lose a worker, but if you have *blat*, you will get your servant." It made excellent sense financially for the factory buyer: his wife earned 300 rubles a month as a typist (in addition to his income), and "we paid our servant 18 rubles a month, plus board and lodging. She slept in the kitchen."[46]

In contrast to the 1920s, there was little public discussion of domestic servants in the 1930s and still less of their exploitation by employers. Some people complained about it privately, claiming that employers abused their servants ("They are even worse than the 'ladies' of earlier times, these wives of engineers, doctors and 'responsible' cadres"), who were forced into servitude and obliged to accept inhuman conditions because of the housing crisis: "The majority have no bed because there is nowhere to put one. They sleep in the 'bathroom,' 'under the table' or 'on chairs.' God help the servant who gets sick—there's nowhere for her to lay her head." [47]

But even convinced Communists often saw nothing wrong with having servants. John Scott, an American working as a worker in Magnitogorsk and married to a Russian, acquired a maid after the birth of their first child. His wife, Masha, a teacher, had no problems with this, despite her peasant background and strong Communist convictions. As an emancipated woman, she was strongly opposed to housework, and considered it both appropriate and necessary that someone with less education should do it for her. [48]

The taboo on public discussion of servants was partially lifted in the late 1930s, when *Krokodil* carried a series of "servant" cartoons and jokes. One, headed "Advice to young housewives," recommended (presumably tongue in cheek) that the best way to find a servant in Moscow was to take a no. 16 tram to Krasnaia Presnia, go to the Textile Combine there, and pick out one of the workers in the spinning shop. Other *Krokodil* cartoons satirized officials who depended on servants to do their shopping and keep them informed on the problems of everyday life, of which they had little firsthand experience. [49]

Dachas (country homes) and passes to elite vacation resorts and sanatoria [50] were other important forms of elite privilege. In Kazan, first secretary Razumov set the pattern by building himself a private dacha in the grounds of the "Livadia" estate that he had turned into a luxurious resthome for party officials. Then the leaders of the city soviet undertook to build a whole dacha settlement—using, as was later alleged, money improperly diverted from other budgetary lines (municipal transport and sewage, parks) and contributed by industrial leaders from the discretionary funds—for a "carefully chosen" list of local bigwigs. [51] This was by no means an isolated case. Genrikh Iagoda, head of the OGPU, was one of a whole array of top party leaders in Moscow who "built themselves grandiose dacha-palaces of 15-20 and more rooms, where they lived luxuriously and wasted the people's money." (As the disapproving tone of this quotation indicates, the dacha privilege, like many others, was subject to revocation without notice when the beneficiary fell out of political favor.) [52]

Writers were particularly favored with regard to dachas. The Politburo's decision to build a new dacha settlement for writers at Peredelkino, a suburban train ride from Moscow, was one of the most dramatic indications of the writer's new status. The construction budget cost was six million rubles, and the settlement was to consist of thirty dachas of four or five rooms each, which were to be allocated by the Board of the Writers' Union for the indefinite use of distinguished writers and their families. The array of literary stars chosen including Boris Pasternak, Isaac Babel, and Ilya Ehrenburg. [53]

Some dachas were in cooperative ownership and could be bought and sold, usually at very high prices. It was also possible to build your own dacha, although that required not only money but also a great deal of *blat* to get permits and building materials. The daughter of a physician working in the public health ministry described how her father had started building a dacha, along with his chauffeur, a man with extensive *blat* connections, and a bookkeeper. They had problems along the way ("Father said that it would cost only about 2,000 rubles but in the end it cost us 12,000 rubles and we had to sell a large carpet, as well as the painting by Shishkin and two Italian engravings"), but in 1937 the dacha was finally built—a brick building with shower and bathhouse, heated by a central stove and habitable all year round, which was divided into three apartments, each with their own separate kitchen, living room, and bedroom." [54]

Crimea was the site of many elite resthomes and sanatoria, to which people came from all over the Soviet Union. The poet Osip Mandelstam and his wife found themselves rubbing shoulders with members of the top political elite, including the wife of future NKVD head Ezhov, in a resthome in Sukhumi. Closer to Moscow, the Barvikha sanatorium was particularly highly regarded. Natalia Sats, director of the Moscow Children's Theater and wife of the trade minister, Izrail Veitser, spent a week there just before her sudden arrest as an "enemy of the people." [55]

Some cultural institutions had their own resthomes. Iurii Elagin, a musician at the Vakhtangov Theater in the 1930s, recalls the idyllic holidays that Vakhtangov actors and musicians spent at the theater resthome on an old noble estate, fully renovated, with a "flotilla of boats and yachts on the river" and the dining room provisioned according to government norms. The Academy of Sciences had had its own resthomes and sanatoria, including the Uzkoe estate near Moscow and the Gaspra estate in the Crimea, since the 1920s. Even before the Union of Soviet Writers officially came into existence, its organizing committee acquired rest homes in the Crimea and elsewhere. [56]

Elite children were provided with special summer camps, differentiated, as so often in the Soviet Union, by the rank and institutional affiliation of their parents. Eugenia Ginzburg, then a member of the regional political elite in Kazan, sent her young son on a winter holiday to a government resort where the children "divided people into categories according to the make of their car. Lincolns and Buicks rated high, Fords low. Ours was a Ford, and Alyosha felt the difference at once." Elena Bonner spent various summers of her childhood in camps under the auspices of the Comintern, where her stepfather worked, and the Moscow party committee, where her mother worked. She also went to the famous Artek camp in the Crimea, a place open to children from around the country who were selected because of some outstanding achievement, but also (of course!) to elite children whose parents could pull strings. [57]

It was standard practice for officials above a certain level to be driven to and from work by a chauffeur. Often these government cars and their drivers were also available for use outside working hours, though this was not officially sanctioned. As Ginzburg's son noted, the make of car varied according to the rank of the official. Natalia Sats recalls that her husband, the minister, "would send his car for me... I also was entitled to a car because of my job, but my husband called it 'a kerosene can on wheels' and tried to steer clear of it at all costs." [58]

Private ownership of cars was rare, though not unknown. In 1937, when the government tried to limit private car ownership, there were at least 400 private cars in Moscow. While cars were sometimes given as prizes and rewards to outstanding managers, scientists, Stakhanovites, and so on, it is not clear that there was any other legal way to acquire them. As for maintenance, service, and spare parts, the only way to get them was through the garage of some institution (which, as a 1937 government decree underlined, was illegal for private citizens). Despite the practical challenges of car ownership, however, officials still used their connections to get custom-made cars straight from the factory and it was alleged that foreign vehicles acquired for experimental purposes routinely vanished from the shops and ended up in the hands of various officials connected with the automobile industry.[59]

Money salary was always a lesser factor in status and well-being in Soviet society than priority access. Nevertheless, the privileges of the privileged classes were also reflected in official pay scales. Before 1934, there was a "party maximum" on the salaries of Communists. When this was repealed, the Politburo approved a series of salary increases for party and Komsomol officials, bringing regional party secretaries, for example, to 2,000 rubles a month in October 1938. According to one report, the salaries of NKVD personnel rose dramatically at the same period, putting them well above other officials at the same level, including party officials. In 1938, the government authorized "personal bonuses" of up to one and a half times basic salary for "particularly valuable specialists" working for various government agencies.[60]

A privilege unique to the unionized cultural professions—writers, composers, architects, artists—was the existence of special funds that provided material help to union members: travel allowances, sickness and disability benefits, help in obtaining living space, passes to sanatoria and resthomes, even loans. The writers' union fund, Litfond, was the first to be set up (June 1934), closely followed by an architects' fund (October 1934). Funds for musicians and artists followed in 1939 and 1940, respectively.[61]

Stakhanovites' Privileges

To say Stakhanovites had privileges is almost a tautology. It was the function of Stakhanovites, as chosen representatives of ordinary people, to be the visible recipients of privilege. They received much the same range of privileges as the political and cultural elites (extra rations, housing, special resort places, priority access of all kinds, and even automobiles).[62] In addition, however, Stakhanovites were often rewarded directly with consumer goods, from lengths of cloth and sewing machines to gramophones and cars. An important part of the ritual of Stakhanovite conferences, especially those for peasants, was for happy Stakhanovites to give a list of the goods they had been awarded:

I received a bed, a gramophone, and other cultural necessities . . .

  Everything I am wearing I got as a prize for good work in the kolkhoz. As well as the dress and shoes, I got a sewing machine in Nalchik. . . . For the harvest I got a prize of a silk dress worth 250 rubles.[63]

Worker Stakhanovites did not necessarily make such crude announcements of their rewards, but these were always listed in newspapers articles about them.

> Aleksei Tishchenko . . . along with his wife Zoia had arrived in Magnitogorsk in 1933 with all their possessions in a single homemade suitcase. By 1936 the couple owned furniture, including a couch and a wardrobe, as well as dress clothes, including two overcoats, some women's dresses, men's suits, shoes. . . . His prizes included a hunting gun, a gramophone, money, and a motorcycle.[64]

A Stakhanovite garment worker from Leningrad was reported to have received a watch, vase, clock, tablecloth, electric samovar, clothes iron, phonograph, records, the works of Lenin and Stalin, and 122 books. Two outstanding Stakhanovite workers were described as wearing their prizes at a New Year's Ball in 1936: "He was dressed in a black Boston suit that fully accentuated his solidly built figure; she was in a crepe de chine dress and black shoes with white trimming." [65]

The function of these awards of material goods was not just to make the Stakhanovites richer and happier, but also to make them more cultured. Often the quality of culture was inherent in the gift itself. "I can report to you that I don't live in my old mud hut anymore—I was awarded a European-style house. *I live like a civilized person*," a Tadjik Stakhanovite told a conference. Beds, gramophones, sewing machines, watches, and radios were all goods that helped raise their possessors out of "Asiatic" backwardness and into "European-style" modernity and culture.[66]

At other times, there was an implied quid pro quo: in return for the goods and services provided to Stakhanovites, it was their obligation to become more educated and more cultured. This is well illustrated in the comments of a leading trade-union official about a Stakhanovite from the Gorky Auto Works, Aleksandr Busygin, and his wife. On the one hand, the official noted all the material privileges Busygin had been given: a new apartment, home delivery of bread after Busygin's wife complained about lines at the bread store, and so on. On the other hand, he emphasized the Busygins' obligation to become more cultured, as was appropriate to their new vanguard status. Busygin's illiterate wife, in particular, had a lot of catching up to do. "A teacher has been sent to work with [her], and now an experienced children's doctor should be made available to her so as to teach her how to bring up a child in a cultured manner, and then she will have time to study." [67]

Thinking About Privilege

Nobody who had privilege in the Soviet Union in the 1930s seems to have thought of himself as a member of a privileged upper class. Rising young managers, upwardly mobile from the working class, were convinced that they remained proletarian at heart. The old intelligentsia, which under the old regime had always resisted the idea that it was an elite, continued to do so: in the wake of the Cultural Revolution, the group's consciousness of being persecuted by the regime was so strong that it seemed to block out any recognition that it was also privileged. While a socialist emigré commentator might conclude that the intelligentsia as a whole had been bribed,[68] members of the intelligentsia in the Soviet Union virtually never generalized in these terms, though they often accused specific fellow intellectuals of having sold out to the regime.

Communists with long memories and sensitive consciences were sometimes uneasy about privilege. There had been concern in Communist circles in the 1920s about the "degeneration" of the party in power and its loss of revolutionary spirit. Trotsky, in emigration, took these concerns further when he wrote in *The Revolution Betrayed* of the emergence of a new privileged class. His criticisms would probably have struck a chord with many Communists of the old guard—if they had had the opportunity to read his book, which of course they did not. In the party as a whole, however, this seems to have been less of a sore point than might have been expected. Many Communists obviously felt they needed and deserved their special treatment.

Soviet Communists of the 1930s practiced what Pierre Bourdieu calls "misrecognition" about privilege.[69] Misrecognition occurs when a group deals with something that might be embarrassing or shameful not only by giving it a different name but also by finding a new mental framework for understanding it. How Soviet misrecognition of privilege worked is illustrated in a memoir of the wife of a high Komsomol official, written half a century later.

> We had, as they say, privileges. There were special food parcels, which were given out on Kirov Street, where there is now a book store. We were cut off from the sufferings of ordinary people, and we thought that's how it had to be. And then, as I reasoned: "Vasilkovskii [her husband] is a senior man, he works a lot, often until late, doesn't spare himself, brings glory to the Native Land, to Stalin." Of course a car came to take him to work. We lived on Sretenka in the apartment house for foreign specialists. Big rooms, a library, furniture which was simply given out from the warehouse. We had nothing of our own, everything was government property. . . . Grishka earned the party maximum, I think it was 1,200 rubles. . . . I earned 5,660 rubles. I couldn't say we had a very glamorous life.[70]

The fact that the amenities of life—car, apartment, dacha—were not owned but were state issue was very important in enabling Communists of the nomenclatura to see themselves as something different from a new nobility or ruling class. On the contrary, they were people who owned nothing! Even their furniture was the state's, not chosen by them but simply issued, each piece with "a small gold oval with a number attached with two nails," as Bonner recalls. It was comparatively easy for elite members to see themselves as indifferent to material things when there was no personal property at stake: in the sarcastic words of a disapproving commentary on luxurious living at the Kazan leadership's dacha, "Lunches, dinners, suppers, snacks and drinks, bed linen—everything was given out free; and the generous hosts, hospitable at the state's expense, paid not the slightest attention to material considerations."[71]

Louis Fischer, an American correspondent sympathetic to the Soviet Union, was worried about signs of emerging privilege. "Perhaps, in fact, a new class is being born," he wrote uneasily in 1935. But then he remembered the

Soviet argument that privilege was only a temporary phenomenon, a step on the way to universal enrichment.

> The recent increase in the supply of goods and perquisites has invested. . . . privileges with considerable importance. . . . But a still further increase will wipe out many privileges altogether: when there are enough apartments it will not be a privilege to get one. *Privilege is the product of scarcity. Yet it also marks the beginning of the end of scarcity and therefore the beginning of its own end.*[72]

Describing workers' newly acquired taste for quality goods, a Soviet writer, Pavel Nilin, wondered whether these should be called luxuries. The answer was no. Luxury, as the *Great Soviet Encyclopedia* "authoritatively explains," is a relative concept. "With the growth of productive forces, luxury items may become necessities," and that was exactly what was happening in the Soviet Union.[73]

Stalin made his contribution to misrecognition by appropriating the term "intelligentsia" to describe Soviet elites as a whole, thus implicitly conferring on Communist officials the cultural superiority of academicians and writers. This conflation of the elites of power and culture was not mere sleight of hand, but conveyed something important about the Soviet mindset of the 1930s. It meant that the social hierarchy was conceptualized in *cultural* terms. Thus, the Soviet "intelligentsia" (in Stalin's broad definition) was privileged not because it was a ruling class or an elite status group, but because it was the most cultured, advanced group in a backward society. It was privileged as a cultural vanguard—and so were the Stakhanovites, whose share in privilege indicated that privilege was not a corollary of elite status. Workers and peasants who had joined the intelligentsia via affirmative action added another facet to the vanguard image, for they, like the Stakhanovites, were forerunners in the masses' upward march toward culture. "We are workers," says the wife of a manager in a novel of the late Stalin period, blithely ignoring both her husband's current occupation and the bourgeois lifestyle of which she has just boasted. "When the government was poor, we too were poor; when the government became richer, we too took heart."[74]

Of course not everybody was convinced by these arguments. Misrecognition was not much practiced outside the circles of privilege, and popular grumbling about privilege was common. "Communists in Moscow live like lords, they go round in sables and with canes with silver handles." "Who lives well? Only top officials and speculators." Some criticism reported by the secret police specifically mentioned the creation of a new privileged class. In the Ministry of Agriculture, for example, there was indignation when separate tables were set up in the cafeteria for people receiving extra rations. According to the police report, people were saying "The point of it is to get rid of equality. [They want] to create classes: the communists (or former nobility) and us ordinary mortals."[75]

During the Great Purges, as we will see in Chapter 8, the regime picked up on this kind of popular objection to privilege, portraying disgraced Communist leaders as abusers of power who had been corrupted by a privileged life style. This appropriation might be viewed as purely cynical, but there is some evidence to the contrary. Judging by his recollections in later life, Viacheslav Molotov, Stalin's closest associate in the 1930s, really did think that many of the high-ranking Communist victims had gone soft in power and were corrupted by privilege. An unpublished Politburo resolution of 1938 on abuse of privileges suggests that this was a collective rather than personal attitude. Some disgraced party leaders, the resolution noted, had "built themselves grandiose dacha-palaces . . . where they lived luxuriously and wasted the people's money, demonstrating their complete degeneracy and corruption in everyday life." Moreover, the resolution continued, "the wish to have such dacha-palaces still survives and is even growing in some circles" of leading government and party officials. To combat this tendency, the Politburo ordered that dachas should not exceed seven or eight rooms, and that dachas exceeding the norm should be confiscated and turned into government resthomes.[76]

The privileges of Stakhanovites were often strongly resented by fellow workers. Stakhanovites were seen as people who "made money at the expense of the other workers" and "took bread from the mouths of working women."[77] Other workers sometimes beat up Stakhanovites or damaged their machines.

> At the "Red Dawn" plant, during a conversation about the Stakhanovite movement among the women workers of the winding department on 17 October, one worker, Pavlova, announced that she was transferring from 12 bobbins to 16. After the break, worker Smirnova hung a dirty rag on Pavlova's machine and said: "There's a prize for your activism in transferring to more intensive work!"

The authorities liked to attribute anti-Stakhanovite behavior to "backwardness," but Smirnova's case was puzzling and distressing in that she was not a raw recruit from the village:

> Smirnova is an old worker, pure proletarian. The factory committee is now trying to find out who could have incited Smirnova and what provoked her to such a protest.[78]

MARKS OF STATUS

In 1934, a mining enterprise in the Moscow region decided to build a fancy dormitory for its best workers. There were to be Oriental carpets and chandeliers, according to a report in the journal *Our Achievements*. Most remarkable was the fact that the dormitory was to have a doorman, who would wear a uniform decorated with gold.[79]

There was something about uniforms that had become deeply appealing to Soviet officials as well as citizens. This was a new departure in the mid 1930s. The Revolution had initially swept away all titles, ranks, and uniforms, regarding them as unnecessary and even absurd marks of status characteristic of an autocratic regime. Epaulettes, insignia, and even military ranks were banished from the Red Army for almost two decades: officers were simply divided into "senior commanders" and "junior commanders." The old uniforms for university and high school students disappeared. Civil service ranks were abolished, as were the different uniforms that had been worn by officials in different ministries. The old engineers' uniforms, including "a cap with a badge of profession: a hammer and spanner," were still sometimes seen in the 1920s. But during the Cultural Revolution they were ceremonially repudiated. A Leningrad resident recalled "a burning scarecrow dressed in the uniform" being paraded along the street, while in Moscow a German correspondent reported that "a technician's cap [was] burned at night with noisy demonstrations, to celebrate the downfall of the 'caste of engineers.'" [80]

Then, in the mid 1930s, the tide turned. Titles, ranks, and uniforms were reinstated, and often bore a strong resemblance to their Imperial predecesssors. In 1934, a government commission recommended that distinctive uniforms be introduced for personnel in civil aviation, waterways and fishing authorities, lumber export, and the polar exploration agency, in addition to those already worn by railroad personnel and militiamen. All uniforms would indicate rank in the same way, by semicircles, circles, pentagons, and stars, and include a greatcoat and field jacket with leather belts at the waist. For managerial (officer-level) personnel, one shoulder strap was to be fastened to the belt.[81]

The dramatic reversal of the mid 1930s has been attributed to a general process of "embourgeoisement" of the Stalinist regime and repudiation of revolutionary values.[82] This is probably true, but we should remember that contemporaries often saw it differently. Communists who had moved up from the lower classes were particularly inclined to see their assumption of distinctions modeled on those of the old regime as simply a proof that the Revolution had finally triumphed: they now had what the old bosses used to have. The Moscow miners evidently felt the same way about their imposing doorman, whose uniform was explicitly modeled on those of the old regime, and gave satisfaction for exactly that reason.

It should be pointed out, moreover, that the appeal of uniforms was not solely connected with status. The return of school uniforms in the second half of the decade, a very popular move, was not a matter of social status, since all pupils went to the same state schools and the only differentiation fostered by the uniforms was between boys and girls. Yet *Izvestiia* reported that "almost every family" was discussing the question of uniforms. A state commission had proposed "electric blue" dresses for high-school girls, but many people had other ideas. The relative merits of berets and caps and long trousers and "sporty knickerbockers" were enthusiastically canvassed. Some people liked the idea of uniforms because they *diminished* social distinctions within the school. Uniforms were associated with order and propriety and the inculcation of responsibility and pride in the collective.[83]

Nevertheless, the policy change of the mid 1930s marked the beginning of a process of restoring ranks and uniforms that transformed the appearance of the Soviet civil and armed services. The Red Army came first, with the re-establishment of the ranks of major, colonel, and marshal in 1935. Five military leaders, including Klim Voroshilov, the defense minister, and Mikhail Tukhachevsky, were immediately appointed to the rank of marshal.[84] New uniforms, with epaulettes and insignia reminiscent of the old Imperial Army, were introduced at the same time. A Communist who watched the first public showing of the new dress uniforms at the November parade in Red Square recorded the event in his diary:

> Voroshilov received the parade on a marvellous horse in a new marshal's uniform. The marshals . . . stood at [Lenin's] mausoleum with members of the Politburo. The troops were also in new uniform. They have got epaulettes, which have not been seen for 18 years. For the junior officer corps, lance-corporals, sergeants, sergeant-majors, stripes have been reintroduced, for the officers, gold epaulettes.[85]

Although the Soviet Union did not go as far as the old regime, in which every civil servant had had his rank as well as the uniform designating branch of service, it took significant steps in this direction. The NKVD acquired a hierarchy of ranks with new military-sounding titles, ranging from sergeant and junior lieutenant to Commissar General of State Security; its members wore insignia and uniforms whose blue trousers, Robert Tucker tells us, were "the same color as those worn by the uniformed police of tsarist Russia." During the war, for the first time, military-style ranks were introduced for state prosecutors. Soviet diplomats went into uniform at the same period.[86]

Science was one of the few spheres in which the traditional hierarchies of rank were not overthrown by the revolution or even by the Cultural Revolution at the end of the 1920s. Full members of the Academy of Sciences, always referred to by their title, "Academician," stood at the apex of the pyramid, followed by corresponding members. The status of academician was attained not through appointment by the regime but through election by the existing members of the Academy, a tradition that survived challenge by Communist militants. The Cultural Revolution, which hit universities particularly hard, temporarily did away with the traditional hierarchy of academic degrees and titles. But these were restored by legislation of 1932 and 1937.[87]

The cultural sphere acquired a new array of titles and honors in the 1930s. This owed relatively little to tradition and Tsarist precedent but instead reflected the Soviet regime's commitment to high culture and recent rapprochement with the old intelligentsia. The title of "Distinguished Artist" or "Distinguished Scientist" was introduced in the mid 1920s. A higher title, "People's Artist of the Russian (or Ukrainian or Uzbek) Republic, was added a few years later, but both titles were still awarded sparingly. It was not until the mid 1930s, with the creation of a still higher title, "People's Artist of the Soviet Union," that titles began to be distributed with a generous hand.[88]

In the last years of the 1930s, the regime became increasingly generous, if not extravagant, in its award of titles and honors to distinguished members of the artistic, scholarly, and scientific communities. After a festival of Uzbek culture was celebrated in Moscow in 1937, thirteen Uzbek musicians and other artists received Orders of the Labor Red Banner and twenty-five received Orders of the Sign of Honor. At the beginning of 1939, a single decree of the Soviet government awarded orders to 172 writers. A month later the Moscow

Film Studio, Mosfilm, received the Order of Lenin (which could be awarded to institutions as well as individuals), and 139 Mosfilm personnel received titles and awards at various levels for their part in making the films *Alexander Nevsky, Volga-Volga, Chapaev*, and other Mosfilm successes.[89]

The creation of the Stalin Prizes in 1939 added a new step at the top of the ladder of cultural honors. Stalin Prizes were awarded for outstanding achievements in the arts, literature, scholarship, and science. In the original formulation, ninety-two prizes were to be awarded annually, carrying prize money ranging from 25,000 to 100,000 rubles in addition to a gold medal. The title "Laureate of the Stalin Prize," established by government decree on 26 March 1941, was pronounced with even greater veneration than "Distinguished Scientist" or "People's Artist." They were the Soviet equivalent of Nobel prizewinners.[90]

The intelligentsia was by no means a monopolist in the matters of orders and titles. Orders of Lenin, Orders of the Red Flag, and titles like Hero of Labor were bestowed on a wide range of people, including outstanding "ordinary people" like Stakhanovites and worker and peasant delegates to the Supreme Soviet. These awards had great status value: their recipients had to be referred to by title or rank on all public occasions, like academicians and professors ("Distinguished Artist of the Russian Republic Alekseeva will sing the role of Tatiana"). In addition, the awards had considerable practical value. Heroes of Labor—who had to have had at least thirty-five years on the job in industry, science, government, or public service—received a pension equalling three-quarters of their full wage or salary. Orders carried small monthly cash payments—25 rubles for an Order of Lenin, 10 rubles for a Sign of Honor—plus release from certain taxes and a 10 to 50 percent reduction in one's apartment rent. Order bearers as well as persons with the title of "People's Artist" and "Distinguished Artist" and the like also had the right to a special pension. In a society where access priority was crucial, bearers of titles and orders had priority in getting railroad tickets, rooms in state resthomes, and a host of other things.[91]

PATRONS AND CLIENTS

It is useful to have as a father-in-law a military commander or an influential communist, as a mother-in-law the sister of a high dignitary.[92]

In the Soviet Union, for all its apparent bureaucratization, many things actually functioned on a personal basis. This was true of government offices, where the joke was that the only way to get in to see an important official was to say your business was personal.[93] It was true in the sphere of supply, where the best way of getting goods was by *blat*, personal connections. It was even true within the sphere of privilege, for commodities like dachas and housing in a ministerial apartment block were in extremely short supply, and mere membership in the eligible group was not enough to secure the prize. To get privileges, you needed contacts with somebody higher up: in short, you needed a patron.

Patronage relations were ubiquitous in Soviet society. Not everybody was fortunate enough to have patrons, of course, but everybody was bound to encounter the phenomenon, if only through the experience of losing out to someone with "protection." Patronage, like *blat*, was often referred to euphemistically, with an emphasis on the friendship between client and patron. Verbs like "help," "support," and "come to the aid of" were often used to describe patronage transactions. Written appeals to patrons requested their "advice" and "help." [94]

For ordinary people without special connections, the most likely source of patronage was one's boss or local party secretary. For a kolkhoznik, the kolkhoz chairman might (or might not) serve as a patron, as in the example given by one Harvard Project respondent: "The accountant of our kolkhoz . . . had very good relationships with the chairman of our kolkhoz. He had protektsiya. . . . If the accountant wanted to fix up his home and protektsiya with the chairman of the kolkhoz he would be able to get the best material." For a journalist, the newspaper editor might serve as a patron; for a worker, the factory director or party secretary or "a friend in the cadres [personnel] department." To become a Stakhanovite in the celebrity sense, a patron, usually a local party secretary, was absolutely necessary.[95]

The intelligentsia—or, strictly speaking, the "creative intelligentsia" of writers, artists, scientists, and scholars—was in a class of its own as far as patronage was concerned. In the first place, patrons were exceptionally highly placed, often at Politburo level. There probably was no Politburo member without his stable of intelligentsia clients, since without them one could not have the reputation as a cultured man that Politburo members, as well as lesser mortals, cherished. In the second place, the system of intelligentsia privileges described earlier in this chapter virtually required a patronage network to allocate them. Finally, it must be said that members of the creative intelligentsia, with centuries of practice with imperial and aristocratic patrons behind them, displayed greater assiduousness and flair as clients than almost any other social group.

Nadezhda Mandelstam, wife of the poet Osip Mandelstam, described her first conscious recognition of the patronage system:

> In 1930 in the little Sukhumi resthouse for bigwigs where we ended up through an oversight of Lakoba's, Ezhov's wife was talking to me: "Pilniak goes to us," she said. "And whom do you go to?" I indignantly reported that conversation to O.M., but he quietened me down: "Everyone 'goes [to someone]'. Obviously it can't be otherwise. And we 'go'. To Nikolai Ivanovich." [96]

"Nikolai Ivanovich" was Bukharin, already a falling star in the party. Ezhov was a rising star, head of the personnel department of the Central Committee and in a few years to become the infamous head of the secret police during the Great Purges. The Ezhovs, it would appear from the wife's comment, were actively seeking intelligentsia friends (clients) who would do them credit. The writer Boris Pilniak was not their only catch. Mikhail Koltsov, famous essayist and editor of the journals *Krokodil* and *Ogonek*, also came into the Ezhovs' orbit in the second half of the 1930s. Ezhov's wife, Evgenia, herself a journalist, had many friends in the cultural world; the writer Isaac Babel was not only a friend but also a former lover.[97]

Many members of the intelligentsia must have recognized their own daydreams in the fantasy sketched by the writer Mikhail Bulgakov of Stalin himself extending his protection:

Motorcycle. . . . brrm!!! In the Kremlin already! Misha goes into the hall, and there sit Stalin, Molotov, Voroshilov, Kaganovich, Mikoyan and Iagoda.

Misha stands in the door, making a low bow.

STALIN: What's the matter? Why are you barefoot?

BULGAKOV (with a sad shrug): Well . . . I don't have any boots . . .

STALIN: What is this? My writer going without boots? What an outrage! Iagoda, take off your boots, give them to him.[98]

In real life, personal meetings of intelligentsia clients with Stalin or other highly placed patrons were relative rare. The usual pattern was to solicit their patrons' help by letter (always hand-delivered), and receive (if they were lucky and the patron was able to help them) a telephone call in return.[99]

Political patrons could assist intelligentsia clients in a number of ways. They could help them obtain scarce goods like apartments or places in an elite resort. They could protect a client who fell into disgrace (though this was of course not always possible: during the Great Purges, such protection became very difficult and dangerous). Finally, they could intervene on behalf of a client in professional disputes. This was a service that clients often requested, and it meant that the incidence of "state" and "party" intervention in cultural affairs was even greater than it would otherwise have been.

Patronage was one of the important mechanisms for distributing scarce goods. The archive of Viacheslav Molotov, head of the Soviet government, is full of appeals for such goods, especially housing. Writers, musicians, scientists, artists, and writers, all approached Molotov, addressing him by name and patronymic in their letters and putting their requests on a personal basis, as befitted clients writing to a patron. The young writer Pavel Nilin, whose thoughts on the relative nature of luxury we encountered earlier in the chapter, was one of those whose appeal to Molotov was successful (he got a one-room apartment of 18 square meters, double the size of his old one). The writer Aleksei Tolstoi, legendary possessor of the "bottomless bank account," got an eight- to ten-room dacha, though to be sure he had asked for eleven rooms.[100]

Requests for protection against defamation or attack were also common in Molotov's mailbag. A non-party scientist appealed for protection against the harassment of a powerful Communist colleague, a historian asked Molotov to help squash a libelous rumor that he had been a friend of a Trotskyite, and a poet complained about a devastating review his work had received in *Pravda*.[101] Other leaders received similar appeals from clients. An actress turned to Iakov Agranov, a high NKVD official, for help when her husband was in trouble. When the composer Dmitrii Shostakovich fell into disgrace over his opera *Lady Macbeth of the Mtsensk District*, he naturally appealed to his friend and patron, Marshal Tukhachevsky.[102]

Clients often appealed to patrons to intervene in professional disputes. Lysenko's feud with the geneticists, for example, was the subject of many appeals from both sides. Physics was also a subject of appeals and counter appeals. For example, a group of Communist philosophers sought Molotov's support for a controversial attack on "idealism" in physics published in their journal, while Kapitsa wrote to Stalin and Molotov in defence of the "idealists," characterizing the journal's intervention in physics as "scientifically illiterate" and deploring the assumption that "if you are not a materialist in physics . . . you are an enemy of the people." Artists, writers, and actors were equally prone to appeal to patrons to resolve professional disputes.[103]

Certain leading members of the cultural and scholarly professions, such as Petr Kapitsa and Sergei Vavilov in the natural sciences, acted as representatives of a whole group of clients in dealing with highly placed patrons. They assumed this broker function because of their professional stature and position (presidents of the Academy of Sciences, secretaries of professional unions, and directors of scientific institutes had it automatically) and their established connections with various government leaders. Sometimes brokering was a matter of representing the professional interests of a group, as when Aleksandr Fadeev, secretary of the Writers' Union, wrote to Molotov to convey the distress of the literary community that no Stalin Prizes had been earmarked for literature (this was quickly remedied) and raise other questions of professional concern such as royalties and taxation of writers' earnings. Sometimes it meant interceding on behalf of subordinates, as when the head of a construction project wrote to the chairman of the Leningrad soviet on behalf of engineers threatened with deportation as "social aliens." [104]

Many "broker" interventions involved arrests within the professional community that the broker represented. Kapitsa, for example, appealed to Stalin twice about the arrest and imprisonment of the physicist Lev Landau. Sergei Vavilov wrote to Lavrentii Beria (head of the security police) in 1944 attempting to gain release from prison of a young astronomer. Maxim Gorky was famous for such interventions on behalf of Petrograd intellectuals during the Civil War and continued the practice in the 1930s. The theater director Vsevolod Meyerhold frequently appealed to his patrons Avel Enukidze and Iagoda on behalf of arrested friends and acquaintances in the theater world.[105]

In his memoirs, Iurii Elagin tells the story of the epic "battle of patrons" between two well-connected theatrical figures, L. P. Ruslanov, administrator of the Vakhtangov Theater, and A. D. Popov, director of the Moscow Red Army Theater. Ruslanov and Popov lived in the same apartment house, and the trouble arose when Popov hung flowerpots from his balcony that Ruslanov regarded as a potential danger to passersby. Using his contacts, Ruslanov got an order from the head of district militia to remove the flowerpots; Popov trumped this by getting permission to keep his flowerpots from the head of militia of the city. Ruslanov then went to the chief director of militia of the whole Soviet Union for a removal order, to which Popov responded with a letter from Voroshilov instructing that he should not be further harassed about his flowerpots. But Ruslanov was the winner: he went to Kalinin, president of the USSR, and obtained an order that the flowerpots should be removed.[106]

Apocryphal or not, this story is a nice illustration of the hierarchies of patronage that could be invoked by persistent and well-connected clients. The Vakhtangov Theater, according to Elagin, had its set of middle-level patrons in the pre-1937 period, including Maxim Gorky, Enukidze, and Iakov Agranov (deputy head of OGPU), who "were always ready to do everything possible for our theater." But there were also even more highly placed individuals, notably Politburo members Voroshilov and Molotov, who could also be called on in extreme cases.[107]

The benefits to clients in Soviet patronage relations are obvious, but what about the benefits to patrons? These seem to have been the same ones that have inspired patrons throughout the ages, namely, a belief that patronage of the arts sheds luster on the patron, enjoyment of social contacts with members of the cultural haute monde, and pleasure in the flattery that it is clients' duty to offer. Voroshilov "loved to play a bit at being, so to speak, a patron of the arts, a protector of artists and so on," according to Molotov, who noted that real friendship existed between Voroshilov and some of his clients, like the painter Aleksandr Gerasimov. To Ivan Gronskii, a serf's son who became editor of *Izvestiia* and patron of a group of old-school realist artists, the fulsomely expressed admiration of "famous old masters of painting" was both flattering and embarrassing. Effusive tributes to politicians emphasizing their cultural expertise were the stock-in-trade of grateful clients: for example, the writer Galina Serebriakova, dacha neighbor of many political leaders, wrote of Politburo member Valerian Kuibyshev that he was "a many-sided man, a great connoisseur of art and literature, enchanting, uncommonly simple and modest in approach," remembering in particular his aesthetic response to a beautiful sunset.[108]

Of course there were perils in being a patron, as well as being a client. Clients might praise their patrons' generosity—but too fulsome expressions of enthusiasm for a local leader could provoke the accusation that he was developing a local "cult of personality," and Stalin was notoriously sensitive to signs that his subordinates were developing their own followings. Voroshilov's friendship with Gerasimov and other artists was not well regarded by Stalin: according to Molotov, he saw dangers in close personal contacts between the political and cultural worlds "because artists, they're irresponsible people. They are harmless in themselves, but around them swarm all kinds of dubious riffraff. They exploit that connection—with Voroshilov's subordinates, with his family." Gronskii's patronage of the realist artists, cited above, could have gotten him into trouble. The day after a group of his "clients" had escorted him home as a gesture of appreciation of his intervention at an artists' meeting, Gronskii received a telephone call from Stalin with the abrupt query (which he understood as a veiled threat): "What kind of demonstration was that yesterday?"[109]

For clients, there were also dangers. Ezhov's patronage was surely danger-ous in the long run to his clients, most of whom perished in the Great Purges after his fall. The patronage of Bukharin blighted the career of a whole cohort of young Communist scholars after he was disgraced as a Rightist. This could also happen at less exalted levels. As a journalist respondent in the Harvard Project put it, "Protection is a dangerous affair. . . . if you have a friend, that's good, but if tomorrow he is arrested, that is bad. Because when your friend is arrested, you also get into difficult straits. The police are not only interested in him, but in his friends as well. When Yagoda was arrested, so were those with whom he had connections. . . . If you work on a newspaper and your editor protects you, that's good, but it is only temporary." [110]

Patronage exists in all sorts of societies. The feature that distinguished So-viet patronage in the Stalin era from other varieties was that the state was the monopoly distributor in a context of shortages of all goods and services. State monopoly meant that *allocation* was a major function of Soviet bureaucracy. Shortages meant that access was a matter of priority and privilege. There were formal rules about priorities, but these did not solve specific allocation ques-tions, all the more since the eligible prioritized group was always larger than the sum of goods available. This was where patronage (and its close relative, *blat*) made their contribution. The ultimate allocational decisions were made by bureaucrats—but on personalistic, not bureaucratic-legal reasons. Mem-bers of the intelligentsia tended to rely more on patronage than *blat* because they had closer personal relations than most citizens with Communist high society. Their privileged status as a group did not automatically confer privi-leges on any single individual. Individual members of the intelligentsia real-ized their claims on privilege the same way would-be Stakhanovites did it—by finding patrons to sponsor them.

5

Insulted and Injured

We have already encountered the power of the "reforging" myth—that in Soviet society every man, no matter what his crimes or the defects of his origins, had the possibility of being remade. The reality, however, was different. If the stigma of past criminal activity could sometimes be shed, other stigmas were essentially permanent. The stigma of "bad" social origin stubbornly refused to disappear even when the regime tried to lift it in the mid 1930s. The stigma of a dubious political past—membership of other political parties before the Revolution, membership of oppositions within the Bolshevik Party, disgrace as an "enemy of the people" during the Great Purges—was similarly indelible.

Soviet society had many outcasts. In the 1920s, they included priests and former priests, members of the prerevolutionary nobility, former capitalists and Nepmen, kulaks, and persons who had been "dekulakized." Most of these people were formally stigmatized by being deprived of the vote. In the 1930s, the ranks of outcasts were joined by a growing population of administrative exiles and political prisoners. The families of all these people usually shared in their stigmatization. Wives, children, and aged parents were deported along with the kulaks; priests' sons and daughters were denied access to higher education; during the Great Purges there were special camps for "wives of traitors to the motherland."

While the new Soviet Constitution of 1936 introduced a new policy on class, it by no means removed the tendency to stigmatize, scapegoat, and outcast that had become deeply rooted in Soviet society since the revolution. In fact, the Great Purges, following on the heels of the Constitution, greatly increased the circle of victims of stigmatization and the panic-stricken viciousness with which other citizens denounced them.

Communists who strayed into opposition were often required to make public confessions and recantations of their mistakes, but confession did not absolve them. Sometimes repentant Oppositionists were allowed back into the party, but their status thereafter was precarious and most were expelled once again after a few years. Similarly, undesirable social origins could not be cast off by statements of loyalty or repudiation of one's class or parents. Priests, to be sure, were sometimes encouraged by local officials to renounce the cloth in a dramatic public gesture. But since they were rarely able to find other employment unless they hid their past, in practice the stigma remained.

Because stigma could so rarely be lifted by legal or other orthodox means, the natural course for a person with a black mark on his record was to try to hide it. This meant creating a new social identity—an identity that was supposed to deceive others, but often ended up being taken extremely seriously by the deceiver himself. Concealment of social identity was very common, but it was considered a serious offense and did not usually work forever. The more desperately people tried to hide damaging facts about themselves, the more eagerly other citizens sought to "unmask" them. To unmask hidden enemies was the duty of every Communist and Komsomol member. But Communists were by no means the only unmaskers, and loyalty to the Soviet regime was only one of many possible motives for denouncing someone. The practice of denunciation served many *private* purposes in the Soviet Union: if you denounced a personal enemy or an unwelcome neighbor as a hidden Trotskyite or a former noble concealing his class identity, there was a good chance that the state would step in to settle your scores for you.

OUTCASTS

The Soviet system of representation was based on the soviets, revolutionary bodies in whose name the Bolsheviks had taken power. Both in 1917 and in their earlier incarnation in 1905, the soviets were class-based institutions: that is, they did not claim to represent the whole citizenry but only "workers" or "workers and soldiers" or "workers and peasants." Once the Bolsheviks had taken power, they broadened the class base of the soviets to include white-collar workers, housewives, and others previously ineligible to vote in soviet elections. But the soviets remained class institutions insofar as they excluded exploiters and people not engaged in socially useful labor and weighted urban votes against peasant ones.[1]

The 1918 Constitution of the Russian Republic excluded the following categories from voting or running as candidates in soviet elections:

- Persons using hired labor with the aim of extracting profit (this covered kulaks, as well as urban entrepreneurs and artisans), persons living off unearned income (dividends from capital, profits from enterprises, rent from property, and so forth)
- Private traders and middlemen
- Monks and priests of all denominations
- Former employees and agents of the Tsarist police, secret police, and special corps of gendarmes
- Members of the former Imperial family, the House of Romanov.[2]

These disfranchised persons constituted the hard core of a wider group of outcasts known collectively as "alien elements" or "social aliens." This wider group included all kinds of formerly privileged— former nobles, former bourgeoisie, former Tsarist bureaucrats, and so on, known collectively as "formers," like the *ci-devants* in the French Revolution—as well as others whose social or political connections were suspect.[3] In practice, even the disfranchised group was both larger and less precisely defined than the Constitution stipulated. In the first place, amendments were added to extend disfranchisement to those who had been officials of the Imperial and White governments, officers in the White Armies, and landlords and capitalists under the old regime, not to mention persons "who were not loyal to Soviet power."[4] In the second place, the local soviets that compiled the lists of disfranchised for their districts often interpreted the law in their own way, disfranchising anyone who looked to them like a "class enemy."[5]

The right to vote in itself may have had little more than symbolic significance. In addition, however, a whole network of class-discriminatory legislation aimed at furthering the life-chances of proletarians and curtailing those of the bourgeois was put in place during the 1920s. Universities and technical schools practiced "social selection" (i.e., affirmative action) in admissions. Housing authorities, rationing boards, and taxation departments followed similar discriminatory practices, and even the courts were supposed to follow principles of "class justice" by punishing "social aliens" harshly and showing leniency to proletarians. Social aliens were barred from joining the Communist Party and the Komsomol, and often from employment in government offices. All this meant that the disfranchised were deprived not only of the right to vote, but also of a host of other rights and opportunities.[6]

For the Bolshevik Party's intellectuals, class was a complex attribute that could not be reduced to class origins. In the party as a whole, however, the "genealogical" approach predominated. If your father had been a noble or a kulak before the revolution, you shared that stigma, regardless of your own social position or political convictions. If you were a priest, the stigma was passed on to your children, even if they renounced you and protested their devotion to the Revolution.[7]

Class War

In the late 1920s, Soviet Communists believed themselves under attack from resurgent class enemies—the old bourgeoisie, the new NEP bourgeoisie, kulaks, even the "bourgeois intelligentsia." To all appearances, however, this was the opposite of the truth. It was the party that had gone on the attack against class enemies, just as it had during the Civil War. Nepmen were being forced out of business. Kulaks were accused of hoarding grain, forbidden to join collective farms, and finally marked for "liquidation as a class," which meant expropriation, eviction, and often deportation or imprisonment in labor camps. At the same time, the church was under attack, with large numbers of priests under arrest and churches closed down. The intelligentsia was in trouble too, harassed by militants of the Cultural Revolution and liable to be accused of disloyalty and even treason.[8]

All this meant hard times for anybody bearing the stigma of bad social origins. During the soviet elections of 1929, conducted under the slogan of class war, more people were deprived of the vote than ever before.[9] In 1929 and 1930, government offices were purged to remove the disfranchised and other social aliens; this process often involved humiliating public cross-examination. A sympathetic reporter described how a taxation official stood up to this:

> A small, clean-shaven old man who was educated in a "respectable" general's family and in the Tsarist Ministry of Finances: he holds himself on the tribune with dignity. Twelve years of the October Revolution changed this man very little. Today from the tribune he makes a statement about his understanding of the purge: "If I am not needed, if I don't suit, tell me and I will go. But why throw dirt on me?"[10]

Children of the disfranchised were expelled from schools; and, as the writer Mikhail Prishvin noted bitterly in his diary, there was even "a class approach to the dying (in the hospital they are throwing out three patients who have been found to be disfranchised)." Increasingly, disfranchised persons found it difficult to get or hold jobs; when rationing was introduced, they were ineligible for ration cards and had to buy food at commercial prices. In the summer of 1929, telephone service to "non-toiling elements" was cut off on the pretext that the system was overburdened. In the fall, Moscow Soviet started to evict "non-toilers" from their municipally owned apartments, though some critics even within the party thought this was illegal.[11]

The drive against class enemies seems to have had more solid support in the lower ranks of the party than in the leadership. The head of the Soviet government, Aleksei Rykov, and other Politburo members soon to be ousted as "Rightists" had serious doubts, as did Mikhail Kalinin, the formal head of state. Avel Enukidze, another highly placed government official who was known for his generosity as a patron to "former people," was outraged, as were leading education officials in Russia and the Ukraine, including Lenin's widow, Nadezhda Krupskaia.[12] But the tide of party opinion was against them. A confidential letter on the plight of priests sent by Kalinin to a fellow

Politburo member, Sergo Ordzhonikidze, complained that local authorities were behaving with "complete arbitrariness" toward priests and other disfranchised persons and ignoring their legal rights:

All the efforts of local authorities are directed towards "dekulakizing" ministers of religion along with kulaks. This illegal "dekulakization" is conducted under the guise of taxation. They try to tax ministers of religion in every possible way and in such amounts that they cannot fulfil the demands made on them, and then all their property is confiscated, even necessities for the family, and the family is evicted . . . Clerics and members of their families have been drafted to work at logging enterprises, regardless of sex, age, or health. Sometimes this harrassment of members of the clergy literally becomes mockery. For example, there have been cases in Barnaul district where ministers of religion were conscripted to clean pigsties, stables, toilets, etc.[13]

A memo to Stalin, evidently from Enukidze, described the position of the disfranchised as desperate—they were often forbidden to work and refused rations, their children were expelled from school, and in the countryside they were often refused shelter at inns. Protests were flooding into President Kalinin's office. In the first two months of 1930 alone, 17,000 complaints of unjustified deprivation of voting rights were received from citizens of the Russian Republic (compared to under 500 in the corresponding months of 1926). Most complaints focused less on disfranchisement per se than on the ancillary penalties: eviction from apartments, expulsion from trade unions and educational institutions, dismissal from work, levying of special taxes, dekulakization, and so on.[14]

Although Enukidze and Kalinin opposed depriving the disfranchised of the right to work, a secret government decree of August 1930 came close to doing this when it ordered that disfranchised persons and other office workers who had lost their jobs in the recent purges should not receive unemployment benefits or be allowed to register for employment at the Labor Exchange along with the general population. "They should be sent to timber camps, peat works, shoveling snow and other jobs and moreover only in places that are experiencing an acute shortage of labor," the decree instructed.[15]

The education ministries of Russia and the Ukraine found that their instructions to local authorities forbidding social purging of schools were simply disregarded.[16] One local soviet (emboldened, undoubtedly, by the active support of the local party organization and the tacit support of the Central Committee) even wrote back to the center describing how beneficial it had been to expel 86 high-school students, almost half of whom had disfranchised parents, and explaining why it proposed to disobey the Russian government's instructions to the contrary:

They are all sons of big hereditary kulaks, and some of their parents have been sent to Solovki.[17] . . . In the great majority of cases, these kulaks' sons were instigators in stirring up nationalism, spreading various kind of pornography, and disorganizing study. . . . All these 38 persons hid their social position while they were in school, registering themselves falsely as poor peasants, middle peasants, and some even as agricultural laborers. . . . At the same time children of workers, poor peasants and agricultural laborers could not get in [to schools] because there were no free places. The population is extremely pleased with what we have done.[18]

The introduction of internal passports by a law of December 1932 brought fresh miseries to the urban disfranchised and other social aliens. Up to this time, passports had been regarded as a symbol of old-regime despotism. But now the Soviet regime faced a desperate situation as famine in the countryside stimulated massive flight to the cities that threatened to swamp the urban rationing system. In addition, the logic of the regime's own practices, notably deportation and administrative exile (discussed below), seemed to require a passport system to enforce restrictions on movement. As in Tsarist times, Soviet passports identified the holder not only by name, sex, age, and nationality, but also by social position. Along with internal passports came a system of urban registration whereby only those who were registered a city had the right to live there.[19]

The actual introduction of passports began at the beginning of 1933. In Moscow and Leningrad, which went through the process first, passportization was the occasion for a purge of the whole urban population. Those residents who did not pass the scrutiny of the OGPU, primarily fleeing kulaks and the disfranchised, were deprived of their rights of residence and expelled from the city. A Politburo Commission did its best to delineate precisely who should be refused passports. Former kulaks and persons who had been dekulakized were to be expelled regardless of their current occupations. The broader group of recent peasant immigrants was also targetted, especially those without skills, fixed occupation, or a settled place to live, and those who had come to the city "exclusively for personal benefit." [20] Priests were on the list too, unless they were associated with functioning churches (a much diminished number since the drive against religion of 1930) or were "dependents of big specialists," engineers, professors, and the like. Then came a general "parasite" category for professional gamblers, drug dealers, brothel keepers, and the like. Finally, criminals with convictions for serious crimes like banditism, smuggling, and currency offences were to be expelled as were those convicted or administratively sentenced by the OGPU for political crimes.[21]

Despite the Commission's best efforts, criteria and categories were, as usual, ambiguous. How could one tell which peasant immigrants had come to town "exclusively for personal benefit"? How "big" did a specialist have to be to save his aged father from expulsion as a priest? An added ambiguity was that persons born in Moscow and Leningrad and living there continuously were supposed to have a right to passports,[22] but whether this right was unconditional was not clear. Was a born-and-bred Leningrader who happened to be a brothel keeper eligible for a passport and urban residence permit? How about a priest, Moscow-born, whose church in Moscow had been closed down during the Cultural Revolution? Nothing was said about the families of those who fell into one of the condemned categories. Were they also to be expelled from the city? If so, how broadly was family to be understood? Finally, the Politburo Commision's ruling did not explicitly state that disfranchisement was in itself a reason for deprivation of passports: was this a mere oversight or should each case of a disfranchised person be judged on its individual merits?

Enukidze, who chaired the commission, favored a much narrower definition of the criteria for expulsion than the other commission members, let alone the OGPU men in charge of the local process of passportization. Local officials generally refused passports to the disfranchised automatically as well as to family members and anybody else they intuitively felt to be "socially alien." According to a complaint from one of Enukidze's subordinates, the OGPU officials in charge of passportization had given verbal instructions to their men to refuse passports to "class enemies" and "former people" in general, failing to communicate an instruction that social origin alone was not grounds for expulsion.[23]

No sooner had the OGPU passportization departments started work than the central government and city soviets were flooded with complaints from persons who had been unjustly deprived of passports. In practice, Kalinin's office reported disapprovingly,

> They are not giving passports to toilers, to many young workers, specialists, and employees, even to Komsomols and members of the party, for the sole reason that they are by origin children of former nobles, merchants, clergy, and so on.[24]

Mikhail Zverev, twenty-six years old and a deputy bookkeeper in a Moscow factory, was refused on the grounds that his father had been a priest, although the younger Zverev had served in the Red Army from 1929 to 1931 and had no recent contact with his father. N. Geld-Fidman was refused on the grounds that her first husband had been shot in 1930 (no further details), even though she had been married to a second husband since 1923. The "recent arrival" clause produced all sorts of anomalies. The Korotkov siblings, two brothers and a sister, were former orphaned street children of Muscovite origin. The state had sent them off for training as weavers in Voronezh, after which they worked first in a Voronezh factory and then, after it was closed down, in a Moscow textile plant. They were all refused passports as recent immigrants to Moscow. In an even more bizarre case, a young man sent from Tashkent to study music at the Leningrad Conservatorium—one of hundreds of students sent from the national republics to the capitals under ethnic affirmative action programs—was refused a passport on the grounds that he was not a Leningrader.[25]

As always, the severity of the law was somewhat tempered in practice by the institutions of petition and patronage. All the cases of arbitrary refusal cited above were protested in written and oral petitions to President Kalinin's office, and such petitions often resulted in a reversal of the original judgments. Patronage acted even more efficaciously. A memoirist tells the story of how Count Nikolai Sheremetev avoided penalties for his noble origins. His wife, an actress with the Vakhtangov theater, invariably got him out of trouble by appealing to one of her powerful patrons.

> The OGPU arrested Nikolai Petrovich ten times. But not once did he sit in jail for more than ten days. . . . There was no way that Soviet power could come to

terms with the fact that a living Count Sheremetev walked freely in the streets of the proletarian capital. But Tsetiliia Lvovna's connections were stronger than Soviet laws.

The connections continued to work in the tense period of passportizat-ion—even though the young policeman who issued Sheremetev his passport was so incensed that higher-ups were protecting a class enemy that he flung it at Sheremetev's feet, hissing "Take your passport, take it, you spawn of the ar-istocracy." [26]

DEPORTATION AND EXILE

Administrative exile to remote parts of the country was a recognized form of punishment under the Tsarist regime. It was not systematically practiced after the revolution until the late 1920s, when it was applied to members of the Left Opposition (including Trotsky himself, who was sent to Alma-Ata for a year before being deported from the Soviet Union altogether), members of certain "counterrevolutionary organizations and groups," and former land-lords still living on their estates.[27] But all these operations were trivial com-pared with the great deportation of kulaks that came with collectivization at the beginning of 1930. In the years 1930–31, almost 400,000 households, or close to two million people, were deported from the villages. Additional kulak deportations, though on a smaller scale, took place in 1932–33.[28]

The question "Who is a kulak?" has been thoroughly canvassed in the liter-ature.[29] In theory, kulaks were prosperous peasants who exploited other peas-ants. In practice, "exploitation" proved an elusive concept, especially when peasants at risk of being identified as kulaks could read the identification crite-ria and take evasive action. From the standpoint of the poor peasant, more-over, the kulak might be seen as a patron, source of loans and support in hard times, rather than an exploiter. An added complication was that the relative socioeconomic positions of households in the village had often changed as a result of the revolution. Families whom other local peasants regarded as real kulaks might have lost much of their prosperity since 1917, while erstwhile poor peasants might have become prosperous through their connections with the Soviet regime; yet it was the former group, not the latter, that the regime sought to disadvantage. Many rural activists thought that in the postrevo-lutionary context "kulak" should be considered as much a psychological cate-gory, applying to embittered and anti-soviet *former* exploiters in the village, as an economic one.

The dekulakization campaign was initiated by Stalin in December 1929 when he called for "liquidation of kulaks as a class." Peasants identified as ku-laks were stripped of their land, animals, and equipment, and evicted from their homes; many of the victims were deported to distant regions of the country by the OGPU.[30] Formal criteria rarely counted for anything. What mattered was who local officials and the incoming collectivization activists *thought* was a kulak. Often that meant prosperous peasants, especially those who had been village leaders not particularly well disposed toward Soviet power, but troublemakers of all kinds were also greatly at risk. Someone who was unpopular in the village for whatever reason might find himself branded a kulak. Where villages were ethnically or religiously divided, for example, between Russians and Ukrainians or Orthodox and Old Believers, one ethnic or religious group might manage to pin the "kulak" label on the other.

Even Communists were somewhat uneasy with the unsystematic expansion of the category of "kulak" during dekulakization. They started to use an additional category, "kulak's hireling," to describe people who deserved a kulak's fate but could not really be called a kulak in economic terms. A Communist reporting confidentially to the head of the West Siberian party organization from the provinces that leadership of a number of collective farms in his district had fallen into the hands of kulaks added in parentheses that he was using the word in its "literal and not metaphorical sense"—in short, that he meant real kulaks.[31]

After dekulakization, the category of "former kulak" began to weigh heavily on Communist minds. In one way it had become easier to identify kulaks: anyone who had been dekulakized was, by definition, one of them. But in another way it had become much more difficult because many peasants potentially in the kulak group had run away rather than wait to be arrested or deported. These people were now in the process of masking themselves and assuming new social identities; that was why it was so vital to the regime to identify and expel them in the process of introducing passports in the cities. But of course many hidden kulaks, and even more children of kulaks, who might be expected to share their parents' bitterness, still eluded the authorities. We will encounter many examples of Communists' fear of these concealed enemies in subsequent chapters.

Meanwhile, a new kind of stigma fell on deportees, most of whom had been sent to the North, the Urals, Siberia, and the Far East, and were either working as laborers on new construction sites like Magnitogorsk or had been settled on uncultivated land as peasant cultivators.[32] Because deportation was an administrative punishment, not a judicial sentence, its duration and terms were uncertain. But one thing was clear: the deported kulaks now belonged to a special legal category of the population subject to various restrictions and loss of rights. At first, they were called "special settlers," then "labor settlers." [33] In a few years, their ranks were joined by other "socially dangerous" people—"kulaks, former traders, former landlords, and so on" who had served out prison or Gulag sentences, but whom the OGPU, for obvious reasons, did not wish to allow to return to their homes.[34]

The kulaks' term of exile, it turned out, had no fixed limits.[35] To be sure, some confusion existed about the regime's policy on this question. The deportees, as exiles and disfranchised persons, were not issued passports after the introduction of the passport regime. Then a government decree of May 1934 returned civil rights, including the right to vote, to those those who had demonstrated their worthiness through "socially useful labor." It might be assumed that civil rights included the right to mobility, but in January 1935, at the request of NKVD head Iagoda, Stalin confirmed that this was not so as far as the deported kulaks were concerned. A public clarification on this question appeared a week later—even so, there were hints at a Kolkhoz Congress in the spring that at least one party leader remained doubtful.[36]

Despite this, deportees still hoped to return home. When the new Constitution of 1936 was announced, many read it as an amnesty and petitioned for release, but in vain. Many others fled from exile over the years—more than 600,000 between 1932 and 1940, according to a Russian historian, of whom two-thirds, over 400,000, were successful. The number of deported kulaks and family members still living in exile as of October 1, 1941 was under 900,000. During World War II, there were further departures: many of the male deportees were called up for military service, which generally meant that their families' exile was lifted. It was not until after Stalin's death that all the kulaks deported more than twenty years earlier were formally released.[37]

Deported kulaks usually lived together in special settlements. For those working in industry, about half the group, the conditions of work with regard to wages, promotions, awards, and benefits was not very different from that of free labor, except that the exiles were ineligible for trade union membership and probably pensions. As of 1938, the NKVD was taking 5 percent of the wages of wage-earning exiles to pay for the cost of administering their exile. We have already seen that deported kulaks recovered the right to vote, subject to good behavior, at the beginning of 1935. This right was publicly confirmed with respect to all special settlers in 1937.[38]

Until 1938, the children of special settlers shared the same restrictions on movement as their parents. They had a right to education, however, and if they were accepted for admission to higher educational institutions outside their place of settlement, they were supposed to be issued passports and allowed to leave, at which point they legally ceased to belong to the category of special settlers. From the autumn of 1938, all children of special settlers became eligible for passports at the age of sixteen and were then free to leave the settlement.[39]

The great majority of special settlers were deported kulaks. But there were other collective deportations, albeit on a smaller scale. The most important were the ethnic deportations that started in the middle of the decade and the Leningrad deportations that followed Kirov's murder in December 1934. The ethnic deportations, curiously at odds with the general Soviet policy of fostering national identity and national territorial bases, involved members of "diaspora" nationalities—people like Finns and Koreans with possible loyalties to a state outside the Soviet Union. They were transported by the NKVD in much the same manner as the kulaks a few years earlier and resettled in the interior. These ethnic deportations foreshadowed the better-known deportations of nationalities like the Volga Germans and Chechens in the 1940s. Although unpublicized and relatively small-scale, the practice of ethnic deportation was sufficiently entrenched in popular consciousness, at least in the Leningrad region, for a man with a Finnish name to refuse to respond to the census-taker in 1939 with the comment: "I know why you are taking a census of the population. That is done in order to find out the Finns and the Estonians and then deport them."[40]

The main victims of deportations from Leningrad after Kirov's murder were "former people" and ex-Oppositionists. Both these categories were held to have some responsibility for the murder—indeed, a number of Oppositionists were executed for the crime, including Zinoviev and Kamenev after the first of the Moscow trials in 1936—although there was no concrete evidence of their involvement, and it is even possible that the timing of their deportations was partly coincidental. The decision to send 2,000 former Communists from Leningrad into provincial exile was presented in internal documents as an outcome of the recent party purge.[41] The exile of over a thousand Leningrad "former people" was described in a brief official announcement as a punishment for "violating residence regulations and the passport law." The popular conclusion on this action, however, was that it was a case of "rounding up the usual suspects" after Kirov's murder; it was even rumored that the NKVD had compiled its list from the Leningrad city directory, in whose prerevolutionary volumes well-born citizens had habitually identified themselves by estate and service rank.[42]

Among those expelled from Leningrad were "former Baron Tipolt [who had] got himself a job in an industrial meal-service as an accountant, General Tiufiasev [who] was a teacher of geography, former Police Chief Komendantov [who] was a technician at a factory, [and] General Spasskii, [who] was a cigarette seller in a kiosk." But some less exalted individuals got pulled into the net, like the man who had worked as a scribe in the Tsarist Ministry of Justice whose deportation order was cancelled only after four years petitioning. Leningrad secondhand stores were swamped with furniture that the deportees had had to sell off. The Leningrad deportees were usually sent into individual administrative exile, not to special settlements like the kulaks, and some were subsequently able through petition and patronage to return to the city. For returnees, however, the recovery of apartments presented almost insuperable problems. Although their right to the apartments was officially acknowledged, in practice these apartments had new occupants whom it was extremely difficult to evict.[43]

Deportation was an even more extreme form of outcasting than the stigmatization involved in depriving people of the vote. Friends and neighbors were supposed to break off relations with a person who was deported; if they did not, they might be charged with "maintaining ties" with anti-Soviet elements. When a group of workers at an electric power station gathered money and goods to send parcels, via a relative, to a deported fellow worker, this was treated as a counter revolutionary initiative that the NKVD ought to investigate.[44] Free residents in the areas to which exiles were sent were encouraged to keep their distance.

Rounding Up Marginals

The Soviet regime, it seems, felt entitled to pick segments of the population up and move them at will, just as serf-owners had been able to do with their serfs under the old regime. Deportations are not the only evidence for this. In addition, the regime was furtively and somewhat tentatively practicing a kind of social cleansing, involving the removal of marginal urban residents, "degenerates" whose presence was regarded as corrupting and disruptive, and their forcible relocation in labor camps or provincial exile. The general term for such marginals was "socially alien and socially dangerous elements," and the process of their removal from society started at the end of the 1920s and reached its peak during the Great Purges.[45]

Prostitutes were one category of victim. From the summer of 1929 the authorities had the legal right to pick up prostitutes or women "on the borders of prostitution" in barracks, restaurants, railway stations, and overnight lodgings and expel them from the city.[46] Beggars and all kind of wanderers such as tinkers and traveling tailors were liable to similar treatment. Beggars were easily construed by the authorities as "church agitators," itinerant tinkers and tailors as spreaders of counter revolutionary propaganda.[47]

The expulsion of marginals from the big cities reached new heights in 1933 with the establishment of the passport regime in Moscow and Leningrad. In Leningrad, a Russian historian of prostitution reports, a "wave of repression" hit the city as "the parasitical element" was rounded up, and the drive against prostitution continued in high gear for the next two years, with almost 18,000 women being detained in Leningrad in 1934–35. Most of these were sent to labor colonies and camps in Leningrad province. In the summer of 1933, "socially degenerate elements," mainly habitual criminals, were rounded up in Moscow and Leningrad. Because of their "corrupting influence" on those around them, they were sent to labor camps rather than allowed to live in "semi-liberty as deportees." Around the same time, 5,000 gypsies "without fixed residence" were picked up in the Moscow region and deported to the Siberian city of Tomsk, along with 338 horses and 2 cows, for relocation in labor settlements. This gypsy operation could be regarded as an early ethnic deportation, but it seems more likely that the authorities conceptualized it differently. The regime made every effort to settle "backward" nomadic peoples, including gypsies, and the gypsies' reputation for stealing and sharp practice no doubt inclined local officials to see them as degenerate troublemakers. In 1937–38, during the Great Purges, another contingent of gypsies was picked up and sent to the East.[48]

This pattern of rounding up criminals and marginals for resettlement was repeated many times in the provinces. Tomsk, recipient of Moscow's gypsies, complained bitterly in 1934 that its streets were full of criminals and juvenile delinquents, many of whom had been brought in by local authorities from other parts of the region and dumped. "As a result," the chairman of the city soviet reported, "the streets of the city of Tomsk, the markets, the stations, the shops and institutions in recent time have been flooded with groups of juvenile and adult delinquents—habitual criminals who are committing all kinds of offences and terrorizing the population."[49]

Perhaps the most remarkable episode of the decade—one that has only recently come to light with the opening of Soviet archives—involved a massive operation to round up social marginals during the Great Purges that resulted in mass executions as well as mass deportations. This episode, still relatively little analyzed, suggests that the Soviet regime had come closer to a Nazi approach to "social cleansing" (though without the racist component) than had hitherto been thought. On July 2, 1937, a secret order from the Politburo called for the rounding up of habitual criminals, troublemakers, and persons who had illegally returned from exile, some of whom were to be executed immediately without trial, others send to Gulag. Each region of the Soviet Union was given a quota; for the Soviet Union as a whole, the target figure for executions was 70,000 (including 10,000 "socially dangerous elements" already in Gulag) and for dispatch to Gulag almost 200,000.[50]

The main thrust of this order was against kulak deportees who had escaped from exile (it will be remembered that there were around 400,000 of these, according to NKVD figures), who were said to be "the chief instigators of all kinds of anti-Soviet and diversionist crimes" in industry, the railroads, state farms, and collective farms. Such people congregated particularly on the outskirts of big industrial towns. In his elaboration of the Politburo order, Ezhov identified three major groups in addition to the escaped kulak exiles. The first consisted of "church people and sectarians who have been repressed in the past." This was probably the largest category of victims taken from the countryside in this operation. The second group were counterrevolutionaries —"persons who were participants in armed uprisings against Soviet power or former members of anti-Bolshevik political parties." The third group consisted of habitual criminals—"repeat offenders who are part of the professional criminal world (horse thieves, cattle-rustlers, robbers, thieves, etc.)"[51]

The results of this operation can be seen in the dramatic rise in the number of Gulag convicts classified as "socially harmful and socially dangerous" in the following year and a half. There were already over 100,000 Gulag prisoners in this category at the beginning of 1937. Two years later, the number had risen to almost 300,000, constituting almost a quarter of all Gulag inhabitants.[52]

RENOUNCING THE PAST

Renunciation was one of the ways people tried to cast off stigma. It was usually unavailing, since social origin was held to be an "objective" taint that could not be removed by a change of heart. All the same, officials sometimes required it of the children of kulaks and priests at the beginning of the 1930s, as they did during the Great Purges of children of "enemies of the people," and sometimes people did it on their own initiative. Two kulak daughters recalled many years later that they had to make statements that they renounced their parents and had no further ties with them. A teacher, Iurii Mikhailovich, inserted a curt announcement in *Izvestiia* that "I renounce my father, a priest." A priest's wife in the Lower Volga tried to repudiate her husband after he was "dekulakized," saying her son had converted her to the cause of Soviet power and led her to hate capitalism. "Starting from today, when as a result of dekulakization I have absolutely no property—I once and for all renounce the old, unneeded and harmful views. Starting from today, I divorce my husband. . . ." The letter was signed "citizeness Dominika Sigaeva." (This appeal almost certainly went nowhere, since the authorities were particularly suspicious of divorces associated with dekulakization, assuming that the motive was to protect the family's assets.[53])

The kind of renunciation that most interested Soviet authorities was when priests renounced the cloth. Such renunciation, if done publicly, provided dramatic support for the Soviet position that religion was a fraud that had been discredited by modern science. Signed announcements that a priest was renouncing the cloth "in response to socialist construction" appeared from time to time as letters to the editor in the local press during the Cultural Revolution.[54] A typical example of this type of political theater took place one Sunday in 1929 in a Catholic church in the Minsk region:

> On the day when believers gathered for religious worship in honor of "God's vicar," they heard with horror from the lips of the priest that religion was a deceit and that he no longer wished to be a weapon in the hands of counter-revolutionaries. At that point, [the priest] threw off his vestments and left the church, accompanied by wails and lamentation from the fanatical old women [in the congregation].[55]

The NKVD reported a wave of renunciations by priests in connection with the Stalin Constitution of 1936. In one case, a priest (Orthodox, in this case) made a public announcement in church of his disillusionment with religion, stating his belief that "science explained nature, not God." In another, a psaltor, announced his renunciation of the faith in the local newspaper; he subsequently entered pharmacy school.[56]

The great drawback to renouncing the cloth was that it was so hard for ex-priests to find jobs. Many, many young priests would leave the church if only this problem could be overcome, a Soviet official reported sadly in 1937. Not only the priests, but also officials of the League of Militant Godless—professional atheist propagandists—wanted renunciation to be a smoother process. "We have priests who renounced the cloth three years ago," said a frustrated official in 1930, "and they don't even take them at the [labor] exchange. . . . We must give people who renounce religion and want to join us the possibility of working, even if it is manual labor." Indeed, the League had whole files of letters from priests who had left the church but were unable to find work.[57]

For victims of disfranchisement as well as deportation and exile, one of the few recourses available was petition. The files of President Kalinin's office are full of such petitions; and at the beginning of 1930, 350 appeals were coming in every day from those requesting reinstatement of rights after being disfranchised by local soviets in the Russian Republic alone.[58] Kalinin's office sympathized with these petitioners and regularly prepared memos on local "excesses" in disfranchisement for circulation to local soviets and central authorities. Among the examples cited of persons incorrectly deprived of the vote were women receiving child support (regarded locally as "living off unearned income"), Tolstoyans, Mennonites, epileptics, and troublemakers (people "who talk a lot at meetings and actively criticize the [local] rural soviet"). One twenty-year-old woman in Penza complained of being deprived of rights "as a nun" because she was not yet married.[59]

In Golfo Alexopoulos' recent study of petitions against disenfranchisement, she found that those seeking reinstatement of rights deployed a range of arguments. Some presented a Soviet persona, stressing their loyalty and contributions as productive Soviet citizens. Thus, a deported "labor settler" wrote that "I have worked as an udarnik and now I work as a stakhanovite, fulfilling many norms in construction three times over"; a young man petitioning on his mother's behalf noted "I am a scientist, an inventor, with honors and awards." Other petitioners stressed their powerlessness and misery, describing themselves as "orphan[s] without a crust of bread," pleading that "I am practically illiterate and have never seen joy in my life," and, in a petition addressed personally to Kalinin, begging that they not be allowed to perish "if only for the sake of the children." [60] Virtually nobody argued about the justice of disfranchising persons who engaged in trade (the main grounds for deprivation of rights in this sample). Rather, they pleaded that they had been wrongly classified, or that their connection with trade was accidental or the result of desperate need.[61]

Petitions were a lottery. We know that quite large numbers were successful, though we have no way of knowing what proportion of the total this was. Some categories of victims, like priests, seem to have produced comparatively few petitions for reinstatement of rights, probably because they knew their chances of satisfaction were small. Others, like widows and small traders, figure prominently in the lists of successful petitioners.

While it was standard practice to petition or write a letter of complaint on one's own behalf, it was unusual to protest on behalf of another person who was not a family member, and even less common to address the issue of stigmatization in principle. Like all rules, however, this one has exceptions.

A woman writing under her maiden name complained to the Ministry of Agriculture about her expulsion from a kolkhoz on the grounds that her husband's father had been a trader before the revolution. She was incensed, in the first place, that her husband's complaint on this score had been answered, while an earlier complaint from her had been ignored, evidently on the assumption that she and her husband were a single entity. She objected to this (correctly, in terms of the law) on the grounds that kolkhoz membership pertained to the individual adult, not to the household. On the substantive issue, she was equally feisty, going straight to the point of principle: "One can't extend responsibility for social origins so far, because I had no connection with my father-in-law Vasilii Gavrilovich, who died in 1922 and whom I never knew, and could not have been infected with his ideology." [62]

A sixty-nine-year-old former revolutionary, Aleksandra Elagina, member of the People's Will terrorist group in the 1880s, went even further beyond the usual bounds when she wrote to Molotov to protest about the fate of "former" people who had served a term in exile and, "despite all decrees and instructions of the government, are hindered from finding employment, studying, and living in those places where they have relatives and housing, for example, in Moscow [and] Leningrad." [63]

Another complaint about stigmatization phrased in principled terms concerned the expropriation of Jewish small traders and artisans in connection with the campaign against private enterprise and Nepmen at the end of NEP. The letter was signed by "Abram Gershberg, worker," and its author claimed to have observed or even participated in the expropriations in connection with his work as an activist in the Kiev region. The letter was in effect a denunciation of anti-Semitism. "When I pointed out this incorrect activity . . . in relation to the small trader and Jewish artisan, then my comrades were not ashamed to say in a joking tone: 'Jews stick together.'" Complaining that these Jews had been deprived of all rights as well as "their last pillow and shirt," the writer asked for an amnesty and permission for them "to work at their trades, for example, as accountants, bookkeepers, salesmen, millers, butter-makers." Who he really was remains a mystery, since a subsequent investigation revealed that no person of that name lived at the address he had given.[64]

"A son does not answer for his father"

The regime's policy on social stigmatization changed in the course of the 1930s, though the practice of most party and government agencies was much slower to shift and there are hints that the change was controversial in high political circles.[65] As early as February 1934, Molotov told the Seventh Congress of Soviets that restrictions on the franchise were "temporary measures" necessary only as long as the old exploiting classes constituted a threat. Now, he said, only about two million people were disfranchised and soon it would be possible to eliminate the category altogether.[66]

The first move concerned the children of the disfranchised, not their parents. At the end of 1935, making an impromptu comment on a speech by a Stakhanovite who claimed that recognition had been withheld from him because his father had been dekulakized, Stalin pronounced that "A son does not answer for his father."[67] He never returned to the issue, but the message was elaborated by others. The Commission for Soviet Control ordered Soviet government and industrial agencies to cease firing and refusing to hire people "for such reasons as social origin, having past convictions, convictions of parents and relatives, and so on." A. A. Solts, a member of the Commission, underlined the importance of lifting past stigmas, "so that a person can forget his social origins and criminal convictions. The offspring of a kulak is not to blame for that, since he did not choose his parents. Therefore they are saying now: don't persecute people for their [class] origins."[68]

Not everyone took these promises at face value. Recalling Stalin's statement that "a son does not answer for his father," one respondent in the Harvard Project added: "But that was not the case because I was and remained the son of a kulak." Another respondent, whose father was a former noble landowner, recalled that a meeting was called at her technical school to discuss the implications of Stalin's new slogan. "The speaker said that since children no longer had to bear the sins of their parents, that those who had hidden their social origin should not be afraid to speak. All students who had hidden their social origin were encouraged to come up to the podium and to talk." The atmosphere was intimidatory, and this respondent sensed a trap and kept silent. One of the few students to respond disappeared from the school shortly thereafter, she claimed.[69]

It may be that local authorities, or even Stalin himself, wanted to use the promise of destigmatization to find out who was concealing what. Neverthless, the formal policy change promised by Molotov went forward, though not smoothly. The commission charged to draft a new Constitution for the Soviet state struggled with the question of just how far to go in removing the stigma from "class aliens." At the eleventh hour, in circumstances that are unclear but suggestive of intervention from the highest level, all the social grounds for disenfranchisement were dropped from the draft Constitution.[70]

The new Constitution—issued after a public discussion of the published draft—affirmed that all citizens of the USSR attaining eighteen years of age, "irrespective of race, nationality, religious confession, education level, way of life, social origin, property status, and past activity," had the right to vote in Soviet elections and also the right to be elected (article 135). In his commentary on the public discussion, Stalin dismissed a proposed amendment "to deprive of voting rights ministers of religion, former White Guards, all former people and persons who are not engaged in socially useful labor." "Soviet power," he said, "had deprived non-toiling and exploiting elements of voting rights not for eternity but temporarily, for a given period." Now that the old exploiting classes had been liquidated, the Soviet regime should be strong enough to remove these limitations. After all, Stalin said (damning with faint praise?) "not all former kulaks, White Guards, and priests are hostile." [71]

The ambivalence of Stalin's comments was reflected in public reaction as well as implementation of the new policy. "I can't accept that priests should be electors or elected," wrote R. Beliaev from the Kalinin region. ". . . in my opinion a priest is not a toiler but a parasite." "It will be very bad for those who were activists during dekulakization and the liquidation of the kulaks [if the latter get the vote]," wrote K. Porkhomenko, a kolkhoznik. "The kulak may now, if he gets into power, press very hard on those people, the activists, because even today the kulaks have great hatred." [72]

While the Politburo duly ruled in the spring of 1937 that all actions "depriving citizens of the USSR of voting rights on the grounds of social origin" must cease,[73] the message that officials and the public were getting was very mixed. The terror of the Great Purges was already underway, and the distinction between the old "class enemies" and the new "enemies of the people" was by no means clear.[74] Social origin was raised time and time again in cases of expulsion from the Komsomol in Smolensk province in 1937, although during the appeals process the following year, persons expelled on these grounds were routinely reinstated. The same was true of the Smolensk party organization during the Great Purges, where accusations of alien social origin or connections with persons of alien social origin were made frequently and with passion.[75] People continued to be discriminated against—or worse—because of their social origins. For example, a secretary of the Stalinsk party committee in Siberia had no hesitation in stating in August 1937 that a certain Shevchenko "was not included in the list of delegates to the Kuzbass Congress of Stakhanovites because his father is a former kulak deprived of voting rights."[76]

As late as 1939, an officer of the Leningrad NKVD was still recommending the dismissal of teachers—daughters of priests, nobles, and Tsarist officials—as "socially alien elements," who were "sullying" the school in which they worked. But the times were evidently changing: the head of the local schools department boldly disputed the NKVD officer's recommendation and his assumption that "social origin is the only criterion of worth," and stated his own opinion that in view of the teachers' record of service and pedagogical qualifications there were no grounds for dismissal.[77]

WEARING THE MASK

Concealment was a normal condition of Soviet life. The authorities regarded everyone who concealed their past as a hidden enemy, but this was not necessarily so. Anyone who had a damaging past more or less had to conceal it, regardless of political sympathies, in order not to be taken for an enemy. Those who concealed their pasts were "masked," in Soviet parlance. And once they were masked, it was necessary to "unmask" them.

Many people had to live a double life. That could mean that they had two personae, an "invented" public self and a "real" private self. But things were not really that simple. One might—in a socialist-realist projection of the future upon the present—passionately desire to become the person whom one publicly claimed to be. One might play the public part so well that it became internalized ("I . . . began to feel that I was the man I had pretended to be"[78]). One might grow to hate the "real" self or see it as a kind of nightmarish Doppelgänger that must be banished from the light of day.[79]

A *Krokodil* cartoonist presented this duality by showing a written resumé behind which could be seen drawings that told another story. In the resumé, the question "Social position before 1917?" receives the answer "Employee"—but the drawing depicts an agent of the Tsarist police. "Did you take part in the civil war? Answer: "Yes"—but the picture shows that it was on the White side. "Do you have specialized education?" Answer: "I have a diploma as a technological engineer"—but this answer is superimposed on a drawing of a man forging a diploma.[80] From *Krokodil's* standpoint, the whole public identity in this resumé was a fraud. In real life, however, it could also be someone's way of remaking himself as a new Soviet man.

For a person suffering social stigma, flight was often the first step to a new life. At the beginning of the decade, peasants who had been dekulakized, or feared that they were about to be, often fled their villages and went to work in towns or new construction sites. Referred to as "self-dekulakization," this was deplored by the authorities but was extremely difficult to prevent. Nepmen facing expropriation at the end of NEP had acted similarly: traders expropriated in Mogilev and Minsk were reported fleeing to Moscow and Leningrad in 1930, and merchants from the Volga moving to Tashkent.[81]

The next step was to get new identity documents. Before passports came in, one of the basic identity documents was a "paper" (*spravka*) from the local soviet attesting to one's social origin, and these remained basic documents for peasants. Many members of kulak families obtained such papers by bribery or "sharing a bottle" with the chairman of the local soviet. Others stole headed paper and stamps from the relevant institutions and made their own. In towns, ration cards, trade-union cards, and party membership cards were all useful identity documents, and there was a lively market in such documents, both genuine and forged. A cartoon on the 1935 review of party membership shows a commission examining the card of a party member with the following caption: "Your last name is written illegibly on your card." "Pardon, in that case I can offer you my other party card. I think it is more legible there." [82]

Sometimes, in the pre-passport days, it was not even necessary to buy your identity documents: "You just lose your documents, and then you ask for other documents and make an oral declaration as to who was your father and mother," said one Harvard Project respondent, recalling a transaction in 1929 or 1930. Kiev was often claimed as a birthplace, since records there had been destroyed during the Civil War. Some people scarcely even remembered the identity change as a problem: "I never acknowledged [my origins] in any application for work. . . . I went by another name, that of my husband. I used the last name of my husband, and so did both my children. Therefore I never acknowledged my past." [83]

Even passports could be bought. A newspaper reported in 1935 that in one Mordovian village buying passports was so easy that forty local disfranchised families did not even bother to petition for restoration of rights:

> "How many of your disfranchised people were reestablished in rights up to the time of the soviet elections?" we asked rural soviet chairman Losev. "Not one! We didn't receive any such petitions. . . . (sic)." And it is true, why petition and beat a path to the rural soviet when in Torbeevo district without any torments you can cheaply buy . . . (sic) "civil rights"! The prices for passports are not high —from 50 to 80 rubles. Many of the disfranchised acquired several passports.[84]

Less drastic ways of making a new identity were through adoption and marriage. It was standard practice for disfranchised persons to send their children to live with unstigmatized relatives.[85] Marriage or remarriage could serve a similar function, whether intentionally or otherwise. A woman of noble origin whose first husband died in the early 1920s chose a lathe operator as her second husband and thereby improved her social position; the daughter of a rich factory owner married the upwardly mobile son of a poor peasant family and, as her son noted, "her marriage saved her from trouble." A kulak's daughter recalled that "my first marriage was a kind of camouflage. I had no place to live. And my husband was from the *bednota* [poor peasants, a socially advantageous status]. He was a member of the Komsomol. . . . Marrying him served as a cover for me. And also we had our own little room. And when I went to bed, I would think to myself, Dear Lord, I'm in my very own bed. . . ." [86]

The building of a new life was sometimes a complex effort of the whole family, using many different ploys. After they were separated in the process of deportation, the dekulakized Tvardovskii family made every effort to keep in touch and get back together again (with the exception of their most famous member, the poet Aleksandr Tvardovskii, who escaped deportation and, to protect himself, concealed his family's fate). The Silaev family in Western Siberia separated several times in the years after Vasilii Silaev, a prosperous peasant, moved to Novosibirsk to avoid dekulakization, but the point of these moves and separations (when they were not purely involuntary) was to preserve the family and some of its property intact. To this end, Silaev formally divorced his wife, after having transferred ownership of two houses to her, and went to another town; after selling the houses, she joined him there. His son, who had an office job in Novosibirsk, journeyed back to their native village to arrange his father's reinstatement in voting rights.[87]

Often families found that dispersal was the only way to survive. "Our social origins weighed on me and my brothers and sisters like a stigma. And all of them, one by one, left Akhansk. . . .Well, and then, you know, things were such that we weren't even supposed to correspond with our parents. It was like having a tie with an 'alien element.' But of course, we continued to correspond with them, and once in a while we visited them, but it was very difficult." [88]

The "unmasking" of individuals hiding their pasts sometimes occurred as a product of police investigations, as happened in Silaev's case. But very often the press or fellow citizens, or a combination of the two, did the job. For journalists, working with severe constraints on "sensationalism," unmasking stories were the liveliest kind of human-interest material available, and they also gave scope for investigative reporting. In the spring of 1935, for example, a Leningrad paper published a series of exposé stories on hidden class enemies in hospitals and schools of Leningrad oblast. The writing, typical of the genre, imparts sinister motives to anyone concealing social origin and makes generous use of emotive words like "refuge," "lurking," and, of course, "enemy."

> Troitskii, a former White officer and son of a priest, has found a refuge [in the hospital]. The economic manager considers that this lurking enemy is "an irreplaceable accountant." Registrar Zabolotskaia, nurse Apishnikova and disinfector Shestiporov are also offspring of priests. Vasileva changed her profession from nun to nurse, and also got a job at that hospital. Another nun, Larkina, followed her example. . . . A former monk, Rodin, got himself a job as doctor's assistant and even substitutes for the doctor in making house calls.[89]

Networks of social aliens were particularly suspect; exposé stories took any opportunity to link social stigma and political deviance, implying a causal connection:

> Bocharov's father was a policeman [in Tsarist times]. He keeps close contact with his relatives—deacons, priests, and kulaks. In 1929, he was expelled from the party as an alien element, but then for some reason reinstated. When he was a student at Moscow University, Bocharov was an active member of the Trotskyite-Zinovievite opposition. During the party purge of 1930, he hid that until he was unmasked.[90]

Denunciation by neighbors, colleagues, and schoolmates was a common hazard in the lives of people with bad social origins. The child of a kulak, adopted and educated by her aunt and uncle, was denounced in a letter from the village to her Komsomol organization. Later, she was denounced again in a letter sent to a newspaper; its publication led to her dismissal from her job and the breaking of her engagement to a Communist, who was given an ultimatum by the party.[91] These denunciations were evidently products of gratuitous malice, but many denunciation had more concrete, self-interested purposes: for example, the wish to rid the communal apartment of undesirable neighbors. The victim of one such denunciation, the son of a priest, complained bitterly about his persecution by neighbors, who want "by fair means or foul to force me and my family to leave—to run away, and then the living space will go to them." "I know that they use my [class] origin as a justification," he wrote. Their denunciations had caused him to be dismissed from three jobs and had also temporarily deprived him of a ration book. Similar denunciations were sent in to the passport commissions in 1933 to prevent neighbors being issued passports and Moscow residence permits.[92]

Some denunciations were written in a spirit of duty, as when a Siberian Communist denounced his own father-in-law, a fleeing kulak, after the latter sought shelter in his apartment in 1930. Others expressed an apparently genuine fear and loathing of the class enemy, as in the case of two workers who wrote separate denunciations of a certain engineer who, they said, had had sailors flogged and workers arrested under the old regime and was only feigning loyalty to Soviet power ("I know his tricks from 1905 as well as I know my own five fingers"). Perhaps the same spirit, or a lynch-mob version of it, inspired workers in a factory in Groznyi after an incident in which the lathes of two Stakhanovite recordbreakers had been sabotaged. They "unmasked the kulak Kruglov, escaped from Kamchatka, and Stepanchuk, a former gendarme, and drove them out of the shop. After that Stakhanovites . . . unmasked another fourteen disfranchised persons who had got jobs in the plant." [93]

There were many circumstances in Soviet life where denunciations were encouraged or even required, such as purges and "criticism and self-criticism" sessions of the workforce at factories and in offices. Sometimes people even denounced themselves for hiding social origins. This happened, for example, at a meeting of a district party organization in the Western oblast where, under the stress of one of the "self-criticism" meetings associated with the onset of the Great Purges, the deputy chairman of the district soviet surprised the meeting by suddenly announcing that "I deceived the party when I joined the Communist Party and during the purge and exchange of party documents, hiding my social position. My father was a rural policeman [under the old regime], not an office-worker." [94]

Unmasking could be a strategy in bureaucratic conflicts. It was rare, however, for an institution to go as far as one government agency did in 1935 when it made a private investigation of the social position of all the residents in two Moscow apartment buildings. The buildings were to be torn down to make way for the agency's new offices, to be constructed on the site, and the agency was therefore legally obliged to find housing for their inhabitants. The investigation turned up a remarkably shady population: no fewer than thirty-seven social aliens, including runaway kulaks, former nobles, former merchants, people with deported or imprisoned relatives, fences for stolen goods, and speculators in goods ranging from auto parts to apartment space to homemade cheese. Having established this social profile, the agency sent the information along to the Moscow police, arguing that since the residents of the buildings were social aliens who had no right to be living in Moscow anyway, it could scarcely be required to rehouse them.[95]

Was it possible to conceal unfavorable social origins in the long term? Harvard Project interviewers asked this question of postwar refugees, as did more recent interviews of elderly women in Russia, and got a variety of answers. Some said it could, citing their own experience or that of relatives and friends. To carry it off, they said, you needed to move away to another part of the country, change jobs frequently, get a false passport, change your name and invent a past for yourself, and avoid making personal enemies who might denounce you. A number of respondents noted, however, that it was dangerous to hide your social origins because once the authorities found out "you will be in worse trouble than before," "[you] will be called a spy and cannot get work at all, or may be arrested." Some said it was possible before passports were introduced, but became very difficult afterward.[96]

Others said that long-term concealment of social origins was simply impossible. Even the question distressed one elderly interviewee, a priest's daughter: "How could I hide that!? How could I hide that?!" "They will find you out because it cannot be hidden permanently," Harvard Project respondents said. "You can hide it for ten years, but in the eleventh you will be found out." But sometimes "impossibility" was a psychological matter, as in the case of the kulak's son who successfully assumed a new identity with false documents and was never caught as long as he stayed away from home. "When I was in Moldavia no one knew me but when I returned to the Don—to my rodina [homeland]—people knew me. I returned because my rodina was calling me. I was homesick." [97]

The psychological strain of concealment was frequently emphasized. "I had always to deny my mother," said an artisan whose mother was a trader. "You know there is a struggle for existence; I said that I did not know about my mother and that she had died. I felt in my head that it was a crime to thus talk against the family, but I felt that I had to do it." Many respondents with taints in their backgrounds emphasized that they had been second-class citizens, deprived of all sorts of opportunities that were available to others, always anxious and on guard. The fear "was with me all the time," one woman said. ". . . I was happy when I was able to retire [in 1965]. Only then did I breathe easy." A teacher whose taint was that he was a priest's son summed up the consensus view: "In the Soviet Union everything is possible. You can, with the help of blat, get false documents and work a few years, but you can never have peace with this kind of affair." [98]

∾ ∾ ∾

We do not know how many lives were scarred by social stigmatization in the 1920s and 1930s, but the numbers must have been great. Four million disfranchised, plus their families, and two million kulak deportees at the beginning of the 1930s; close to 300,000 "socially harmful elements" in Gulag, almost a million "special settlers," and perhaps several hundred thousand more administrative exiles at the end of the decade—these overlapping and incomplete figures provide us with no usable totals but at least suggest the magnitude of the phenomenon.[99] Moreover, the affected group was always larger than the figures show, both because whole families were affected by the stigmatization of one member and because of the shadowy contingent of people who were successfully, but fearfully, concealing social origin. In a recent collection of interviews with elderly Russian women, no less than half the interviewees experienced stigmatization based on social origin. This is probably a sample bias, but there were also many (though proportionately fewer) respondents in the Harvard Interview Project who reported that social stigmatization was a central fact of their prewar lives as well as others for whom class origin was a lesser or occasional problem.[100]

What did it mean for the society to have so many people stigmatized or fearful of becoming so? Probably the most important consequence was large-scale concealment of social origin and misrepresentation of identity. This was certainly the aspect that weighed most heavily on the political leaders, who assumed that a person stigmatized is automatically an enemy. This made it necessary to punish him further and isolate him from society, to prevent him retaliating—thus, of course, setting up a vicious circle. Some people thought that the liquidation of "enemy" classes—capitalists, old nobility, merchants, kulaks—had removed a source of enmity to the Soviet regime, Stalin said a few years after dekulakization. "Wrong! Thrice wrong! Those people exist . . . we did not physically destroy them, and they have remained with all their class sympathies, antipathies, traditions, habits, opinions, world views and so on."[101]

It would be hard to disagree with one implication of Stalin's comment, namely that the Soviet regime had a genius for making enemies. A kulak might have been hostile to the regime in the 1920s, but he was likely to feel infinitely greater hostility after being dekulakized. The regime had reason to be concerned about the bitterness of thousands of former kulaks many of them had assumed new identities and were successfully hiding both their past and their thoughts. But not all the victims of social stigmatization reacted in this way.

It was common, especially for the children of stigmatized parents, to feel that their social origins shut them out of a community they desperately wanted to join. "Do my 'social origins' really put a wall between me and the [Komsomol]?" wrote a twenty-three-year-old rural teacher, the illegitimate son of a priest's daughter, to Stalin. This man was indignant at the unfairness of it, pointing out that as an illegitimate child he would have been stigmatized under the old regime too, and asserting his devotion to the Soviet cause. "From when I was a little boy I was penetrated to the [marrow] of my bones with revolutionary Leninist ideas and I will be convinced of them forever!" [102]

Exclusion often produced misery and a sense of inferiority rather than indignation or anger. "I was always sad and unhappy because I was alien," a priest's daughter remembered. "I could not belong because of my father and my brother [who died fighting for the Whites in the Civil War]." The daughter of a well-placed intelligentsia family, a great Soviet patriot in her youth, recalled that rejection by the Komsomol on grounds of social origin made her miserable, but that she did not question its justice. She began to feel "that there was something inferior and insufficiently firm within me. I was an 'intellectual,' and had to struggle against it without fail. I had to weed it out." [103]

Stigmatization could produce exaggerated feelings of loyalty and devotion to the Soviet regime and its values. Stepan Podlubnyi, whose peasant father had been dekulakized, struggled to overcome the "sick psychology" of his origins and remake himself, despite loneliness and self-doubt, as a model Soviet citizen. Another "interloper" developed "a pronounced complex that I was inferior to the other young workers whom I regarded as 'real Soviet people.'" When he was finally accepted into the Komsomol, "my fear turned into overwhelming relief, exaltation, and faith in myself." He became a Komsomol enthusiast and an idealistic supporter of the Soviet cause. "By entering the Komsomol I had acquired my full rights as a Soviet citizen. From then on I felt an integral member of the school community and realized with pleasure that I was now 'like the rest.' . . ." [104]

The fact that the Komsomol, at least up to 1935, was an exclusive organization that rejected many applicants on grounds of immaturity or social origin was obviously part of its appeal to Soviet youth. It is possible that there was a similar dynamics of Soviet citizenship and patriotism: the more people were excluded from full citizenship or could imagine the possibility of exclusion, the more prevalent a certain type of anxious, intense, exaggerated Soviet patriotism became.

"Just a suggestion." Caption: "The mass character of parachute sport in our country raises the challenge of servicing the parachutists without removing them (the parachutists) from the air. That is exactly what our artist Iu. Ganf suggests." Artist: Iu. Ganf. From *Krokodil*, 1937, n. 25, back page.

P. P. Konchalovskii, *A. M. Tolstoy as Guest of the Artist.* From *Agitatsiia na shchast'e. Sovetskoe iskusstvo stalinskoi epokhi*, Düsseldorf-Bremen: Interarteks-Edition Temmen, 1994. By permission of the State Russian Museum, St. Petersburg.

"What Cabbage Again?" From David Low, *Low's Russian Sketchbook*, London: Victor Gollancz, 1932. By permission of Solo Syndication Limited. Reproduced by the Department of Special Collections, University of Chicago Library.

T. S. Kuchkina, A Clock Stand with Figures of Pioneers (porcelain, late 1930s). From *Agitatsiia na shchast'e. Sovetskoe iskusstvo stalinskoi epokhi*, Düsseldorf-Bremen. Interarteks-Edition Temmen, 1994, p. 177. By permission of the State Russian Museum, St. Petersburg.

БОЛЬШИЕ ИЗДЕРЖКИ

Рис. К. Ротова

— Третью пару обуви изнашиваю и никак не могу найти пару детской обуви.

"Big Holdups." Caption: "That's the third pair of shoes I have worn out and I just can't find a pair of children's shoes." Artist: K. Rotov. From *Krokodil*, 1935, n. 24, p. 8.

"A Gentleman." Caption: "Did you really leave your wife completely alone?" "What do you mean? I left her with the child." Artist: Iu. Ganf. From *Krokodil*, 1935, n. 30–31, p. 2.

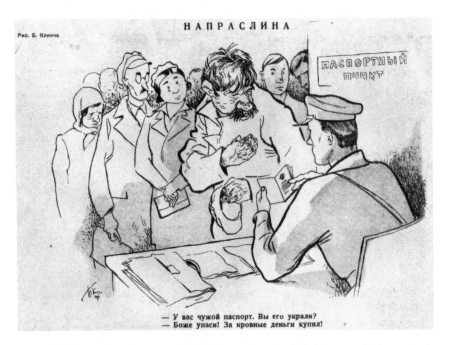

"Wrongful accusation." Caption: "You have someone else's passport. Did you steal it?" "God forbid. I bought it with my own money." Artist: B. Klinch. From *Krokodil*, 1935, n. 23, p. 14.

"Alexander Sirin, young worker-aviator, takes his mother for a joyride. Sirin works in an auto-repair shop in Stalino and learned to fly at the local air club, without leaving the job." From *Soviet Russia Today*, April 1937, p. 15.

"Shock brigade of women workers on a construction site, 1931." From *Moskva. Illiustrirovannaia istoriia,* Moscow: Mysl', 1986, p. 135. By permission of Mysl' Publishing House.

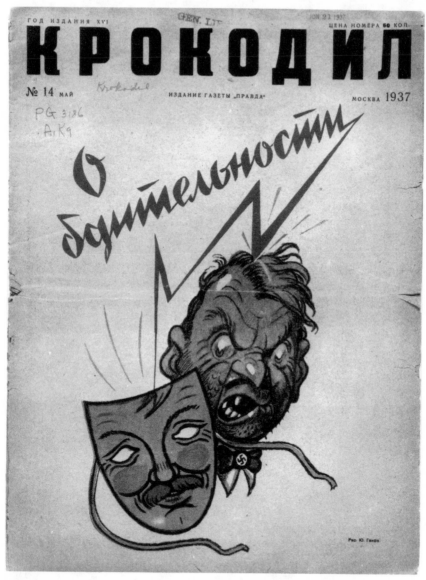

"On vigilance." Artist: Iu. Ganf. From *Krokodil*, 1937, n. 14, front cover.

6

Family Problems

The early 1930s were a period of great disruption and upheaval in Soviet society. Thus it is not surprising that the family was shaken too, just as it had been during the Civil War. Millions of men left home during collectivization; some kept in touch with their families in the village, others did not. Divorce was easy—one urban respondent in the Harvard Project remembered an "epidemic" of divorces at this time—and in any case there was no pressure to register marriages.[1] The incredible difficulty of urban housing conditions forced families into miserably confined spaces and contributed to the high rate of desertion by husbands, especially after the birth of a child. Almost ten million women entered the labor market for the first time in the course of the 1930s and many of them ended up as the sole breadwinner for families that often consisted of a mother, one or two children, and the irreplaceable *babushka* (grandmother) who ran the household. The task of the woman breadwinner was not made easier by the fact that women tended to be clustered in low-skill, low-paying jobs.[2]

Families bearing a social stigma had particular problems: the children might be sent away to protect them from the taint or they might feel obliged to keep their distance from their parents for the same reason. Deportations and exile sometimes kept families together whether they wanted it or not, but often one or more family members managed to escape the sentence. Sometimes children of stigmatized parents felt obliged to renounce them, following the example of the legendary Pavlik Morozov. More families were torn apart by the Great Purges, which left spouses and children stigmatized for the connection with "enemies of the people." Some wives of victims were sent to camps themselves, others were exiled. Their children often ended up with relatives and friends or, worse, in orphanages under new names.

But there is another side to the story, namely the resilience of the family. At the most basic level, people continued to get married. The Soviet urban marriage rate remained very high by both prewar and contemporary European standards, especially assuming that not all de facto marriages were registered; in 1937, 91 percent of all men aged 30 to 39 and 82 percent of women reported themselves married.[3] In some respects, the uncertain and dangerous conditions of life in the 1930s seemed even to make families stronger as their members drew closer together for self-protection. "The Soviet Union is a mass of individual family units isolated from each other," one Harvard Project respondent from the intelligentsia said. "Families are not broken up, rather, they try to draw close to each other." "We lived separately before, but after the revolution we all came together," said another respondent from the same social group. "We talked freely only in our own family. In difficult times we came together."[4]

According to the Harvard Project's analysis, based on a question about whether the family became more or less cohesive under Soviet conditions, the great majority of urban respondents said that the family had grown closer or stayed the same. Intelligentsia respondents gave the strongest positive responses, with 58 percent saying families had grown closer and only 7 percent saying they had grown apart, while blue-collar workers were more divided in their answers. This suggests that the "drawing closer" effect could be counterbalanced by tensions associated with poverty and difficult living conditions. Collectivized peasants were more evenly divided on this question than urban residents, but even in this group 45 percent said the family drew closer, compared with 30 percent who thought it grew apart. The researchers concluded that the main reason for the higher negative response was "the physical separation and geographical dispersion of the peasant families."[5]

There is no doubt that the impact of "Soviet conditions" on the family could be contradictory. Consider the example of Stepan Podlubnyi, son of a dekulakized Ukrainian peasant, who went to Moscow with his mother after his father's arrest at the beginning of the 1930s. Podlubnyi was extremely close to his mother, with whom he lived, and felt great loyalty to her; when she was arrested in 1937, his faith in the Soviet regime was seriously shaken. With his father, it was the opposite: they were pulled apart not only geographically but also psychologically as Podlubnyi tried to make himself into a good Soviet citizen and push his father and his father's anger out of mind.[6]

Another kind of contradiction is illustrated in the family of a woman doctor interviewed in the Harvard Project. Married sometime in the early 1930s, the mother of a son, she and her husband divorced but continued to live in the same apartment. She described this as a calculated survival strategy ("We did it [divorced] so that we would not be responsible for each other. If we had been married when my husband was arrested [in 1938], I would not be sitting here today"), but her narrative suggests that some degree of personal estrangement may also have played a part. Whatever the real reason for the divorce, the continued cohabitation had practical reasons. "We lived together for material purposes. He often had a chance to get into the villages and he would bring back foodstuffs." Yet this same woman, who was greatly attached to her only son and had excellent relations with him, was one of those who considered that the family had become more cohesive in Soviet times.[7]

"The family" was a very diverse and flexible unit in the 1930s, often with several generations of women as its backbone. Memoirs of communal apartments describe families of all types living side by side in their separate rooms. One memoirist grew up in a room in an apartment on the Arbat to which his grandmother had brought her three grown daughters from the provinces after the Civil War. In the 1930s, the household consisted, besides himself, of his mother, a single parent since the arrest of her husband, and her sister, a typist who was the only legal inhabitant of the apartment and apparently the main breadwinner, whom he thought of a "second mother." But they were in close contact with an extended family:

> Uncle Vasia, the husband of Aunt Nina, used to come from Lugansk and then from Nizhny Tagil, and usually stayed with us for a while. Uncle Volodia used to visit from Leningrad. His relatives the Matveevs used to come regularly twice a year, four of them, with two children (in our small room!). They were coming from the Gorky region, where Uncle Alesha Matveev worked, on vacation to their native Leningrad and back. Some second cousins of Mama's and Aunt Tania's came from Iaroslavl came more than once. Our Kiev relatives [on his father's side] used to visit.[8]

With them in the same apartment were several single women, either living alone or with one child, and some families with two parents and children, which the memoirist shows no sign of regarding as more "normal" than his own family. One of these, a working-class family headed by a telephone linesman who had lost both legs in an accident, consisted of the linesman's wife, son, mother, younger sister, and another relative who was periodically hospitalized for psychiatric problems—all of them living in one dark, stuffy room without a window.[9]

A grandmother, in this case on the maternal side, was also the lynchpin of Elena Bonner's much more prosperous and privileged family, in which both mother and father worked and were Communist activists. The same was true of the family of Sofia Pavlova, a university teacher whose mother lived with her from the time of the birth of her first child through two marriages (one unregistered), the arrest and disappearance of her second husband in the Great

Purges, wartime evacuation, and other upheavals. "Mama saved me . . . I was completely free. I didn't breast-feed my baby long. Mama in fact bottle-fed him." Her mother took total charge of the household, not only bringing up the two children but also doing the shopping and making all the household's financial decisions (her daughter and son-in-law simply turned their salaries over to her).[10]

In the 1920s, Communist attitudes toward the family were often hostile. "Bourgeois" and "patriarchal" were two words often coupled with "family." The conventions observed by respectable society before the revolution were dismissed as "petty-bourgeois philistinism," and the younger generation in particular made a point of its sexual liberation and disrespect for the institution of marriage. "Free" (unregistered) marriages were common, as was post-card divorce; abortion was legal. Communist women and men alike believed in equality of the sexes and women's emancipation (though women were and remained only a small minority of party members). For a woman to be nothing but a housewife was shameful. Some enthusiasts went so far as to suggest that children would be better brought up by state children's homes than at home with their parents.[11]

Nevertheless, the social radicalism of the 1920s can be exaggerated. Lenin and other party leaders were much more conservative on family and sexual questions than the younger generation. Soviet interest in communal as against family child-rearing was never anything like as strong as in Israeli kibbutzim thirty years later. Abortion was never encouraged, and in the latter part of the 1920s there was an active campaign against abortion, casual divorce, and promiscuity.[12] Moreover, Soviet laws on divorce, alimony, property rights, and inheritance were based on quite different assumptions about the family, even in the 1920s. These laws strongly emphasized the mutual responsibility of family members for each other's financial welfare; the consensus of Soviet legal experts was that, since the state lacked the resources for a full social welfare system for the time being, the family remained the basic institution of social welfare for Soviet citizens.[13]

In the mid 1930s, the Soviet state moved to a positively pro-family and pro-natalist stance, outlawing abortion in 1936, making divorce harder to obtain and more costly, rewarding mothers of many children, stigmatizing irresponsible fathers and husbands, and reinforcing the authority of parents vis-à-vis the school and the Komsomol. This change seems to have been primarily a response to falling birthrates and alarm at the failure of Soviet population figures to show the robust growth expected under socialism. Free marriage still existed as an institution (it was to be abolished only in the 1940s), which meant that a residual fuzziness remained about what constituted a marriage: in the 1937 census, one and a half million more women than men declared themselves to be currently married, implying that the same number of men were in relationships considered by their partners, but not themselves, to be marriages.[14] By the end of the 1930s, however, free marriage was becoming a less popular option, and even those who had previously been in free marriages were tending to register their unions.

One chronicler of Soviet social attitudes labeled this "the great retreat," meaning retreat from revolutionary values.[15] Aspects of this process, especially the organization of a volunteer movement of elite wives discussed later in this chapter, certainly have a strong flavor of embourgeoisement. But we should also note some other important characteristics. First, insofar as we can make any judgments about popular opinion in Stalin's Russia, the regime's change in attitude toward the family seems to have been well-received. Disintegration of the family was widely perceived as a social and moral evil, a sign of the disorder of the times; consolidation of the family was interpreted as a move toward normalcy.

Second, the family propaganda of the second half of the 1930s is even more notable for being anti-men than for being anti-revolutionary. Women were consistently represented (as they were and would continue to be in Soviet-Russian popular discourse) as the nobler, suffering sex, capable of greater endurance and self-sacrifice, pillars of the family who only in the rarest instances neglected their responsibilities to husband and children. Men, in contrast, were portrayed as selfish and irresponsible, prone to abusing and abandoning their wives and children. In the inevitable conflict between women's interests, construed as altruistic and pro-family, and men's interests, read as selfish and individualistic, the state was unquestionably in the women's corner. At the same time, this did not prevent it from adopting an anti-abortion law that made the lives of urban women even more difficult than before and appears to have been deeply unpopular with this group.

ABSCONDING HUSBANDS

The family may be viewed as a private sphere whose separateness from the public sphere constitutes a large part of its value to its members. This is how the Harvard Project interviewers approached the topic, and respondents from the intelligentsia usually shared their assumptions. It is not clear, however, that these same assumptions were strongly held at lower levels of Soviet urban society. Another possible view of the family is that it is an important institution that the powers that be (state, church, or both) should actively uphold, as indeed they had always done in Russia until the revolution. Many Soviet citizens, particularly women, seem to have held this view in the 1930s, judging by their appeals to the state to intervene in family problems. The most common type of appeal from urban citizens was a written request for help in tracing an absent husband and collecting family support payments.

Aleksandra Artiukhina, chairwoman of a large trade union with many women members, reported that "thousands of letters come to me at the union from worker women about seeking their husbands." These women wanted the authorities to find their absent husbands and collect family support payments from them. Some wrote sober and factual letters like this one, sent to the women's journal *Rabotnitsa*:

> I am a worker, Aleksandra Ivanovna Indykh. I earnestly request the editors of the journal *Rabotnitsa* to advise me how to find my husband, Viktor Ignatevich Indykh, who is a bigamist and at the present time is working at Feodosiia station

(Crimea). As soon as he realizes that I have found him, he quits his job and moves to another place. Two years have passed in this way, and he has given me nothing for bringing up the child, his son Boris.[16]

Other letters were more plaintive or more accusatory. In the first vein, a Siberian woman, Aleksandra Sedova, a poorly educated candidate member of the party, wrote to the regional party committee to complain about her husband, a district secretary of the Komsomol, who "leads a dissolute life, was a double-dealer as a Trotskyite and infected me with gonorrhoea so I was deprived of [the possibility of having] children." When Aleksandra was away on vacation to recover her health, her husband had written to inform her that he was marrying a Komsomol girl; on her return, he had frightened her with a pistol and "suggested that I should leave the apartment because it will be too big for you and they will give you [housing] where you work." Aleksandra mentioned that she was left penniless, but her letter stressed her need for understanding and moral support rather than her material needs. "I am not asking . . . for Sedov to live with me, but I am a human being I don't want to be thrown overboard and I don't want people to make fun of me. I am suffering if [you] push me away there will be no point to my life." [17]

A veterinarian wrote to her party committee in a spirit of vengeful indignation. Working in the provinces, she had met and married a Communist from Leningrad. They had quit their jobs early in 1933, when she was eight months pregnant, to return to Leningrad, but he had gone on ahead, taking their shared savings of 3,000 rubles and all her possessions, including 200 rubles in state bonds, while she waited in the provincial town of Oirat-Tura to have her baby. After the baby was born, she wrote to him that she was coming on to Leningrad, but he put her off. This went on for six months, until she finally wrote to acquaintances in Leningrad who told her that her husband "had calmly acquired a family" in the city and did not intend to return to her. She now concluded that he had married her solely for gain, which was "the act of a swindler," ill becoming a party member. She wanted the party to discipline him and presumably (though this was not explicitly stated) to make him recompense her and pay child support.[18]

The authorities responded to these appeals in different ways. Some were extremely helpful. Artiukhina, for example, took the deserted wives' cause to heart (though complaining that the state procurator's office, especially at the district level, did not do enough to help).[19] The West Siberian party committee, headed by Robert Eikhe, was also notably sympathetic and helpful. (It received an unusually large number of letters about absconding husbands, perhaps because Siberia seemed a good place to disappear in.) "In response to your complaint," Eikhe's office wrote to one woman,

we inform you that . . . your former husband Aleksei Goldobin is working at the Moshkovo logging cooperative. . . . We sent your complaint to the secretary of the Moshkovo district party committee, comrade Iufit, so that he can put pressure on Goldobin through the party. But in order for you really to receive child support payments regularly, regardless of whether Goldobin wants to pay, you need to find out what his salary is, present proof to the court that he is really the father of your child, and get a court order against him, which should be sent to Goldobin's place of work. Then you will really receive alimony regularly, since it will be withheld from his salary.[20]

In one Siberian district, local officials took the unusual step of organizing a conference of young peasant women and encouraging them to express their grievances against the men in their lives, revealing "a series of cases of intolerably caddish treatment of girl-friends and wives." The examples cited were all Komsomol members: one "deserted his wife with a baby at the breast," others were unfaithful and abusive, and a flagrant offender had "changed wives five times in the recent past." [21]

Party committees were not always helpful. Many appeals went uninvestigated and unanswered (as was probably the case with the veterinarian), while others were dismissed by local committees whose members sympathized with the husband (as Aleksandra Sedova complained in her letter to the regional authorities). An example of the latter is the dismissal of a wife's request that her husband be forced to pay child support by a party committee that justified this decision on the grounds that the husband was a good man, a Communist in the Red Army reserves, and an amateur aviator.[22]

Still, the weight of central instructions and propaganda was on the side of the deserted wives, not the husbands. The trade-union newspaper *Trud* was particularly active in its campaign against erring husbands in the mid 1930s. An article with the unambiguous title "Base Conduct" lambasted a certain Svinukhin, a bank manager who had abandoned a household consisting of his wife, three young children, and his seventy-year-old mother. Svinukhin refused to pay any family support, and as soon as the court order reached him at his place of work, he would move to another city. This had gone on for three years, and *Trud*, like Artiukhina, faulted local prosecutors for lack of diligence. The article described Svinukhin as one of those who abused the freedom of Soviet marriage laws and understood it as a right to "wildness, degeneracy, and baseness," which was all the more outrageous since the man was a senior official, a trade-unionist, and a member of the party. "Enough!" the journalist concluded. "Arrest Svinukhin! Hold him fast! Hold him so that he will not get away again. Take away his party card! Bring him to justice! Judge him sternly! Before all honest people, in the biggest club in Mtsensk, let this criminal answer for his vileness." [23]

Many of the deserted wives complained that their husbands had not only absconded but "found another wife" in another town. The problem of bigamy—or, to be more exact, polygamy—received attention in the mid 1930s. There were some show trials, like this one in Moscow:

A. V. Malodetkin, a worker at Moscow Instruments Plant, in a short period made the acquaintance of three young female workers, Petrova, Orlova and Matina. He proposed marriage to each of them in turn, and, receiving their agreement, began affairs with them. They all considered themselves his wives, since they did not know of his cheating. . . . [In addition], it turned out that Malodetkin had married back home in his village.

Although the one thing Malodetkin had refused to do with his Moscow girlfriends was go through the formalities of marriage, this behavior was characterized and condemned as polygamy. At his trial, Malodetkin denied any guilt and stated that he took up with these women "because he had nothing better to do." Indignant at this flippant response, the court sentenced him to two years imprisonment "for deception and insult to women." Polygamy was also occasionally cited among the grounds for expulsion from the Communist Party. One party member was expelled in Smolensk in the mid 1930s for having been married too often (three times, serially) and being unreliable in his payments of child support to the first two wives as well as for drinking and unsatisfactory performance on the job.[24]

In discussions of marriage and family questions, it was almost always assumed without question that it was men who sinned and women who were sinned against. If written complaints about deception, betrayal, and general bad treatment are any guide in this context, the assumption was, broadly speaking, correct: there were few men's letters of this kind to offset the enormous numbers of women's letters. (This may be because the chances of collecting family support money from an absconding wife, who had very likely gone off with another man, were close to zero.)

Still, we should not forget the other side of the picture. In at least one case, a court awarded child support to a father whose wife had left him and their child, ignoring her counter-plea for custody and a half share of the father's apartment.[25] And it is salutary to note that the Siberian party committee's investigation of one pathetic letter from an abandoned wife concluded that the "husband" from whom she demanded child support barely knew her (they lodged at one time in the same house) and almost certainly never had an affair with her. The investigator concluded that it was an extortion attempt by a confidence trickster.[26]

In addition to adultery, a range of other male delinquencies came under attack from wives, girlfriends, and neighbors as well as from the state. The state's intervention was frequently prompted and solicited by injured women. "I beg the party to check up on personal life, even if it is just the personal life of party members," pleaded a deceived wife, Anna Timoshenko. Anna's distress was occasioned by the conspicuous affair her husband, a party leader in Gzhatsk, was having with a female colleague. Anna had gone to her rival to offer to give him up, despite their eighteen-year marriage and children, but her rival had dismissed this idea with insulting condescension ("She answered thus: in the first place, you love him madly, in the second place, he loves the children, and in the third place, you would be left a beggar, so stop pestering him"). Anna had followed the pair secretly at night; when she surprised them exchanging "passionate kisses," her husband, in Anna's colorful description, "started running like a forty-three-year-old Pioneer; he didn't even run like that from the bullets of the White enemy at the front." The children took their father's side, saying "once he gives me money and does not beat me why do I undermine Papa's authority and thus ruin myself and [them]." Semiliterate and lacking any work experience except on the kolkhoz, she did not know where to turn. She begged the regional party secretary, "as a father, as a friend of the people," to take time to see her and help her to bear her torment.[27]

Accusations of adultery alone were virtually never acted on by the authorities. As for wife-beating, a common or even standard practice in lower-class milieus, especially when the husband was drunk, wives rarely complained about it in letters to the authorities. Neighbors were also generally reticent on the subject, although the authorities' objection to wife-beating was well known. One exception was the prosecution of a certain Rudolf Tello for mistreatment of a servant. Tello was accused of "unmercifully exploiting" the young and inexperienced family servant, Katia, and then, when his wife was away on vacation, forcing her to have sex with him. When she became pregnant, he drove her out of the house, but she was forcibly returned after the intervention of neighbors and the militia. Then Tello and his wife began to beat her, and even invited two friends to participate. Tello was sentenced to five years in prison for these offenses.[28]

Neglected Children

The upbringing of children is normally considered women's business, and so it was in Soviet Russia in the 1930s. It was women, not men, who wrote again and again to the authorities asking for help for their children, "barefoot and hungry." It was women too who occasionally despaired and wrote to the authorities begging them to have their children taken into state care or adopted as mascots by army regiments. It was a woman who, on hearing her younger children cry for bread after two weeks of hunger in the winter of 1936–37, "got up and went into the kitchen and ended her life"; and it was even a woman, a widowed kolkhoz chairman with two young children, who cabled the regional party secretary that if bread was not sent "she would be obliged to abandon the children to the kolkhoz and run away." [29]

If women were the main providers of child care, it would seem to follow that they would also be the ones held primarily responsible for child neglect. Sometimes this was the case, although it was more common (at least in the press) to find stepmothers charged with cruelty and neglect than natural mothers. But there were other cases where men incurred more blame than women, even when both were apparently responsible. Child neglect was a major problem of urban Russia in the 1930s, linked with casual marriage and divorce, women working, and above all the housing problem.

Housing was the key factor in one of the more vexing case of child neglect and abuse encountered by party leaders and judicial authorities. Rosa Vasileva was a fourteen-year-old Moscow schoolgirl in 1936 when she wrote an earnest letter to Stalin suggesting a "child tax," to be paid by all Soviet citizens, from which the state would pay each child a stipend from birth to age eighteen. This was to protect children from possible neglect and abuse by their parents. Although Rosa's letter was couched in abstract terms and contained no direct personal appeal, she did indicate that she had firsthand knowledge of problems associated with divorced parents and contested living space. Perhaps this was what caught the eye of Stalin's assistant, Poskrebyshev, and prompted him to forward the letter to Andrei Vyshinsky, a legal expert who was deputy head of the Council of People's Commissars.

Vyshinsky had the Moscow city prosecutor's office investigate Rosa's situation, and a sad story emerged. Like so many sad Soviet stories, it revolved around housing. Rosa and her parents had once lived together in a room of 11 square meters. Then her parents got divorced, and Rosa stayed on in the room with her father, Aleksandr Vasilev. When his job took him outside Moscow, he found a woman, Vronskaia, to look after Rosa on a live-in basis. But the militia would not register Vronskaia as a separate occupant because the room was too small, so (as he later explained) he was forced to marry her to get her registered. The Prosecutor's Office put almost all the blame for Rosa's subsequent sufferings on Vronskaia, "a hysterical personality" who, in her father's absence, abused Rosa, interrupted her homework, refused to allow her to have a bed, and finally—one month after obtaining her own registration as a resident—tried to throw her out on the street. A battle royal of competing eviction orders then ensued between Vronskaia, Rosa's father, and Rosa's mother. (The orders were all ignored, and after three years of effort, when Rosa was in her last year of high school or already graduated, Vyshinsky finally gave up on the case.[30])

The most famous of all child neglect cases in the mid 1930s was the "Geta" case, publicized extensively by the labor newspaper *Trud* and the subject of a show trial in a large Moscow factory. This was a case of problems associated with divorce and remarriage rather than housing. Geta Kashtanova was born in Bezhitsa in 1930 to Kashtanov, a technician, and Vasileva, a worker. They had met and married in 1929 at the "Red Profintern" plant. Around the time of Geta's birth, Kashtanov left. Vasileva tried to trace him to get child support payments, but was unsuccessful. Not wanting or able to bring up the child herself, she handed her over to her mother. After a time, Vasileva married again, a Communist named Smoliakov who had a good job in the trade unions, and they had two children. Then the grandmother became ill and sent Geta, aged five, back to her mother. The Smoliakovs had moved to Kaluga, where Smoliakov was editor of a newspaper; he was well paid, and they kept a servant, Marusia, in their three-room apartment (spacious, by Soviet standards, for a household of six). But Vasileva did not want Geta, whom she evidently disliked, and started to beat her. Smoliakov did not join in, but neither did he interfere to protect the child.[31]

Somehow at this point Vasileva learned the address of her former husband, Kashtanov, now an engineer living in Moscow. She decided to solve the problem by sending the child to live with her father. Accordingly, the servant Marusia took Geta up to Moscow to Kashtanov's address, but Kashtanov refused to take her, saying that his apartment was too small and he did not earn enough to support himself and a child. "The child's return provoked a new outburst of rage from Vasileva, and she at once started to beat Geta again." Then she ordered Marusia to take Geta to Kashtanov's a second time, and abandon her on the street if he refused to take her in. "She told Geta: 'Auntie Marusia is going to leave you. Don't cling to her. If you come back, I will kill you.'" The urgency of Vasileva's desire to get rid of the child was evidently related to the fact that Smoliakov had gone to a new job in Millerovo, much further from Moscow, and she was about to follow him—minus Geta.

On the evening of January 21, 1935, Marusia and Geta turned up again on Kashtanov's doorstep. Again, Kashtanov refused to take her, though he did escort the two to the bus stop and give them a ruble for the fare. This was presumably not a happy position for Marusia either, since as a result of Vasileva's departure for Millerovo she was unemployed as well as burdened with responsibility for Geta. So Marusia followed Vasileva's orders, taking Geta to a toy shop and then (according to one account) vanishing into the crowd. (According to another account, Geta was left knowingly and did not object "because her mother had told the nanny that if Geta came back, she would suffocate or poison her.") Four days later, Geta was brought into the 22nd precinct of the Moscow militia, dirty and ragged. "The girl said that she had no passport, her mummy lived in Bezhitsa (sic), that she didn't know anything about her daddy, and that she was hungry." A pencilled note found on her read:

[Geta] Kashtanova, five years old. Father is an engineer living on the 11th lane of Marina Roshcha, no. 30, apt. 2. He drove the girl out on the street. Have pity on her, good people![32]

Following the script established by this note, the militia-men tried to persuade Kashtanov to take the child, Kashtanov continued to refuse, and a highly colored report in *Trud* tagged him as the villain of the piece: "Let engineer Kashtanov be brought to justice!" On the same day, the district prosecutor announced that he was bringing charges against Kashtanov under article 158 of the Criminal Code and Kashtanov was arrested.[33]

As the investigation proceeded, however, attention switched to Vasileva—as well it might, on the evidence—and she too was arrested on May 6. By the time the Geta case actually came to court, Vasil'eva had become the main defendant, with Kashtanov and Ustinova ("Auntie Marusia") also charged with neglect and abuse but in lesser degree. The trial was held as a show trial in the club of the Trekhgornaia textile plant in July, with a woman prosecutor, Niurina, and an audience consisting largely of women workers from the plant. Niurina originally asked for a three-year sentence for Vasileva, but in the event "Vasileva's case was separated in view of her illness" and she received no sentence at this time. Kashtanov got six months' imprisonment, and was obliged to pay 125 rubles a month (more than a third of his salary) to Geta's grandmother, who was once again to act as Geta's guardian. After the sentence was pronounced, the audience of women workers remained in the hall and "a unanimous cry arose: 'Too little!'" Prosecutor Niurina then took the floor again and said she would petition for "a more severe law for people who do not pay child support"—meaning, of course, men.[34]

The reaction to the Geta case suggests that women's resentment against men's refusal to recognize family responsibilities ran deep. This was presumably recognized by the authorities, as witnessed by the decision to hold a show trial with a female prosecutor before an audience of female workers. Around the same time as the Geta case, a much less serious propaganda event with a somewhat similar message was held in a Leningrad publishing house. In this case, no child abuse had occurred and the family in the spotlight was clearly prosperous, even enlightened. The event consisted of a report by a Communist, comrade Zharenov (evidently an official at the publishing house), on "how he brings up his children." The report focused on his inadequacies:

> "I must confess," said Zharenov, "that up to this time I paid very little attention to the upbringing of my children. I became particularly acutely aware of this now when I am telling the comrades about myself as a Communist father. In our family up to this time the arrangement was that my wife alone concerned herself with the upbringing of the children, and I had almost nothing to do with it."

The audience took up the "self-criticism" tone and pushed further.

> They asked: "Is your daughter a Pioneer?" "Does the child see people drunk in the family?" "Do the parents use bad language in front of the children?" "Does the child have its separate dishes to eat from?" "With whom do your children socialize?" "Who are their closest friends?" "What grades did the children receive in school for the second quarter?" and so on.

Comrade Zharenov was unable to answer any of these questions: "He did not know how his children were doing in school, or what they did in their free time." As a result, he was "sharply criticized" by those present "for bringing up his children badly." The strange thing about this story is that Zharenov's wife (present at the meeting with her daughter Lida) received no criticism that was reported, indeed was scarcely even mentioned. This could be taken to imply that she too was neglectful, but the more plausible reading is that the intended message of this meeting was that *men*, not women, were inclined to neglect their children and should change their ways. Zharenov's wife's moment, and his daughter Lida's, presumably came at the happy end of the meeting when "comrade Zharenov and his family enlisted in the competition for the best upbringing of children." [35]

Homeless and Delinquent Children

Among the biggest social problems associated with family breakdown were homeless children and teenage hooligans. Homeless children—orphaned, abandoned by parents, or runaways—formed gangs, living by their wits in towns and railway stations and riding the rails. There had been hundreds of thousands of such children in the country after the Civil War, and efforts to get them into orphanages and educate them continued through the 1920s. By the end of the decade, partly because that cohort of children grew up, the problem started to ease. But then came collectivization, dekulakization, and famine in the countryside, and a new wave of orphans appeared—kulaks' children, children whose parents had died in the famine, children whose parents had disappeared to cities. [36]

The network of juvenile institutions—collection centers for children taken off the streets, juvenile affairs commissions, orphanages, colonies for juvenile offenders like Makarenkos's—was strained to the utmost. Villages often abandoned traditional practices of caring for orphans, partly because of the taint associated with kulaks' children, and "immediately send children whose parents have died to the town or the nearest orphanage." Rural authorities were reported to be ridding their areas of young beggars and vagabonds by giving them "attestations of vagabondage and begging" and taking them to the nearest railway stations and towns. Officials in small towns often acted similarly, forcibly putting abandoned children on trains bound for the big cities.[37]

To complicate the situation still further, parents often put their children in orphanages temporarily because of poverty or when they were in transit. This practice went back to the Civil War (it is described in Gladkov's famous novel *Cement*, where Dasha leaves her child in an orphanage that burns down, killing the child), and appears to have been common. The outcomes were various. For two malnourished children of dekulakized parents, who left them as an act of despair on the orphanage doorstep, the orphanage was a life saver; in a material sense, they were better off there than with the family that ultimately reclaimed them. For another child, brought up in a Siberian orphanage after his family fled the Volga famine of 1921, the experience was also positive; his mother did not reclaim him, but he managed to keep in touch with her and his siblings and get an education. But there were also tragedies. A Siberian worker put his small children in the Barnaul orphanage after his wife died and found when he came to claim them that one had died and the other was missing—perhaps sent out to a kolkhoz, but no one knew where.[38]

Juvenile crime, from pickpocketing to hooliganism and violent attacks, was perceived as an increasing problem in the first half of the 1930s. Until 1935, however, the law was relatively lenient on juveniles: for hooliganism, for example, the maximum penalty was two years imprisonment and rehabilitation was preferred to imprisonment for juvenile offenders.[39] The authorities dealing with juvenile crime tended to focus on family circumstances and how to improve them. But this "liberal" approach was abruptly discredited in 1935, after what was perceived as an upsurge in random violence, including murder, on city streets, with juveniles prominent among the perpetrators.

Klim Voroshilov, Politburo member and Minister for Defence, raised the alarm. Citing Soviet newspaper reports on a series of murders and violent assaults in Moscow by two sixteen-year-olds who got only five-year sentences, he claimed that Moscow authorities had on their books "about 3,000 serious adolescent hooligans, of whom about 800 are undoubted bandits, capable of anything." He deplored the courts' mildness toward young hooligans and suggested that, to make the streets of the capital safe again, the NKVD should be instructed to clear Moscow immediately not only of homeless adolescents but also of delinquents out of parental control. "I don't understand why we don't shoot these scoundrels," Voroshilov concluded. "Do we really have to wait until they grow up into still worse bandits?"[40]

Voroshilov's sentiments were fully shared by Stalin, who reportedly was the main author of the law of the Politburo decree of 7 April 1935 "On measures of struggle with crime among minors," which made violent crimes committed by juveniles from twelve years of age punishable as if they were adults.[41] The decree was followed by a law optimistically titled "On the liquidation of child homelessness and lack of supervision," which increased the NKVD's involvement in the handling of homeless and delinquent juveniles and attempted to speed up the process of getting such people off the streets and into appropriate institutions. The law also attempted to protect orphans from exploitation by their guardians (citing particularly illegal taking over of living space and property left after the death of parents) and authorized the militia to fine parents up to 200 rubles for "mischief and street hooliganism" of their children. Parents who did not adequately supervise their children risked having them taken away by the state and placed in orphanages, where the parents would have to pay the cost of their maintenance.[42]

THE ABORTION LAW

There ought to be a law forcing men to take marriage seriously, wrote an Armenian kolkhoznik (male) to President Kalinin. They should not be allowed to keep getting divorced and leaving their children orphaned.[43]

This was the view of many people in the Soviet Union, and by the mid 1930s it was also the regime's view. In May 1936, the government put out a draft law to strengthen the family whose most notorious aspect was the prohibition of abortion. This came as a shock to many party and intelligentsia members, since the removal of Tsarist prohibitions had been a conspicuous part of early Soviet "liberationist" legislation. The announcement was also surprising in its form, for instead of issuing the law in the normal manner, the government was first publishing a draft for public discussion.[44]

The draft law dealt with four main topics: abortion, divorce, child support, and rewards for mothers of many children. It proposed to prohibit abortion except when the mother's life or health was threatened, and punish doctors who performed abortions and persons forcing women to have abortions with up to two years imprisonment. The women themselves were to be "exposed to public contempt"—that is, shamed by having to suffer public discussion and criticism of their conduct, usually at the workplace—and fined for repeat offenses. Divorce was to be made harder to obtain by requiring both parties to be present at divorce proceedings and raising the fee for registering a divorce to 50 rubles for a first divorce, 150 rubles for a second, and 300 rubles for any subsequent divorce. The level of child support was raised to one-third of the absent parent's earnings for one child, half for two children, and 60 percent for three or more children; the penalty for failure to pay child support increased to two years in prison. Finally, mothers with seven children were to receive cash payments of 2,000 rubles a year—a really substantial amount—for five years, with additional payments for each child up to the eleventh (5,000 rubles).

Because the draft that was the basis for discussion presumably contained the government's own position on family issues, there were obvious constraints on the free expression of opinion. Some discussions at workplaces were reportedly formal and unproductive, with those present treating attendance as a duty: at the Moscow "Red Seamstress" factory, for example, "the only person who spoke at the general factory meeting was the one who read out the draft," and a reporter found that at least one of those who remained silent had a strongly negative attitude to the law. But critics were not always so reticent. The labor newspaper *Trud*'s coverage of the discussion, which focused heavily on the abortion issue, included a range of opinions, both positive and negative, even though the debate was accompanied by editorials that took a firm anti-abortion stand based primarily on damage to women's health and ability to bear children.[45]

It would be hard to imagine a greater contrast between the Soviet debate on abortion in the 1930s and the contemporary American debate. The Soviet debate was not at all about the foetus's "right to life" and only marginally about women's right to control their own bodies. Participants on all sides of the urban debate spoke as if it were a given that all right-thinking women would naturally want to have children (though men and some young, irresponsible women might feel differently). The big question at issue in the Soviet debate was what to do about women whose material circumstances were so bad that they felt obliged to deny themselves the happiness of being a mother: should they or should they not be allowed to have abortions? There was virtually no philosophical aspect to the Soviet debate, and not much about ideology. Among the central topics of discussion, as it turned out, were Soviet housing and health-care problems.[46]

One woman told a reporter that, despite having a husband and a good income, she would "do literally anything not to have a second child" and was "prepared to have an abortion under any circumstances." The reasons were her first child's health problems, which required enormous attention, and her housing: "My family lives with another family in a room of 30 meters. Have I the right to allow myself the luxury of bringing a second child into this environment? I think not." Other women (and even the occasional man) wrote in to the newspaper making similar arguments. "I live with three children in a 12-meter room," wrote a Moscow woman accountant. "And however great my desire to have a fourth child, I cannot allow myself to do so." Only a partial ban on abortions was appropriate, a Leningrad engineer (male) argued: decisions should be made on a case-by-case basis after "authoritative commissions" have investigated the pregnant woman's living and housing conditions.[47]

Almost all participants in the discussion agreed or gave lip-service to the idea that access to abortion ought to be restricted. A number of people suggested that the outright prohibition on abortion ought to be restricted to women without children, while the rules for women who already had children should be more lenient. Others suggested a variety of exemptions: for women with three or four children, for young women who wanted to finish their education, for women over forty. There were many suggestions that banning legal abortions would increase the number of underground abortions "and thus the number of crippled women."[48]

The strongest support for the ban on abortion came from women whose past experience with abortion had left them in poor health or made it difficult for them to bear children.

I am 39 years old. But only yesterday I bore my first child. Many years ago I had an abortion. And the result was this. Twice I was pregnant, but could not carry to term. My health, worsening after the abortion, interfered with the proper course of the pregnancy. How ardently I wanted a child! How I cursed myself and that doctor who agreed to give me an abortion.[49]

With regard to the divorce provisions of the law, many women expressed approval for the punitive features, namely increased registration fees for divorce (which were seen as directed primarily at men) and more severe punishment for fathers who did not pay child support. "It's already five years since my husband abandoned the family," said a Stakhanovite woman worker, "and he does not pay any support for the children. Now he won't be able to get out of it. The new law will force such fathers to take care of their children."[50]

Some men spoke against the high charge for registering divorce, arguing that then "divorce will turn into a luxury, accessible only to highly paid categories of workers." But others expressed support for these charges. In discussions at one electrical plant in Moscow, a worker suggested *tripling* the proposed tariff for divorce, so that a first divorce would cost 200 rubles and a third, a thousand rubles. "Men with many wives ought to be prosecuted like criminals," said another worker. But this same man suggested that each divorce must be approached individually by the court, implying that charges should be levied only on "guilty" parties. Another worker made this point explicit, suggesting that a special court should establish who is to blame for the collapse of the marriage and that the cost of the divorce be paid by the guilty party.[51]

The draft law proposed extraordinarily high rates of child support—up to 60 percent of wages. Understandably, this worried many men. As a male office worker from Voronezh wrote:

What if the man has married a second time and has children from the second marriage? That would mean that the second family would live on 40% of his wages. Why should the children of the second family be in worse circumstances? In my opinion, the size of child support payment must not exceed half the wages of the payer.[52]

It also worried women married to men with children from earlier marriages, presumably a sizeable group. One wrote that "the wife in a second marriage is in an exceptionally severe material position," especially if she herself has several children. Such wives, she added, should have the right to have abortions.[53]

Despite the publication of many positive responses to the draft law, the final impression from reading the discussion was that many and perhaps most urban women were deeply dismayed by the proposal to ban abortion. The reaction to other aspects of the draft law was more positive, although some questioned the high child support payments proposed and even those who supported them seemed doubtful of their feasibility. Tightening up of divorce had support, and indications are that at least some participants in the discussion would have welcomed the abolition of "free marriage." (In fact, it was not until 1944 that "free marriage" was abolished, along with very substantial restrictions on divorce.)[54]

After a month of discussion, the decree on abortion became law on 27 May 1936. It was substantially the same as the draft, meaning that the evident public uneasiness, especially among women, about a total prohibition on abortion was disregarded. Of all the exemptions to the abortion ban proposed, the only one adopted (apart from the original "threat to women's life and health") was for women with hereditary diseases. But there was one relatively significant concession, mainly benefiting men: child support payments dropped from a third (stipulated in the draft) to a quarter of wages or salary for one child, from half to a third for two children, and from 60 percent to 50 percent for three and more children.[55]

The outlawing of abortion had a very substantial impact on women's lives. It was sufficiently toughly enforced to produce a noticeable effect on urban births, temporarily reversing their decline and raising the birth rate from under 25 per thousand in 1935 to almost thirty-one per thousand in 1940. Considering that there was no improvement in housing conditions in this period, the associated suffering and discomfort must have been very great. Many women resorted to illegal abortions, but these were dangerous in both the medical and the police sense. Newspapers regularly published short reports of prosecutions of doctors and unqualified medicine women who performed abortions as well as of those who forced women to have abortions (usually their husbands). According to the law, the women themselves were supposed to be subjected to public contempt but not prosecuted. But some memoirs claim that women were sent to prison for having abortions. While this could be a confusion of memory between the 1930s and the tougher postwar period, at least one newspaper report seems to confirm it.[56]

Rewards for Mothers With Many Children

Rewards for mothers was not a burning topic in the public discussion, at least not in its published version. This was presumably because the kind of person who was likely to express opinions on public policy was not the kind of person to have seven or more children. Most people who commented on this provision suggested that the number of children necessary to qualify should be lowered because, as a Moscow electrical worker put it, "When only one person in the family is working . . . it is hard to bring up five or six children without the help of the state." [57] This was one of the suggestions on the draft that was incorporated (albeit in milder form than it was often put) into the final law, where the minimum number of children necessary to qualify was lowered from seven to six.

It was only after the passage of the law that this aspect became a real focus of attention. But it was a different kind of attention than had been given to the proposed prohibition on abortion: this was an issue of *entitlements*, and all over the Soviet Union women started thinking about how to get their share. A month after the law was passed, the head of the Moscow registry office proudly told the press that more than 4,000 applications had already been received in Moscow oblast. Of these families 2,730 had eight children, 1,032 had nine or ten children, and 160 had more than ten. The record was held by a mother in Shakhovskoi district who had fifteen children.[58]

The archives reveal how lively the interest in cash benefits for mothers was: they are full of letters from women (and even a few men) asking about their eligibility. The framers and bureaucratic implementers of the law had obviously given little thought to the subtleties of this issue, but of course it was crucial from the perspective of the individual citizen. Was it necessary to have six *living* children to get the benefits? (The answer to this frequent query was yes.) Did adopted children count? Stepchildren? Children who were foreign citizens? (No.) Was it possible to get the benefit as a father of many children when their mother had died? (No.)[59]

Among the most complicated issues were those involving civil rights. A query of 16 October 1936 from a local soviet official whether families of disfranchised persons were eligible received no answer from central authorities. An inquiry as to whether women whose husbands were in prison were eligible received the answer that they were, provided the husband was imprisoned for a criminal offense and would soon be released. This curious answer opens a window on one of the strangest by-products of the law—the bureaucratic dispute during the Great Purges about whether wives of enemies of the people who happened to have many children were eligible for cash benefits. In October 1937, the Finance Ministry issued a secret instruction that benefits would no longer be paid to women whose husbands had been exposed as enemies of the people. But Vyshinsky, the state prosecutor, protested that the finance ministry had exceeded its competence in giving this instruction.[60]

It is not clear how or even whether the issue was resolved. However, somewhat surprisingly, there really were wives of enemies of the people who tried to collect the benefits. In June 1938, an Armenian peasant woman sent the following plea to Kalinin's office:

> I have seven children. My husband has been arrested and sentenced to be shot with confiscation of property. After my husband's arrest, they expelled me from the kolkhoz. My children are going hungry. They would not give me the benefit for having many children in 1938, citing my husband's arrest. Please mitigate the punishment of my husband and revoke the confiscation of our property.[61]

Her letter received no reply.

THE WIVES' MOVEMENT

"Wives" were an almost unrecognized entity in the first decade and a half after the revolution. An emancipated woman did not define herself by her status vis-à-vis her husband but by her work and activity outside the home. Educated revolutionary women despised housework and tended to consider the upbringing of children as a community rather than family responsibility. For a woman to concern herself primarily with home and family was "bourgeois." Although housewives had the vote, they often seemed to be treated as second-class citizens. "Sometimes I thought that we housewives were not even considered human," one woman complained. Another wrote:

In all my documents it says: housewife. It has been ten years since I graduated from high school and got married, and here I am still putting it down as my meaningful "occupation." During the elections to the soviets I, a healthy young woman, was sitting together with the old people and retired invalids. I suppose that's fair. I am "unorganized population." [62]

In addition to resenting the inferior classification as "housewife," the wives of high-powered industrial managers were often bored, especially when their husbands were posted at new plants in the middle of nowhere with no amenities. In a little volume of personal stories put out by some of the wives (mainly from southern steel plants), they wrote with feeling of the emptiness of life before the wives' movement, when the only events were visiting the hairdresser and going to parties with the same guests and nothing to talk about. Time hung heavy on the wives' hands, and they often quarreled with their husbands because of the latters' involvement in their work. Wives from a prerevolutionary intelligentsia background—as many of the engineers' wives still were—suffered particularly from the loneliness and lack of culture around them, all the more if their husbands developed close relationships with the Communists with whom they worked. One of them recalled her chagrin at finding that, while her husband had a common language with the Communist managers, she had none:

> The more time [my husband] spent at the factory, the more he participated in construction, the larger was the distance between us. He made new acquaintances. They were not just engineers—industrial administrators and party workers began to frequent our house. . . . Ever since childhood, I had been taught to entertain guests. . . . I remember the time when I was an expert at this art. But it turned out that it was not enough to be able to make conversation; one had to know what to talk about. . . . Once, as I was trying to carry on a conversation [with a Communist], I looked at my husband and stopped short. His eyes were full of anxiety and terrible pity. [63]

For wives like this one, seeking an occupation and a way of connecting with the new Soviet society, the emergence of the wives' volunteer movement was a godsend. The movement, known by the name of its journal, *Obshchestvennitsa*, which means woman activist, originated in heavy industry under the patronage of Sergo Ordzhonikidze, Minister of Heavy Industry, and went national in May 1936, when a "conference of wives of managers and engineers in heavy industry" was held in the Kremlin. Stalin, Ordzhonikidze, Voroshilov, and other leaders attended the conference and graciously accepted gifts and effusive tributes from the delegates. Wives of army officers and railroad managers were soon organizing in a similar manner. [64]

One of the problems of organizing housewives in the past had always been the lack of a good basic unit of association on which to build. "Street committees," mobilizing women on the basis of residence, had not been a success. The great discovery of the wives' movement was that wives, like everyone else in Soviet society, could be organized through the workplace—in this case, the *husband's* workplace. Not only the husband's workplace but also his work status was crucial to the movement's internal structure: in any local branch of the movement in industry, it was usually the enterprise director's wife who took the lead.

It was the wives' task to make society in general and their husband's workplace in particular more "cultured." According to one account, the whole movement started when Ordzhonikidze was touring the Urals and noticed a square that the wife of a local industrial manager, Klavdia Surovtseva, had planted with flowers and bushes. Wives were encouraged to furnish workers' dormitories and barracks, organize kindergartens, nurseries, and camps and sanatoria for children, set up literacy schools, libraries, and public baths, supervise factory cafeterias, plant trees, and in general do their best to improve the quality of life at their husbands' plants. Their work was generally unpaid, and the (generally unstated) premise on the financing of their projects was that it would be done by a domestic version of *blat*, that is, getting the director-husbands of the wives to release funds from the enterprise budget.[65]

The wives also did their best to improve their own quality of life, which at distant provincial construction sites, railroad depots, and military bases was often extremely dismal. In Magnitogorsk, the local wives (headed by Maria Zaveniagin, the director's wife) set up a "cultured" cafe in the local theater and acted as patronesses of the arts. At the "Red Profintern" plant, wives set up a fashion atelier. At Krivorog, wives set up a dressmaking shop where a worker could have a dress made for 7 or 8 rubles, and then added a more fashionable atelier for elite women where a dress might cost from 40 to 100 rubles.[66]

A good deal of what the wives did was reminiscent of the charitable activities of upper-class women under the old regime. Some of them, indeed, had been involved in philanthropy before the revolution. Of course the analogy was firmly denied by spokeswomen for the movement, even though the Old Bolshevik Nadezhda Krupskaia (Lenin's widow) came close to making it explicit at the founding conference. "We do not have charity. We have social activism," asserted the movement's journal defensively.[67]

But the high-society, "charity ball" aspect of philanthropy in "bourgeois" society was certainly not absent from the Soviet version. The Magnitogorsk wives organized masked balls that were by invitation only, with "undesirable elements" excluded. Moreover, both local and national branches of the movement cultivated close relations with local political leaders, whom they often addressed in gushing and adulatory tones. The choice of tasteful gifts for political patrons like Lazar Kaganovich, Minister for Transport, was a major concern of the wives, as Galina Shtange's diary attests. In Leningrad, seamstresses at the "Rabotnitsa" factory complained to the local party committee that the local managers' wives were only interested in getting themselves honors and publicity and had wasted the workers' time and the state's money by having workers embroider a picture of comrade Stalin at a cavalry parade as a gift to him. All the workers were indignant at being exploited for the glory of the "wives," the letter claimed.[68]

As this letter implies, the wives' movement had a distinct class base: it was explicitly a form of organization for elite wives, not ordinary working women.

The wives' upper-class manners could grate on Communist managers and workers. Even within the movement, it was sometimes admitted that the wives' relationship with their husband's workforce left something to be desired, since they "still behave in an arrogant manner . . . and speak in the tone of a boss." The addition of wives of Stakhanovite workers to the roster of volunteers did not significantly change either the movement's actual upper-class character or popular recognition of it.[69]

Nevertheless, the wives' movement really did provide an important Soviet socialization experience for many of its members. The wife, quoted above, whose husband had felt "anxiety and terrible pity" for her earlier efforts to entertain Communist visitors now had something to talk about with them and found new common interests with her husband. She and the other volunteers were also inducted into specifically Soviet rituals that their lack of contact with a Soviet workplace had previously denied them. The diary of Galina Shtange, wife of a railroad engineer, chronicles her growing acquaintance with the world of meetings, conferences, publicity photos, and even business trips to other cities, and makes it clear that these rituals were a source of particular enjoyment, satisfaction, and self-respect. Meetings and other formal gatherings of the wives (like those of Komsomols, Young Pioneers, and other voluntary associations) were conducted strictly according to Soviet conventions for "real" business meetings. As Galina Shtange reported her official visit as representative of the wives' movement:

> The room . . . had been decorated with flowers and slogans. In the middle of the room stood a large table, covered with a red tablecloth. The whole Wives' Council, plus stenographers, was already there waiting for us. . . . They seated me at the center of the table, and we had our picture taken. . . . Then the activists from each brigade reported on their work.[70]

One of the major themes of the wives' movement was the obligation of wives to make a comfortable and well-ordered home life for their husbands. "Becoming volunteers, these women did not cease to be wives and mothers," said one delegate at a conference of Red Army wives, and this motif was repeatedly emphasized, particularly in the early phases of the movement. The ideal was represented by someone like the wife of Professor Iakunin, a member of the Moscow regional council of scientists' wives, who did not let her new volunteer duties interfere with her basic vocation as a support to her husband:

> Neither the important and serious business, nor the bulging briefcase, nor the endless telephone calls, give Professor Iakunin any reason to complain about lack of attention to the home from his wife. In her room there is exemplary order and warm, feminine comfort. As before she and she alone manages all the housework; as before, arriving home, her husband meets a welcoming, attentive wife.[71]

But it was not so easy to combine these things in real life. "N. V."—wife of an engineer in Magnitogorsk—started a lively discussion when she wrote in to *Obshchestvennitsa* to ask how she could reconcile her husband's strong desire that she remain at home, look after their child, and, above all, look after him as his "secretary, adviser, nanny, and confidante," and her own feeling that she was wasting her education and being left out of all the exciting things happening in the country.[72]

Readers reacted in various ways. Some were sharply critical of the husband. One critic was reminded of "the country nobleman who will not go to sleep unless a serf scratches his heels" and recommended that N. V. liberate herself as soon as possible from a suffocating, exploitative marriage. Another thought the husband would cope better than N. V. feared if she became active outside the home, citing the example of her own husband, who had learned to shop, cook, and clean now that she worked, without cost to their relationship ("If there has been a change, it has been for the better. We have become closer. We have more in common.") If N. V. did decide to liberate herself, readers were divided as to whether she should go out to work or just become an activist in the wives' movement.[73]

The tentative and sometimes disapproving approach of the wives' movement to women's paid employment was one of its most curious features. After all, this was a decade in which millions of women were entering the workforce and being encouraged to do so. The regime was doing its best to increase the number of women in higher education and the professions and, with less success, to promote women to administrative positions. Women in the Soviet Union were brought up to think they should have careers: as a Harvard Project respondent reported, "at meetings and lectures they constantly told us that women must be fully equal with men, that women can be flyers and naval engineers and anything that men can be." [74]

In "backward" groups, like peasants and Central Asians, the regime was still urging women to stand up for their rights against oppressive husbands and fathers; "wifely duty" was not a theme commonly discussed in Soviet propaganda (outside the wives' movement) in this context. Indeed, even *Obshchestvennitsa* recognized that in the lower classes men were likely to retain attitudes so unenlightened that the issue of women's emancipation still had priority, reporting with respectful sympathy on the hard lives of working-class women who had had to contend with abusive, bullying husbands. All this underlines the elite nature of the wives' movement and suggests that the movement's characteristic themes and attitudes came at least as much from the elite wives themselves as from the regime.

By 1939, in any case, the earlier homemaking emphasis of the wives' movement was giving way to a focus on women learning to do men's work and entering the workforce. This was both an internal development within the movement and a response to the imminence of war and the likelihood that men would soon be conscripted. The journal *Obshchestvennitsa* gave readers many accounts of daring, path-breaking women, high achievers in formerly "male" professions and activities, like the ship's captain Anna Shchetinina, Polina Osipenko's team of female aviators, and the dauntless female automobile drivers who participated in the long-distance race Moscow-Aral Sea-Little Kara-Kum-Moscow. Toughening the body on skis, bicycles, and long hikes was particularly favored in the military branch of the wives' movement. But the women volunteers of the Kuznetsk metallurgical plant were not far behind: under the theme "Ready for anti-chemical [warfare] defence," eleven women activists set off for a hike wearing gasmasks.[75]

Women learned to shoot, drive a truck, and fly planes in the wives' movement. They studied in courses to become "chauffeurs, communications operators, stenographers, accountants." Early on, this was usually represented as a means of making the wives fit partners for their husbands, but it soon became an end in itself, closely linked with preparation for war. Even in 1936, sixty engineers' wives in Gorky learnt to drive "so that at a crucial moment for the native land they can militantly take the wheel." In 1937, Kaganovich told the transport wives (in Galina Shtange's diary rendition) "how we need to be aware of the international situation and be ready at any moment to take the places of our husbands, brothers and sons if they go off to war." By 1939, getting ready to take the men's places in time of war had become one of the central motifs of the volunteer movement, with exhortations directed to mothers as well as wives of prospective soldiers.[76]

By 1938, *Obshchestvennitsa* was writing almost as if a stint as a volunteer was a preparatory stage for wives bound for further education or promotion to administrative work—a kind of elite wives' equivalent of the "workers' faculties" that used to prepare worker promotees for university entrance. Wives' councils sought support for various kinds of training courses that would give the women specialized skills and thus enable them to move into paid employment. Under the heading "A battle plan for women volunteers," *Obshchestvennitsa* editorially deplored both the reluctance of industrial managers to appoint women volunteers to responsible administrative positions and the fact that the leaders of the movement themselves had "limited the range of activities and [had] not prepared the activists for permanent positions in the economy. . . . It is important to understand that a woman who has spent, say, two years as a volunteer, receives training roughly equivalent to one year of political education, and that the experience of volunteer work will be of great help when she gets a permanent position." [77]

When promotion of women occurred in real life, there were likely to be conflicts with husbands and the concept of wifely duty fostered by *Obshchestvennitsa* in its early phase. In the case of Klavdia Surovtseva, the original volunteer gardener noticed by Ordzhonikidze back in 1934–35, this meant getting rid of the husband. Their married life had suffered from her public success with the gardening project ("like many people, he lost his perspective from close up"), and he had been unhappy when she went to Moscow for the 1936 meeting in the Kremlin. At that meeting, Klavdia had taken the pledge to study (following a Stakhanovite rather than volunteer model: in 1936, nobody was stressing study for activist wives), promising "that she would study, would become an engineer. That would be her expression of gratitude to the country for the high award—the order of the Labor Red Banner." In a "Where are they now?" article in 1939, *Obschestvennitsa* revealed that Klavdia was indeed studying in Moscow at the Stalin Industrial Academy. Moreover, she had a new husband, also studying, with whom her relations were on a much more equal basis than her old one: "My husband has taught me how to organize my studies. He is a good friend and a sensitive comrade. We are at the same level. . . ." Showing her college transcript to the reporter, Klavdia said happily, "This is my passport to a new life." [78]

∾ ∾ ∾

There was a gulf between the elite women of the wives' movement and ordinary working women, or even the wives of ordinary workers, and it was not only social but also ideological. For elite wives, duty to husband and family and the task of homemaking were seen as paramount, particularly in the early stage of the movement. Yet these ideals could hardly be applied without qualification to lower-class women who (it was acknowledged) still had to defend themselves against abuse and oppression by unenlightened husbands and fathers. Moreover, such ideals were at least potentially in conflict with an economic goal dear to the regime's heart—that of expanding the labor force by drawing in large numbers of urban women who had not previously worked for wages.

Of course the regime's message about the importance of family responsibilities was not limited to or even mainly directed toward elite wives. As the law against abortion made clear, it was the responsibility of women of all social classes to bear children, whether or not they worked or had adequate housing for their families; and it was the responsibility of their husbands to support them in this endeavor. As far as lower-class women were concerned, however, it was the duty to family, not the duty to husbands, that was usually emphasized. Lower-class husbands were too often delinquent in their own performance of family duties to be a suitable object for too much wifely duty—with the interesting exception of Stakhanovite workers who evidently deserved the same level of support as elite husbands.[79]

At all levels of the society, though most notably at its lower levels, women took the brunt of the manifold problems of everyday life in the Soviet Union—feeding and clothing the family, furnishing and organizing its dwelling space, achieving a modus vivendi with neighbors in communal apartments, and so on. In some cases, the woman who performed these tasks was not the wife and mother of the family, especially if she was educated and worked outside the home, but the grandmother or domestic servant; it should be noted that for all *Obshchestvennitsa*'s efforts, emancipated Soviet women of the younger generation did not take at all kindly to housework. Still, women were increasingly accepting the role of the family's specialists on consumption and taste as well as the upbringing of children. This meant knowing how to get goods, both legally and by *blat*, and how to judge their quality.

A voice noticeably muted, if not silent, in the 1930s was that of educated women with a profession, a job, and an ideology of women's emancipation who did *not* define themselves as wives. Such women had been visible and vocal in the 1920s, often in connection with the Communist Party's Women's Department (closed down in 1930); Stalin's young wife, Nadezhda Alliluyeva, was one of them until her suicide at the end of 1932. They were a minority, to be sure—only about 10 percent of senior administrative jobs were held by women, who constituted about 15 percent of party membership—but then they had also been a minority in the 1920s. Their much lower profile in the 1930s is often attributed to a withdrawal of regime support for the women's cause; yet, if the cause is defined in terms of support for women's entry into higher education, the professions, and responsible administrative jobs, support was *not* withdrawn, at least at the rhetorical level, though it obviously was not one of the regime's top priorities. It seems at least as likely that the muting of this group had practical causes, notably the great difficulties and hardships of everyday life that fell with particular force on working women with dependents. After marriage, or more precisely after the birth of a child, women who worked usually had no time to be activists, regardless of ideology. For this reason, the percentage of Komsomol members who were women (34 percent in 1935) was more than double that of Communists.[80]

7

Conversations and Listeners

The Soviet regime was wary of allowing citizens to express uncensored opinions about matters of public import in public. At the same time, it was extremely anxious to know what people were thinking. This is a contradiction that all repressive, authoritarian regimes must try to resolve. For regimes that consider it too dangerous to allow organized opposition, a free press, or elections in which voters have a real choice of candidates, let alone use the techniques of mass opinion polling that were developing in the capitalist West, the options are limited. The Soviet regime had two ways of finding out about popular opinion: secret police reports and politicians' mail.[1]

The NKVD collected information about public opinion the same way it collected much other information—namely, through snooping by its agents. It is often clear from the content of local reports how the agent (usually anonymous, sometimes identified by a nom de guerre) collected his information: standing in a queue outside a store, frequenting the kolkhoz market, listening to workers' complaints in the factory cafeteria, relaxing in a sauna or bathhouse, or talking to academics at the university. These reports were collated into summaries, which were sent up to the next level. Finally, the central NKVD and its regional branches produced summaries of "the mood of the population" that were circulated regularly to the top leaders.[2]

It was the NKVD's brief to present the bad news —what people in Leningrad were *really* thinking about price rises, what the true (uninflated) industrial production figures for Sverdlovsk were—in contrast to the good news about popular satisfaction and plan fulfillment in their bailiwicks that party and soviet officials habitually presented to the center. Something of this slant can be felt in the NKVD summaries of popular opinion: if the NKVD reported local discussions of the Constitution, for example, seditious and heretical comments were likely to figure prominently.

The second source of information was politicians' mail, that is, the letters individual citizens wrote to central and regional political leaders and institutions like the procuracy, the NKVD, and the newspapers. The newspapers did not often print these letters, but they took them seriously. Complaints were often investigated, denunciations noted, and appeals forwarded to the proper authorities. Newspapers regularly summarized readers' letters on particular issues and sent their summaries to the party leaders.

Most letters were written in the hope of provoking a specific action (provision of a good or service, in the case of appeals; investigation, in the case of complaints; punishment of an enemy, in the case of denunciations). The reason people went on writing them was that the authorities reacted to them: as Jan Gross has suggested, one of the paradoxes of the totalitarian state was that its responsiveness to denunciations made it readily manipulable by individual citizens.[3] But not all letters were written with the intent of furthering the writer's personal interests. A surprising number of people wrote letters to express an opinion about a matter of public policy—and most of these letters were even signed. We cannot tell for sure, any more than Soviet officials could, how representative these letter-writers were of the population as a whole. But at least it can be said that the world of opinion that emerges from citizen's letters is recognizably related to the one that emerges from the NKVD summaries of popular mood.

From the regime's standpoint, a great virtue of citizens' letters was that they provided information on the society in general and bureaucratic malfunctioning in particular. In the first decade after the revolution, the function of exposing local bureaucratic and other abuses belonged to a special corps of volunteer activists known as worker and peasant correspondents who provided this information to newspapers. The correspondents were still active in the collectivization period, and quite a number were murdered for their zeal in exposing kulaks and corrupt officials in their villages. From a local standpoint, of course, the correspondents were often viewed simply as informers and traitors to the local community. Maxim Gorky questioned the wisdom of encouraging so much grass-roots criticism of local bureaucracy, arguing that the constant harping on what was wrong with the Soviet Union undermined people's sense of accomplishment and spoiled the country's reputation in the outside world. But Stalin firmly rejected Gorky's argument, saying the criticism was an essential control over local officials and their habits of arbitrariness and incompetence.[4]

Soviet elections were regular occasions for gathering information on the popular mood. This did *not* mean (as might be assumed in "bourgeois" Western democracies) that the voters expressed their opinions by voting for the candidates of their choice, for these were one-candidate elections. But there were election campaigns, known as "preparation for the elections," in which meetings were held and more or less compulsorily attended by the local population. What was said about issues of the day at the meetings, and still more what was said privately in the corridors afterward, was considered useful information and constituted a regular reporting subject.

Channels of communication between ordinary people and the regime existed in the Soviet Union, but because they were embedded in complicated processes of surveillance and control they can scarcely be considered neutral. People knew they could get arrested for expressing "anti-Soviet" opinions; thus they tended either to refrain from doing so or to express such opinions outside the range of state surveillance (as they hoped). What people "really" thought was hard for the NKVD to get at, and it is no easier for the historian. Some genres of popular expression existed, however, that were less constrained than the official venues of expression (even though the NKVD monitored them too). Jokes, rumors, and the topical songs known as *chastushki* all belonged to a literally subversive realm of popular culture—one in which official values and clichés were turned on their heads.

Meetings of writers, composers, scientists, and professors—particularly off-the-record discussions in the corridors—were the subject of detailed, almost verbatim reports by informers. Conversations in private homes, over the kitchen table, were also reported. All these reports went into the summaries that the NKVD regularly distributed to the party leaders. An example of a "kitchen table" report was the one on the death of Academician Pavlov, a scientist feted by the regime but also feared because of his known distaste for Communism. Like a good gossip columnist, the NKVD agent seemed to have personal access to his celebrities, and this report came directly from the apartment of the deceased. There, "confusion" reigned among the "anti-Soviet types" in Pavlov's family and entourage. Even before the funeral, family, friends, and colleagues were fighting about what to do with his archive and who should succeed him as Institute director. Hostilities continued at the funeral, which was a religious ceremony at the Volkov cemetery. Pavlov's daughter wanted the scientist Leon Orbeli to be Pavlov's successor at the Institute; other family members opposed this.[5]

Agents were equally diligent in reporting on the writers' discussions of "formalism," meaning essentially Western-inspired modernism, in the spring of 1936. These discussions were organized by the Writers' Union after *Pravda*, speaking as mouthpiece for the leaders, condemned Shostakovich's opera, *Lady Macbeth of the Mtsensk District*; they were occasions for the literary community to assimilate the new message, work out how to translate it into practical directives for the field, and, above all, decide which of their members should be scapegoated as "formalists." NKVD informers reported both on the public discussions and on the talk in the corridors. In Leningrad, they said, writers found the task of "drawing conclusions" from *Pravda*'s article on Shostakovich onerous and pointless. Some naive souls like the humorist Mikhail Zoshchenko suggested that "we must stop the discussion since we have all got completely confused." Other more worldly writers wanted to find a way of appearing to satisfy the Kremlin's new anti-formalist line without actually doing anything ("We need to hold a final meeting at which five or six good orators will speak and get out of this episode with honor," Konstantin Fedin suggested.) Aleksei Tolstoy accepted the official premise that formalism was bad, and confessed to having been a formalist himself in earlier works, but did this in such a lively manner that he entertained rather than instructed the audience and thus trivialized the issue. "Alesha has chutzpah," commented the writer Olga Forsh in a conversation in the corridor—speaking, as it turned out, to a wider audience than she thought.[6]

The informers who compiled these reports were obviously insiders, members of the writers' community as well as agents of the police.[7] The complexities of the double role are evident in the next report on the Moscow discussions on formalism. The Muscovites had settled on an obscure young writer—L. I. Dobychin, author of a play called *The Town of N*—as sacrificial lamb. Some were worried about the impact of such sharp criticism on Dobychin; others about its impact on themselves. And indeed Dobychin was shattered; he confided this to his friend—who, under the code name "Seaman," was an NKVD informant. Seaman listened to and duly reported Dobychin's threats of suicide and his wild statements that he would leave Leningrad immediately and abandon his vocation as a writer forever. Then (as Seaman reported) Dobychin vanished, leaving his apartment keys and all his documents including his passport inside the apartment. This disappearance and the suicide threats brought the top brass of the Leningrad NKVD into the picture. Accompanying Seaman's report in the summaries circulated to party leaders was a memo from Leonid Zakovskii, head of the Leningrad branch of the NKVD, noting Dobychin's threats of suicide and stating that he had reportedly gone home to his mother in Briansk and that the police were looking for him.[8]

While Dobychin might have taken some comfort from the thought that his threats of self-destruction were not going unheeded, members of the intelligentsia usually had an understandable dislike for having their private conversations recorded. There are occasions, however, where the substance of a report on intelligentsia conversations leads one to wonder whether somebody (the NKVD informant? the other participants in the discussion?) was sending a message to the people "up there." A case in point is the report of disparaging comments by Leningrad artists on the honors bestowed on participants in the "Ukrainian week" recently held in Moscow, one of a series devoted to the reworked folk art of different republics. The Leningraders thought "ethnics" were being unduly favored and it appears that the informant shared this opinion, since his report presents their arguments as reasonable and contains no negative evaluation. The whole Leningrad artistic community (the informant reported) was saying that the Ukrainian Theater of Opera and Ballet had got awards not for merit but for political reasons, as part of a campaign to exalt non-Russian artists at the Russians' expense. "The Ukrainians presented folk songs and dances [at the week of Ukrainian art held in Moscow in the spring of 1936] and they had no high, serious, art," the respected conductor Samuil Samosud was quoted as saying. "Now in general they [the regime] are praising and rewarding ethnics," said Distinguished Artist Rostovtsev less diplomatically. "They give medals to Armenians, Georgians, Ukrainians—everyone except Russians." [9]

The intensity of the NKVD's surveillance of the intelligentsia was matched by the Politburo's diligence in attending to cultural issues—often issues so specific or even trivial that it is a surprise to find them on the Politburo agenda. Academician Pavlov's funeral, for example, was a Politburo agenda item, and so was theater director Konstantin Stanislavsky's seventy-fifth birthday and the closure of the Meyerhold Theater. It was by Politburo decision that the young violinists Busia Goldshtein, Marina Kozolupova, and Misha Fikhtengolts were added to the list of Soviet violinists competing at the Brussels international competition in 1937; and the Politburo similarly approved the selection of Emil Gilels and other competitors for the international pianists' competition in 1938.[10]

In the late 1920s, the Politburo's agenda had contained many items having to do with the censoring of various plays. This became less common in the 1930s, but a Moscow Arts Theater production of Bulgakov's play *Molière* made the Politburo agenda in 1936, as did Eisenstein's film *Bezhin Meadow* (which the Politburo ruled should not be shown).[11] The Bolshoi Theater was a constant object of worried scrutiny: in 1932, for example, we find the OGPU reporting highly critically on its political condition, appending a long list of "antisoviet elements" working for the theater, including religious believers, anti-Semites, persons with foreign ties, and people who criticized Soviet power.[12]

In January 1935, the Politburo decided to establish a high-level permanent commission to supervise the activity of state theaters under the chairmanship of opera buff Klim Voroshilov. The Politburo also ruled in May 1936 that modern paintings of "a formalist and crudely naturalist character" should be removed from the general exhibition halls of the Tretiakov Gallery in Moscow and the Russian Museum in Leningrad, recommending at the same time that a special exhibition of "realist" artists Repin, Surikov, and Rembrandt should be mounted.[13]

LISTENING IN

The NKVD's reporting function was separate from its punitive function, although the two sometimes overlapped when the NKVD decided to arrest someone for expressing a particularly egregious anti-Soviet opinion. But the NKVD was not the only government agency involved in reporting the popular mood. The party, the Komsomol, and the Army's political administration all made regular reports on the mood of their particular constituencies; these agencies and might feel called on to discipline individual members whose mood was conspicuously disaffected. Even agencies like the census bureau and local electoral commissions were drawn in to report on the popular mood.

The basic analytical categories that the NKVD and other agencies used to distinguish subgroups of the population were workers, intelligentsia, kolkhozniks, and youth. Popular opinions were generally characterized as "favorable" or "hostile" to the regime. Reactions to economic crises like the famine of 1932–33 and the bread shortages of 1936–37 were particularly closely watched. Special reports were also commissioned on major policy changes like the end of rationing, and on big public events like a national show trial or the death of a political leader.

The reports on the popular mood of 1929–30 include a much greater variety of critical comments, especially criticism based on an explicit ideological position, than was the case later in the 1930s. This probably reflected both a decline in political consciousness in the course of the 1930s and a greatly increased fear of the consequences of careless political talk. In 1930, *Pravda*'s summary of unpublished letters ("the most characteristic extracts" was how it explained its choices) showed this variety. Food shortages and complaints about breadlines figured prominently, expressive not only of the population's indignation but also (in contrast to later complaints) of its surprise that goods should suddenly be so scarce. From Odessa came reports that housewives had attacked local cooperative stores with cries of "Down with industrialization, give us bread." From Novorossiisk came statements of outrage that grain was being exported while the workers went hungry.[14]

There were reports of rising popular anti-Semitism associated with the economic crisis: "People say that 'Yids' are buying up silver. The disappearance of change coins is the work of 'the hands of Yids.'" Jewish artisans, for their part, complained of being victimized by the regime's social discrimination policies: their artels had been closed down as part of the drive against private business, they had been stripped of their civil rights and evicted from their premises, and, as disfranchised persons, they found it very difficult to find work.[15]

Stalin's letter "Dizzy with success," blaming local officials for excesses in collectivization, came in for a lot of comment in the *Pravda* summaries. Some said it was Moscow, not local officials, that was responsible for collectivization excesses. Others said Stalin was a Rightist and his statement "a powerful tool in the hands of the hostile camp," in the words of a signed letter from Odessa that *Pravda* decided to include in full. If Stalin was going to destroy everything that had been achieved, all thinking citizens, especially old revolutionaries, were bound to rebuke him, the Odessa writer stated. "I hope that comrade Stalin recognizes his error and returns to the correct path."[16]

Policy changes like the one announced in "Dizzy with success" were often the subject of special opinion summaries. These described both favorable and unfavorable reactions, the latter often in more detail, and also sometimes discussed the way people interpreted the intent and likely consequences of a new law or policy. Apropos of the law of May 1932 on the legalization of peasant markets, for example, a summary of the opinions of agricultural experts noted that some approved the law as a return to NEP and "a break with the general line of the party," while others said it was too late and would have no effect "since there is no food in the village and they don't have anything to trade with anyhow." [17]

Some policies provoked uniformly negative reactions. When prices on consumer goods doubled in 1939, popular comments were hostile and resentful. Many complained that Molotov had deceived them in his earlier statements: "Molotov says that prices on everything will get lower, but in fact they get higher and by a great deal." One woman worker quoted Stalin's "Life has become better" slogan with heavy irony: "Life has become better, life has become more cheerful—everything [is] for the bosses, they raised their salaries." Reactions of workers to the 1940 labor discipline law were equally outraged. One lathe operator who had been prosecuted under the law for being 30 minutes late for work told interrogators "the law is oppression for the workers, as in a capitalist country" (he was sentenced to three years). Other workers were overheard saying "This law is rotten; Trotskyites wrote it." [18]

Kirov's murder, like President Kennedy's in the United States, provoked endless popular speculation and discussion, both at the time and later. The contemporary reaction may even have been magnified by the intensity of the regime's monitoring of it. Certainly the reports are likely to have shaken up the leadership, because they revealed a depth and breadth of hostility to the Communist regime that is quite striking, especially in view of the fact that Kirov was supposed to be one of the most popular party leaders.

One sailor was arrested after stating, "I am not sorry for Kirov. Let them kill Stalin. I will not be sorry for him." Reactions like that sailor's abounded in the Komsomol organizations of the Smolensk region, whose reactions were the subject of a detailed report early in 1935. At a teachers' college, some students admired Kirov's murderer: "Nikolaev was a bold man, decisive, brave. In general, Nikolaev is a hero because he did such a deed, like [the nineteenth-century terrorist] Sofia Perovskaia." Many considered it as a judgment on and warning to the party leadership. Songs with variants of the refrain "They killed Kirov / They [we] will kill Stalin" went the rounds, and other remarks on the desirability of killing Stalin were reported. "Down with Soviet power, when I grow up, I will kill Stalin," said a 9-year-old schoolboy. [19]

NKVD reports also monitored public opinion about international affairs, a subject that was extensively covered in the Soviet press and, it appears, read with more interest than might be expected by the general public. [20] Although the heavy newspaper coverage of Hitler and the Nazi party was unrelentingly hostile, some readers had drawn other conclusions. Recording various reactions among the Soviet public to Hitler's march into the Rheinland in 1936, the NKVD mood-watchers noted the opinion that Soviet foreign policy was too soft and Hitler's boldness was to be admired. Hitler was described as charismatic, "very intelligent," and a man who had worked his way up from the bottom; a student said, "The Fascists are constructing socialism in a peaceful way. Hitler and the fascists are clever people." In the hungry winter of 1936–37, approving comments on Hitler multiplied. "People say 'Better in Germany.' 'If Hitler takes power, it will be better in Russia. Only Hitler can give life to the people.'" [21]

The Spanish Civil War was the international event of the decade for the Soviet public, heavily covered in the newspapers and provoking some real enthusiasm among the young as well as some more dubious responses. An NKVD report on public opinion of November 1936 said that many workers were enthusiastic, volunteering to go and fight in Spain, and willing to sacrifice up to 1 percent of their pay in the Spanish cause. Inevitably, there was resentment at the thought that the Soviet government was spending money on Spain while people at home were in want. "Your children don't see chocolate and butter, and we are sending them to Spanish workers"; "How can we sell grain. We ourselves are starving. Let the government stop sending grain to Spain, then there will be a lot of extra grain." There were also more profoundly hostile comments: one worker was quoted as saying, apropos of aid to Spanish workers, "Let them only arm our workers, then 50–60% would take up arms against the Soviets." [22] That Spain lingered in the popular memory is evident from the references to it that continued to be made in other contexts. During the 1937 elections, for example, a Dnepropetrovsk kolkhoznik commented sadly: "If the workers of Spain knew how we live, they would not have struggled for freedom." [23]

The NKVD kept a careful eye on youth, both Communist and other. The fictional Sasha in Rybakov's novel *Children of the Arbat* was not the only young Komsomol member to fall into its hands, even before the Great Purges. Periodically, the NKVD discovered small "counterrevolutionary" organizations of young people. In Leningrad, for example, between December 1933 and 15 May 1934 police discovered eight such groups of schoolchildren and young workers, including the Fascist "Society for the Rebirth of Russia," a nationalist organization of ethnic-minority students who wanted to found a "Great Finnish republic," and various "terrorist" organizations (that did not accomplish any terrorist acts). In Voronezh, the police reported some support for terrorism, fascism, and Trotskyism among high school pupils in 1937, and noted swastikas painted on walls and the prevalence of anti-Soviet rumors, especially in connection with the food shortages of the past winter. A technical student said, "If only war would start soon, I would be the first to destroy the Communists." [24]

The Leningrad police was also concerned about the demoralizing influence gangs of homeless children were having on schoolchildren in the city. Criminal and hooligan behavior was still surrounded by a "romantic oreole" in the eyes of Leningrad's young people, the police reported. Knife-fights and gangs were common, and young people "at the great majority of enterprises and schools" were carrying knives, knuckle-dusters, and other weapons. The homeless children corrupted other young people by organizing drinking parties with them, "as a result of which children started to leave their parents to go and live with the homeless children." [25]

The NKVD took these signs of disaffection among youth seriously, although the frequency and content of their reports do not indicate that this was regarded as a top-priority problem. Some of the events that alarmed the authorities seem trivial or even laughable. One such case was the "counter revolutionary game" organized among local children in Leningrad by a twelve-year-old troublemaker, Aleksei Dudkin, son of a Communist. Dudkin Jr. had a history of ingeniously disruptive behavior—drawing swastikas on the foreheads of other children, organizing public prayers in class, inciting his friends to steal money from their parents and run away into the taiga, and taking them to beg at the Finland Station. The exploit that got the NKVD involved was the game he organized called "counterrevolutionary Trotskyite-Zinovievite band." This was a kind of cops and robbers game in which Dudkin himself played the part of Zinoviev, while other children took the roles of Trotsky, Kirov, Kamenev, Nikolaev (Kirov's killer), and an NKVD official. The first part of the game reenacted the murder of Kirov. The scenario for the second—presumably the really alarming part to the authorities, though the gang never got to play it—was to have been the murder of Stalin by the same terrorist gang of counterrevolutionary terrorists.[26]

Suicide

Suicides were a matter of great concern to the authorities. We have already seen one case (that of the young writer Dobychin) where the NKVD reacted with alarm to a suicide threat conveyed to them by an informant. Actual suicides—of Communists and Komsomol members, but also of ordinary citizens—were carefully investigated, for this was one of the regime's indices of social and political health: suicides were understood as signals that something had gone wrong. This concern went back to the 1920s, when social statisticians had gathered and published quantitative data on suicide. The poet Sergei Esenin's suicide in the mid 1920s, which allegedly turned the thoughts of many young people to suicide, sparked one of the more curious political debates between Stalinists and Oppositionists, in which each side accused the other of responsibility for the "degeneration of the revolution" and the consequent disillusionment of idealistic youth. In the 1930s, the public debate and the publication of statistics on suicide ceased, but the authorities' concern remained. The Red Army's political administration was particularly diligent in monitoring and investigating suicides within its ranks.[27]

Any suicide of a Komsomol member, Communist, Red Army man, worker, or rural teacher was likely to be closely investigated, usually with a view to seeing if local officials had driven the victim to the act by persecution or refusal of support in difficult conditions. Even suicides of kolkhozniks were regular reporting subjects, which is surprising given the regime's general lack of interest in the village's internal culture and social problems. In 1936, the NKVD circulated a report on investigations of sixty suicides in Ukrainian villages that found that twenty-six were associated with harsh treatment by officials and activists, nine with harassment and slander, eight with illegal expulsion from the kolkhoz, and seven with loss of reputation. A similar report on seventeen suicides in a district of Karelia over a fifteen-month period (1933–34) found that hunger ("shortage of bread") was the most frequent cause (three cases), followed by drunkenness (two) and persecution and intimidation (two). The other reasons for suicide were heavy taxes, embezzlement, family quarrels, publish shaming, and "lack of desire to live under Soviet power" (one case each). The circumstances of each case were briefly summarized in the reports. In the 1936 report, for example, one of the suicides was that of a brigade leader of a tractor brigade who cut his throat with a razor because he had used up his allowance of fuel and therefore could not fulfill his plan.[28]

The attempted suicides of five women working on a state farm were the subject of another investigation. These women were in the award-winning Stakhanovite category whose troubles always rated special attention. The suicide attempts were found to be associated with extremely poor living and working conditions, cruel abuse and insults from other workers, and a demoralizing atmosphere of "sexual depravity and licentiousness."[29]

Sex and disappointed love figured, as one might expect, in suicide reports. An investigation of the suicide of a woman tractor-driver found that her motive was despair on being abandoned by a faithless married lover, who was subsequently charged with responsibility for her death. A romantic tragedy lay behind one of the suicides investigated by Siberian authorities. A Komsomol official, teacher of history and social studies, fell in love with the daughter of a kulak deprived of voting rights. She refused to marry him because of his party connections (or so the report claims: it may have been vice versa) and he killed himself. He was much admired locally, and other suicides followed among the young, as well as a cult of his memory, à la Mayakovsky, the famous revolutionary writer who committed suicide in 1930.[30]

Although some suicides turned out to have personal motives, the underlying premise of Soviet suicide investigations was that the person who killed him- or herself was likely to be sending a message to the state. This seems to have been literally true in a surprising number of cases: it was a culture in which the equivalent of "Look what you made me do!" (directed at the regime) was a common form of self-justification. A suicide might give "lack of desire to live under Soviet power" as his motive; a man who murdered his children might greet the police with the accusatory statement "Look what Soviet power has brought us to!" Of course, this is not to say that these were the "real" motives. But they were plausible motives, which would not have been the case in many societies. It made sense to Soviet citizens that whatever went wrong was the regime's fault, just as it made sense to the Soviet regime that any action by a citizen, however personal and individual it might appear, had an underlying political meaning.[31]

A case of a double suicide that was overtly and unmistakably a message to the regime was recorded in the diary of a Communist sent out to investigate. Two activist brothers, village-dwelling workers who were serving as rural soviet chairman and kolkhoz chairman, became embroiled in conflict with the district authorities in the winter of 1930 because the brothers favored voluntary collectivization and the district officials wanted to force the pace. "I went to the izba of rural soviet chairman Peter Anikeev," recorded the diarist. "A cold body was awaiting burial. I went to Andrei Anikeev. He was alive, but it was his last hours. He said that the district people were going against the party. He and his brother decided to protest and shoot themselves with a revolver so as to call the attention of the center to this arbitrary behavior." The pathos of this message was all the greater for the fact (prudently not remarked on by the diarist) that it was not the district officials but rather the idealistic Anikeevs who had misunderstood the party line.[32]

Another kind of message, an apology for not having the stamina to make it to the end, was left by a woman student in a military academy who killed herself in the early 1930s. Although her suicide note was formally addressed to her husband, its tone and content suggest that the party was the true addressee ("I die because I have not enough strength for further struggle to correct the general line of the party")—and indeed the suicide was investigated in painstaking detail by the authorities of the Airforce Academy in which she was studying. Polina Sitnikova, born in a white-collar family in Riga in 1900, had joined both the Communist Party and the Red Army during the Civil War, when she was eighteen. Her first husband died at the front; a second, a pilot, was killed in a plane crash in which Polina also suffered serious injuries. She had an apparently happy family life with her third husband, described as devoted to her, and her young daughter, in a comfortable apartment shared with a servant with a daughter of the same age who looked after the two girls. All of Polina's problems had to do with the Airforce Academy where she had been sent to study in the early 1930s. She found the work hard, and constantly complained of poor health (she had had pulmonary tuberculosis) and tiredness. She thought the other (male) students mocked her and had no respect for her revolutionary pedigree. At the Academy, she wept whenever her work was criticized or she was needled by other students (as in the ironic greeting, "How's comrade Sitnikova feeling today?"). The investigation found no hint of political content in her conflicts at school, so the meaning of her reference to the "general line of the party" remains unclear: probably it was just an effort to dignify her death and diminish her sense of personal failure.[33]

Political suicides were in a category of their own. In Bolshevik revolutionary tradition, suicide was an honorable way of registering a moral protest or exiting from an impossible situation; it had a heroic ring. The suicide of the Trotskyite Adolf Ioffe in December 1927 was a moral protest suicide. So, in part, may have been the suicide of Stalin's wife, Nadezhda Alliluena, at the end of 1932. By the mid 1930s, however, the party leaders started trying to squelch this tradition by either refusing to publicize political suicides or representing them as cowardly or despicable acts. Suicide still sometimes served to rescue a besmirched reputation. But increasingly it was being publicly interpreted as a sign of guilt: Panas Liubchenko, former chairman of the Ukrainian Sovnarkom, was said to have been "entangled in his anti-soviet connections and fearing responsibility before the Ukrainian people for betraying the interests of the Ukraine" when he killed himself in September 1937, and a similar formula had been used on the suicide of Red Army leader Ian Gamarnik a few months earlier.[34]

The hard-line interpretation of suicide was stingingly put forward by Stalin, speaking at the December 1936 plenum of the Central Committee on the death of a Moscow party official named Furer, whose suicide was noteworthy in that he himself had not been accused; the act was a protest against the arrest of a friend and colleague that he regarded as unjust. Some might see this gesture as noble, Stalin said.

> But a person arrives at suicide because he is afraid that everything will be revealed and he does not want to witness his own public disgrace. . . . There you have one of the last sharp and easiest means that, before death, leaving this world, one can for the last time spit on the party, betray the party.[35]

WRITING TO THE GOVERNMENT

Soviet citizens were great writers of complaints, petitions, denunciations, and other letters to the authorities. They wrote (generally individually, not collectively), and the authorities often responded.[36] It was one of the best-functioning channels of communication between citizens and the state, offering ordinary people without official connections one of the few available ways of redressing a wrong or provoking official action on the writer's behalf. To some degree, the widespread practice of writing to the government—old-fashioned and redolent of premodern petitioning though it might be—filled the gaps left by the restriction of association and collective action and the weakness of legal processes in the Soviet Union. With only a hint of embarrassment at the paternalist implications of the practice, Soviet official spokesmen boldly claimed that it demonstrated the strength of Soviet democracy and the uniquely direct nature of the link between citizens and the regime.

Writing letters to the authorities was a way in which Soviet citizens participate in the "struggle with bureaucratism" and the "struggle for socialist legality," wrote one Soviet commentator in the mid 1930s. Bourgeois democracies had no equivalent form of direct citizen action, he claimed. "Feeling themselves masters of the country, workers and kolkhozniks cannot pass by violations of the general interests of their state": they write to Stalin, Molotov, Kalinin, and other leaders about "theft of socialist property, administrative abuses, class enemies in the bureaucracy, and all kinds of injustices." Of course these injustices were usually personally experienced rather than abstractly deplored:

> Someone has been incorrectly evicted from an apartment, someone was refused an apartment to which he had undoubted right, someone was fired from an institution, blamed for offences he did not commit. Someone shows unreasonable zeal, shows "vigilance" and throws an innocent man off the deck of Soviet life. Another pays back for a bold word of self-criticism with repressions.[37]

Party leaders spent a lot of time on letters. Kalinin, one of the biggest recipients, was said to have received more than one and a half million written and oral petitions over the years 1923–35. Mikhail Khataevich, regional party secretary in Dnepropetrovsk, described this kind of correspondence as a major part of the regional secretary's workload: "Not counting business correspondence, I receive 250 letters of, so to speak, a personal character every day, letters from workers and kolkhozniks. Out of those letters I can and do read 30, and reply personally to the majority." Khataevich's claim may have been somewhat exaggerated, but his basic point about the volume of citizens' letters was correct. Andrei Zhdanov, regional party secretary in Leningrad, received an average of 130 letters a day throughout 1936, according to a careful accounting by his office, and another 45 letters a day were going to the Leningrad soviet. The Leningrad procurator's office, the largest recipient of citizens' letters in Leningrad, was handling almost 600 a day.[38]

Many Soviet citizens evidently shared the authorities' belief that letter-writing was a democratic practice that brought citizens closer to their government. This is how a young Russian (post-Soviet) historian interprets letters complaining about food shortages in the late 1930s. "Although they criticize and sometimes abuse the existing ways of doing things, all the same they appeal to the regime as 'their own people's [power],'" she writes. "The authors are convinced that the government not only can but must help people. The recognition of the regime as legitimate, 'their's,' determines the form of appeal to the leaders and also the system of argumentation—references to authorities held sacred by that regime (Marx, Lenin, Stalin, *The Short Course of History of the Communist Party* and so on)." While it would clearly have been counterproductive for citizens making complaints and appeals to deny the regime's legitimacy, this comment nevertheless rings true for many citizens' letters. It could also be argued that leaders like Khataevich themselves felt more "legitimate" as a result of the letters they received and responded to, playing the role of "benevolent father" and corrector of injustices that many of the letters required.[39]

The authorities strongly encouraged letters from individual citizens but were less enthusiastic about collective ones. "Let's say you write an application, and that you put in a request for something and several men sign it," said one former Soviet citizen in a postwar interview. "That's *gruppovshchina* [pejorative term for group action]. Immediately, the local Communist Party and trade union people will call one guy after another and reprimand him. But they will not call the whole group, they will deal with each individual, separately."[40] People sometimes did write collective letters, however, despite this danger. In Zhdanov's Leningrad files for 1935, the ratio of collective to individual letters is roughly 1:15, with the collective letters addressing such subjects as closing of bars, late payment of wages, need for clean water, street crime, and reinstatement of a colleague who had been fired.[41]

Some letters, including signed ones, were written to state an opinion or offer advice on public policy. To take a fairly random sample: a worker wrote to Molotov (recently appointed Minister for Foreign Affairs) to advise him on diplomacy ("Don't trust the British, the French or the Germans. They all want to harm the USSR"). A Soviet employee from Pskov wrote to Kirov suggesting that measures be taken to prevent malnutrition among schoolchildren. A Leningrader wrote to another Leningrad party secretary bemoaning the defeats of Leningrad's two football teams and asking him to do something about it.[42]

In the Leningrad letter files, writers of "opinion" letters were often workers whose letters showed both a degree of identification with the Soviet regime and readiness (even in the mid 1930s) to admonish it. One worker wrote to Kirov in 1932 to complain about food shortages: "Is it known to you, comrade Kirov, that among the overwhelming majority of workers, and not bad workers, there exist great discontent and lack of confidence in the decisions that the party is taking?" Such workers often criticized the emergence of a privileged class of bureaucrats. The bosses have become a "caste," wrote one of them in 1937; the party has "got too big for its boots." Among workers, "all I hear is cursing Soviet power." Another writer deplored the fact that the party had lost its contacts with the masses, the party leaders from the party rank-and-file, factory managers from the workers: no wonder so much wrecking had been uncovered—and there was more to come! The leaders were risking the fate of Antaeus in the Greek myth, who perished after he lost contact with the earth.[43]

The practice of letter-writing involved two-way surveillance, for it was both part of popular surveillance over bureaucracy and of the regime's gathering of information on citizens. But the authorities also used citizens' private correspondence as a source of information, and here the surveillance was only one way. The regime's purpose in perlustration (which it began to practice shortly after the revolution) was both to catch individual wrongdoers and get a different angle on social processes and popular opinion. A kolkhoznik, Nikolai Bystrov, was one of those whose letter was opened and found its way into the Leningrad party archive. Bystrov had been drafted from the kolkhoz to work on timber cutting in Karelia and, as was usual for draftees, he had taken a kolkhoz horse. Finding that there was no food in the logging camps and many people were running away and abandoning their horses, he wrote to the leaders of his kolkhoz to tell them that he too was thinking of running away and needed their advice about what to do about the horse.[44]

Sometimes citizens forwarded private letters they had received to the authorities. For example, a Communist student sent on to the Central Control Commission a private letter he had received from another Communist, with whom he had worked on the sowing campaign in 1932. The letter was full of anguish at the famine ("the muzhik is starving," there is "cannibalism in Kazakhstan"), the disarray of the leaders ("Stalin is frantic"), and repression ("writers are being driven into the grave"). After Stalin himself read the letter, adding some indignant comments in the margins, the forwarder was called in for questioning. (Probably the author was arrested, but this is not clear from the file.[45])

On rare occasions, the Leningrad NKVD compiled summaries of data from intercepted private correspondence and sent them in along with their regular summaries from informants' reports. This happened during the food crisis in the winter of 1936–37, which was a top priority reporting subject for the

NKVD for months. The correspondence quoted, intercepted on its way into and out of the city of Leningrad, contained harrowing descriptions of hardship—including what the NKVD labeled "provocative information" on the absence of basic foods from Leningrad stores—as well as reports of rumors. "They are saying here [in Kostroma] that the whole of Peter [Leningrad] is to be put on bread rationing and they also say something about a Bartholomew Day's massacre—only don't tell anyone," a father wrote to his daughters in Leningrad. The writers used language they would not have used in writing to the authorities: for example, "I don't know how the Lord will help us to bear this." They discussed, albeit delicately, the regime's responsibility for the crisis. "You come and see what is happening in the city from the morning," wrote a wife in Vologda, clearly an educated woman, to her scientist husband in Leningrad. "They get in line from 12 o'clock at night and even earlier. What do you think, who is to blame for this. I wonder if they know about it in the center. There is not a single word about bread in the paper."[46]

PUBLIC TALK

"Public discussion" (*narodnoe obsuzhdenie*) was an experiment that was tried twice, both times in 1936. The subjects were the abortion law (discussed in Chapter 6) and the new Constitution. It may have been part of an unsuccessful effort at democratization, as Arch Getty has argued, or simply a new form of information gathering about public opinion.[47] In any case, it was not repeated. As we have seen in the case of the abortion debate, "public discussion" had many constraints. There was always the danger that the statement of unorthodox views would bring trouble from the NKVD. Moreover, the regime had stated its position at the beginning, with the publication of the draft law on abortion and the draft Constitution, and major changes were scarcely to be expected and did not in fact occur.

From the standpoint of the NKVD (and of later historians), however, the Constitution discussion was definitely worthwhile, for it generated a mass of useful information on popular opinion on a wide variety of topics, including some that were rarely addressed in other forums. This was not so much because people spoke up at the meetings as because they talked in the corridors (reported, as always, by the NKVD) and wrote large number of letters about the Constitution to newspapers and government agencies. These letters were summarized by the recipient agencies and sent up to the party leaders, according to standard procedure. In some cases, the summaries distinguished a special category of "hostile" comments.[48]

Public discussion meant that meetings were organized at all workplaces, with attendance virtually compulsory. People often came to the meetings unwillingly and complained that the whole process was a waste of time. "The workers are all literate, they read the papers, there's nothing to discuss," workers at some Leningrad factories complained; some refused to attend the meetings. At the Maxim Gorky Weaving Plant in the Ivanovo region, management locked the doors and posted a guard beside them to prevent workers from leaving the meeting, which took place after work. This was deeply resented by the workers, most of whom were women with duties awaiting them at home. "You have posted a guard and are holding us by force," one woman protested. Another complained: "My children are left at home, and you don't let me out." This meeting went completely awry when a group of workers got past the guard by a ruse and "opened the doors with a shout," at which forty people immediately left, "Those who didn't manage to leave sat on the staircase and slept until the end." [49]

One of the substantive policy issues raised in the Constitution discussion (primarily in letters rather than public meetings, it seems) was the abolition of discrimination, including deprivation of rights, on grounds of social class. The draft Constitution incorporated this important policy change, which was subsequently enacted into law (see Chapter 5). But not everyone approved—in fact, the majority of letters dealing with this issue were uneasy about ending discrimination. One writer was dubious about giving vote to former kulaks, who might use their new status in society to take revenge on activists. Another said he was not opposed to giving the vote to some disfranchised persons who had earned it, but drew the line at allowing priests to vote or run for office. "Celebrating a religious service is not socially useful labor." [50]

Similar reservations were expressed about article 124 of the Constitution guaranteeing freedom of religion, which one writer proposed replacing with an injunction "to categorically forbid the work of churches that stupefy the people" (by which he evidently meant all churches) and "convert the buildings of churches into houses of culture." But article 124 also had its articulate defenders, namely priests and religious believers. They not only praised the Constitution's guarantee of religious toleration but immediately sought to put it into practice, petitioning for the reopening of churches that had been forcibly closed earlier in the decade, seeking jobs in the collective farms and rural soviets that had hitherto been closed to them, and even trying to run religious candidates in the national soviet elections of 1937. [51]

Although the public discussion of the Constitution did not produce important changes, it would be misleading to assume that it had no benefits for the populace. As Sarah Davies has pointed out, this discussion brought a new vocabulary of rights into popular use. A young kolkhoznik asserting his right to leave the kolkhoz for further education wrote: "I consider that each citizen, including the kolkhoznik, has the right to education. *It says so in the draft of the new Constitution.*" Such assertions became common, and this represented a real change. The old (1918) Constitution had never been used in the same way as a touchstone in popular pleading, and law-based arguments in general had not been much in favor since the Revolution. [52]

The change, undoubtedly, was not altogether a happy one from the regime's standpoint. The new Constitution was remarkably generous in the rights it promised the population: article 125 guaranteed freedom of speech, freedom of the press, freedom of assembly, and freedom of street processions and demonstrations, none of which in fact existed in the Soviet Union either before or after the promulgation of the new Constitution. [53] Judging by the comments reported from the public discussion, people did not take these

promises seriously (in contrast to those on religious toleration, which some
hoped and others feared would be kept), but the discrepancy between promises and reality provoked indignant and satirical reactions.

> It's all lies what they write in the draft of the new constitution, that each citizen
> can write in the press and speak out. Of course it isn't so, you try speaking up,
> tell how many people died of hunger in the USSR and you'll get 10 years.

(This pungent comment was rightly classified as "hostile" in the summary.[54])

The Constitution was a fraud, many agreed: "They publish laws and they all
lie." Equality of rights was an empty promise. "We don't have equal rights and
won't have. Our business is to work like horses and get nothing for it, and the
Jew does nothing, sits in power, and lives at our expense." Even if equal rights
were not a fraud, the Soviet regime should get no credit for them: they were
just put in the Constitution because "foreign powers put pressure on the Soviet Union" (this speaker added ominously that soon "the regime will change
altogether"). Even the right to possess and inherit personal property —which
actually existed in practice, even if not fully reliably—aroused the wrath of
some: a former member of the Socialist-Revolutionary Party described it as
"advantageous only for communists, who have seized for themselves many
valuables at the time of the revolution and want to hang on to it." [55]

The satirical instincts of the population were strongly aroused by the clause
in the Constitution that, following Marx, affirmed the principle that "he who
does not work, does not eat." "It's not true," said one wit, "in practice we
have the opposite: he who works does not eat, and he who does not work,
eats." Another suggested that "He who does not work, does not eat" should
be replaced with the slogan "He who works *should* eat." [56] These comments
were mainly from kolkhozniks, and their frequency no doubt owed something to the fact that this was the beginning of the hungry winter after the bad
harvest of 1936. Still, kolkhozniks had other bones to pick with the Constitution. It did not escape their attention that the old age and disability pensions
and vacation arrangements promised, as if to the whole population, in art.
120 were in fact available only to wage and salary earners in the towns. "This
Constitution is good only for workers," one kolkhoznik complained.[57]

Elections

Elections in the Soviet Union were single-candidate affairs, with one partial
exception to be discussed; and the national parliament to which deputies were
elected had no real political power. The authorities nominated the candidates,
doing their best to give due representation in each district to workers, peasants, intelligentsia, women, Stakhanovites, Communists, non-Communists,
and Komsomol members, and local meetings were held to discuss their candidacy and other questions of the day.[58] As we know, a proportion of the population was disenfranchised on social grounds, and urban votes were heavily
weighted over rural.

Election day was organized as a celebration, but strong pressure was put on
the population to vote and turnouts were always high (at least according to
official figures). Some people found the ritual of voting uplifting: "I felt a kind

of excitement in my soul, I don't know why, and there was even a lump in my throat," wrote Galina Shtange in her diary after voting in the 1937 elections. Galina's sister Olga, living in miserable and penurious circumstances in Leningrad, wrote to her in similar vein: "This morning at 8 a.m. I went to vote and with a clear conscience I turned in my ballot for Litvinov and Kalinin. As I dropped my envelope into the ballot box I felt with my whole being the truth of the Arabic saying 'The tiniest little fish can stir the depths of the ocean.'" [59]

Since voters could not choose between candidates, the elections themselves did not yield much information for the regime about popular mood, except for some marginal variations in the number of nonvoters or ballot-spoilers. The preparatory meetings before the elections did yield information, however, and were the subject of regular reporting. Nor should we exaggerate the non-eventfulness of Soviet elections: in the prewar years, they were not always as humdrum and conflict-free as their later counterparts. Out of four national (All-Union) soviet elections in the period from the First Five-Year Plan to the Second World War, two—the election of 1929 and that of 1937—had their own elements of drama.

The 1929 elections were noisy and tumultous, with many "anti-Soviet" statements and attempts at organized opposition from religious and party Opposition groups. More people were disfranchised in this election than in any previous one, and the onset of collectivization and the drive against religion generated an exceptionally tense atmosphere. In addition, members of the defeated Left Oppositions (Trotskyite and Zinovievite) were still active and made their voices heard during the election campaign. In Slavgorod, for example, Trotskyites put out statements saying "the existing system of party dictatorship suffocates everything vital," while in Moscow Trotskyite groups in factories tried to nominate their own candidates to run against the official ones. [60]

Peasant demands for the organization of peasant unions (on a par with trade unions for the urban population) were reported from locations as far apart as Krasnoiarsk and Khabarovsk. Kulaks, religious sectarians, and other disfranchised persons were said to be using the elections as an occasion for "agitation" against the Soviet regime, and there were reports of threats and physical assaults on Communists. In a village in the Tarsk region, people deprived of rights marched down the street with flags, and peasants joined them. Orthodox and sectarian activity was also widely reported, with an emphasis on Tolstoyan and Baptist activity. Comments to the effect that the regime had become cut off from the working class, that it was not true Soviet power, and that the Communists were suppressing freedom were reported. People complained that Communists were a new privileged class, who "live like lords, they go round in sables and with canes with silver handles." In Tula, one man protested against the regime's international revolutionary commitments, asking why the regime supported the Sun Yat-Sen Chinese University in Moscow (which he called "the factory of yellow dynamite") and how much it cost the Soviet state. [61]

The 1937 elections, following on the heels of the new Constitution, were initially announced as *multi*candidate elections—that is, elections where voters actually had a choice. This idea fell by the wayside sometime in the first half of the year, presumably a victim of the extreme suspiciousness and political uncertainty attendant on the Great Purges, and the elections, which took place at the end of the year, were ultimately conducted on a single-candidate basis. But this sequence of events was mysterious and bizarre rather than humdrum. At least for Galina Shtange, the 1937 election retained its sense of specialness (it was the first under the new Constitution and deputies were being elected to a new body, the Supreme Council of Soviets). "We were the very first of the first voters at the first such election in the world," she recorded with satisfaction.[62]

The 1937 election campaign, held in the autumn, was very subdued because of mass arrests of those who had sought to utilize the multicandidate promises made the previous winter as well as continuing terror. A single nominee from "the bloc of Communists and non-party people" (the euphemism covering reversion to single candidacy) ran for each place, and the NKVD monitoring of election discussions turned up little substantive discussion of policy (much less than in the Constitution discussion the previous autumn). As usual, there were some expressions of impatience with the whole election procedure since "anyway the Communists will appoint who they want." Some voters also seemed dubious, in view of the recent disclosures that "enemies of the people" were everywhere, that these candidates for high office would prove any more reliable than their predecessors. "How can you climb into the soul of a man?," one woman asked at a Moscow pre-election meeting in October. "After all we also elected the former Communists and thought they would be good, but they turned out to be wreckers."[63]

But popular feistiness was not totally absent. There were cases of objection to the official nominees, especially those who were central politicians and celebrities. In Kuibyshev (Central Volga), there were objections to the candidacy of a Ukrainian for the Soviet of Nationalities (upper house of the Supreme Soviet): "Let the Ukraine elect him, and we will put forward our own [Russian] candidate."[64] In Leningrad, objections were voiced to the candidacies of Mikoyan (on grounds of his "dissipated personal life"), Kalinin ("too old"), and the writer Aleksei Tolstoy ("really fat"). In Novosibirsk, one pre-election meeting even objected to Stalin's candidacy, on the grounds that he was standing for nomination in many constituencies; instead, the candidacy of Alekseev, Novosibirsk party secretary was proposed—and passed by a vote of 150, as against 50 for Stalin.[65]

TALKING BACK

As we have seen, Soviet surveillance of the popular mood had its consultative aspect in the forms of public discussions, election meetings, and the authorities' willingness to accept individual complaints and petitions. But all these public consultative forums were constrained and to varying degrees unsatisfactory to both sides, the watchers and the watched. Knowing that the regime might punish somebody who said the wrong thing in public, citizens preferred to discuss public affairs outside these forums and in different ways from the officially prescribed one. Suspecting that citizens were unlikely to say what they really thought in public, the authorities—in particular, the NKVD—sought to extend their surveillance to citizens' "off-the-record" discussions, those that were outside the range of state surveillance. That meant attempting to monitor not only conversations in private homes and private correspondence, but also anonymous and subversive public communications like jokes, songs, rumors, verbal outbursts against the regime, and abusive letters to the authorities.

Anonymous public exchanges on issues of the day, like those that occurred in every Soviet queue or railroad compartment, in markets, and in the kitchens of communal apartments, are the hardest of all types of communication for the historian to get at. Some Soviet ethnographers collected *chastushki* (songs on topical subjects, usually set to well-known melodies), but the heavy censorship of the 1930s made it impossible to publish them without bowdlerizing them completely. We therefore have to rely mainly on contemporary NKVD "ethnography," based on listening in queues and markets and writing down the jokes and rumors, and Russian popular memory, which is good for jokes even at half a century's remove but less good for the other forms of anonymous public communication. The peculiarity of the NKVD "ethnographers," it should be remembered, is that when they heard a really good subversive joke or rumor, they sometimes arrested the teller for "anti-Soviet conversation."

Rumors disseminate information, or alleged information, on public matters to those who hunger for it, but they also express popular hopes and fears and attempt to explain puzzling events. Thus, Soviet rumors in the 1930s constantly dwelt on the imminence of war, which was feared by many and hoped for by some. They brought "news" of popularly desirable policy changes, like amnesties and religious toleration. They spoke threateningly of the "Bartholomew's Day massacres" that were imminent if food shortages continued. They offered various explanations of Kirov's murder, including an ingenious one that implied a causal link, based on chronological conjuncture, between the murder and the indignation of working folk at the abolition of rationing.[66]

According to a diarist of the 1930s, the majority of jokes were about politics. One Harvard Project respondent, who valued Soviet rumors as having "true information," remembered rumors about new laws, imminent arrests ("some big man would be imprisoned and . . . it would not be in the newspapers, but people knew it"), price rises, and food shortages ("they would say that soon there would not be any sugar or any bread, and this is how it usually happened, the rumors were justified"). But others were less confident of the reliability of rumors. One, reporting rumors of the early 1940s that collective farms would be abolished after the war and bells rung in the churches, suggested that NKVD agents themselves "passed these rumours out because they knew that the people liked to hear them." Another recalled that there were many false rumors, especially during the Great Purges. For example, "we heard two or three times that supposedly Molotov had disappeared." [67]

It was the essence of Soviet anonymous communications to the authorities to be subversive.[68] They were subversive in the most literal sense of overturning Soviet clichés, as well as the political sense of being "anti-Soviet." The official way of characterizing subversive comment was "hostile," but a more exact description might be "defiant." Jokes, outbursts, and the rest were a way that citizens could thumb their noses at Soviet power—an action whose appeal was all the greater because of the pious right-mindedness that was normally required of public utterances.

Among the most attractive targets for subversive comment were Soviet slogans. These phrases, generally derived from Stalin's obiter dicta, tended to be infinitely repeated in newspapers and propaganda speeches, sometimes even written up on banners. "Life has become better." "Technology decides everything." "Cadres decide everything." "Catch up and overtake the West." "There are no fortresses that Bolsheviks cannot storm." Like advertising jingles, they were easy to memorize and also easy to despise and satirize. We have already seen how irritated people got at the constant iteration of "Life has become better." "Catch up and overtake the West" (which sounds better in Russian) was the basis for frequent witticisms: for example, "When we catch [the capitalist countries], can we stay there?" "When we come abreast of America please let me off. I don't want to go any farther." [69]

Acronyms and initials, another favorite of Soviet officialdom, were the occasion for many jokes, usually variant readings. The initials of the Communist Party in the 1930s, VKP, were read by peasant wits to stand for "Second serfdom" (*Vtoroe Krepostnoe Pravo*), while in the reading of some Leningrad youths the initials of the USSR itself—SSSR [CCCP] in Russian—became "Stalin's death will save Russia" (*Smert' Stalina Spaset Rossiiu*). The OGPU was spelt out as "O Lord! Help us to flee" (*O, Gospodi! Pomogi Ubezhat'*) and (back to front) "If you flee they'll catch you and cut off your head" (*Ubezhish'—Poimaiut, Golovu Otrubiat*)." [70]

The same love of wordplay and inversion of Soviet clichés expressed itself in what in a less authoritarian context might be called practical jokes (the Soviet authorities called them sabotage). Despite the harsh punishments for such actions, the censors had to be constantly on the lookout for small changes in texts of newspapers, brochures, and books that could have been typographical errors but played havoc with the sense. "Liquidation of illiteracy," a favorite slogan, somehow became "liquidation of food" in one provincial newspaper. In another paper, portraits of Politburo members appeared in unfortunate proximity to a story on economic statistics entitled "Heads of cattle in the USSR." Place names honoring leaders like Kirovgrad and Stalingrad were transmuted into Kirov*gad* and Stalin*gad* (*grad* = city, *gad* = scoundrel). One jokester (saboteur) in Bashkiria did not even bother to make his joke look like a typographical error when he inserted the slogan "He who works more and better gets nothing!" on the cover of 10,000 labor books for kolkhozniks in 1933.[71]

Communists were much reviled in Soviet jokes, with Stalin and Lenin, and to a lesser extent leaders like Molotov, Voroshilov, and Kalinin, frequently featured. One of many Lenin-Stalin jokes circulating in the mid 1930s played on the fact that both Lenin's wife, Krupskaia, and Stalin's wife, Allilueva, were named Nadezhda, which means hope, and that Stalin's wife had died. "Lenin had Nadezhda [hope] and she remained, but Stalin has no Nadezhda." Riddles and back-to-front readings were popular: "Read Kirov's name backward, that is, from right to left" (*vorik* means petty thief).[72]

In the mid 1930s, there were many variants and elaborations of the *chastushka* prompted by Kirov's death: "They killed Kirov/ They (we) will kill Stalin." One variant was as follows: "When they killed Kirov/They opened trade in bread/When they kill Stalin/They will disband all the collective farms." Another *chastushka* of the same period ran: "When Lenin was dying/ he ordered Stalin/Not to give bread to the workers/Not to show them meat." But this *chastushka* was somewhat unusual in equating Lenin and Stalin rather than contrasting them. A *chastushka* from the Ukraine in the famine years of 1932–33 drew the contrast as follows: "Lenin defended our class/So that we had enough to live on./Stalin destroyed us all/So that we lay down in the grave."[73]

Stakhanovites, viewed as the teachers' pets of the regime, were the butt of many jokes. "What are they giving out?" asks a deaf old lady, joining a queue. "A slap in the face," someone replies. "To everyone, or just Stakhanovites?" Another joke concerns the awarding of prizes to Stakhanovite milkmaids. In a formal ceremony, the first milkmaid gets a radio receiver, the second a gramophone, the third a bicycle. Then comes the fourth, the "leading pig-tender" of the kolkhoz, to whom with much emotion the kolkhoz director presents "the complete works of our beloved comrade Stalin." Awed silence. Then a voice is heard from the back: "Just what the bitch deserves."[74]

There were many jokes about repression and terror, the unmentionables of Soviet society. The following two became classics of Soviet folklore.

> 1937. Night. A ring at the door. The husband goes to answer. He returns and says: "Don't worry, dear, it is bandits who have come to rob us."

> "What are you in for?—For being talkative: I told some jokes. And you?—For laziness. I heard a joke and thought: I'll tell them tomorrow, but a comrade didn't waste time."[75]

Some jokes emphasized the powerlessness of Soviet citizens to protect themselves against state violence; others turned the cliché contrasting the happy present and the miserable past on its head, or subverted Soviet images of heroism and dedication. In one joke,

> [A] worker is taken to the top of the Kremlin wall and asked if he will prove his devotion to the Soviet system by leaping to what seems certain death. He jumps without a moment's hesitation, is caught in a net prepared for the emergency and congratulated on his devotion. But one of the witnesses of the scene, asking the worker why he leaped with so little hesitation, gets the disillusioned reply: "Oh, to the devil with the life we are leading."[76]

Outbursts like the one above—brief public explosions of anger, when the individual threw away normal caution and inhibitions—happened often in real life too. This was no doubt related to the exceptional discomfort and tensions of everyday life, but it may also have been a reaction against the constraints associated with surveillance. One real-life outburst was reported from a village meeting on the perennial favorite topic of Soviet propagandists—the international situation and the danger of war. One member of the audience, who had heard all this once too often, "jumped from his place and cried out, shaking with anger: 'To hell with this kind of life! Let there be war! The sooner the better! I'll be the first to go!'" A similar outburst was triggered at a factory discussion on the new Constitution by mention of Stalin's "Life has become better" slogan. "When discussion turned to the fact that life has become better, life has become more cheerful, [one worker] threw the brochure of the draft constitution on the floor and began to trample it with his feet, shouting: 'To hell with your constitution, it has given me nothing. . . . I am going hungry. . . . My whole family is going hungry. . . . I have begun to live worse. . . . It was better before." [77]

Public outbursts were often associated with drunkenness, which served as a partial excuse for outrageous behavior in Soviet terms, even though this did not necessarily save the offender from punishment. A desire to mock the authorities, as well as defy them, was often evident. A respondent in the Harvard Project related this episode: "In Stalingrad I had a friend who was drunk and he was walking in the street. He saw a man who looked like a Party worker and he jostled this fellow and said: 'I have no time because I have to fulfil the 5 Year Plan.' He got arrested and received 3 years because he made fun of the 5 Year Plan." An official report on the popular mood during the 1937 elections included a story of a "very drunk" citizen at a Moscow polling booth who announced: "I will only vote for comrade Ezhov [head of the NKVD], I won't vote for the rest. Arrest me if you want to, I will only vote for Ezhov, and Gudov [the Stakhanovite worker who was official candidate for this district] does not satisfy me." [78]

Anonymous letters to the authorities containing abuse and invective against the regime expressed the same pent-up anger as outbursts. Because anonymity was a better cloak than drunkenness, they were not as risky as public outbursts. Writing such letters was not a risk-free pastime, however, since the NKVD routinely tried to trace the authors, often successfully. The writers were clearly aware of this, since some anonymous letters contain challenges to the NKVD to identify their authors.[79] Some anonymous letters contained outright threats, as when the "Committee for the Salvation of the People" warned Zhdanov that he and other leaders had better watch out or they would go the same way as Kirov, or when an anonymous individual warned that if prices were not lowered, the rest of the leaders would share Kirov's fate. Sometimes the threats were veiled, as in the letters that warned that Soviet policies were inexorably leading to uprisings, revolution, and civil war.[80]

Ethnic slurs, particularly but not solely anti-Semitic ones, were common in anonymous letters. Although this was no doubt an expression of prejudices that ran deep in Russian society, it also constituted a violation of a strong Soviet taboo in the prewar period against their expression, thus giving an extra bite to the letters. Anonymous letters frequently stated that Jews—or Jews, Georgians, and Armenians—were running the country. "We, unfortunate citizens of a Jewish-Armenian country," began one anonymous letter to *Pravda*, protesting church closings. The Russian revolution was run by Jews, said another, and Jews want to run the world. "Who needs internationalism—only Jews." Authors of anonymous letters accused the regime of being dominated by Jews, and its non-Jewish members like Stalin and Kirov of selling out to the Jews. Stalin's nationality did not escape attention: one anonymous letter mocked him as "Caucasian prince Stalin." [81]

One writer expressed his anti-Semitic sentiments in verse, calling on the reader to remember that the USSR was

A country without rights and without law,
Of innocent victims and brazen slaughterers.
A country where the slave and the spy reign
And Jews triumph over the holiness of the idea.

The verse was part of an anonymous letter, addressed to Otto Schmidt, head of the agency in charge of arctic exploration, whose main purpose was to gloat over the crash of one of the much ballyhooed Soviet Arctic flights. "No Jewish advertisement helped. Instead of San Francisco your famous airplane, made [at] 'famous' Soviet factories and out of Soviet materials, that is to say rubbish, shamefully crashed on to the rocks." [82]

The risk involved in writing any anonymous abusive letter was greatly increased if the anonymous communication was passed up as a note to an official speaker at a meeting. Nevertheless, such things happened. Molotov read out one such note as that he received after his speech at a party conference in Moscow in 1929:

Comrade Molotov! You shout about self-criticism, but . . . if someone would criticize the dictatorship of Stalin and his group, then tomorrow he will fly from his post, from his job, to the devil, to prison, and further. (Noise) Don't think that people follow you and vote for you unanimously. Many are against you, but are afraid to lose a crust of bread and their privileges. Believe me, all the peasantry is against you. Long live Leninism! Down with the Stalinist dictatorship! [83]

Surveillance was not a totally one-sided activity. The very fact of the regime's gathering of information on the citizenry created a channel of communication for popular opinion. But there was another sense in which surveillance had two sides. Citizens practiced their own form of surveillance on the regime, notably in trying to decode its public pronouncements to find out what was really going on. Newspapers and other official texts—even census forms—were routinely subject to close scrutiny, not only by intellectuals but also, it appears, by a large part of the whole reading population, including peasants.[84] Thus, the watchers were watched in their turn.

Skepticism about the reliability of what was written in the papers—as expressed in the joke that there was no truth in *Pravda* (which means truth) and no news in *Izvestiia* (which means news)—was widespread. The reaction that "It's all lies" was not uncommon: for example, "There are no real Stakhanovites, all that is just written in the paper, but doesn't exist in life, they make it all up." But most newspaper readers, while distrusting the press, assumed that some of what appeared in the papers had a relationship to reality. One Harvard Project respondent, a skilled worker with a high-school education, said that he did not believe the boasting about economic achievements in the Soviet press, but he did believe the articles that described "disorder, nonfulfillment, and spoilage of production." If the press published a denial by TASS, the Soviet international news agency, of a foreign report, he believed it, for "if they deny something [there] must be [something] to it." [85]

Aesopian reading of texts was as deeply ingrained in Russian/Soviet culture as Aesopian writing, and practiced by a much larger community. Some texts were written for Aesopian reading by journalists and politicians trying to convey a message that the censors or the Politburo were likely to block. But that was not a prerequisite for Aesopian reading: Soviet readers did their best to discern the hidden meaning behind texts that were not written with the intention of communicating anything beyond their face value. The Aesopian reader used his skills to try to work out what was happening on the international scene, in the Soviet Union, and even in the Politburo. He looked for hints and subtexts to divine exactly what was intended by the often obscure "signals" that came down from on high. Although he assumed that the regime was often trying to deceive him, he also assumed that there was a possibility of reading through the deception and getting at some kind of truth.

To illustrate this point, we must return to the NKVD summaries on popular mood discussed earlier in this chapter. There is a real pattern of mirrors here, for embedded in the NKVD's pictures of popular opinion are the pictures of regime behavior and intentions drawn in popular discourse. When the NKVD collected data on popular reactions to the Kirov murder, for example, these data included popular speculation about who had done the murder, and why, and what it signified—in other words, citizens' attempts to decode and interpret the public announcements on the murder. "Maybe he [Kirov] got drunk and shot himself," some suggested. Maybe it was part of a bureaucratic power struggle in which Kirov and Nikolaev [the assassin] were on different sides. Maybe it was a consequence of the end of rationing (which occurred within a few weeks of the murder) since "the position of workers did not improve and that angered the workers—after all, Nikolaev came from the working class." [86]

All these speculations of course contradicted the official version that Oppositionists were behind the deed, and some comments made this explicit. So who *was* behind the murder? Some comments suggested that "Kirov was killed on Stalin's orders," although this speculation seems to have been less widespread at the time than it was to become later, when in the Khrushchev period stories of Stalin's guilt became a staple of Moscow folklore. More common was a less specific sense that the murder had something to do with high politics: "They are shooting up at the top, and at the bottom they are crying for order," as one comment had it.[87]

The 1937 population census provided a flurry of popular speculation about the regime's intentions and the meaning of certain questions on the census form. According to NKVD reports, people were saying that the taking of the census meant that war and military conscription was imminent: its purpose was to "identify young people and send them off to war." The 1937 census was unique among Soviet censuses in including a question on religion.[88] This aroused enormous discussion, since its unexpected appearance could be read either as a threat or a promise. Was the purpose of the census "to identify believers for the purpose of repressing them"? People talked about the possibility of a slaughter of believers—a "St Bartholomew's Day massacre"—and noted that it was "no accident" that the census was being carried out "on the night of the seventh of January, that is on the birthday of Christ." But others thought the question about religion provided an opportunity for believers to show their true numbers and force the Soviet regime to change its policy on religion. Some thought that a high "vote" for religion would lead to religious freedom, speculating that the question had been included at the insistence of the League of Nations or of foreign powers.[89]

The final example of popular decoding belongs to the tense months at the beginning of 1937, as the Great Purges were just getting under way. When a popular Politburo member, Sergo Ordzhonikidze, died suddenly early in February (by his own hand, as most historians now think), the official version was that he died of "paralysis of the heart." But the death occurred just a few weeks after one of his deputies, Iurii Piatakov, had been charged with treason and sabotage in the second of the Moscow show trials, convicted, and executed.[90] Although the obituary notices for Ordzhonikidze were fulsome and extensive, there was a note of confusion and disarray likely to alert Aesopian readers. As the NKVD noted in its report on popular reaction to Ordzhonikidze's death, "quite a large part of the materials reflect the comments of non-soviet, philistine elements who link the death of comrade Ordzhonikidze with the 'unpleasant things' and 'moral shocks'" associated with the Piatakov trial.[91]

A number of quoted comments indicated that the tone of announcement makes people suspect something fishy. Was Ordzhonikidze a victim of terrorism? Suicide? Poisoning by Piatakov's men or by persons unknown? Had he died of worry because of the Piatakov trial? (Murder on Stalin's orders was not one of the speculations reported by the NKVD, in contrast to the Kirov case; this rumor, persistent in the post-Stalin period was evidently of later genesis.) Many people thought that Ordzhonikidze's death heralded more repression. "He who lives through 1937 will be a happy man," said a worker who belonged to a religious sect. "That is written in the Bible. They are destroying all the Red rulers, and after that Tsar Mikhail will rule." This was not the only comment anticipating more deaths in the political leadership. "Now it's the turn of other leaders, of Stalin." As the population correctly read the signs at the beginning of 1937, a new "time of troubles" lay ahead.[92]

8

A Time of Troubles

"You know they are putting people in prison for nothing now."
Comment of local official, 1938.[1]

Surveillance means that the population is watched; terror means that its members are subject on an unpredictable but large-scale basis to arrest, execution, and other forms of state violence. A society under surveillance does not have to be a society under terror: for example, the German Democratic Republic of the 1970s and 1980s was relatively free of terror, although it was watched over by the Stasi—that overachieving pupil of the NKVD—with a thoroughness unparalleled in the history of state security.[2] But there is obviously a relationship between surveillance and terror; the same institutions are used and many of the same processes are involved. In the Soviet Union, where waves of terror against different groups of the population started with the Civil War and occurred periodically thereafter throughout the prewar period, the relationship was particularly close. Surveillance was an everyday reminder of the possibility of terror.

It is instruments of the state that conduct surveillance and organize terror. In popular Soviet parlance, these are things that "they" do to "us." It is very important to understand that this was how Soviet citizens perceived these processes, but it is also important to realize that this analysis is in many ways unsatisfactory. In a society with almost a million office-holders, ranging from powerful figures to petty, poverty-stricken officials out in the countryside, where does the boundary-line between "them" and "us" lie? Moreover, if "they" are the people who have access to state power through office-holding, how can a terror like the Great Purges, in which office-holders were the primary victims, be understood in "them" against "us" terms?

For a society, the experience of terror is more complicated than just the suffering of the victims and their families and the fear of others in the population that they will become victims. The societal experience of terror involves victimizing as well as being victimized, inflicting violence as well as suffering it. This is also true of the individual experience of terror: even people who never voluntarily denounced their fellow citizens in the Great Purges failed to defend friends who were publicly pilloried, cut off contact with the families of "enemies of the people," and in a host of ways found themselves becoming participants in the process of terror. One of the most useful functions of the "them" and "us" framework for Soviet citizens—and a major reason why historians should approach it warily—was that it obscured this unbearable fact.

There were many waves of terror, to use Solzhenitsyn's image, each sweeping victims from different groups into prison and Gulag. At the end of the 1920s and the beginning of the 1930s it was kulaks, Nepmen, priests, and, to a lesser extent, "bourgeois specialists" who were the main victims. In 1935, after Kirov's murder, Leningraders—particularly members of the old privileged classes and former Oppositionists in the Communist Party and the Komsomol—suffered. Then came the Great Purges, focused especially on the Communist elite, which hitherto had not been a target, as well as on the intelligentsia and all the "usual suspects" like kulaks and "former people."

The subject of this chapter is one specific wave of terror, the Great Purges of 1937–38. This was the quintessential episode of Stalinist terror, a historical moment that crystallized and at the same time reconfigured the accumulated experience of terror over the past two decades. Terror against enemies of various kinds was a familiar though intermittent part of Soviet life. But until the Great Purges, the word "enemies" was usually bracketed with the word "class." That notion of "class enemies" implied that there were certain fixed categories of persons in Soviet society who were liable to be victims of terror: kulaks, priests, disfranchised "former people" from the old privileged classes, and the like. It seemed to imply also that those who did not belong to these categories were free of vulnerability to terror—although in practice few Soviet citizens would have put total confidence in that premise, knowing how infinitely flexible stigmatizing categories like "kulak" and "bourgeois" could be.

The Great Purges introduced a new definition of the target of terror: "enemies of the people." In one sense, this was simply a code term indicating that in this terror, in contrast to previous ones, the hunt for enemies should focus particularly on the Communist elite. But in another sense, it marked a destruction of the previous conceptual boundaries of terror. "Enemies" no longer had any specific attributes like class; anyone could turn out to be an enemy, Soviet terror was random. In the words taken as an epigraph for this chapter, "They are putting people in prison for nothing now."

For social pathologies like the Great Purges, there are no fully satisfactory explanations. Every individual knows that he is powerless, an actual or potential victim. It seems impossible, at least to minds brought up on Enlightenment principles, that something so extraordinary, so monstrously outside normal experience, could happen "by accident." There must be a reason, people think, and yet the thing seems essentially unreasonable, pointless, serving no one's rational interests. This was basically the framework within which educated, Westernized, modern Russians, members of the elite, understood (or failed to understand) the Great Purges. The dilemma was all the more agonizing in that these were the very people who were most at risk in this round of terror, and knew it.

For the majority of the Russian population, less educated and less Westernized, the conceptual problems were not so acute. The terror of 1937–38 was one of those great misfortunes, like war, famine, floods, and pestilence, that periodically afflict mankind and simply have to be endured. There is no specific reason for such misfortunes (although some religious believers will always say they are a judgment on sinners), and no way to prevent them. Moreover, what happened in 1937–38 affected the lower classes of the population—excluding outcasts and marginals[3]—much less than the elites. For peasants, there was no comparison with the great trauma of the decade, collectivization. For urban workers, the hunger at the beginning of the decade and the punitive tightening of labor discipline at the end of it loomed larger on the scale of misfortune.

By the beginning of 1937, both educated and uneducated Russians were seeing signs that a time of national misfortune was at hand. The most important proximate cause for this perception was the failure of the 1936 harvest, which in the following winter and spring led to hunger in the countryside, breadlines in the towns, and a panicky fear that things would get still worse, as in 1932–33. In the countryside, rumors of imminent famine, turmoil, and war flew around, as they had during collectivization.

There were other contributing factors. Since the beginning of the First Five-Year Plan and collectivization, the regime and the society had been under constant stress, strained to the utmost by the industrialization drive, the disaster of collectivization, and apprehension about the international situation that had put the country on a pre-mobilization footing. Within the Communist Party, the atmosphere became increasingly tense as the process of "small-p" purging, begun in 1933–34, was repeated in 1935 and again in 1936. After Kirov's murder, former Oppositionists became targets of terror, and Zinoviev and Kamenev were twice tried and, in 1936, executed for alleged responsibility. As the party continued to purge itself of undesirable members, the process became more and more vicious—no longer just a matter of expulsion but often of arrest. Almost 9 percent of those expelled in the most recent party purge—a total of more than 15,000—had been arrested as spies, kulaks,

White Guards, and scoundrels of various kinds, Ezhov told the Central Committee in December 1935. And there would have to be more arrests. As one speaker at this meeting put it, as soon as those expelled from the party get home, they start getting involved in counterrevolutionary activity: they should be "smoked out" before real trouble occurs.[4]

The pool of ex-Communists members grew, until by early 1937 worried party leaders were pointing out that in some regions and enterprises the number of *ex*-Communists equalled or exceeded the number of current party members.[5] These people, it was assumed, were enemies—part of that inexorably expanding group that included not only everyone who had ever opposed the regime but also everyone whom the regime had ever injured, not to mention the entire capitalist world whose hostile "encirclement" threatened the survival of the Soviet state. Soviet political culture had developed no effective mechanisms for allowing errant sheep back into the fold. The need for such mechanisms was recognized, or so one might conclude from actions like the party's readmission of former Oppositionists, the return of civil rights to deported kulaks, and the attempt to de-stigmatize "social aliens" in the 1936 Constitution. But these efforts rarely succeeded for long: deportees remained tied to their places of exile, formerly disfranchised persons were still objects of discrimination regardless of the Constitution, and almost all the former Oppositionists were again expelled and arrested as "enemies of the people" within a few years of their readmission. Stigma was essentially permanent; black marks on the record could not be expunged.

Worse, from the Communists' standpoint, was the fact that many of these enemies—victims of the regime's punishment and stigmatization—were no longer readily identifiable because they had "masked" themselves. Kulaks and their children had fled to towns and become workers, hiding their former identities. Former nobles had changed their names and taken work as humble accountants. Former priests and priests' children had moved to other parts of the country and become teachers. Persons expelled from big cities at the time of passportization had come back with forged passports and were posing as respectable citizens. Even Communists expelled from the party for various derelictions had re-entered the party with forged cards. Was it not likely that within this huge community of the disaffected, networks and conspiracies would grow? Was not this a new class of enemies, mutually linked, like the old privileged classes, by invisible bonds of sympathy and shared grievances?

The suspicion and conspiratorial mentality that had always characterized the Soviet Communist Party had not declined, as might have been expected as a revolutionary party consolidated power: the failure of collectivization and the shock of Kirov's murder had seen to that. Nor had the party's great fear of disunity and intolerance of disagreement grown less; indeed, it had increased, and open disagreement in the upper ranks of the party had been silenced. But this produced its own problems: if everybody claimed to agree, how could one know what they were really thinking? Party membership must be reviewed yet again, denunciation encouraged, surveillance increased.

The party had always required its members to be vigilant. But now there was a difference: they should be vigilant not only against the enemies without but also the enemy within. "Within" meant, in the first instance, inside the Communist Party. But there was also a hint of something even more disturbing, the possibility that the enemy might lie within oneself. "Each man . . . feels that somewhere in the depth of his soul is a little kernel of wrecking," writes a student of Stalinist culture. The diarist Stepan Podlubnyi, son of a dekulakized peasant, knew this feeling of self-distrust and struggled to erase the tainted birthmark his origins had imprinted on him. As the party's collective self-examination continued, becoming ever more hysterical, certainties dissolved. It was possible, evidently, to be a wrecker without meaning to be one or even knowing it. It was possible to wear a mask that deceived even oneself.[6]

THE YEAR 1937

There had been rumblings ever since Kirov's death and the localized waves of terror that followed it. The first of the three great Moscow show trials of former Oppositionists, the trial of Zinoviev and Kamenev in August 1936, initiated a round of arrests of former Oppositionists, but this was still on a relatively small scale. Mass arrests in the Communist elite and the episode of hysterical witch-hunting we now know as the Great Purges began in the first months of 1937, with the January show trial of Iurii Piatakov and other former Communist leaders for counterrevolutionary wrecking and sabotage and the bloodthirsty plenary meeting of the Central Committee that followed. Although it was almost two years before the terror started to wind down and Nikolai Ezhov was removed as head of the NKVD, the whole episode was long remembered by Soviet citizens as "the year 1937."

The three trials had a strong structural resemblance to the show trials of the Cultural Revolution, the Shakhty trial of 1928 and the Industrial Party trial of 1930. The difference was that then the defendants had been "bourgeois specialists," charged as representatives of their class as part of a campaign against the old intelligentsia. This time the defendants were high Communist officials, very recently removed from top positions. The inference that they too were on trial as representatives of a class was there to be drawn—but the question was, what class? One possible reading was that it was the class of former Oppositionists. The other, considerably more disturbing in its implications, was that it was the whole Communist managerial class that was now on trial.

The theme of the Piatakov trial was wrecking, meaning intentional sabotage of the Soviet economy by highly placed officials who were secret enemies of Soviet power. Iurii Piatakov, one of the chief defendants, was a former supporter of Trotsky who had recanted in the early 1930s, been readmitted to the party, and become the right-hand man of Sergo Ordzhonikidze at the Ministry of Heavy Industry. He was accused of "treason against the country, espionage, committing acts of diversion, wrecking activities and the preparation of terrorist acts." Prosecutor Vyshinsky put on a dramatic performance, describing in astonishing detail the awful outlines of the conspiracy of former Oppositionists, their master, "Judas-Trotsky," and German and Japanese intelligence agencies against Soviet power. They were "a brigand gang," "murderers," "toadies and cads of capitalism," Vyshinsky claimed. "This is not a political party . . . it is merely a gang of criminals . . . hardly to be distinguished from gangsters who use blackjacks and daggers on the high-road on a dark night." Fearful of the masses, "from which it runs like the devil from holy water," the gang "conceals its brutal claws and ferocious fangs. The roots of this gang must be sought in the secret recesses of the foreign espionage agencies which bought these people, which kept them, paid them for their loyal, flunkey service." [7] The trial was reported almost verbatim in all the national newspapers, with banner headlines, photographs of the cowed defendants, and boxed statements by indignant Soviet citizens calling for the death penalty.

Stalin, Molotov, and Ezhov spelled out the message to a terrified Central Committee at the plenary meeting that began in February. Their speeches lent considerable weight to the reading that the class on trial in the Piatakov trial was the Communist managerial elite. It turned out, they said, that Piatakov and Co. were not the only wreckers in industry. In fact, wreckers were flourishing everywhere in the industrial and transport apparats, overlooked by complacent Communists who had forgotten about vigilance; and not all the wreckers were former Oppositionists. There were enemies of the people in other branches of the Soviet government too. In addition, wreckers and traitors had wormed their way into top positions in the regional party administrations. (This was particularly distressing news for the Central Committee, many of whose members were themselves regional party secretaries.[8])

Over the next few months, the newspapers carried a wealth of startling information about the sins of leading Communists in the center and the regions. These news items usually refrained from stating outright that the subject, unmasked as an "enemy of the people," had been or would shortly be arrested, but this was obvious to any experienced reader of the Soviet press. The stories were written in such a way as to arouse all the latent hostility of Soviet citizens to elite privileges and arbitrary exercise of power. Enemies of the people had practiced patronage and favoritism, bullied subordinates and been rude to ordinary citizens, developed their own local "cults of personality," used state funds to support a luxurious lifestyle of banquets, dachas, cars, foreign consumer goods, and expensive clothes.

The atmosphere of the time, strongly anti-elitist and anti-bossist, was encapsulated in Stalin's toast in October to "little people" in which he remarked that "Leaders come and go, but the people remain. Only the people are eternal." [9]

In this highly charged atmosphere, standard practices suddenly became fraught with sinister meaning. Take the "families" of clients and connections that every central and regional political figure gathered round himself. It was natural (most people, in normal times, would have agreed) to want to be surrounded by your own people; to bring trusted lieutenants with you when you changed jobs; to protect your people if some Moscow busybody started to make trouble for them; to cooperate with others in your Ministry or regional party organization to show the achievements of the institution or region in the best possible light. But now all such efforts seemed suspect, smacking of conspiracy.

A provincial newspaper had a field day with the clientelist tendencies of G. P. Savenko, director of the local coke-chemical plant, when he was exposed as an enemy of the people. Savenko, the paper reported, had brought "his own people" with him, including class enemies and former Trotskyites, when he moved to Dnepropetrovsk from the Donbass and given them all sorts of perks, "cossett[ing] these confidence men and rascals in every way." Over two years, 1935 and 1936, he spent 114,000 roubles from discretionary funds for bonuses, whose recipients included an unmasked wrecker, the son of a White Cossack officer, a former Trotskyite, the son of a big prerevolutionary manufacturer who had been expelled from the party for speculating in gold, and other undesirables. Savenko also spent money from the director's fund for lavish banquets. This (the newspaper pointed out) was in sharp contrast to the miserly amount available for cultural purposes, workers' housing, and other worthy causes.[10]

"Humility adorns a Bolshevik," a *Pravda* editorial underscored. Alas, many leaders had forgotten this lesson. A critic of the Ukrainian leadership accused Pavel Postyshev (former head of the Kiev party organization) of creating his own cult. "An atmosphere having nothing in common with Bolshevism reached its apogee when comrade Postyshev headed the Kiev organization. 'Postyshev's guidelines,' 'Postyshev's slogans,' 'Postyshev's kindergartens,' 'Postyshev's gifts' etc. Everything began and ended with Postyshev." The industrial leaders were no better: at the big Makeevka metalworks (whose director, G. V. Gvakhariia, was unmasked as a member of a German-Japanese-Trotskyite conspiracy at this time), a newspaper reported that the plant leaders, "surrounded by acolytes, began to sing each other's praises" and "things got to the point that on revolutionary holidays the portrait of Gvakhariia was hung at the entrance to the plant, and they carried his picture at the head of the march."[11]

Luxurious lifestyles were the target of other stories. A Kazan newspaper, for example, chose this ground of attack in writing of the recently disgraced leaders of the city soviet, including P. V. Aksenov, former soviet chairman and husband of the later Gulag memoirist Eugeniia Ginzburg, who faced criminal charges for misuse of government funds. It was alleged that they built themselves an elite dacha settlement, taking the funds from local building trusts as well as soliciting contributions from factory directors (who would be among the users of the dachas) out of their directors' funds. The dolce vita at these dachas was described as follows:

> Life at the dacha was lavishly appointed. Breakfasts, dinners, suppers, snacks and drinks, bed linen—everything came free. The hospitable hosts, generous at the expense of the state, did not have to bother with any financial calculations. . . . Here, in the shadow of pines and fir trees, no-one worried about accounts and accountability; they spent money as they wished, without the usual formalities. Altogether, about 225,000 roubles of state funds were wasted on "exploitation" of the dachas.[12]

A similar description of luxurious living accompanied *Pravda*'s attack on the director of a Komsomol publishing house, E. D. Leshchintser, who was described as "a bourgeois degenerate" who "unceremoniously ripped off the state" by furnishing his apartment in expensive Karelian birch and providing himself a luxurious apartment in the publishing house's dacha.[13]

What was striking about these stories was not their revelations about the behavior of highly placed Communists: the family networks and regional leader cults were features of Soviet governance well known to Soviet citizens and it came as no surprise either to learn that such people were materially privileged. The striking thing was that *Pravda* and other official organs had appropriated some themes of popular complaint that, if uttered by a citizen in normal times, would have risked being labeled "anti-Soviet" or "hostile." The behaviors it described were characteristic, as many of its readers surely knew, of the whole cohort of Communist cadres, even though they were being attributed only to certain scapegoated "enemies of the people."

Because the two groups were linked in so many ways, it was inevitable that the intelligentsia should get involved in a terror against the political elite. The intelligentsia included Communists, many of whom held important institutional positions and some of whom had been Oppositionists. There were personal and familial ties between the political and cultural elites: Galina Serebriakova, for example, was the wife of one defendant in the Piatakov trial and the former wife of another; the Communist journalist Leopold Averbakh, leader of the Association of Proletarian Writers (RAPP) until its dissolution by the Central Committee in 1932, was a friend and brother-in-law of Genrikh Iagoda, Ezhov's predecessor as head of the NKVD; the poetess Vera Inber was the daughter of a cousin of Trotsky's, and so on. A web of client-patron connections linked politicians and leading members of the creative intelligentsia—writers, artists, theater people, scholars, scientists. As for engineers, they often worked so closely with Communist bosses in industry that they were liable to share their bosses' fate if the latter were disgraced. Finally, the intelligentsia had elite status and privileges comparable with those of the Communist managerial class. If there was to be terror against elites and denunciation of privilege, the intelligentsia was unlikely to escape unscathed.

The first "plague-bearers" in the intelligentsia were Communists with an Oppositionist past or Oppositionist connections. Richard Pikel, a drama critic and member of the Union of Writers who had once headed Zinoviev's Secretariat at the Comintern and had been active in the Left Opposition, was a defendant in the Kamenev-Zinoviev trial in August 1936. Within a week of that trial, Central Committee cultural officials had sent party leaders a memo about Oppositionists and other possible enemies in the Union of Writers. As the memo made clear, arrests among the writers had already started (Serebriakova and several former members of the RAPP leadership were among those named as under arrest), and there was reason for serious concern about others—Vera Inber, for example, for her family connection with Trotsky; Ivan Kataev, because he had given money and friendship to various disgraced Trotskyites; Ivan Gronskii, editor of the journal *Novyi mir*, because he had published Pikel's work, and so on. In "self-criticism" in the Writers' Union, other names had surfaced, including those of well-known writers who were not members of the Communist Party. The poet Boris Pasternak was in trouble for not signing a collective request from well-known writers for the execution of Kamenev and Zinoviev; the prose writer Iurii Olesha was in trouble for defending Pasternak and having been a drinking companion of one of the show-trial defendants.[14]

In the early months of 1937, Leopold Averbakh emerged as the center of vilification in the literary community. Averbakh became totally demonized, a satanic figure like "Judas-Trotsky" himself, polluting everything and everyone he had ever come in contact with. Although he was called a Trotskyite, Averbakh had not really been an Oppositionist in the 1920s, although he had admired Trotsky. His real sin was the close connection with Iagoda, together with the fact that as former leader of RAPP, the main instrument of persecution of writers during the Cultural Revolution, he had made many enemies who welcomed the opportunity to settle scores. One of Averbakh's fellow leaders of RAPP, the playwright Vladimir Kirshon, who was also a member of Iagoda's social circle, was excoriated with almost equal vigor as Averbakh. One of his attackers was his former wife, who complained that he had physically and morally abused her.[15]

Contacts with Bukharin—personal and institutional as well as professional—damaged many reputations in the literary and scholarly worlds. As one commentator in a literary weekly put it, it was necessary to "burn out" Bukharin's influence. Bukharin was not yet under arrest, but he was already disgraced and isolated, and at the February–March plenum he had been subjected to a devastating cross-examination by Stalin, Molotov, and others, and the plenum had expelled him from the party. Young Communist intellectuals who had been his disciples (your "little school," as Molotov contemptuously put it) had already been arrested and testified against him. In May, Bukharin was expelled from membership of the Academy of Sciences. Nikolai Gorbunov, the Bolshevik chemist who was permanent secretary of the Academy and thus had the distasteful task of acting as "prosecutor" in Bukharin's expulsion, did not survive him long.[16]

The beginning of the Great Purges in the Red Army came in June 1937 when a new and shocking plot was disclosed—that of Marshal Mikhail Tukhachevsky, General Iona Iakir, and other top military leaders. None of these men had belonged to the Opposition in the 1920s. A closed court martial convicted all of them of treason, specifically of organizing a political-military conspiracy with the support of Germany, and they were immediately executed. They had been "caught redhanded" as spies, *Pravda* said. In a rambling speech at the closed discussion of party leaders that followed the executions, Stalin noted that those hunting for "enemies of the people" would not necessarily find them among former Oppositionists. That may or may not have comforted former Oppositionists, but it surely intensified the fear felt by party leaders with irreproachable political pasts.[17]

A week after the execution of the military leaders, *Pravda* announced that it had "received a letter from the former wife of Iakir . . . in which she re-nounces and curses her former husband as a traitor." [18] This letter, presumably coerced, did not save Sarra Iakir from punishment; she ended up in Gulag with her teenage son, encountering among other old acquaintances the young wife of Bukharin. The wives of big "enemies of the people" were rou-tinely arrested along with or shortly after their husbands. Natalia Sats ended up in a whole room of "wives" in Butyrki prison, including the wife of Marshal Tukhachevsky. There were even special camps in Gulag for "wives of traitors to the motherland." [19]

By mid 1937, terror was in full swing and most of the basic contours of the Great Purges were set. There was, of course, much more to come—waves of arrests of different categories of elite members like diplomats, foreign Com-munists, Communist "nationalists" in the non-Russian republics, Komsomol leaders, and finally even members of the security police; the July order for mass arrests and executions of social marginals was discussed in Chapter 5. But this is not the place for a detailed descriptive history of the Great Purges.[20] Our primary concern is the impact of the Great Purges on everyday life and practices, and for that we must turn to the processes and spreading mecha-nisms of terror.

SCAPEGOATS AND "THE USUAL SUSPECTS"

In the terror of 1937, there was a clear sense that "enemies of the people" were likely to be found in the elites, especially Communist administrators. But enemies might be found anywhere; even within the elites there were no clear guidelines as to which persons needed to be unmasked. Of course someone with black marks on his record—past Oppositionism, bad social origins, for-eign connections—was particularly at risk, and prepared lists of victims played a role in the Great Purges. But there was a large element of randomness in the selection process too. Finger-pointing at "self-criticism" meetings in offices and enterprises, public accusation in newspapers, and private denunciation by citizens were among the selection mechanisms. Chains of associations were also very important. The NKVD would pull in one person and interrogate him, asking him to name his criminal associates; when he finally broke down and named some names, they would be pulled in in turn, and the process contin-ued. When anyone was arrested as an "enemy of the people," family, friends, and work associates all became high-risk candidates.

One of the key processes of terror in the Great Purges, particularly in the first half of 1937, was public scapegoating. This took place at meetings at the workplace whose function was to "draw conclusions" from some signal from above, for example, the Piatakov trial or the February–March plenum of the Central Committee. There would be a report explaining the significance of the signal, followed by a collective discussion on the conclusions that should be drawn. This was a well-established Soviet practice, but in the context of ter-ror it acquired a new purpose: "drawing conclusions" came to mean pointing the finger at hidden enemies within the institution. These meetings were sometimes described as "criticism and self-criticism" sessions, but "self-criticism" was really a misnomer.[21] Apologies and recantations by individuals occurred (though they rarely affected the outcome), but the drama of the occasion lay elsewhere. The institution, not the individual, was the subject of self-criticism. The point of "criticism and self-criticism," Great Purges style, was collective discovery of a hidden enemy within the ranks, usually one of the leaders of the institution. The outcome was not generally predetermined; the implicit requirement was only that a scapegoat should be found, and that he should not be an insignificant person whom the institution could easily sacrifice. Tension could mount intolerably in these sessions just because of the uncertainty about who the ultimate victim(s) would be.

One model for this form of scapegoating came out of the Stakhanovite movement, which in 1936 had developed strong anti-management overtones, with Stakhanovites in local management collectives taking the lead in denouncing managers as wreckers and saboteurs. A secret instruction from the Politburo early in 1937 instructed factory managers to hold monthly meetings with Stakhanovite workers so the Stakhanovites could vent their criticisms and accusations. The newspapers reported dramatic occasions, when workers hurled abuse at unpopular managers (the epithets "Goebbels," "bureaucratic barbarians," and "donkey's ears" were used at one meeting). But this zest for denunciation was not universal. In some plants, it seems, workers grew weary of giving up their free time to wrestle with the question of which of the managers were wreckers. We know of several cases where workers tried to short-circuit the process by simply nominating a list of candidates for "wrecker" status and voting to approve it.[22]

Another scapegoating mechanism was the re-election of party officers called for in the name of "party democracy" at the February–March plenum of the Central Committee. The label sounded innocuous, but every party secretary present must have recognized it as part of the complex of threats to his security that were offered on that occasion. It must be remembered that, in normal circumstances, "party democracy," like "soviet democracy," existed only as a fiction. The convention in both contexts was that elections were essentially uncontested; the candidates were nominated according to lists sent down from a higher authority, which were then duly confirmed by voting. When it became clear in the spring of 1937 that party elections under the rubric of "party democracy" meant that there would be *no lists*, that was a major shock, and not a welcome one. On what basis were candidates for party office to be selected if the central party organs refused to indicate whom they favored? In a context where more Communist officials were being unmasked as "enemies of the people" every day, how could one avoid the ultimate horror of electing someone who turned out to be an enemy (which meant showing oneself to be an enemy-by-association)?

The party elections proceeded slowly and with great difficulty. In the absence of lists, each candidate had to be discussed individually and the presumption was that at least some of the candidates—notably those who were incumbents—would be unmasked as enemies in the course of the discussion. The incumbent officers were understandably intimidated and paralyzed; the rank and file often showed little inclination to take the initiative into their own hands. Sometimes there was difficulty getting the show off the ground at all because nobody wanted to speak; some elections lasted for weeks. At one Iaroslavl plant, for example, the 800 members of the factory party organization attended meetings *every evening for more than a month* before they managed to elect a new committee.[23]

The party elections were no simple matter in the Ministry of Heavy Industry, where it took a week of careful weighing of eighty candidacies to produce a list of eleven names. Some candidates were discredited in the course of discussion, among them the incumbent party secretary Andrei Zykov, who was alleged to have contacts with "Trotskyite counterrevolutionaries" and to have participated in a "leftist group" at the Institute of Red Professors in 1928–29. When Zykov failed to win re-election, that did not just mean he lost his job but also that he was in acute danger of being arrested as a counterrevolutionary, which was indeed his fate. The same fate awaited others criticized at the prolonged meetings at the Ministry: for example, Georgii Gvakhariia, head of the Makeevka metallurgical plant, whose definitive unmasking as an "enemy" came only a few weeks after he had been worked over in this forum.[24]

The party elections of the spring of 1937 were a one-shot event, but other kinds of electoral meetings were held periodically during the Great Purges and these occasions were often perilous for the nominees. In January 1938, for example, the trade union of government employees held its national conference and, according to the rules, proceeded to elect a new central committee of the union. Whether a list of candidates had been provided for this election is not clear from the minutes of the conference. Most likely it was, but in the climate of the Great Purges that did not prejudge the outcome. Each candidate was required to make an autobiographical statement to the conference, and delegates cross-examined them on it. In a series of meetings that grew increasingly tense, delegates savaged several members of the old central committee who had been nominated, causing two of them to be knocked off the list, and cross-examined other candidates in an aggressive and threatening way about their Civil War military records, social origin, kulak connections, and so on. The scapegoating instincts of the delegates fastened on one hapless woman with relatives abroad and a failed marriage she was unwilling to discuss; she escaped being dropped from the list and declared an "enemy of the people" only through a dramatic last-minute intervention by a senior delegate.[25]

Regional and other "family circles" had their own tried and tested methods of defending members from outside threat; indeed, this was one of the main purposes of their existence. Thus, in response to the threats to individual "family" members early in 1937, the heads of the families—industrial managers, regional party secretaries—sprang to defensive action. For example, the head of a metal trust let some subordinates go "at their own request" when the heat got too great and moved others to new jobs in different cities where they would be safer. Another industrial leader let his right-hand man be prosecuted for sabotage after a bad accident, but at the same time gave him 12,000 rubles for legal defense; yet another, a regional representative of the Ministry of Heavy Industry, tried to rescue a disgraced factory director by appointing him as his assistant. In Sverdlovsk, the party committee rallied to the support of the director of a local plant when he came under attack as a "wrecker" and blocked his expulsion from the party. In the Far East, regional officials resisted attempts to expel one of "their own," Matvei Khavkin, who was secretary of the Jewish autonomous region, Birobidzhan. When it became clear that Khavkin could not be saved by action at the regional level, his friends encouraged him to go to Moscow to plead his case, giving him 5,500 rubles from party funds for the purpose and issuing him a pass that secured him a place on the Moscow train.[26]

By mid 1937, however, the usual methods were proving increasingly ineffective and dangerous because of the "guilt-by-association" mechanism of the terror. The center made clear its determination to prevent family circles protecting their own by declaring such protection to be "counterrevolutionary" and treating those who offered it as enemies of the people. Most of the cases described above are known because the would-be protector was being indicted as an enemy of the people, with his acts of protection constituting the indictment.[27] The Communist Aleksandr Solovev recorded another typical case in his diary in April 1937. His old acquaintance, Ivan Nosov, head of the party committee in Ivanovo, was being pressured by the NKVD to sanction the arrest of some former Trotskyites working in Ivanovo. When he refused, he was accused of protectionism.[28]

Show trials were one of the most characteristic forms of scapegoating of the Great Purges era. But their forms and the messages they conveyed were more various than might be assumed from the three big Moscow trials alone. Local trials had a different resonance, although they were also orchestrated from the center to some degree. In his memoirs, Aleksei Adzhubei, editor of *Izvestiia* in Khrushchev's time, took one issue of the newspaper from June 1937 and pondered the message contained therein. On the one hand, there were the reverberations from the recent court-martial of the military leaders, with comments like "A dogs' death to the dogs" quoted from members of the public, which to Adzhubei epitomized the bloodthirsty irrationality of the terror. On the other hand, there was a report of a local show trial from the rural district of Shiraievo in which corrupt and abusive officials were brought to answer for their mistreatment of the local population. The Shiriaevo message, as Adzhubei read it, was that "before Stalinist justice, everyone was equal—Marshal Tukhachevsky and the secretaries of district party committees and chairmen of rural soviets." [29]

The Shiriaevo trial was one of the first of a series of show trials of local officials that were held in many localities in the summer and autumn of 1937. In contrast to the Moscow trials, with their melodramatic tales of spying, international intrigue, and conspiracy, the local trials featured accusations that were wholly plausible: local officials were accused of a range of abusive, arbitrary, and incompetent administrative behaviors that were typical of lower-level Soviet officials in real life. In one Iaroslavl show trial, for example, workers from the Rubber Combine testified against managers and foremen who had allegedly insulted and beaten them, harrassed women, and given bonuses to favorites; in another, housing officials were accused of allowing substandard conditions in factory barracks. In Smolensk and Voronezh, officials were blamed for shortages of bread and sugar. In the local trials, the accused did not always confess, and their chief accusers were not state prosecutors but ordinary citizens called as witnesses. There was an overtly populist aspect to the local trials that was almost entirely missing in their Moscow counterparts.[30]

Both local and central show trials were heavily publicized. Whole workforces from local factories and collective farms attended each local trial, and long accounts appeared in local newspapers. The Moscow show trials received saturation coverage in the central press, including verbatim reports of proceedings, as well as being broadcast on radio and filmed.[31]

The show trials, which were themselves political theater, spawned imitations in the regular theater, both professional and amateur. Lev Sheinin, whose cross-over activities between criminal investigation and journalism we have already encountered,[32] was coauthor of one of the most popular theatrical works on the themes of the Great Purges, a play called *The Confrontation*, which played in a number of theaters throughout the Soviet Union in 1937. Since Sheinin was reputed to be the author also of the scenarios of the big Moscow show trials, this switch to "legitimate" theater, using the same themes of spies and their unmasking and interrrogation, is intriguing. Some reviewers found fault with the play as being too close to journalism, but others were more appreciative. John Scott, who saw the play in Magnitogorsk, was impressed by its dramatic tension and the force of its message of suspicion and vigilance and reported that the local audience applauded wildly at the end.[33]

One can see why. The villains have black hatred in their hearts ("I lived in Russia all my life and all my life I have hated it," says one old man who is discovered to be a hidden German agent. "I hate your space, your people, your self-confident youth poisoning the whole world with the poison of their teaching. Hatred for you replaced everything for me, even love, and became the sense and meaning of my whole life.") They are part of a mighty force poised to crush the Soviet Union. But they are defeated by the vigilance of the Soviet people. "How many secret agents has the counter-intelligentsia of the country bordering us to the West [that is, Germany]?" the spy is asked. Eight to ten thousand, he estimates, and another fifteen thousand agents of the country on the Eastern border (Japan). "But we have 170 million overt agents," that is, the whole population of the Soviet Union, comes the triumphant reply.[34]

At a more mundane level than show trials, the terror gathered momentum through the rounding-up and imprisonment or execution of "the usual suspects." A particularly egregious example was the massive action against escaped deportees, religious sectarians, habitual criminals, and other marginals ordered by the Politburo in the July 1937.[35] But the process was not limited to major punitive actions and total outcasts. Anybody whose name was on any

of the lists of dubious characters kept by local organizations—former Oppositionists, former members of other political parties, former priests and nuns,
former White Army officers, and the like—was liable to be picked up at this
time. In villages, families that had lost one member to deportation in the early
1930s were likely to lose another in 1937–38. In factories, workers who had
fled the villages to escape dekulakization a few years earlier were liable to be
"unmasked" during the Great Purges. In universities, students were denounced as "socially dangerous" elements for having kulak fathers or having
been "brought up by a merchant." [36]

"Former people" exiled from Leningrad in the wake of Kirov's murder in
1935 were often picked up again in their place of exile—this time bound for
Gulag, if not a death sentence—for alleged participation in "counterrevolutionary conspiracies." A. A. Siniagin, son of a prosperous businessman who
had been exiled from Leningrad in 1935 and taught at Tomsk University, was
rearrested and shot in Tomsk in August 1937 as "a member of a counter revolutionary anarcho-mystical and terrorist organization"; two months later in
Orenburg the same fate befell Sergei Rimsky-Korsakov, an economist deported from Leningrad in 1935 who was a grandnephew of the composer
Tchaikovsky.[37]

For Communists and Komsomol members, any stains on the record—
association with the Oppositions of the 1920s, contacts with Oppositionists,
party reprimands, past suspensions or expulsions—were likely to float to the
surface again in the 1937–38, either through finger-pointing at self-criticism
meetings or secret denunciations. "Trotskyite waverings" in 1923 might be
recalled by a former classmate, a suspicious friendship with a foreigner or
"softness on Trotskyism" remembered by a colleague, possible Oppositionist
connections suspected by a former's wife's best friend.[38] No charge could be
convincingly disproven, and a Communist's previous good deeds, as well as
his bad, did not go unpunished. A man who, in the spirit of party duty, had
denounced his father-in-law as a kulak years earlier was expelled from the
party for "socially alien" connections in 1937. A Communist who had once
reported his mother-in-law for anti-Soviet conversation found himself
accused of being related to an undesirable element, namely his mother-
in-law.[39]

The story of a Jewish Communist named Zlatkin illustrates all the compro-
mises and betrayals that family taints produced as well as their ultimate point-
lessness. Zlatkin, who worked in state insurance, had no black marks in his file
on his own account, but his sister's husband had been deported as a Trotskyite. An investigator sent from Zlatkin's local party organization to his home-
town early in 1937 came back with more damaging allegations: he claimed
that Zlatkin's father, once a Communist but now expelled, had been an elder
of the synagogue (so unlikely for a Communist as to be surely untrue) as well
as a police agent of the old regime. What could Zlatkin say? His sister's husband, he admitted, was a Trotskyite; after the man's second expulsion from
the party, Zlatkin had "suggested to my sister that she should get a divorce,
but she didn't listen." As for his father, Zlatkin testified that when he was ex-

pelled from the party, "I didn't even help him with his appeal." "I thought that I had gone a long way away from the family," said Zlatkin gloomily. "I thought I would be clean." No such luck. He was expelled from the local party organization by majority vote.[40]

Information about the operation of NKVD troikas in Saratov at the end of 1937 suggests that the victims here—ordinary townsmen and peasants convicted after the briefest trials—may well have been rounded up on the basis of lists of various kinds of undesirables, from White Army personnel to churchmen.[41] They were charged with "anti-Soviet activity," which seems to have meant anti-Soviet conversation, plus a blot on the record; almost no evidence was presented, but seventeen out of twenty nine received the death sentence and the rest ten years. The "Saratov Nine," eight of whom came from the same village, were peasants among whom (according to the docket) were five former kulaks (four of whom had been deported and escaped from exile or served out sentences in Gulag), two former landowners, a Tolstoyan, and two active members of the Orthodox community. The "Saratov Twenty," all townsfolk, included eleven former White Army officers or volunteers, three members of the old Socialist-Revolutionary party, four sons of traders or prosperous bourgeois, three former Tsarist policemen, one former prison guard, and a member of the prerevolutionary City Duma.

The troikas did not even bother to record the anti-Soviet remarks for which the "Saratov Nine" and the "Saratov Twenty" were so harshly punished. But they probably resembled those of another group charged with "counterrevolutionary activity" in Saratov a year earlier. This was a real group, unlike many others so called; it consisted of religious believers, all comparatively elderly men and women, some of them former priests and nuns, who had gathered around a priest by the name of Rubinov and met in his home in Volsk. Rubinov told his followers that they should encourage kolkhozniks to leave the kolkhoz because famine was returning (this was October 1936), and that they should take advantage of the new Constitution to elect believers to the soviets. His followers reportedly made the same kind of remarks that the NKVD so often included in their summaries on popular mood: "Soon there will be war" and the Soviet regime will collapse," the Soviet leaders were "Jews who had sold out Russia," and "the time will come when we will take revenge on the Communists, "Germany and Japan . . . will begin the war, and we will help them." [42]

SPREADING THE PLAGUE

Terror spread in many ways. It was disseminated through denunciation in a climate of popular suspicion and spy mania. It spread through the NKVD's practice of interrogation, in which arrested "enemies of the people" would be forced to write confessions naming their conspiratorial associates. It could be spread by "plague-bearers," people who for one reason or another infected all around. A notable plague-bearer was Leopold Averbakh, the former leader of the proletarian writers, whose sinister reputation has already been remarked.[43] One less typical, because he himself was not arrested, was a young astronomer from Central Asia, an "affirmative action" beneficiary who was discovered to have faked experimental data in an article published in a foreign scientific journal. The reverberations from this scandal were sufficient to bring down virtually everyone with whom the young astronomer had had contact in two institutes, while he himself apparently escaped arrest through a nervous breakdown.[44]

Another type of plague-bearer was the Communist administrator who, though tainted in reputation, had not yet been arrested and was desperately trying to avoid this fate. Pavel Postyshev, the Ukrainian party leader, by reputation a moderate, was criticized and demoted in the early months of 1937, but remained at liberty. His new job was in the Kuibyshev region on the Volga where he "hunted for enemies everywhere with a magnifying glass," causing a panic that spread through the local bureaucracy and into the population. Postyshev completely dissolved thirty district party committees, on the grounds that they were irreparably corrupted and had sixty-six district officials arrested as enemies of the people. At the January 1938 plenum of the Central Committee (where "excesses" of terror were criticized, though without lasting effect), Postyshev stood by his story that Kuibyshev had been full of enemies even under hostile questioning—one could almost call it teasing—from Molotov and others.[45] Perhaps Postyshev's was an extreme case, since his heels were held to an exceptionally hot fire over an unusually long period before he was, in his turn, unmasked as an enemy. But the practice of moving a discredited official and having him involuntarily "infect" a whole institution by his presence for a few months was not uncommon.

> Help! What kind of place are we living in, and what do we have to look forward to tomorrow. It reminds me of when I first learned about microbes and bacteria; I was reading some science book, and it said that everything, even the air, was made up of living creatures. And after that I kept seeing little creatures everywhere, and I couldn't even stand to take a drink of water. That's the way it is now: you look at a man and suddenly he turns into a swindler or a traitor before your very eyes.[46]

Andrei Arzhilovsky wrote these words in his diary in February 1937 after reading Vyshinsky's speech for the prosecution at the Piatakov trial. A tough-minded man who had served time in prison, Arzhilovsky succumbed only temporarily to this mood of suspicion. But for many others, suspicion became a daily companion. This attitude is reflected in the letters ordinary people sent to the authorities during the Great Purges describing suspicious events and persons. An Ivanovo worker wrote to party leaders expressing his dismay that the new 30-ruble notes had image of Lenin on them—meaning that his image was likely to be profaned. Was this arranged by the same enemies who had been committing all sorts of sabotage in Ivanovo? An economist wrote to Molotov warning him not to underestimate the threat from internal enemies, citing anti-Soviet conversations he had overheard in Kuntsevo. A radio listener heard Chopin's Funeral March played the day Zinoviev and Kamenev were executed and wrote in to share his suspicions that it was a signal from Trotskyite conspirators.[47]

The newspapers added fuel to the fire with their constant stories of unmasking of enemies and spies. The spy motif became particularly strong after the Tukhachevsky trial: the military leaders were accused of having fallen into the clutches of German spies; and in a speech behind closed doors on the affair Stalin painted a vivid picture of the dangers to high Soviet officials posed by female spy-seductresses. Many stories of such seductions circulated. Men were warned against sexual entrapment, as in the case of an engineer who was seduced by a "citizenness, young and pretty, who had not long ago come from Harbin"—really, of course, a Japanese spy. Lonely women were also warned, with citations of cases like the recently deserted young wife whose confidence was won by a smooth talker who pretended to be as lonely as she was but was really a spy.[48]

For children, catching spies seemed like great sport. "How I caught a spy, recounted by Ukrainian Pioneer, Lena Petrenko," was the heading of one such newspaper story. Returning from Artek children's camp, Lena recognized that a fellow traveler on the Nikopol-Dnepropetrovsk bus was a suspicion type when she heard him whispering in German about "rails" and "signal." As she followed him to the station buffet, he dropped an envelope, which turned out to be a letter in German giving directives on committing "a diversionary act." Lena informed the police and the man was quickly arrested.[49]

The nightmarish consequences of adolescent spy mania were exemplified in the case of Igor Lazich, an eighth-grade pupil in Moscow. Igor was a problem child, something of a delinquent, who had twice run away from home. He was jealous of the more successful and popular son of one of his neighbors in the communal apartment, seventeen-year-old Konstantin Retinskii, who was a Komsomol leader at a prestigious military cadet school, and on at least one previous occasion had denounced him to the police but was not taken seriously. He was vaguely Russian nationalist and anti-Semitic, with an admiration for fascist organizations with storm troopers. Apparently to prove his boast to friends that he had connections with an underground conspiracy, Igor sent a letter allegedly from a co-conspirator identifying himself as a spy (the letter was intercepted by the post office). At the same period, he went out one night with two friends (who subsequently confessed to the deed) and stuck up "counterrevolutionary posters" in Moscow. When he was arrested for these two acts, he claimed that Konstantin was a member of his subversive group. Konstantin was accordingly arrested, confessed under interrogation, and was convicted along with Igor. Konstantin's anguished mother wrote to Vyshinsky explaining that this was just one more of Igor's malicious pranks, but Konstantin's conviction was not reversed—after all, he had confessed.[50]

Denunciation was one of the most important mechanisms for spreading the plague. This practice was endemic in Soviet life, but it became epidemic during the Great Purges. Colleagues denounced colleagues: for example, a joke in *Krokodil* in 1939 has a man in court pleading "Comrade judges, how could I have written 75 denunciations when there are only 63 persons working in our institution?" Neighbors denounced neighbors: in another *Krokodil* joke of the same period, a husband complains to his wife, "Just think, Masha, how unpleasant. I wrote a denunciation on Galkin and it turns out that Balkin has the bigger room." [51] Workers denounced factory managers; students denounced professors; kolkhozniks denounced kolkhoz chairmen. Communists were denounced by Communists, often on political grounds like past links with the Opposition, and by non-Communists, usually for abuse of power. These denunciations accumulated in the dossiers of all Soviet citizens holding official position and many who did not. Sometimes they were ignored or dropped, but in the conditions of 1937–38 they often provided the stimulus for NKVD actions that led to imprisonment, Gulag sentences, and even execution.

People denounced celebrities they read about in the paper like the aviator Mikhail Babushkin and the polar explorer, Otto Schmidt; they denounced political leaders and their wives. After an elderly photographer told his apprentices that the quality of photographic paper had been better before the revolution, one of them denounced him; he was arrested and, in December 1937, executed. A Leningrad artist got drunk in a bar and "slandered the Soviet Constitution and the punitive policies of Soviet power," expressing sympathy for those who had been repressed as enemies of the people; he was denounced by a fellow drinker and got seven years. A young leatherworker was arrested on the basis of a denunciation from his estranged wife (though freed after his aunt appealed his sentence). [52]

Feuds, bureaucratic rivalries, and professional jealousies often produced denunciations. This could happen in industry, for example, between protagonists of different types of equipment or product design. It occurred very frequently within bureaucracies, where members of competing factions denounced each other. It happened in the cultural and scientific worlds, where different professional groups were often vying for the regime's patronage. Undoubtedly one reason why leaders of the proletarian literary organization RAPP were hit so hard was that they had been such vicious faction fighters themselves, accumulating a mountain of enemies with long-standing grievances not only in the center but also in the provinces where they had thrown their weight around. [53] In general, as one Harvard Project respondent told his interviewer, it was very important not to make enemies in the Soviet Union because of the danger of denunciation. "You should never step on anybody's toes. Even a minor incident may be fatal. Your wife has an argument with her neighbor and that neighbor will write an anonymous letter to the NKVD and you will have no end of trouble." [54]

Some people became virtually professional public denouncers during the Great Purges. Sometimes they did this because they had decided that super-vigilance was the way to save their own skins and thus made a point of writing denunciations of everyone in their environment to the NKVD and speaking up with denunciations at public meetings. This worked well at the height of the terror, but later, when the Purges were dying down, such behavior was often characterized as slanderous and counterrevolutionary. As a result, we have some intriguing confessions from super-denouncers, for example, one Poliakovskii, employed at the "Bolshevik" factory, who described how he and an associate, Vorozheikin,

> began to go to party meetings . . . with readymade lists of persons whom we intended to accuse of being enemies. Everybody already knew Vorozheikin and me; when we appeared it only not caused embarrassment at the meeting, but frightened party members would quietly run out of the building, since it often happened that we would add to the prepared lists names that happened to come into our heads there at the meeting.[55]

In one district of the Tatar Republic Sapiakh Minachev, a party investigator, "gave slanderous denunciations on half the members of the district party organization. In almost every file started on a Communst there were Minachev's 'signals.' Communists were afraid to speak against this slanderer. And how could one not fear: he himself wrote the denunciation, himself checked them, himself reported on the results of the investigation at the party bureau. . . . Minachev was finally himself arrested as an enemy of the people; but the regional newspaper asserted that "similar things happened in almost all the organizations of Tataria." In Leningrad, one senior official in the procuracy systematically wrote denunciations of his colleagues and superiors, as a result of which several were arrested by the NKVD. When some of them were subsequently released, he hanged himself in a hotel room. "A whole volume of denunciations"—175 pages—was found in his apartment after his death.[56]

Some of the compulsive denouncers were evidently emotionally disturbed. For example, a man named Sukhikh, who worked in a district party committee,

> smeared the reputations of dozens of honest Communists and non-party people. In autumn of last year Sukhikh appeared without invitation or mandate at a regional conference of workers of public health workers and, [seized by] the "oratorical itch," demanded the floor. "I am a representative of the city party committee," he announced. The floor was given to him even without any restriction on time. However soon it became evident that the orator was spewing out incredible rubbish. Actually he was talking about everything and nothing substantive. The delegates looked round in bewilderment, and a wave of murmuring went through the hall. But the orator continued. . . .[57]

LIVING THROUGH THE GREAT PURGES

Even in terror, there are rituals. Arrests were made at night, so that the sound of a car stopping, feet going up the stairs at 2 or 3 a.m., and knocks on doors, are vividly remembered by most memoirists. The NKVD men would conduct a search, perhaps take some papers, and march out the victim, allowing him or her to take the packet of warm clothing that many families had long ago prepared for such an eventuality.

Memories of this traumatic event varied. One woman wrote to Vyshinsky protesting the impoliteness of the NKVD man who conducted a house search the night they came to take her husband—they addressed her, a Soviet pedagogue, disrespectfully, using the familiar form.[58] Another woman, an official in a ministry, recalled her own bizarre behavior. During the NKVD's four-hour search of her apartment before she was taken away under arrest, she sat obsessively finishing the paperwork for a forthcoming Stakhanovite conference:

> I wrote and pasted, put the materials in order, and as I wrote, it seemed to me that nothing had happened, that I will finish the work and hand it over, and then my [minister] will say to me: "Good girl, you didn't lose your head, didn't attach any importance to that confusion." I myself don't know what I was thinking about at that time, the inertia of work, or perhaps confusion from fear, were so great that I worked for four hours precisely and effectively as if I were in my own office in the [ministry]. The detective in charge of the search finally snapped: "You'd do better to say goodbye to the children." [59]

Like many convinced Communists, this woman had refused to make any arrangements to protect herself or her children even after her husband's arrests and a warning from an older comrade—after all, she and her husband were innocent! Another woman Communist wryly recalled her lack of common sense both when her husband was arrested and at her own arrest some months later:

> Grishka [her husband] didn't even have time to get dressed, and I was in a dressing-gown, four months pregnant. We had Hitler's *Mein Kampf*, and they took it. Why not, it was proof of ties with Hitler. They sealed up two rooms, left me in the bedroom. . . . I should have given him things to take with him, food, and didn't think of it—only a few handkerchiefs, how stupid. They said he didn't need anything. I thought that he would be back soon, after all, he wasn't guilty of anything, it was some kind of mistake. On the night of 5 September they came for me... (sic) "Get dressed!" I left my son sleeping, fool that I was. So as to phone my sister. Well, what do you want, I had no time, I had to get to prison as quickly as possible![60]

Non-Communists were more practical. Elena Bonner's grandmother had the whole procedure organized:

> I dressed in silence but couldn't get my feet in my stockings; Batanya whispered to herself and hurriedly got out new warm socks, new mittens, her down shawl, new stockings, a shirt, underwear, undershirts, and put them all on the table. I dressed, and as I put my felt boots on, Batanya said quietly, but in almost her usual voice, "Put on heavy pantaloons. and galoshes over your boots." Then I took my coat and my knit cap from the closet, but Batanya silently took away the cap. "Wear my shawl.". . . I put it on somehow. And my coat. Batanya got her traveling bag from the closet, shook out its contents, and stuffed in the things she had prepared for me. Then she handed me some money—five thirty-ruble notes. I was going to stick them in the bag, but she said, "Put it in your bra." [61]

Often the non-arrested members of the family were evicted a few days later and the apartment sealed by the NKVD—a vivid visual reminder to all other residents of what had happened. Bonner described this at the Hotel Luxe:

> On the right-hand side of the corridor, there was a big reddish brown seal on the third door from the lobby. A weight hung from a tiny string embedded in the wax. . . . Those seals that jumped into your eyes appeared on many doors on every floor of our building over the winter of 1936–37, and especially in the spring of 1937. The seals were broken in a few days. Under the supervision of Commandant Brant, two or three suitcases and bundles of books were removed. The furniture and things that had the Comintern tags were cleaned. The floor polishers showed up, and in a few days a smiling Brant welcomed the new tenant.[62]

Like the Hotel Luxe, some big apartment blocks in Moscow became almost ghost towns as a result of the terror, notably Government House diagonally opposite the Kremlin across the river, whose fate in 1937 was described by the novelist Iurii Trifonov in his novella *House on the Embankment*. In both Government House and the Hotel Luxe, which housed Comintern employees, survivors report a series of moves to different apartments and rooms in the same building after the first arrest, until finally the whole family had been picked up or dispersed, or the NKVD finally kicked them out into the street.[63]

Once an arrest had occurred, the family's job was to try to find out where the prisoner was and if parcels could be sent. There were lines outside the offices that gave this information: "Sofia Petrovna had seen many lines, but never one like this one. People were standing, sitting and lying on every step, every landing, and every ledge of the enormous, five-story staircase. It was not possible to climb this staircase without stepping on someone's hand or someone's stomach. In the corridor near the little window and the door to Room No. 7, people were standing as crowded together as on a streetcar."[64]

The sending of parcels was a miserably complicated and uncertain affair.

> They didn't take parcels at Lubianka. They only said whether he was or wasn't [on the lists]. They took parcels only in the prisons, but there they didn't give information about whether the arrested person was there or not. You found out where the relative was from the parcel. If they took the parcel, that means he was there. But if they didn't take the parcel, that still doesn't mean that he was not in that prison. They could be punishing him, depriving him of the right to parcels. But they won't tell you that. They simply didn't take the parcel, not explaining anything. And then you waited a whole month until the next parcel.[65]

Families were not routinely informed when the arrested relative was moved from prison to labor camp. If they managed to discover it, however, there were new routines to follow. Only relatives could send parcels to Gulag prisoners: the limit was 10 kilograms every three months. In Leningrad, for some reason, such parcels had to be mailed from a post office more than 100 kilometers from the city, which meant arduous journeys in crowded trains for the relatives.[66]

As the victims, if still alive, were making their way along the "conveyor belt" to Gulag so vividly described by Alexander Solzhenitsyn, Eugenia Ginzburg, and other memoirists, their relatives outside were also struggling to survive. Wives of the most important "enemies" got arrested too, and their children sent (under other names) to orphanages if relatives did not step in immediately and (at risk to themselves) assume legal guardianship. Lesser wives remained at liberty, but had enormous difficulty keeping jobs because of their husbands' fates. But there were wives whose petitioning and string-pulling on behalf of husbands actually worked: witness the interesting case of a Communist woman lawyer who at the time of her husband's arrest was having an affair with another man and thinking of divorce, but dropped the affair to devote her full energies—successfully!—to getting her husband out of jail in 1937.[67]

Children of arrested parents were liable to be expelled from university and even from high school after a ritual public humiliation by their peers, at which some tried to defend the parent. If the mother was taken as well as the father, some brave relative or even former servant sometimes took over care of the child, although this was not without its own dangers. One memoirist describes the night of her mother's arrest. After her mother was taken away at 5 a.m., the NKVD men wanted to take her (aged twelve) and her younger siblings to an orphanage, but the nanny fiercely resisted and there was a loud scene— nanny shouting, children sobbing. The NKVD men finally left the children with the nanny on the strength of her assurance that she took responsibility and would obtain a signed statement from the children's grandmother assuming legal guardianship.[68]

Reactions

Looking back on 1937 from a distance of more than three decades, Solzhenitsyn wrote:

> How could we know anything about those arrests and why should we think about them? All the provincial leaders had been removed, but as far as we were concerned it didn't matter. Two or three professors had been arrested, but after all they hadn't been our dancing partners, and it might even be easier to pass our exams as a result. Twenty-year-olds, we marched in the ranks of those born the year the Revolution took place, and because we were the same age as the Revolution, the brightest of futures lay ahead.[69]

This statement, which few other survivors of the Stalin period would have the confidence and moral capital to make, reminds us that the terror was not a terror for everyone. The attitude Solzhenitsyn describes was common among—perhaps even typical of—young people, as long as their own families were not affected. That caveat is very important, however, for the arrest of a family member changed everything overnight. A world of difference existed between what the terror meant for those who were personally touched by it and what it meant for others. Nina Kosterina was a fifteen-year-old schoolgirl in 1937, happy, busy, and full of idealism and energy. But then the unthinkable happened: Nina's father was arrested. Her life plunged into a downward spiral of withdrawal, isolation, and depression, even though the ostracism and school problems she encountered were comparatively mild for someone in her situation. Her diary became a melancholy record of broken friendships, lost opportunities, and deteriorating family relationships. "I keep feeling that it is all a dream—a nasty, ugly dream," she wrote. "In a moment I'll wake up and everything will be as before, fine, straight, and clear... I want to howl with despair. Why, why isn't it a dream?"[70]

The first reaction of many victims and their relatives was that an innocent person had been arrested by mistake and would soon be released. Sometimes this was coupled with the belief that all the other people under arrest were guilty, causing people just arrested to shun their fellow prisoners. Wives almost invariably continued to believe in their husband's innocence, sent them parcels, and wrote endless petitions to the authorities pleading for them. Despite the counterexample of Iakir's wife offered in *Pravda*, nobody really expected them to do otherwise; even officials considered it normal for them to petition, not a sign of their own guilt.

There were wives whose reactions were more ambivalent, of course. One such case was that of Julia Piatnitskaia, wife of the Old Bolshevik and Comintern official Osip Piatnitskii, whose diary records her anguish after his arrest. One of her strongest early reactions was anger—how could he have let this happen to them?—and she blamed him for not having denounced colleagues she regarded as suspicious. Then she began to have graver doubts: perhaps he really was a spy and always had been; perhaps "that's why he lived like that, . . . so withdrawn and severe. Evidently it was a weight on his soul." In this mood, "I would be capable of spitting in his face, giving him the name of a spy." [71]

The children of arrested parents were under more pressure than the wives to renounce them, for this was a popular ritual in schools and Pioneer and Komsomol organizations. Most succumbed, although every memoirist seems to remember one instance where a child refused. [72] But of course this tells us little of their inner feelings. Most memoirists with arrested parents report an unshakeable belief in their parents' innocence, and the small number of diaries available convey the same. When his mother was arrested, the kulak's son Stepan Podlubnyi, who had tried so hard to make himself a good Soviet citizen, not only dismissed the idea of her guilt out of hand but lost his faith in Soviet power: "I would never have dreamt that they would consider an almost illiterate woman like Mama as a Trotskyite. . . . In my worst nightmares I couldn't have imagined that she should be arrested for these old sins [the kulak past], when her present life is completely blameless." [73]

Podlubnyi, however, was already a young adult with some experience of the world. It seems likely that younger children were sometimes more influenced by the collective judgment on their parents, especially if both were arrested. Before nine-year-old Egor Alikhanov was scolded out of it by his elder sister, Elena Bonner, his first reaction after his father's arrest was to accept his guilt. "Look what those enemies of the people are like," Bonner quotes him as saying. "*Some of them even pretend to be fathers.*" [74]

Whatever friends, relatives outside the immediate family circle, and colleagues of those arrested privately felt about their guilt, the prudent course was to sever all contact. That was what almost everyone did, leaving the immediate family isolated. Exceptions are cited, but they have the same heroic and atypical quality as the stories of Gentiles sheltering Jewish children in areas under Nazi occupation during World War II. As long as the terror continued, members of the victims' families were likely to be shunned as plague-bearers. But even after the terror subsided at the end of the 1930s, the spouses and children of Purge victims remained stigmatised for many years, carrying notations in their personal dossiers at work, university, and so on. It was extremely difficult to hide the fact of an arrested relative, other than by assuming a totally new identity; those with this disability were required to include it in their official resumés.

Among those not personally affected by the Great Purges, a wide range of reactions is reported. Some people believed in the guilt of the officials who fell victim to the Great Purges, and thought they deserved their punishment. The comment that "Ordzhonikidze shot people, and now he has died himself," though provoked by a suicide that was not directly a Purge death, illustrates a popular attitude that the death of any Communist leader, no matter what the circumstances, might be a matter of indifference or a blessing, but was certainly not a loss. In some factories, a collective suspicion of management developed during the Great Purges as workers started to feel that managers were tainted with disloyalty as a class. In Leningrad, workers' reactions to the show trials included concern that enemies of the people should not get off too lightly, and assertions that the ruling elite had become corrupted because it contained no workers and too many Jews. "All the leaders in power and Stalin should be shot," was one summation of this attitude.[75]

A postwar refugee, looking back on his Soviet life as a teacher in Kazakhstan, remembered reacting with approval to the show trials because his personal acquaintance with some arrested government officials convinced him that they deserved anything they got.

> I will quote a typical case. In 1932, I had to ask for the help of the Kazakhstan People's Commissariat of Education. I was sent to Tashtitov, the Deputy Commissar for Education. He was a young Party member, short in stature, with a pockmarked face. He received me, sprawling all over his chair. When I told him that there were no copy books, textbooks, nor kerosene in the school for illiterates, he jumped up and shouted at me: "Why bother me with your copybooks! I know all about it anyhow! You don't have to tell me! You have put in your requisition—well, just wait! Every Tom, Dick, and Harry can't come pestering the Deputy Commissar for Education about kerosene."
>
> Five years later Tashtitov, who by then had become First Secretary of the Central Committee of the Kazakhstan Komsomol, was unmasked as an "enemy of the people." I must admit that I felt no sympathy whatever for him.[76]

But other postwar refugees had different memories. A housepainter reported that in the show trials "the papers kept yelling 'enemies of the people,' but the plain people did not believe it." A blacksmith had been heartened to learn that there *were* enemies of the Soviet regime when the show trials were broadcast on the radio. He and everyone else in his kolkhoz liked these broadcasts, and he believed that "there were many people who were fighting the Soviet power who got encouragement from these court scenes because they realized that the people on trial were opposing the Soviet power." Others felt similar sympathy with the accused on the grounds that any enemy of Stalin's must be their friend. Obviously Trotsky and the rest were in favor of liberating the enserfed peasantry and that's why they were tried, wrote one anonymous commentator after the Piatakov trial. Peasant sectarians prayed for the souls of Zinoviev and Kamenev after their show trial and execution in 1936.[77]

For Communists, of course, nonbelief was not so simple. A middle-ranking Moscow Communist writing in his diary in 1937 reported the doubts of an old Party comrade that after twenty years the party had so many active enemies. In addition, he reported, Nadezhda Krupskaia (Lenin's widow) complained in his presence of "the abnormal atmosphere, poisoning everything," and another prominent Old Bolshevik expressed the opinion that Ezhov had been misled by irresponsible denunciations and disinformation from foreign counterintelligence, and was misleading the party leaders in his turn. But the diarist himself could not make up his mind to doubt, or at least to admit to doubting in his diary. "How can I judge, a rank-and-file party man? Of course, sometimes doubts sneak in. But I cannot fail to believe the party leadership, the Central Committee, Stalin. Not to believe the party would be blasphemy." [78]

People's reactions to the Great Purges often changed over time. In the diary of Andrei Arzhilovsky (a peasant and former political prisoner under Soviet power, banished to a provincial town in 1937), the first reaction to the Piatakov trial was approval: "I read the prosecutor's indictment in the case of the Trotsky Center. It was wonderful! Vyshinsky is pretty smart." This was quickly followed by the feeling that the defendants' crimes indicated the corruption of the whole regime: "If hundreds of sincerely dedicated, battle-scarred Communists . . . ultimately turn out to be scoundrels and spies, then who can guarantee that we're not completely surrounded by swindlers? Who can guarantee that the greatest and dearest of them won't be sitting down there on the defendants' bench tomorrow?" Within a few months, Arzhilovsky had completely dismissed the thought that there was any real treason. In June, apropos of the announcement of treason among the military leaders, he made the following comment in his diary:

The GPU has uncovered a whole group of high-ranking secret agents, including Marshall Tukhachevsky. The usual executions. A replay of the French Revolution. More suspicion than fact. They have learned from the French how to kill one's own. [79]

Liubov Shaporina, a member of the Leningrad artistic intelligentsia, made a strange entry about the Piatakov trial in her diary for 30 January 1937. In a passage that appears to combine ironic skepticism, genuine hatred of Communists, and the desire to mislead any unauthorized reader, she wrote:

Each [Ministry] has in its leadership a traitor and a spy. The press is in the hands of traitors and spies. They are all party members who have made it through all the purges. . . . There's been a continual process of decay, treachery and betrayal going on, and all of it in full sight of the Chekists [NKVD men]. And what about the things that are not being said at the trial? How much more terrible they must be. And worst of all is the very openness of the defendants. Even Lafontaine's lambs tried to justify themselves before the wolf, but our wolves and foxes—people like Radek, Shestov, Zinoviev, old hands at this business—lay their heads down on the block like lambs, say "mea culpa" and tell everything; they might as well be at confession.

The same entry takes a sharp and disconcerting turn into anti-Semitism.

Suddenly it turns out that Mr. Trotsky already had everything figured out in advance, it was all ready to go, the machinery was already in place. Amazing! But as always with the Jews, it hadn't been planned carefully enough and was bound to fall through. . . . They took it into their heads to eat the Russians for dinner, figuring they're just pigs anyway. Just you wait, my dearies, the Russian people will show what it's made of yet. [80]

Maria Svanidze, the sister-in-law of Stalin's first wife who continued as a member of Stalin's social circle until her arrest in the Great Purges, registered a series of reactions in her diaries. Around the time of the Zinoviev-Kamenev trial in 1936, she focused on the corruption of privilege: "I never trusted [those people] and didn't hide it, but what turned out exceeded all my conceptions of human baseness." Everything—terror, wrecking, embezzling—was done "only out of careerism, out of greed, out of the desire to live, to have mistresses, foreign trips, the good life and cloudy perspectives of taking power by a palace coup." In a later diary entry, she contemplated some of the disasters of Soviet everyday life and saw that they must be caused by wrecking. How else could it be that the textile factories were full of Stakhanovite overachievers but there were still no textiles to buy in the stores? "They [the wreckers] are getting in the way, hindering in every branch of construction and we have to struggle ruthlessly with that."

Then the subject disappeared from Svanidze's diary for a long time, recurring only in one of the last entries (7 August 1937), by which time she had obviously begun to feel extremely frightened and depressed. She still did her best to see all the "enemies" as people quite different from herself—social "aliens," class enemies:

> Often, going along the street and looking at the people and the faces I used to wonder where had they gone, how had those millions of people masked themselves, those who by their social position, education and psyche could not accept the Soviet regime, could not march together with the workers and poor peasants, together with socialism to communism. And now those chameleons in the 20th year of the revolution have emerged in all their false vestments (sic).

But the terror was coming inexorably closer, and her belief that all those arrested were actually guilty was clearly wavering: "A heavy mood has settled. Distrust and suspicion, and what's surprising about that when yesterday's acquaintances today turn out to be enemies, for many years lying and wearing the mask." Maria Svanidze's husband was arrested in December, and her own arrest followed; after a few years in prison, both were executed.[81]

Little is known so far of the reactions to the Great Purges by the NKVD men who actually carried them out. But occasional vignettes crop up in unexpected connections like pension claims. One NKVD officer, Dmitrii Shchekin, head of a district police department in the Kursk region, spent the last week of his life in the summer of 1938 visiting the families of Purge victims and drinking with them. On 4 August, he killed himself. (We know this because his sons subsequently petitioned for his pension and were refused on the grounds that he died a suicide.) In the Volga region of Kuibyshev in the second half of 1937, another district NKVD head was charged with removing a convoy of "unmasked enemies of the people" who were to be deported. Under the pretext of holding a meeting about the upcoming soviet elections, he allowed more than 200 members of the "Giant" kolkhoz to gather and bid farewell to their relatives and neighbors. For this defiance, he was himself unmasked as an enemy and arrested.[82]

Officially, the "excesses" of the Great Purges were repudiated at the 18th Party Congress in the spring of 1939, a few months after Ezhov's demotion and subsequent execution. No doubt it was a difficult process to stop, since the first signs of an attempt to change course went back as far as January 1938. At the January plenum of the Central Committee, Politburo member Georgii Malenkov delivered a report "On mistakes of party organizations in expulsion of communists from the party, on a formal-bureaucratic attitude to the appeals of persons expelled from the VKP(b), and of measures to get rid of these failings" in which he offered some hair-raising examples of terror going out of control.[83] Stalin must obviously have approved this report, although he did not contribute to the discussion. His close associates did, however: Zhdanov called for an end to irresponsible accusations against persons and made some criticisms of the NKVD, and Molotov stated that it was important "to distinguish people who have made mistakes from wreckers." Kalinin tried to reintroduce the notion of proof of guilt, suggesting that what was needed was "not to look into someone's eyes or [say] who is his friend, brother, or wife, or who has been arrested, but [ask] what has he done." [84]

Despite the admission in 1939 that many Communists had been wrongly accused, few purge victims were actually released from prison or Gulag at this time, or for many years thereafter. The Great Purges left deep scars on Soviet society, not just because of their dimensions,[85] but also because for decades they remained a taboo subject. It was not until after Khrushchev's indictment of Stalin's crimes at the 20th Party Congress in 1956 that most of the surviving Great Purge victims were released. Even then, as in 1939, the public apology went to unjustly punished Communists, not to the many non-Communists who were also victims.

The unwillingness to allow purge victims to return probably had the same roots as the decision earlier in the decade to keep the deported kulaks in exile—it seemed too dangerous to let back into society those whom the regime had grievously injured. The presumption that enemies always remained enemies was deeply ingrained in Soviet Communist mentalité, as we have seen in connection with "social aliens" in an earlier chapter. So was the belief that enemies who had been punished became doubly hostile. Yet, if enemies had to be isolated and punished, and punishing enemies only created more enmity, where was there an end to it? Fortunately, the Soviet Union was large— "Broad is my native land," in the words of the song—making it possible to use space as a solution for social problems, as the British had done a century and a half with their policy of transporting convicts to Australia. If all the enemies could only be rounded up, there was room in the Soviet Union to banish them to distant corners of it, where they would be out of sight and, it was hoped, out of mind. The hidden enemies, unmasked, could be hidden once more—but this time, hidden somewhere the state could find them.

Conclusion

A popular joke of the 1920s and 1930s concerns a group of rabbits that appear at the Soviet-Polish frontier, applying for admission to Poland. When asked why they wish to leave, they reply: "The GPU has given orders to arrest every camel in the Soviet Union." "But you are not camels!" "Just try telling that to the GPU." [1] This is one of many rueful jokes of the period that emphasize the arbitrariness of terror. But terror was not the only thing that was arbitrary in Stalin's Russia. Rewards—for example, those that fell in the laps of celebrity Stakhanovites and other famous ordinary people—were also arbitrary. The whole bureaucracy acted in a arbitrary manner, minimally guided by law and only sometimes manipulable via personal connections. Political leaders made abrupt switches in state policy, often discarding without explanation a course that had been ruthlessly pursued for years and substituting something completely different, even contradictory. Every time this happened, some arbitrarily chosen scapegoats were punished for overzealousness in carrying out the old policy.

These were circumstances that encouraged fatalism and passivity in the population, instilling a sense that the individual was not and could not be in control of his own fate. These attitudes were often evident in Harvard Project interviews, notably with respect to questions about how Soviet citizens could protect themselves or advance their interests in a variety of hypothetical situations. "They could do nothing" was the favorite response—even though this was often contradicted when, under further questioning, the respondents suggested things the hypothetical citizen *could* do.[2] In the real world, of course, Soviet citizens were by no means totally without strategies of self-protection, however rooted their sense of dependency and lack of agency. Indeed, to assure the authorities of one's own powerlessness—as the Harvard Project respondents were doing to their American interviewers—was exactly such a strategy.

"I feel I've lived someone else's life," said one woman interviewed in the post-Soviet period, referring to the disruptions that propelled her out of the village at the time of collectivization. This was part of the complex of feelings that led Harvard Project respondents to say that life in the Soviet Union in the 1930s was not "normal," that one could not "make a normal life." Respondents never accepted individual or collective responsibility for this; the situation was squarely blamed on "them," on the government, on all those external forces that put one's own life out of one's control. Abnormality had many aspects, including unpredictability, dislocation, and state violence against citizens, but one motif was constant: it was an abnormal life because of the privations and hardships. Some respondents even used the phrase "living normally" to mean living a comfortable, privileged life—the life to which everyone was entitled, not the life that most people had. "Normal life" was an ideal, not a statistical concept.[3]

The sense of unpredictability was heightened by the sharp breaks, relocations, and deracinations that were part of Soviet lives. The pattern started with the First World War and Civil War, when huge numbers of people were uprooted geographically and socially, losing touch with family and friends, working in occupations different from the ones that had seemed marked out for them. The Revolution opened doors for advancement to some people, closed them for others. Then, at the end of the 1920s, came the new upheavals of Stalin's revolution, shattering routines and expectations once again. Peasants stigmatized as kulaks were deported or ran away to the cities, often with little sense of what they wanted out of their new lives. Their sense of dislocation is conveyed in the response of one Harvard Project interviewee, son of a kulak expropriated in 1930, who had difficulty answering a question about what his father had wanted him to be. "When we lived on the land he wanted me to become a peasant," he said finally. "When we were chased from the land we lost all orientation of what we wanted to become. *I was left up to my fate.*"[4]

Life could seem just as unpredictable to those who were beneficiaries of Soviet opportunities. All those dazzling success stories (related in Chapter 3) of Cinderella-like ascents from the humblest position to the heights express a sense of astonishment as well as satisfaction and self-congratulation. In addition, rising to the heights had its own risks. It could happen that the same person experienced both a sharp ascent and a sudden fall, as was the case with a young man selected by the Komsomol for training as an aviator, whose good fortune was abruptly cut short when his father was arrested and the family exiled. There was a recognized trade-off between the benefits of a career and its disadvantages: as one Harvard respondent put it, "Veterinary work in general in the Soviet Union is good. A veterinarian has the possibility of getting products [i.e., food]. On the other hand it is like work of every employee and specialist. It is dangerous. There is planning; the plan is high, and a man can be brought to court at any moment." Some people refused to accept promotion because of the greater responsibilities and dangers. "To raise one's position means more responsibility. The greater the responsibility, the nearer the unmasking. To sit at the bottom was safer." [5]

In one of the few peasant diaries we have from the Stalin era, the writer's main subject was the weather, which in his world was the primary arbitrary determinant of good and bad fortune; the government was virtually ignored. Urban diarists, by contrast, carefully recorded the government's major initiatives, presumably for the same reason the peasant diarist noted changes in the weather. These Stalin-era diaries are particularly interesting for the amount of time and thought their writers gave to public affairs, especially if one defines that concept broadly to include the economy and the availability or otherwise of consumer goods. Private life and personal emotions are of course present in the diaries, but they seem confined and crowded by public events and pressures, always liable to be thrust from center stage by some external crisis. [6]

Stepan Podlubnyi wanted to find friends, but they should be friends who could help his project of becoming a good Soviet citizen, free of the taint of his kulak past. Liubov Shaporina, former wife of the composer Iurii Shaporin, wrote obsessively of the loss of her young daughter, but conflated that loss and the destruction of her personal happiness with the intelligentsia's and Russia's sufferings at the hands of state during the Great Purges. In Arkadii Mankov's diary, public affairs, viewed with a deeply jaundiced eye, were the main topics, and even when he mentioned family matters, discussion of the state often intruded. For Galina Shtange, an activist in the wives' movement, a major theme for her diary reflections was the conflict of family obligations and public ones. For the schoolgirl Nina Kosterina, a dedicated chronicler of first love and friendship in the early part of her diary, private life became hopelessly compromised and entangled with public issues after the arrest of her father as an "enemy of the people." [7]

Little wonder that Russians looking back on their lives in the Stalin period often use public events, not private ones, as markers and framing devices. When an American scholar interviewed old Russian peasant women about their lives at the beginning of the 1990s, his interviews "were designed to capture their experiences with childbirth and child care, on the assumption that the birth and nurture of children are defining events of a woman's life." He found, however, that public events dominated both the lives and the women's way of remembering them. "The life of virtually every woman I interviewed was . . . shaped more powerfully by the events of the early 1930s. Nearly every woman had a broken life, with the break dating to that time (although for some the war played an even bigger role). Their children were important to them, but their identity and the places they ended up in life were defined much more by the upheavals of the 1930s." [8]

When respondents in the Harvard Project were asked how to get ahead in Soviet society, some said education and proletarian origins, some said time-serving and informing, many said connections, and a few said luck.[9] Luck was indeed extremely important. For this reason, Stalinist citizens, although generally passive, were also intermittent risk-takers—people who bought lottery tickets and played the potentially dangerous game of denouncing their bosses; people who were liable to tell anti-Soviet jokes, and who sometimes, when drunk, made obscene gestures at sacred images in public places. They were by no means as cautious as one might expect of persons living under a highly repressive regime, perhaps because they had no confidence that caution would ensure survival.

Risk-taking was sometimes a necessity for effective functioning. Industrial managers, for example, could not get the raw materials, spare parts, and labor they needed without breaking rules and taking risks, despite the ever-present possibility that they would be punished. The economic historian Joseph Berliner pointed out that in the Soviet Union "the successful manager, the one who climbs swiftly to the top and makes a brilliant career, is the one who is willing to hazard arrest and prison sentence. There is a selective process at work which raises the risktaker to the top, and causes the timid to fall by the wayside." [10]

Risk-taking (as opposed to prudent calculation) was held in high popular esteem. Even the literary intelligentsia, one of the most intimidated and risk-averse groups in Soviet society, made heroes of its risk-takers as well as its martyrs. Writers like Mikhail Bulgakov who sailed right up to (or beyond) the limits of the permissible in their writings were admired for doing so; journal editors and theater directors won prestige with their peers, as well as risking punishment, when they tried to publish or stage such works.

The gambling mentality, it should be noted, was a direct antithesis of the rational planning mentality that the regime in principle approved and tried to inculcate in its citizens. In official discourse, there was nothing more glorious than the Five-Year Plan and the regularity and predictability suggested by the phrase "according to the plan." Spontaneity or happenstance, the opposite of predictability, was something that had to be overcome; accident (in the sense of unpredicted occurrence) was not only deplorable but epistemologically trivial; the term "accidental elements" was used for people who had no right to be there, or simply no rights. Yet all this stood in a dialectical relationship to the mentality of most Soviet citizens, who looked to "spontaneity" (an agentless concept in Russian) to deliver them when they were headed for trouble with the regime's plans, and knew that what "planned distribution" of goods really meant was shortages.[11]

A propensity for occasional or even regular risk-taking did not mean that people were not frightened of the regime. Of course they were frightened, given the regime's proven willingness to punish, the strength of its punitive arm, its long and vengeful memory, and the unpredictability of its outbursts. Hence, the normal posture of a Soviet citizen was passive conformity and outward obedience. This did not mean, however, that Soviet citizens necessarily had a high respect for authority. On the contrary, a degree of skepticism, even a refusal to take the regime's most serious pronouncements fully seriously, was the norm. Of all the Soviet citizen's repertoire of everyday resistance, the popular phrase "This too will pass," said with a shrug in response to some new policy initiative from above, was one of the most devastating from the regime's standpoint. Although the literature of socialist realism did its best to provide exemplars of purposeful, dedicated, effective leadership, other images of authority proved at least as durable.[12]

In two of the most widely read and best-loved literary classics of the prewar Stalin period, Ilf and Petrov's *Twelve Chairs* and *The Golden Calf*, the hero is a confidence man whose stock in trade is his ability to out-talk and out-think slow-witted local officials. In the film *Lieutenant Kizhe* (1934), now best remembered for its score by Prokofiev, the authorities (from the time of Emperor Paul) are so stupid that they appoint a man to the Guards, disgrace him and sentence him to Siberia, pardon him, and promote him once again to the rank of general—all without noticing that he never existed. In the great popular literary success of the Second World War, Aleksandr Tvardovski's *Vasilii Terkin*, the eponymous protagonist is an anti-hero who possesses all the foraging and survival skills needed by *Homo Sovieticus* and has the same good-humored contempt for authority as Jaroslav Hasek's *Good Soldier Schweik*.[13]

The antithesis of "us" and "them" was basic to Soviet subaltern mentality in the 1930s. "They" were the people who ran things, the people at the top, the ones with power and privilege. "We" were the ones at the bottom, little people without power or privilege whom "they" pushed around, exploited, deceived, and betrayed. Of course, the dividing line shifted according to the speaker's own position. Just as no Soviet professional of the Brezhnev period ever admitted to being a "bureaucrat,"[14] so no Soviet citizen of the 1930s was likely to identify himself as one of "them," either with respect to power or privilege. "They"—the ones with *real* power and privilege—always existed in a higher sphere than the speaker.[15]

For one kolkhoznik, writing to express his views on the Constitution, there were two classes in society: "[white-collar] employees and the workers are one class, and the second class is kolkhozniks [who] bear all the burdens, all the hard work and all the taxes, and the employees have no [burden], as the ruling class." But workers who addressed this topic always saw their own class as the one that was exploited. "Comrade Zhdanov, at all the meetings they talk about the classless society, but in fact it isn't like this, you have a handful of people who live and forget about Communism. It is time to stop feeding [senior officials], it is time to close the 'Torgsins,'" wrote one aggrieved group anonymously. Administrators "live in the best conditions and live at the expense of the labour of the working class," complained another worker, noting that "new classes have developed here, with the only difference being that they are not called classes." [16]

For many Soviet citizens, it seems, privilege and political power became so closely linked in the 1930s that there was little room for other kinds of class hostilities. Resentment of privilege was very strong, but it seems to have been directed almost solely against the privileges of office-holders, that is, against the state and the Communist Party, not against the privileges of the intelligentsia. When Harvard Project interviewers, looking for data on class antagonisms within the society, asked which of the basic social groups (intelligentsia, employees, workers, peasants) received "less than they deserved," they received a remarkable response—in effect, ironically, a rousing endorsement for Stalin's claim that class antagonism had been eliminated in the Soviet Union. *All* social classes, even the intelligentsia, were considered to receive "less than they deserved"—by a majority of respondents of all classes, although admittedly only about half the working-class and peasant respondents had this opinion of the intelligentsia. In addition, many respondents hastened to remind the interviewers that there was another relevant group that had been omitted from the question, namely "party people": they were the ones who got *more* than they deserved. [17]

This tenderness toward the intelligentsia on the part of workers and peasants is surprising, since anti-intelligentsia feeling had apparently run strong in the working class in the revolution and throughout the 1920s, when "bourgeois specialists" were frequently attacked as survivors of the Tsarist privileged classes who had managed to hang on to their privileges despite the Revolution. During the 1928 Shakhty trial, workers not only accepted the state prosecutor's view that the engineers charged were guilty of sabotage and treason, but even tended to go further ("Ripping their heads off would be soft treatment"; "We must shoot all of them or else we'll have no peace." [18]).

If these attitudes went into remission in the 1930s, this may have been because the regime's "war against the nation," as Adam Ulam has called it, focused popular anger exclusively on the party and its leaders, or it may have been a response to the fact that the intelligentsia had been substantially renewed through state-sponsored and other upward mobility from the lower classes since 1928. [19] It should also be noted, however, that the Harvard Project respondents probably understood the "less than they deserved" question as an inquiry about victimization rather than about privilege. The notion of collective victimization was much favored by Soviet citizens, and they were not exclusionary in their application of it. There was more satisfaction in pointing out that virtually everyone suffered than in quibbling about degrees.

So far, I have been describing popular attitudes to the regime that fall mainly in the range between passive acceptance and cautious hostility. Lack of personal security, suppression of religion, the emergence of a new privileged class, and police surveillance and terror no doubt contributed to this broadly based popular criticism of the regime in the 1930s. But the primary cause of it was surely economic: people were living badly, worse than they had done ten or twenty years earlier. "We were better off before" (during NEP, under the Tsars) was probably the most frequently reported of all critical comments in the NKVD's summaries of popular opinion. Under such circumstances, it would have been extraordinary if people had not blamed the government, all the more in that the privation ordinary citizens experienced was so clearly related to government policies like collectivization and crash industri-alization.

Despite its promises of future abundance and massive propaganda of its current achievements, the Stalinist regime did little to improve the life of its people in the 1930s. Judging by the NKVD's soundings of public opinion, a problematic source but the only one available to us, the Stalinist regime was relatively though not desperately unpopular in Russian towns. (In Russian vil-lages, especially in the first half of the 1930s, its unpopularity was much greater.) Overall, as the NKVD regularly reported and official statements re-peated, the ordinary "little man" in Soviet towns, who thought only of his own and his family's welfare, was "dissatisfied with Soviet power," though in a somewhat fatalistic and passive manner.[20] The post-NEP situation was com-pared unfavorably with NEP, and Stalin—despite the officially fostered Stalin cult—was compared unfavorably with Lenin, sometimes because he was more repressive but more often because he let the people go hungry.

This is not to say that Stalin's regime was without support from its citizens. Active support came from the young, the privileged, office-holders and party members, beneficiaries of affirmative action policies, and favored groups like Stakhanovites. Of these, the young are perhaps the most interesting category. Less inclined than their elders to react to economic hardship, urban youth, or at least an impressive proportion of that group, as well as many young peas-ants with some schooling, seem to have assimilated Soviet values, associating them with a rejection of all that was boring, corrupt, unprincipled, old, and routine, and identified, often passionately and enthusiastically, with Soviet ideals. They were ready to go adventuring in the Soviet cause: they grew up wanting to go on polar expeditions and volunteer to build Komsomolsk in the Far East. This was the cohort that, as Solzhenitsyn put it, had grown up under Soviet power and regarded the revolution as "ours." Even young people who had experienced stigmatization on the grounds of their social origin often shared this "Soviet" orientation of their more fortunate peers. "I didn't join the party, but I was a Communist at heart," said a teacher, who suffered much in the 1930s for being a priest's daughter, in a recent interview.[21]

The attitudes of the majority of urban citizens who were not active sup-porters of the regime are much harder to get at than those of the activists and youthful enthusiasts. The working class, to which the regime had looked for support in the 1920s, had changed so much as a result of peasant influx and the upward mobility of "old" workers that both its coherence as a class and the workers' sense of a special connection with the regime must be called into question. A number of labor historians see the dominant motif of the 1930s as state exploitation and worker resistance. It is likely, nevertheless, that many workers retained a residual feeling of connection with the Soviet cause, especially in cities with a strong revolutionary tradition like Leningrad, and that this constituted passive support for the regime.[22]

It has recently been argued that it makes no more sense to ask whether Soviet citizens did or did not accept the Soviet worldview than to ask whether medieval people accepted the Christian worldview: there was simply no other available.[23] The analogy has obvious weaknesses since in the Soviet case everyone over thirty in 1937 could perfectly well remember a pre-Soviet world, and in the census of that year more than half the population identified themselves as religious believers, thus rejecting a basic tenet of the Soviet worldview. Nevertheless, the argument is useful in reminding us that most people most of the time do accept their governments, and the chances are that the Russian urban population in the 1930s was no exception.[24]

In the first place, the Soviet government had positioned itself as the repository of national sentiment and patriotism; its nation-building and national-strengthening projects could appeal even to citizens who complained about shortages and resented the privileges of the office-holding elite. In addition, in the course of the 1930s the Russian element in Soviet patriotism came increasingly to the fore, with the return of Russian history to the school curriculum, of uniforms and insignia for the Soviet Army that resembled those of the former Russian Imperial Army, and so on.[25] This was likely to raise passive-approval rates as far as the Russian population was concerned, though it may have had other consequences in the non-Russian republics.

In the second place, this was a regime that had apparently successfully associated itself with progress in the minds of many of its citizens. If the Soviet worldview was not literally the only one available to Russians in the 1930s, it was the only available worldview linked to modernity. Whether or not the Soviet regime had broad legitimacy with the population, its modernizing (civilizing) mission appears to have done so. As far as we can tell, most people accepted the dichotomy of "backwardness" and "culture" and the proposition that the regime was helping the population to become less backward and more cultured that lay at the heart of the Soviet message. They may personally have cherished some aspects of their own backwardness (e.g., getting drunk and beating their wives), but this was quite compatible with accepting that drunkenness and wife-beating were bad and signs of an uncultured, undeveloped human being. It could even be that the same person who grumbled one day about the disappearance of fish from the market was capable the next day of telling his neighbor that grumbling about shortages was a sign of backwardness and lack of political development.

In the third place, the Soviet state was becoming a welfare state, however incomplete and spasmodic its delivery of benefits in the 1930s. The state was the monopoly distributor of goods and services, which meant that allocation—the power to decide who got what—was one of its most important functions. As Janos Kornai puts it, in Soviet-type systems the population is under the "paternalistic tutelage" and care of the party and state. "The bureaucracy stands *in loco parentis*," he writes, "all other strata, groups, or individuals in society are children, wards whose minds must be made up for them by their adult guardians." The citizen's natural posture toward a state that controls distribution of goods and benefits is one of supplication, not resistance. It may also be one of passive dependence; indeed Soviet officials frequently complained about the "dependent" habits of *Homo Sovieticus*, his lack of initiative, and his stubborn expectation that the state would and should provide.[26]

The Soviet state, with which citizens' everyday lives were so entangled, was a peculiar hybrid. On the one hand, it remained revolutionary, committed to changing the world and shaking up the lives of its citizens, and retaining all the violence, intolerance, and suspicion that pertain to those aims. On the other hand, it was moving toward the welfare-state paternalism that would characterize Soviet-type systems in the postwar period, and was already perceived by its citizens in these terms. These two facets of the state seem very different, but they had important elements in common. First, both the revolutionary and the paternalist states disdained law and bureaucratic legalism, preferring voluntarist solutions in the first case and personalistic ones in the second. Second, both had a very strong sense of the responsibilities of leadership. In revolutionary terminology, this was the vanguard concept. In the paternalist state, the vanguard concept became, in effect, "Father knows best."

If we consider what models or metaphors of the Soviet state might help us understand the practices of *Homo Sovieticus*, several possibilities present themselves. In the first place, Soviet society may be conceptualized as a prison or a conscript army. This catches the elements of regimentation, strict discipline, and confinement within a closed institution with its own strict codes of behavior, often bewildering to outsiders. The behavior of prisoners and conscripts reflects their fear of punishment, which may be incurred by failing to follow orders or random mischance. A sharp dividing line separates guards and officers in such institutions from inmates and recruits: these are "us" and "them" situations. Bullying by guards/officers produces resentment, though it is also seen as part of the natural order of things. There are informers among the inmates, but "ratting" to the authorities on other inmates is nevertheless strongly condemned in the inmate community. Desertion/attempting to escape is severely punished. In the case of the army, patriotism and the spirit of patriotic duty are strongly inculcated.

Another way of conceptualizing Soviet society is as a school of the strict type, probably a boarding school. The school is also a closed institution with its own conventions and discipline. School spirit, the local form of patriotism, is inculcated. A social gulf separates teachers and pupils; tattling to the teachers is prevalent, but disapproved of in the pupil community. Teachers often speak in homilies, recommending virtues such as cleanliness, quietness, politeness, and respect for elders and school property that pupils may or may not inwardly accept but in any case regard as suitable only for the teacher-dominated public sphere, not for private intercourse with fellow pupils. Many activities in the school that are described as voluntary are in fact compulsory, and in general pupils often observe and privately ridicule the hypocrisy of the school's public discourse and the divergence from it of the teachers' conduct.

There is, however, an important difference between schools and other closed institutions—schools have the function of education. The school is a civilizing institution: its raison d'être is to impart the learning and behavioral skills appropriate to the adult (cultured) society that the children will eventually have to join. Most pupils accept the premise that, however unpleasant the educational process may be, it is ultimately for their own good. This model undoubtedly comes closest to the Soviet regime's self-conception as an enlightened vanguard carrying out a civilizing mission. Education was one of the regime's core values; school—as in the epithet "school for socialism," applied to a variety of Soviet institutions from the trade unions to the Red Army—was a key metaphor.

Finally, there is another less exalted model of the Soviet state that may help illuminate Soviet everyday practices: the soup kitchen or the relief agency. Soviet citizens were masters of self-representation as the deserving poor; they regarded it as the state's obligation to provide them with food, clothing, and shelter. Very likely, being deserving poor, they also feel an obligation to work, but the relationship of work to welfare is not seen as reciprocal. The whole range of supplicatory and dependent behaviors characteristic of Soviet citizens outlined above fits the soup kitchen model better than any of the others. The client of a soup kitchen does not feel that he or she is involved in a self-improvement project, in contrast to the school pupil, nor has he the strong fear of punishment and sense of loss of freedom characteristic of prisoners and army recruits. He may or may not feel grateful to the organizers of the soup kitchen, although periodically he is likely to reproach them for not providing enough soup or saving the best meals for favorite clients. But basically he sees the soup kitchen just as a source of goods he needs, and judges it primarily by the quantity and quality of the goods and the convenience of obtaining them.

This book has described a wide range of practices of everyday life in Stalin's Russia: "getting" goods legally and illegally, using patrons and connections, counting living space in square meters, quarreling in communal apartments, "free" marriage, petitioning, denouncing, informing, complaining about officials, complaining about privilege, enjoying privilege, studying, volunteering, moving up, tumbling down, confusing the future and the present, mutual protection, self-criticism, scapegoating, purging, bullying subordinates, deferring to officials, lying about social origin, unmasking enemies, hunting spies, and many others. It was a life in which outward conformity to ideology and ritual mattered, but personal ties mattered even more. It was a life of random disasters and of manifold daily irritations and inconveniences, from the hours wasted in queues and lack of privacy in communal apartments to the endless bureaucratic rudeness and red tape and the abolition, in the cause of productivity and atheism, of a common day of rest. There were fearful things that affected Soviet life and visions that uplifted it, but mostly it was a hard grind, full of shortages and discomfort. *Homo Sovieticus* was a string-puller, an operator, a time-server, a freeloader, a mouther of slogans, and much more. But above all, he was a survivor.

Notes

Introduction

1. The term *Homo Sovieticus*, used critically and as condemnation of a social type, became popular in the Soviet Union in the 1980s. Aleksandr Zinoviev took it for the title of his book *Homo Sovieticus* [*Gomo sovetikus*], trans. Charles Janson (Boston, 1985). My usage, in contrast, is not meant to be pejorative but rather to call attention to the existence of a characteristic set of "Soviet" practices and behaviors related to the peculiarities of Soviet institutions and social structure.

2. On private life, see Michelle Perrot, ed., *A History of Private Life* IV: *From the Fires of Revolution to the Great War*, trans. Arthur Goldhammer (Cambridge, 1990) and Philippe Ariès, *Centuries of Childhood: A Social History of Family Life*, trans. Robert Baldick (New York, 1962); on the workplace, see Alf Lüdtke, ed., *The History of Everyday Life. Reconstructing Historical Experiences and Ways of Life*, trans. William Templer (Princeton, 1995) (esp. articles by Lüdtke, Kaschuba, and Niethammer); on resistance, see Detlev J. K. Peukert, *Inside Nazi Germany. Conformity, Opposition, and Racism in Everyday Life*, trans. Richard Deveson (New Haven, 1987); on everyday resistance, see James C. Scott, *Weapons of the Weak. Everyday Forms of Peasant Resistance* (New Haven, 1985), and Sheila Fitzpatrick, *Stalin's Peasants. Resistance and Survival in the Russian Village after Collectivization* (New York, 1994).

3. For a theoretical discussion of practice, see Michel de Certeau, *The Practice of Everyday Life*, trans. Steve F. Rendall (Berkeley, 1984).

4. See Jerry F. Hough, *Russia and the West* (New York, 1988), ch. 4. On "pre-mobilization," see N. S. Simonov, "'Strengthen the Defence of the Land of the Soviets': The 1927 'War Alarm' and its Consequences," *Europe-Asia Studies* 48:8 (1996), 1355–64.

5. On cultural revolution, see Sheila Fitzpatrick, ed., *Cultural Revolution in Russia, 1928–1931* (Bloomington, 1978).

6. For purge figures, see Chapter. 8, n. 85. Given the relative size of the groups, however, the Great Purges have to be regarded as the more intensely traumatic for the urban elites affected.

7. See I. A. Benediktov, "O Staline i Khrushcheve," *Molodaia gvardiia*, 1989 no. 4, for a vigorous defense by a *vydivzhenets* of the meritocratic basis of Stalin's cadres policy.

8. See Roger R. Reese, *Stalin's Reluctant Soldiers* (Lawrence, Kans., 1996), 4–5, 147–58.

9. Aleksandr Zinoviev, *The Radiant Future* [*Svetloe budushchee*], trans. Gordon Clough (New York, 1980).

10. For a more detailed discussion, see "Becoming Cultured: Socialist Realism and the Representation of Privilege and Taste," in Sheila Fitzpatrick, *The Cultural Front. Power and Culture in Revolutionary Russia* (Ithaca, 1992).

11. On Soviet Potemkinism, see Fitzpatrick, *Stalin's Peasants*, 262–68.

12. *Tolkovyi slovar' russkogo iazyka*, D. N. Ushakov, ed., III (Moscow, 1939): *Otstalost'*.

13. On "friendship of peoples," see Terry D. Martin, "An Affirmative Action Empire: Ethnicity and the Soviet State, 1921–1938," Ph.D. diss., University of Chicago, 1996, 932–81; on backwardness, see Yuri Slezkine, *Arctic Mirrors* (Ithaca, 1994), ch. 7.

14. Letter to Molotov, 1935, in "The Letter as a Work of Art," Sheila Fitzpatrick, ed., *Russian History,* no. 1–2 (1997).

15. See Alex Inkeles and Raymond A. Bauer, *The Soviet Citizen. Daily Life in a Totalitarian Society* (New York, 1968) (1st pub. 1959).

16. On working-class work experiences, see Solomon M. Schwarz, *Labor in the Soviet Union* (New York, 1951), Donald Filtzer, *Soviet Workers and Stalinist Industrialization* (Armonk, NY, 1986), and particularly Vladimir Andrle, *Workers in Stalin's Russia. Industrialization and Social Change in a Planned Economy* (New York, 1988); also Lewis H. Siegelbaum, *Stakhanovism and the Politics of Productivity in the USSR, 1935–1941* (Cambridge, 1988). There are as yet few studies of the life experiences of white-collar groups, although Inkeles, *Soviet Citizen,* provides an excellent overview and introduction.

17. On the disintegration of the urban working class, see Daniel R. Brower, "'The City in Danger': The Civil War and Russian Urban Population," and Diane P. Koenker, "Urbanization and Deurbanization in the Russian Revolution and Civil War," both in Diane Koenker et al, eds., *Party, State, and Society in the Russian Civil War. Explorations in Social History* (Bloomington, 1989), 58–80 and 81–104. On the impact of the vanishing proletariat on the Bolsheviks, see Sheila Fitzpatrick, "The Bolsheviks' Dilemma: The Class Issue in Party Politics and Culture," in Fitzpatrick, *The Cultural Front.*

18. On this question, see Fitzpatrick, "The Problem of Class Identity in NEP Society," in Sheila Fitzpatrick, Alexander Rabinowitch, and Richard Stites, eds., *Russia in the Era of NEP* (Bloomington, 1991).

19. I use Bolshevik and Communist more or less interchangeably. The party changed its name from the former to the latter in 1918, but the former usage persisted for some years, particularly with respect to the party's old guard.

20. For a fuller discussion of Stalinist "estates," see Sheila Fitzpatrick, "Ascribing Class: The Construction of Social Identity in Soviet Russia," *Journal of Modern History* [henceforth *JMH*] 65:4 (December 1993).

21. See E. A. Osokina, *Ierarkhiia potrebleniia. O zhizni liudei v usloviiakh stalinskogo snabzheniia 1928–1935 gg.* (Moscow, 1993).

Chapter 1

1. I use this term broadly to encompass both the state in the strict sense and the Communist Party, since their administrative and organizational functions were completely intertwined. Some scholars use the cumbersome but accurate term "party-state" for the same reason.

2. In his speech on the draft Constitution, in which he described Soviet society as consisting of two basic classes, workers and collectivized peasantry, and a stratum, the intelligentsia. I. V. Stalin, *Sochineniia,* Robert H. McNeal, ed., vol. I (XIV) [henceforth, Stalin, *Soch.*] (Stanford, 1967), 143–45.

3. Nicolas Werth, *Etre communiste en URSS* (Paris, 1981), 42. On party admissions, see T. H. Rigby, *Communist Party Membership in the U.S.S.R. 1917–1967* (Princeton, 1968); on education, see Sheila Fitzpatrick, *Education and Social Mobility in the Soviet Union, 1921–1934* (Cambridge, 1979).

4. See Michael David-Fox, *Revolution of the Mind. Higher Learning among the Bolsheviks, 1918–1929* (Ithaca, 1997).

5. Kaganovich quotation from *XVII syezd V. K. P. (b). 20 ianv.–10 fev. 1934 g. Stenograficheskii otchet* (Moscow, 1934), 565. Out of just under two million Communist party members at the beginning of 1937, 88% were in urban cells and 85% were men. Rigby, *Communist Party Membership,* 52–53, 233, 361.

6. *Stalin's Letters to Molotov,* Lars T. Lih, Oleg V. Naumov, and Oleg V.

Khlevniuk, eds. (New Haven, 1995), 232.

7. Lev Kopelev, *The Education of a True Believer*, trans. Gary Kern (New York, 1980), 90.

8. Dimitrov report in A. G. Solov'ev, "Tetradi krasnogo professora, 1912–1941 gg." in *Neizvestnaia Rossiia. XX vek* IV (Moscow, 1993), 183–84.

9. Quoted in Werth, *Etre communiste*, 225.

10. *Trinadtsatyi syezd RKP(b). Mai 1924 goda. Stenograficheskii otchet* (Moscow, 1963), 158; Zelensky, in *Report of the Court Proceedings in the Case of the Anti-Soviet "Bloc of Rights and Trotskyites" heard before the Military Collegium of the Supreme Court of the U.S.S.R. Moscow, March 2–13, 1938* (Moscow, 1938), 749.

11. On loss of privileges, see Werth, *Etre communiste*, 261.

12. Solov'ev, "Tetradi," 183–84. See also *Sto sorok besed s Molotovym. Iz dnevnika F. Chueva* (Moscow, 1991), 409–11, 429–30.

13. *Report* (1938), 777–78.

14. Quoted in Werth, *Etre communiste*, 264.

15. *Chistka*. The "small-p" distinguishes it from a different phenomenon, the Great Purges of 1937–38.

16. Contemporary reports quoted by Iu. K. Shcheglov, "Kommentarii k romanu "Zolotoi telenok," in I. Il'f and E. Petrov, *Zolotoi telenok. Roman* [henceforth Shcheglov, *ZT*] (Moscow, 1995), 378.

17. Elena Bonner, *Mothers and Daughters*, trans. Antonina W. Bouis (New York, 1993), 148–49.

18. Sheila Fitzpatrick, "Lives under Fire. Autobiographical Narratives and their Challenges in Stalin's Russia," in *De Russie et d'ailleurs. Mélanges Marc Ferro* (Paris, 1995), 225. On confession in Soviet culture, see also Oleg V. Kharkhordin, "The Collective and the Individual in Soviet Russia: A Study of Background Practices," Ph.D. diss., Berkeley, 1996, chs. 2, 5, and 6.

19. See Kendall E. Bailes, *Technology and Society under Lenin and Stalin. Origins of the Soviet Technical Intelligentsia, 1917–1941* (Princeton, 1978), 69–121.

20. Martin, "Affirmative Action Empire," 411, and see Stalin's letter to Menzhinskii in *Revelations from the Russian Archives. Documents in English Translation*, Diane P. Koenker and Ronald D. Bachman, eds. (Washington, 1997), 243, and Lars Lih, "Introduction," in *Stalin's Letters to Molotov*, 42–49. On Shakhty reactions, see Matthew E. Lenoe, "Soviet Mass Journalism and the Transformation of Soviet Newspapers, 1926–1932," Ph.D. diss., University of Chicago, 1997, 309–15.

21. Victor Serge, *Memoirs of a Revolutionary 1901–1941* (London, 1963), trans. Peter Sedgwick, 203–04.

22. On this subject, see Gabor T. Rittersporn, "The Omnipresent Conspiracy: On Soviet Imagery of Politics and Social Relations in the 1930s," in J. Arch Getty and Roberta T. Manning, eds., *Stalinist Terror. New Perspectives* (Cambridge, 1993), 99–115.

23. Stalin's views, as reported by State Prosecutor Krylenko, are in *Sovetskaia iustitsiia* [henceforth *Sov. iust.*] (1934) no. 9, 2.

24. *Konspiratsiia* and *konspirativnost'* (note that a different term, *zagovor*, was used for counterrevolutionary conspiracy). See, for example, the Politburo resolution of 16 May 1929 "O konspiratsii" in *Stalinskoe Politbiuro v 30-e gody. Sbornik dokumentov* (Moscow, 1995), 75; for a detailed survey, see Jonathan Bone, "Soviet Controls on the Circulation of Information," paper presented at a conference "Assessing the New Soviet Archival Sources," New Haven, May 16–18, 1997.

25. "O konspiratsii" and Khlevniuk, *Politbiuro*, 250; Smolensk Archive (SA), WKP 178, 61; Lenoe, "Unmasking, Show Trials, and the Manipulation of Popular Moods," unpub. ms., 123.

26. Gosudarstvennyi arkhiv Sverdlovskoi oblasti (GASO), f. 52 (88), op. 1, d. 66, l. 78 (secret instruction on handling classified documents, 1931); Gosudarstvennyi arkhiv Rossiiskoi Federatsii (GARF), f. 5446, op. 81a, d. 337, l. 12 (secret instruction from Vyshinsky, deputy chairman of Sovnarkom, to the People's Commissariat of Health, 1940).

27. Stephen F. Cohen, *Bukharin and the Bolshevik Revolution* (New York, 1973), 92; L. Kritsman, *Geroicheskii period velikoi russkoi revoliutsii* (2nd ed., Moscow-Leningrad, 1926), 81–82.

28. Lenoe, "Unmasking," 124.

29. Dzhambul, "Narkom Ezhov," *Pravda*, 3 December 1937, 2. For the anniversary, see ibid., 20 and 21 December.

30. See Jerry F. Hough and Merle Fainsod, *How the Soviet Union Is Governed* (Cambridge, 1979), 128–32 and 144–46, for a good short description of this process.

31. For deprecation, see Dmitri Volkogonov, *Stalin. Triumph and Tragedy*, trans. Harold Shukman (Rocklin, CA, 1992), 241; Lion Feuchtwanger, *Moscow 1937*, trans. Irene Josephy (New York, 1937), 75–77; Stalin, *Soch.* I (XIV), 274.

32. The boss = *khoziain*. See O. V. Khlevniuk, *1937-i: Stalin, NKVD i sovetskoe obshchestvo* (Moscow, 1992), 30.

33. *Khrushchev Remembers*, trans. Strobe Talbott (Boston, 1970), 58–62; O. V. Khlevniuk, *Stalin i Ordzhonikidze. Konflikty v Politbiuro v 30-e gody* (Moscow, 1993); *Stalinskoe Politbiuro*, 91.

34. *Stalinskoe Politbiuro*, 97 (quotation from Sergei Syrtsov), 99, 178–79; Ivan Gronskii, *Iz proshlogo . . . Vospominaniia* (Moscow, 1991), 135–36.

35. Khlevniuk, *Politbiuro*, 240–42; Arkady Vaksberg, *The Prosecutor and the Prey. Vyshinsky and the 1930s Moscow Show Trials*, trans. Jan Butler (London, 1990), 278.

36. *Iosif Stalin v ob"iatiiakh sem'i. Iz lichnogo arkhiva* (Moscow, 1993), 32–33. My emphasis.

37. Examples in Solov'ev, "Tetradi," 177; Khlevniuk, *Stalin*, 86. See Khlevniuk, *Stalin*, 106–07, for an exception proving the rule.

38. The genesis of the letter is discussed in John Barber, "Stalin's Letter to the Editors of *Proletarskaya revolyutsiya*," *Soviet Studies* 28:1 (1976).

39. For examples in the realm of education policy, see Fitzpatrick, *Education*, 220–26.

40. GARF, f. 1235, op. 141, d. 130, l. 18. On the drive against religion in 1929–30, see Fitzpatrick, *Stalin's Peasants*, 59–63.

41. GARF, f. 1235, op. 141, d. 435, ll. 3, 8–9.

42. Steven D. Richmond, "Ideologically Firm: Soviet Theater Censorship, 1921–1928," Ph.D. diss., University of Chicago, 1996, 380–81.

43. Rossiiskii tsentr khraneniia i izucheniia dokumentov noveishei istorii (RTsKhIDNI), f. 142, d. 461, l. 13. Stalin ignored Lunacharsky's plea.

44. Vitalii Shentalinskii, *Raby svobody. V literaturnykh arkhivakh KGB* ([Moscow], 1995), 124–25.

45. See Lynne Viola, *Peasant Rebels under Stalin. Collectivization and the Culture of Peasant Resistance* (New York, 1996), 171–72; Fitzpatrick, *Stalin's Peasants*, 287–90.

46. See, for example, *Krokodil* (henceforth, *Krok.*), 1935 no. 21, 6; 1940 no. 16, 8–9.

47. *Krok.*, 1935 no. 28–29, 17. See also ibid., 1934 no. 9, 2; 1934 no. 13, 7; 1935 no. 6, 10; 1939 no. 1, back page; 1939 no. 28, 14.

48. See Peter H. Solomon, Jr., *Soviet Criminal Justice under Stalin* (Cambridge, 1996), 127–28, 139–40, and passim.

49. Sarah Davies, "The 'Cult' of the 'Vozhd': Representations in Letters from 1934–1941," *Russian History*, 24(1997): 1–2.

50. "Diary of Andrei Stepanovich Arzhilovsky," in *Intimacy and Terror. Soviet Diaries of the 1930s*, Véronique Garros, Natalia Korenevskaya, and Thomas Lahusen, eds. (New York, 1995), 118.

51. For city name changes, see E. M. Pospelov, *Imena gorodov: vchera i segnodnia (1917–1992)* (Moscow, 1993); on Moscow street names, see also P. B. Sytin, *Iz istorii moskovskikh ulits (ocherki)* (Moscow, 1958). Data on renaming industrial enterprises from *Alfavitno-predmetnyi ukazatel' k. prikazam i rasporiazheniiam NKTP za 1935 g.* (Moscow, 1936). The town of Gatchino, later Gatchina, was named Trotsk in Trotsky's honor from 1923 to 1929; the city of Elizavetgrad was named Zinov'evsk for Zinoviev from 1923 to 1934; the Donbass industrial center Enakievo was named Rykovo for Aleksei Rykov, the Rightist leader, from 1928 to 1937.

52. B. Starkov, "Kak Moskva chut' ne stala Stalinodarom," *Izvestiia TsK*, 1990 no. 12, 126–27; *Krasnaia Tatariia* [henceforth *Kras. Tat.*], 26 March 1937, 2.

53. E. Pramnek, *Otchetnyi doklad V Gor'kovskoi oblastnoi partiinoi konferentsii o rabote obkoma VKP(b)* (Gorky, 1937). Stalin outlined "six conditions" in a famous speech on economic development in 1931.

54. Eugenia Ginzburg, *Into the Whirlwind*, trans. Paul Stevenson and Manya Harari (Harmondsworth, Mx, 1968), 18.

55. *Trud*, 22 Mar. 1937, 1 (Iaroslavl); Tsentral'nyi gosudarstvennyi arkhiv istoriko-politicheskoi dokumentatsii Sankt-Peterburga (TsGAIPD), f. 24, op. 2v, d. 727, l. 290 (Leningrad). For other depictions of abusive bosses, see Fitzpatrick, *Stalin's Peasants*, 183–85.

56. On risk-taking, see Conclusion.

57. Khlevniuk, *Stalin*, 36–37; *Stalinskoe Politbiuro*, 154.

58. See "Neotraditionalism," in Ken Jowitt, *New World Disorder. The Leninist Extinction* (Berkeley, 1992), 121–58; Graeme Gill, *The Origins of the Stalinist Political System* (Cambridge, 1990), 129–30, 324.

59. Speech of 5 March 1937 in Stalin, *Soch.* I (XIV), 230–31; draft cited Khlevniuk, *1937-i*, 77.

60. James R. Harris, "The Great Urals: Regional Interests and the Evolution of the Soviet System, 1917–1937," Ph.D. diss., University of Chicago, 1996, 283–84.

61. See Marc Raeff, *Origins of the Russian Intelligentsia. The Eighteenth-Century Nobility* (New York, 1966), 78–79; Richard Pipes, "The Russian Military Colonies, 1810–1831," *JMH* 22:3 (September, 1950).

62. From an article in *Severnyi rabochii* [henceforth *Sev. rab.*], 11 April 1937, 1. The same Chekhov story ("Unter Prishibeev," 1885) is cited in *Krok.*, 1939 no. 14.

63. *Krok.*, 1934 no. 14, 10.

64. Nadezhda Mandelshtam, *Hope Abandoned*, trans. Max Hayward (New York, 1974), 288.

65. *Sov. iust.*, 1937 no. 20, p. 22; *Kommuna*, 22 Jul. 1937, 2.

66. GARF, f. 8131, op. 27, d. 107, ll. 155, 156, 135

67. GARF, f. 8131, op. 27, d. 107, ll. 97–99.

68. *Tolkovyi slovar'* I: *Aktiv, Aktivizirovat', Aktivizm, Aktivist*.

69. Russian Research Center, Harvard University, *Project on the Soviet Social System. Interview Records*, "A" Schedule Protocols [henceforth HP], #385 (XIX), 11–12.

70. *Krasnyi Krym*, 30 March 1939, 4.

71. N. Khvalynsky, in *Soviet Youth. Twelve Komsomol Histories*, ed. Nikolai K. Novak-Deker (Munich, 1959): Institut zur Erforschung der UdSSR, Series 1, no. 51 [henceforth *Soviet Youth*), 120–21.

72. Abdy Kurmanbekov, in *Soviet Youth*, 174–75.

73. Peter Kruzhin, in ibid., 196, 198.

74. W. I. Hryshko, in ibid., 98.

75. Nikolai Lunev, in ibid., 34.

76. Partiinyi arkhiv Novosibirskoi oblasti (PANO), f. 3, op. 9, d. 952, ll. 211–12.

77. GARF, f. 3316. op. 2, d. 1615, l. 57.

78. On Bykov, see *Izvestiia* [henceforth *Izv.*], 26 June 1935, 4; ibid., 27 June 1935, 3. As in many of these stories, the circumstances surrounding the Bykov murder are murky and the official characterization of it as an act of "class vengeance" may not be fully accurate. It is clear, however, that Bykov was an activist on his way up and that his murderers, described as lumpen proletarians, resented this. On Morozov, see below, ch. 3.

Chapter 2

1. John Carswell, *The Exile: A Life of Ivy Litvinov* (London, 1983), 101.

2. The Russian for the terms in inverted commas is *dostat'* (instead of *kupit'*); *trudno dostat'*; *defitsitnye tovary*; *avos'ki, Chto daiut?* (or *Chto vybrasyvaiut?*); *na levo*; *znakomstva i sviazi*; *blat*. For commentary on new usages involving acquisition of goods, see *Krok.*, 1933 no. 13, 4–5; 1934 no. 29–30, 10, and no. 26, 10; 1935 no. 25, 7, and no. 33–34, 21; and HP, #3 (I), 47, and #4 (I), 11.

3. W. A. Rukeyser, *Working for the Soviets: An American Engineer in Russia* (New York, 1932), 217.

4. See data cited by Stephen G. Wheatcroft in Getty, *Stalinist Terror*, 282–89, and Alec Nove, *An Economic History of the U.S.S.R.* (Harmondsworth, Mx, 1972), 177.

5. See Osokina, *Ierarkhiia potrebleniia*, 39 (Table 4).

6. Nove, *History*, 259.

7. *Izmeneniia sotsial'noi struktury sovetskogo obshchestva 1921–seredina 30-kh godov* (Moscow, 1979), 194. *Sotsialisticheskoe stroitel'stvo SSSR. Statisticheskii ezhegodnik* (Moscow, 1934), 356–57; *Sotsialisticheskoe stroitel'stvo Soiuza SSR (1937–1938 gg.). Statisticheskii sbornik* (Moscow, 1939), 12–15. Note that 1926 figures are from the census of 17 December 1926.

8. This argument is put in Janos Kornai, *Economics of Shortage* (Amsterdam, 1980), 2 vols.

9. GARF, f. 3316, op. 16a, d. 446l, l. 36.

10. TsGAIPD, f. 24, op. 2v, d. 1869, ll. 49–50; *Intimacy and Terror*, 139; TsGAIPD, f. 24, op. 2v, d. 2487, l. 90.

11. Letters published in E. Osokina, "Krizis snabzheniia 1939–1941 gg. v pis'makh sovetskikh liudei," *Voprosy istorii* [henceforth *Vopr.ist.*], 1996 no. 1, 8–12; Alma-Ata report from GARF, f. 8131, op. 27, d. 165, l. 307.

12. Osokina, "Krizis," 6, 25.

13. On the temperance movement, see T. P. Korzhikhina, "Bor'ba s alkogolizma v 1920-e — nachale 1930-kh gg.," *Vopr. ist.*, 1985 no. 9. For local reports and petitions in favor of prohibitions of alcohol sales in the period 1929–32, see GANO, f. 47, op. 5, d. 120, l. 155; ibid, f. 33, op. 1, d. 223, l. 105, and Stephen Kotkin, *Magnetic Mountain. Stalinism as a Civilization* (Berkeley, 1995), 189. For Stalin's note, see *Stalin's Letters*, 209. On vodka production, see Julie Hessler, "Culture of Shortages. A Social History of Soviet Trade, 1917–1953," Ph.D diss., University of Chicago, September 1996, 82 and 85, n. 52.

14. *Melkaia promyshlennost' SSSR. Po dannym perepisi 1929 g.*, vyp. 1 (Moscow, 1933), v; Smolensk Archive [henceforth SA], WKP 178, 4; RGAE, f. 3429, op. 1, d. 5162, l. 19. See also Sheila Fitzpatrick, "After NEP: The Fate of NEP Entrepre-

neurs, Small Traders, and Artisans in the "Socialist Russia" of the 1930s," *Russian History* 13: 2–3 (1986).

15. *Leningradskaia pravda*, 8 April 1937, 3; *Sov. iust.*, 1932 no. 2, 18; V. A. Tikhomirov, *Promkooperatsiia na sovremennom etape* (Moscow, 1931), 15–17; *Vecherniaia Moskva* [henceforth *Vech. Mosk.*], 1 October 1934, 2 (on household repairs); Leonard E. Hubbard, *Soviet Trade and Distribution* (London, 1938), 151–53. *Krokodil* kept up a running commentary on bad workmanship and defective products: see, for example, *Krok.*, 1934 no. 4, 11; no. 10, 11; no. 12, 2 and inside back cover; no. 26, 12; no. 29–30, 17.

16. Hubbard, *Soviet Trade*, 151–53; *Sobranie uzakonenii i rasporiazhenii rabochego i krest'ianskogo pravitel'stva RSFSR* (henceforth *Sobr. uzak.*), 1931 no. 41, art. 284.

17. *Puti industrializatsii*, 1931 no. 5–6, 78; "Kalosha" (1926) in Mikh. Zoshchenko, *Rasskazy, fel'etony, povesti* (Moscow, 1958), 33–6; *Sev. rab.*, 26 August 1935, 4.

18. Stalin was the Politburo's rapporteur on consumer goods (*shirpotreb*) in June 1936: RTsKhIDNI, f. 17, op. 3, d. 978, ll. 1–2.

19. Sarah Davies, *Popular Opinion in Stalin's Russia. Terror, Propaganda, and Dissent, 1934–1941* (Cambridge, 1997), 38–43,.and TsGAIPD, f. 24, op. 2v, d. 3553, ll. 223–24 (Leningrad NKVD reports, 1939); GARF, f. 5446, op. 82, d. 112, l. 220 (1939 letter to Molotov).

20. Osokina, *Ierarkhiia*, 36; *Trud*, 14 July 1933, 4 (and see Kotkin, *Magnetic Mountain*, 258–61, for a similar show trial in Magnitogorsk); *Rabochii put'* [henceforth *Rab. put.*], 22 July 1937, 4; *Kommuna*, 23 November 1937, 3, and 24 November, 3; GARF, f. 5446, op. 82, d.56, l. 331; *Kras. Tat.*, 22 January 1937, 4.

21. Osokina, "Krizis," 10, 12, 16–17.

22. Although most residential housing units were state owned, some small one-family wooden houses still remained in private hands in the 1930s. This was especially common in provincial towns that had not experienced rapid industrial expansion. Toward the end of the decade, some municipalized housing was returned to private hands, evidently in the hope that this would improve maintenance, and local authorities "in some places" (outside the major cities?) were instructed to make building materials and bank credits available to citizens who wished to build their own homes. It is not clear how much came of these initiatives. See GARF, f. 8131, op. 27, d. 165, ll. 365, 376, and 404; *Sov. iust.*, 1937 no. 23, 45; Gosudarstvennyi arkhiv Novosibirskoi oblasti [GANO], f. 47, op. 1, d. 3407.

23. Timothy J. Colton, *Moscow. Governing the Socialist Metropolis* (Cambridge, Mass., 1995), 798; Kotkin, *Magnetic*, 161 (1935 figure); V. I. Isaev, "Formirovanie gorodskogo obraza zhizni rabochikh Sibiri v period sotsialisticheskoi rekonstruktsii narodnogo khoziaistva," in *Urbanizatsiia sovetskoi Sibiri*, ed. V. V. Alekseev (Novosibirsk, 1987), 48 (1933 figure).

24. Consolidation = *uplotnenie*; superintendent = *upravdom*; yardman = *dvornik*. From 1931 to 1937, many apartment houses in Moscow and other big cities were formally rental cooperatives, known by the Soviet acronym of "*Zhakty*" (*zhilishchno-arendnye kooperativnye tovarishchestva*): see Colton, *Moscow*, 159.

25. *Sov. iust.*, 1936 no. 31, 7; Colton, *Moscow*, 343; *Sov. iust.*, 1939 no. 11, 64; *Krasnyi Krym*, 28 April 1939, 4.

26. GARF, f. 5446, op. 82, d. 42, ll. 47–51; ibid., d. 64, l. 161.

27. Colton, *Moscow*, 342.

28. Kotkin, *Magnetic*, 174. After residents' protests, one kitchen was added to each apartment block (which contained up to eighty apartments).

29. GARF, f. 5446., op. 81a, d. 94, ll. 207–09.

30. "Nervnye liudi," in Zoshchenko, *Rasskazy*, 22–24; *Sov. iust.*, 1935 no. 22, back page. For firsthand accounts of communal apartments, see Raissa L. Berg, *Memoirs of a Geneticist from the Soviet Union*, trans. David Lowe (New York, 1988), 129–45; Svetlana Boym, *Common Places. Mythologies of Everyday Life in Russia* (Cambridge, Mass., 1994), 121–67; Paola Messana, *Kommunalka* (Paris, 1995).

31. Messana, *Kommunalka*, 173–74.

32. TsGAIPD, f. 24, op. 2v, d. 1514, ll. 114–20. Another similar case is in ibid., d. 727, l. 174.

33. Liubchenko, "Arbat, 30, Kvartira 58," *Istochnik*, 1993 no. 5–6, 24–36. See also Berg, *Memoirs*, 141–44; Messana, *Kommunalka*, 27–30, 159–630.

34. Kotkin, *Magnetic*, 167; Colton, *Moscow*, 308. Although exact figures for Moscow in the 1930s are not available, the trend can be discerned from the fact that share of company-owned housing rose from 25 percent in the 1920s to 40 percent in the 1940s.

35. Isaev, "Formirovanie," 47 (on Kuznetsk); Kotkin, *Magnetic*, 136.

36. John Scott, *Behind the Urals. An American Worker in Russia's City of Steel* (Bloomington, 1973; original ed. 1942), 39–40.

37. Kotkin, *Magnetic*, 135–36; Isaev, "Formirovanie," 47; Kotkin, *Magnetic*, 135–36; Colton, *Moscow*, 342.

38. Colton, *Moscow*, 342–43; GANO, f. 33, op. 1, d. 346, ll. 43–48.

39. *Kommunist* (Saratov), 8 May 1935, 1; *Trud*, 3 January 1935, 2; ibid., 4 January 1936, 2; Kotkin, *Magnetic*, 171; Colton, *Moscow*, 342–43.

40. Zara Witkin, *An American Engineer in Stalin's Russia. The Memoirs of Zara Witkin, 1932–1934*, Michael Gelb, ed. (Berkeley, 1991), 55–56.

41. Svanidze diary, in *Iosif Stalin*, 173–75 (entry for 29 April 1935).

42. On sewage, see Colton, *Moscow*, 853, n. 193; on bathing habits, see ibid., 342, and Messana, *Kommunalka*, passim. For a panegyric to Moscow's bathhouses (established before the revolution), see Vl. Giliarovskii, *Moskva i moskvichi* (Moscow, 1979; 1st pub. 1926), 246–74

43. *Pravda*, 11 June 1938, 2; *Trud*, 8 May 1935, 3; *Kommuna*, 6 September 1937, 3; Isaev, "Formirovanie," 47; M. A. Vodolagin, *Ocherki istorii Volgograda 1589–1967* (Moscow, 1968), 268, 271; GANO, f. 33, op. 1, d. 223, ll. 49, 57–59. Note that reliable published figures on services and amenities in the provinces in the 1930s are extremely hard to come by.

44. GARF, f. 5446, op. 82, d. 25, ll. 231–34; *Sots. stroi.* (1934), 356–57.

45. GANO, f. 47, op. 5, d. 206, l. 10.

46. Kotkin, *Magnetic*, 132–33, 137–39.

47. Betty Roland, *Caviar for Breakfast* (Sydney, 1989), 67–68; Louis Fischer, *Soviet Journey* (New York, 1935), 62; *American Engineer*, 131–32; *Krok*, 1932 no. 8, 9; *Sov. iust.*, 1933 no. 9, 13.

48. Vodolagin, *Ocherki*, 271; *Narodnoe khoziaistvo Pskovskoi oblasti. Statisticheskii sbornik* (Leningrad, 1968), 269; *Penzenskaia oblast' za 50 let sovetskoi vlasti. Statisticheskii sbornik* (Saratov-Penza, 1967), 218; Kotkin, *Magnetic*, 132–33.

49. *Sovetskoe gosudarstvo*, 1933 no. 4, 68. See also ibid., 1932 no. 9–10, 152, and *Sov. iust.*, 1934 no. 2, 16. On ethnic conflicts on the Turksib and in Moscow barracks, see Matthew J. Payne, "Turksib: The Building of the Turkestano-Siberian Railroad and the Politics of Production during the Cultural Revolution, 1926–1931," Ph.D. diss., University of Chicago, 1994, ch. 4, and *Vech. Mosk.*, 29 September 1934, 3.

50. *Sov. iust.*, 1934 no. 2, 16. On the meaning of hooliganism in early twentieth-century Russia, see Joan Neuberger, *Hooliganism. Crime, Culture, and Power in St. Petersburg, 1900–1914* (Berkeley, 1993), 1–8 and passim.

51. *Sov. iust.*, 1934 no. 2, 16 (quotation); ibid., 1934 no. 2, 16; 1935 no. 26, 4.

52. *Gor'kovskaia kommuna*, 20 July 1937, 3 (quotation); *Tikhookeanskaia zvezda* [henceforth *Tikh. zv.*], 14 May 1937, 4.

53. *Krest'ianskaia pravda* [henceforth *Kr. pr.*], 27 May 1935, 3, and 17 March 1935, 3; PANO, f. 3, op. 9, d. 9, l. 126.

54. I include cooperatives and trade unions in this category.

55. The partial exception was health care, since physicians were still allowed to maintain a limited private practice.

56. On chronic scarcity, see Kornai, *Economics of Shortage*; on the allocative function, see Katherine Verdery, *National Ideology under Socialism. Identity and Cultural Politics in Ceausescu's Romania* (Berkeley, 1991), 74–83.

57. For ideological justifications, see A. N. Malafeev, *Istoriia tsenoobrazovaniia v SSSR (1917–1963 gg.)* (Moscow, 1964), 147–48 (rationing) and M. Chamkina, *Khudozhestvennaia otkrytka* (Moscow, 1993), 217 (closed distributors as a weapon against the class enemy); on leaders' attitudes, see Hessler, "Culture of Shortages," 268–69, and Khlevniuk, *Politbiuro*, 126–27 (Stalin). For evidence of popular support for rationing, see Davies, *Popular Opinion*, 25–31, Osokina, "Krizis snabzheniia," 8, and GARF, f. 5446, op. 82, d. 112, l. 220 (letter to Molotov, 1939).

58. See Osokina, *Ierarkhiia*, 15; E. H. Carr and R. W. Davies, *Foundations of a Planned Economy, 1926–1929* I (London, 1969), 702–04; Malafeev, *Istoriia*, 138. Peasants did not receive ration cards, although rural officials and some other wage and salary earners in the countryside did.

59. *Biulleten' Narodnogo Komissariata Snabzheniia SSSR*, 1931 no. 5, 22–24.

60. On priorities, see Hessler, "Culture," 74–80.

61. These were officially called "closed distributors" (*zakrytye raspredeliteli*) and informally referred to by the usual bewildering range of Soviet initials and acronyms—ZRK for closed factory cooperatives (later replaced by ORSy), ZVK for their counterpart in the armed forces, and so on. On ZRK (closed workers' cooperatives) and ORSy (departments of worker supply), see *Istoriia sotsialisticheskoi ekonomiki SSSR v semi tomakh*, I. A. Gladkov, ed. [henceforth *Ist. sots. ek.*] (Moscow, 1977), III, 453, and Hessler, "Culture," 92–108. ORSy, established in 1932, served the same function as ZRK but were subordinate to the individual factory rather than the central cooperative union. The ORSy were also responsible for producing food for the plant on state farmland and distributing allotments (*ogorody*) to workers's families for individual cultivation.

62. *Ist. sots. ek.*, III, 454; G. Ia. Neiman, *Vnutrenniaia torgovlia SSSR* (Moscow, 1935), 159.

63. See Scott, *Behind the Urals*, 86–87, and John D. Littlepage with Demaree Bess, *In Search of Soviet Gold* (New York, 1938), 68.

64. *Izv.*, 26 Sep. 1935, 2; *Trud*, 8 Feb. 1936, 4; GARF. f. 8131, op. 27, d. 165, ll. 304, 320–21. On the supply crisis of the late 1930s, see E. Osokina, "Liudi i vlast' v usloviiakh krizisa snabzheniia 1939–1941 gody," *Otechestvennaia istoriia*, 1995 no. 3, 16–32.

65. Decree of 20 May 1932, "O poriadke proizvodstva torgovli kolkhozov, kolkhoznikov i trudiashchikhsia edinolichnykh krest'ian . . . ," in *Resheniia partii i pravitel'stva po khoziaistvennym voprosam (1917–1967 gg.)* II (Moscow, 1967), 388–89.

66. See Hessler, "Culture," ch. 4, esp. 183–97. The phrase "oases of private trade" is Osokina's in *Ierarkhiia*, 108.

67. Osokina, *Ierarkhiia*, 117–18. According to the 1932 decree, kolkhoz trade should be conducted at prices "forming themselves at the market"

(*skladyvaiushimsia na rynke*), though these prices should not exceed "average commercial prices" in state trade. *Resheniia* II, 389.

68. See E. A. Osokina, "Za zerkal'noi dver'iu Torgsina," *Otechestvennaia istoriia*, 1995 no. 2, 86–104; Malcolm Muggeridge, *Winter in Moscow* (London, 1934), 146. In their first year of existence, the Torgsins were closed stores selling only to foreign tourists; hence the name (= *torgovlia s inostrannymi turistami*).

69. *Ist. sots. ek.* III, 454–55; Hessler, "Culture," 82–83; Osokina, *Ierarkhiia*, 109.

70. *Ist. sots. ek.*, IV, 429–30, 433; Hessler, "Culture," 269–72.

71. Quotation from Davies, *Popular Opinion*, 30; TsGAIPD, f. 24, op. 2v, d. 3553, ll. 62 and 223–24 (1939 reports).

72. On "pushers" (*tolkachi*), see Joseph Berliner, *Factory and Manager in the Soviet Union* (Cambridge, Mass., 1957), and his "*Blat* is Higher than Stalin," *Problems of Communism* 3:1 (1954). Berliner, *Factory and Manager*, and "*Blat*."

73. Note that persons disfranchised for trading and petitioning for restoration of rights often wrote of their resort to trade as a last expedient, forced on them by extreme need and contrary to their better natures—the kind of rhetoric one might expect in connection with prostitution or some other truly shameful activity. See Golfo Alexopoulos, "Rights and Passage: Marking Outcasts and Making Citizens in Soviet Russia, 1926–1936," Ph.D. diss., University of Chicago, 1996, 465–75.

74. *Sov. iust.*, 1936 no. 26, 9; *Gor'kovskaia kommuna*, 23 November 1937, 4.

75. *Vecherniaia krasnaia gazeta*, 27 February 1936, 3; *Groznenskii rabochii*, 30 January 1938, 6.

76. *Kommuna*, 4 August 1936, 4.

77. TSGAIPD, f. 24, op. 2v, d. 3553, ll. 223–24.

78. *Krok.*, 1939 no. 2, 8–9.

79. *Krok.*, 1933 no. 1, back page; ibid., 1932 no. 13, back page; *Sov. iust.*, 1932 no. 3, 33.

80. *Zvezda*, 25 July 1937, 4; HP, #431 (XXI), 25; ibid., 26; *Sov. iust.*, 1936 no. 26, 9.

81. See discussion in Hessler, "Culture," 235–40.

82. *Zvezda*, 3 July 1937, 3.

83. *Sov. iust.*, 1936 no. 24, 15.

84. GARF, f. 5446, op. 81a, d. 24, ll. 49–48.

85. Edward Crankshaw, *Khrushchev's Russia* (Harmondsworth, Mx., 1959), 71–72.

86. *Tolkovyi slovar'* I.

87. HP, #386 (XX), 24; #4 (I), 36; #431 (XXI), 7; #432 (XXI), 16; #518 (XXVI), 29; #358 (XIX), 18; #396 (XX), 12; #386 (XX), 24; ibid., #338 (XXXVIII), 8; Berliner, "*Blat*," 23.

88. HP, #166 (XIII), 44; and see Alena Ledeneva, *Russia's Economy of Favours: Blat, Networking and Informal Exchanges* (Cambridge, 1998) for a study of *blat* based largely on 1980 interview data from 1994–95.

89. This is one of the characteristic reticences of the project, probably the result of the respondents' desire to present a good moral character in connection with their applications to emmigrate to the United States.

90. HP, #421 (XXI), 17–18.

91. Ibid., #338 (XXXIII), 6–7.

92. Ibid., #338 (XXXIII), 6–7; #407 (XX), 11; #358 (XIX), 13; #2 (I), 16. On *sobutyl' nichestvo*, see ibid., #407 (XX), 11.

93. Ibid., #147 (v. 34), 6–7; Harry Rosenberg, *The Leica and Other Stories* ([Canberra,] 1994). Thanks to Yuri Slezkine for elucidating the passage and T. H. Rigby for introducing me to the book.

94. *Krok.*, 1933 no. 3, 3. The Russian title is *"Blat-not,"* a play on the word *bloknot*, which means notebook. Thanks to Yuri Slezkine for assistance in translating the slang terms in this poem.

95. HP, #338 (XXXIII), 6–7; #518 (XXVI), 37.

96. Ibid., #7 (I), 23; ibid., #10 (I). 6. In the latter case, the interviewer noted the discrepancy in his report.

97. Ibid., #385 (XIX), 99; #416 (XXI), 3–4; #395 (XX), 9–10; #431 (XXI), 28–29; ibid., #96 (VII), 18; #517 (XXVI), 36; ibid., #398 (XX), 31.

98. *Krok.*, 1935 no. 30–31, 18 (college); 1935 no. 17–18, 11 (resort); 1940 no. 14, 2 (restaurant); 1937 no. 8, 12 (medical certificate).

99. *Krok.*, 1935 no. 25, 13. "Sells" = *otpuskaet* (literally, releases).

100. The continuous work week (*nepreryvnaia proizvodstvennaia nedelia* or *nepreryvka*) was established in the fall of 1929, initially only in industry; it meant that everyone worked four days and then took a day off, with staggered schedules so that four-fifths of the employees were always at the workplace and the machines were always running. In 1931, the *nepreryvka* was dropped for most jobs, and a fixed six-day week took its place. This was an improvement, since most people had the same day off, but the scheduling chaos associated initially with the *nepreryvka* and later with the bewildering succession of "5-day weeks (*piatidnevki*)," "6-day weeks (*shestidnevki*)," and "10-day weeks (*dekady*)" was never entirely overcome in the 1930s. It was not until 1940 that the seven-day week with the Sunday holiday returned. See Schwarz, *Labor*, 268–77, and Shcheglov, *ZT*, 414–15.

101. Quoted in H. Kent Geiger, *The Family in Soviet Russia* (Cambridge, Mass., 1968), 128.

Chapter 3

1. The epigraph and the chapter title are from a children's book set in the Soviet Union of the 1930s, Marjorie Fischer's *Palaces on Monday* (Harmondsworth, Mx., 1944, 1st pub. 1937).

2. The phrase is from Zinoviev, *The Radiant Future*.

3. For an interesting discussion of space and its meaning in the 1930s, see Emma Widdis, "Decentring Cultural Revolution in the Cinema of the First Five-Year Plan," paper delivered at annual meeting of AAASS, Seattle, November 1997.

4. *Nashi dostizheniia* [henceforth *Nash. dost.*), 1932 no. 11–12, 6, 16.

5. Ibid., 1932 no. 11–12, 6.

6. Ibid., 1934 no. 5, 81–82.

7. Ibid., 1934 no. 1, 7 (the print run had been cut from 100,000 to 30,000–40,000); James van Geldern and Richard Stites, eds., *Mass Culture in Soviet Russia* (Bloomington, 1995), 235.

8. *My nash, my novyi mir postroim.*

9. Aleksei Adzhubei, *Te desiat' let* (Moscow, 1989), 194–95.

10. Raisa Orlova, *Memoirs*, trans. by Samuel Cioran (New York, 1983), 27.

11. "O general'nom plane rekonstruktsii goroda Moskvy," 10 June 1935, in *Resheniia* II, 573–76; Janina Urussowa, "'Seht die Stadt, die leuchtet': zur Evolution der Stadtgestalt in den sowjetischen Filmen der 20er und 30er Jahre," paper delivered at Universität Tübingen, 6 May 1997 (*Chabarda!* excerpts); Richard Stites, *Russian Popular Culture. Entertainment and Society since 1900* (Cambridge, 1992), 84, and *Trud*, 20 December 1935, 4 (Moscow Hotel).

12. Urussowa, "Seht die Stadt" (*New Moscow* excerpts).

13. Orlova, *Memoirs*, 28; Solov'ev, "Tetrady," 205; and Sytin, *Iz istorii*, 212, 215, 224–25.

14. Quoted *Nash. dost.*, 1932 no. 11–12, 6.

15. Figures from *Izmeneniia*, 194, 196; *Narodnoe obrazovanie, nauka i kul'tura v SSSR. Statisticheskii sbornik* (Moscow, 1971), 21, 44–45; *Vsesoiuznaia perepis' naseleniia 1939 goda. Osnovnye itogi* (Moscow, 1992), 39. Note that all Soviet figures for the 1930s are likely to be inflated: I cite these to convey the dimensions of change. The 1939 literacy rate should be taken with a grain of salt: the figure in the suppressed census of 1937 was six points lower (75 percent): Iu. A. Poliakov, V. B. Zhiromskaia, I. N. Kiselev, "Polveka molchaniia (Vsesoiuznaia perepis' naseleniia 1937 g.)," *Sotsiologicheskie issledovaniia*, 1990 no. 7, 65–66.

16. On the Agricultural Exhibition, see Stites, *Russian Popular Culture*, 84; Jamey Gambrell, "The Wonder of the Soviet World, *New York Review of Books*, 22 December 1994, 30–35; and Vladimir Papernyi, *Kul'tura 'dva'* (Ann Arbor, 1985), 158–63.

17. Stalin, *Soch.* XIII, 38–39 (speech of 4 February 1931).

18. Texts of *Esli zavtra voina* (1938), *Marsh veselykh rebiat* (1934), *Sportivnyi marsh* (1936), and *"Zhit' stalo luchshe"* (1936) texts in van Geldern, *Mass Culture*, 317, 235, 236, 237. On Stalin's slogan "Life has become better," see ch. 4.

19. *Nash. dost.*, 1932 no. 4, 56–57.

20. Van Geldern, *Mass Culture*, 235.

21. "Po Soiuzu Sovetov" (1932–33) and "O p'esakh" (1933), in M. Gor'kii, *Sobranie sochinenii v tridtsati tomakh* (Moscow, 1949–55) XVII, 190, and XXVI, 26, 420. Master = *osvoit'*.

22. Frank J. Miller, *Folklore for Stalin* (Armonk, N.Y., 1990), 32, 56; Katerina Clark, *The Soviet Novel. History as Ritual* (Chicago, 1985), 138; *Pravda*, 3 December 1937, 2, and 11 November 1937, 2 (Ezhov, as *geroi*, with *podvigi*). The honorific title "Hero of Labor" was established by government decree in 1927: see Iu. K. Schcheglov, "Kommentarii k romanu 'Dvenadtsat' stul'ev'", in I. Il'f and E. Petrov, *Dvenadtsat' stul'ev* [henceforth Shcheglov, *DS*] (Moscow, 1995), 478–79.

23. On polar explorers, see John McCannon, *Red Arctic: Polar Exploration and the Myth of the North in the Soviet Union, 1932–1939* (New York, 1998), and idem, "Positive Heroes at the Pole: Celebrity Status, Socialist-Realist Ideals, and the Soviet Myth of the Arctic, 1932–9," *Rus. Rev.* 56:3 (1997); on aviators, see Bailes, *Technology*, ch. 14; on the heroic myth, see Clark, *Soviet Novel*, 136–41.

24. Sokolov, "Tetradi," 175, 188 ("eagles"); *Rab. put.*, 16 July 1937, 1 ("Hail to Stalin's bogatyrs!" on the Chkalov flight); Clark, *Soviet Novel*, 124–29 ("father"); RTsKhIDNI, f. 17, op. 3, d. 999 (funeral).

25. Sokolov, "Tetrady" (diary entry 26 July 1937), 195–96; McCannon, "Positive Heroes," 359–63. On Central Committee monitoring, see GARF, f. 5446, op. 82, d. 51 (note of 7 August 1937 to Molotov from B. Tal', head of the press department, reporting rebuke to *Izvestiia* for printing Papanin's telegram from the North Pole in an abbreviated version on the back page); on *Izvestiia*'s investment in the Arctic story under Gronskii's editorship, see Gronskii, *Iz proshlogo*, 127–29, 160–61.

26. Miller, *Folklore*, 111, 117, 121, 123, 125, 127, 129, 135–37.

27. This was produced at the Kamernyi Theater in Moscow in 1935: *Vech. Mosk.*, 10 November 1935, 4.

28. Jay Leyda, *Kino. A History of the Russian and Soviet Film* (London, 1973), 358; Stites, *Popular Culture*, 87–88.

29. Surveys from *Komsomol'skaia pravda* [henceforth *Koms. pr.*], 22 October 1937, 3, and 7 November 1937, 4 (no further information on first group; second group consisted of 865 workers from the Stalin Auto Plant in Moscow). The films were *Chapaev* (1934, dir. Sergei and Georgii Vasil'ev); *Shchors* (1939, dir. Aleksandr Dovzhenko).

30. For the Pavlik Morozov legend, see "Pavlik Morozov," excerpted from *A Poem about Hate* (1933) by Mikhail Doroshin in van Geldern and Stites, 153–56. For the reality behind the legend, see Iurii Druzhnikov, *Voznesenie Pavlika Morozova* (London, 1988).

31. See examples of real-life Pavlik emulators in Fitzpatrick, *Stalin's Peasants*, 256.

32. *On the Waterfront* (1954) was directed by Elia Kazan, who had recently named names of former Communists before the House Un-American Activities Committee. It may be considered part of a running polemic with Arthur Miller, one of the Hollywood Ten, whose plays *The Crucible* (1953) and *A View from the Bridge* (1955) presented denunciation and informing in a strongly negative light. For further discussion of "discourses of denunciation," see Sheila Fitzpatrick and Robert Gellately, eds., *Accusatory Practices. Denunciation in Modern European History 1789–1989* (Chicago, 1997), 17–20.

33. *The Moscow Theatre for Children* (Moscow, 1934), 44.

34. See Katerina Clark, "Little Heroes and Big Deeds: Literature Responds to the First Five-Year Plan," in Fitzpatrick, *Cultural Revolution*; A. Volkov, *A. M. Gor'kii i literaturnoe dvizhenie sovetskoi epokhi* (Moscow, 1958), 333–34. For an overview of Stakhanovism, see Siegelbaum, *Stakhanovism*.

35. The Soviet term, *znatnye liudi*, translates literally as "renowned people," but in fact it was applied only to heroes from the masses, not famous elite members.

36. On Stakhanov's mentor, Konstantin Petrov, see Siegelbaum, *Stakhanovism*, 67–69; on Angelina's mentor, Ivan Kurov, see P. Angelina, *O samom glavnom* (Moscow, 1948), 13.

37. Angelina, *O samom glavnom*, 5 .

38. *Geroini sotsialisticheskogo truda* (Moscow, 1936), 168 (my emphasis).

39. See, for example, the highly appreciative comments on a young Stakhanovite female mountain-climber from the North Caucasus, encountered at an airshow, in the diary of Vladimir Stavskii, a top cultural appratchik: *Intimacy and Terror*, 234.

40. Pasha Angelina, *Liudi kolkhoznykh polei* ([Moscow, 1948), 26.

41. *Geroini*, 25; *Nash. dost.*, 1934 no. 5, 161; *Krok.*, 1936 no. 4, 13.

42. "Perepiska s chitateliami," in Gor'kii, *Sob. soch.* XXV (Moscow, 1953), 221.

43. Cited in Raymond A. Bauer, *The New Man in Soviet Psychology* (Cambridge, 1952), 81.

44. See Thomas Lahusen, *How Life Writes the Book, Real Socialism and Socialist Realism in Stalin's Russia* (Ithaca, 1997), 46–52.

45. Charles Kingsley, *The Water-Babies. A Fairy Tale for a Land Baby* (London: Macmillan & Co, 1903). 1st ed. 1863. On bandit tales, see Jeffrey Brooks, *When Russia Learned to Read. Literacy and Popular Literature, 1861–1917* (Princeton, 1985), ch. 5.

46. *Belomorsko-Baltiiskii kanal imeni Stalina: Istoriia stroitel'stva*, M. Gor'kii et al., eds. (Moscow, 1934). The English translation appeared as *The White-Sea Canal* in London and *Belomor. An Account of the Construction of the New Canal between the White Sea and the Baltic Sea* in New York in 1935. On the propaganda project, see Joachim Klein, "Belomorkanal. Literatur und Propaganda in der Stalinzeit," *Zeitschrift für slavische Philologie* 55:1 (1995/96), 53–98. On the construction project, see I. Chukhin, *Kanalarmeitsy. Istoriia stroitel'stva Belmorkanala v dokumentakh, tsifrakh, faktakh, fotografiiakh, svidetel'stvakh uchastnikov i ochevidtsev* (Petrozavodsk, 1990).

47. *Belomorsko-Baltiiskii*, 252–56.

48. Katerina Clark, "Little Heroes," in Fitzpatrick, *Cultural Revolution*, 192–93.

49. On *Putevka v zhizn'*, written and directed by Nikolai Ekk and based on the Liuberets commune, see Leyda, *Kino*, 284–85, and *Ocherki istorii sovetskogo kino* I

(Moscow, 1956), 296–301, 479. On *besprizornye*, see Alan M. Ball, *And Now My Soul Is Hardened. Abandoned Children in Soviet Russia, 1918–1930* (Berkeley, 1994).

50. *Pedagogicheskaia poema* (1934–35) in A. S. Makarenko, *Sochineniia v semi tomakh* I (Moscow, 1957). Note that the 1951 English-language edition published in Moscow used the title *Road to Life*, and gave an amended version of the Russian title—*Putevka v zhizn'*. *Pedagogicheskaia poema*—not used in the Makarenko's collected works. Despite the similarity of title, the Ekk film was not based on the book, which it preceded.

51. A. Zorich, "Otets. Zaiavlenie Sergeia Ivanova," *Izv.*, 15 January 1936, 4; ibid., 17 January 1936, 4. According to the first story, Ivanov's search for his daughter was unsuccessful, Then, remarkably, a mere two days later, *Izvestiia* announced that the child had been found in a Moscow orphanage and would be reunited with her father.

52. A. Zorich, "Serdtsa chekista," *Izv.*, 4 October 1935, 4. The Bol'shevo commune is described in Louis Fischer, *Soviet Journey* (New York, 1935), 97–105.

53. "Iavka s povinnoi," in Lev Sheinin, *Zapiski sledovatelia* (Moscow, 1965), 93–95. The original publication was in *Izvestiia*, 15 March 1937, 3, and a version of the whole "reformation of thieves" story (misdated to 1935) appears in Arvo Tuominen, *The Bells of the Kremlin. An Experience in Communism*, Piltti Heiskanen, ed., trans. Lily Leino (Hanover and London, 1983), 128–35. Whether or not Sheinin's claim about the rash of voluntary confessions was true, at least one such incident had been reported in *Izvestiia*'s chronicle section the previous year: according to the report, a habitual thief, I. Astakhov, had unexpectedly appeared at the Moscow Criminal Investigation Department and confessed his crimes, stating his wish "to serve the appropriate term of imprisonment and then engage in honest labor" (*Izv.*, 8 May 1936, 4).

54. "Razgovor na chistotu," in Sheinin, *Zapiski*, 98–104, first published *Izv.*, 18 March 1937, 4. Tuominen adds the detail that the amnesty Vyshinsky promised was for theft and minor crimes, not for political crimes or, in most cases, murder (Tuominen, *Bells*, 130, 133).

55. Interview with Vyshinsky, *Izv.*, 20 March 1937, 4; "Krupnoe rukopozhatie," in Sheinin, *Zapiski*, 105–10, first pub. in *Izv.*, 28 March 1937, 4. On Count Kostia's fate, see Tuominen, *Bells*, 134–35. Another (real-life) version of a repentant criminal claiming artistic skills, and having his claim taken seriously, is in Golfo Alexopoulos, "Portrait of a Con Artist as a Soviet Man," *Slavic Review* [henceforth *Slav. Rev.*], forthcoming.

56. See above, p. 86.

57. A. S. Makarenko, "Flagi na bashniakh" (1938), in Makarenko, *Soch.* III. The irredeemable character is Ryzhikov. The statement that he was "vermin by nature," together with a promise to explain at some future date how this could be, was made by Makarenko in a conference with readers included in an appendix to the English edition: *Learning to Live (Flags on the Battlements)*, trans. by Ralph Parker (Moscow, 1953), 646.

58. "Culture" is used here both for the Russian *kul'turnost'* and *kul'tura*. On mastery, see the definition of *kul'turnyi* in *Tolkovyi slovar'* II, as (2) "standing on a high level of culture, having mastered (*usvoivshii*) culture." On arguments of the 1920s, see Fitzpatrick, *Cultural Front*, ch. 1.

59. *Izv.*, 28 May 1934, 3.

60. Yuri Slezkine, "From Savages to Citizens: The Cultural Revolution in the Soviet Far North, 1928–1939," *Slav. Rev.* 51:1 (1992), 71, 74–75.

61. *Krok.*, 1936 no. 28, back page.

62. See the agreements teachers concluded with parents at the Reutovskaia knitting plant: *Trud*, 17 July 1935, 2.

63. *Zhenshchina—bol'shaia sila. Severnoe kraevoe soveshchanie zhen stakhanovtsev, Arkhangel'sk 1936* (Arkhangelsk, 1936), 54.

64. See Kotkin, *Magnetic*, ch. 5 ("Speaking Bolshevik").

65. Autobiography of Marusia Rogacheva, in O. N. Chaadaeva, ed., *Rabotnitsa na sotsialisticheskoi stroike* (Moscow, 1930), 79.

66. Busygin quotation from Catriona Kelly and Vadim Volkov, "Directed Desires: *Kul'turnost'* and Consumption," in Catriona Kelly and David Shepherd, eds., *Construction Russian Culture in the Age of Revolution: 1881–1940* (Oxford, 1998), 303–04; Komarova comment from Chaadaeva, *Rabotnitsa*, 144.

67. *Zhenshchina—bol'shaia*, 74, 43; Kotkin, *Magnetic*, 192 and 487, n. 179.

68. Kelly and Volkov, "Directed Desires," 297; Fischer, *Soviet Journey*, 70.

69. *Za ind.* [henceforth *Za ind.*], 17 January 1937, 2.

70. See Kelly and Volkov, "Directed Desires," 298–99; Vera S. Dunham, *In Stalin's Time. Middleclass Values in Soviet Fiction*, enlarged edition (Durham, 1990), 41–58.

71. *Obshchestvennitsa* [henceforth *Obshch.*], 1937 no. 1, 14.

72. HP #167 (XIII), 26.

73. *Krok.*, 1940 no. 24, 5 ("*Na vy*"); ibid., 1940 no. 22, 9.

74. On revolutionary names, see Papernyi, *Kul'tura*, 150. For Stalinka, see Angelina, *Liudi*, 117. For a rare decision to call a child Iosif after Stalin, see Sats, *Zhizn'*, 307.

75. This discussion of name changes is based primarily on the announcements published in *Izvestiia* over the period 10 March 1935 to 27 May 1928. For name changes in the late Tsarist period, see Andrew M Verner, "What's in a Name? Of Dog-Killers, Jews and Rasputin," *Slav. Rev.* 53:4 (1994). For political name changes, see *Izv.*, 8 September 1938, 4.

76. *Izv.*, 10 May 1936, 3 (comment of B. M. Tal': his word is "*poshlost'*").

77. *Trud*, 8 March 1936, 2. The reference is to Chekhov's story "Van'ka" (1886).

78. Promotion = *vydvizhenie*: see *Tolkovyi slovar'*, vol. 1 on the word "*vydvizhenets*, a new coinage meaning "a worker appointed or promoted to a responsible position (in the organs of state and economic administration; a student chosen . . . for training for scientific work." On affirmative action, see Fitzpatrick, *Education*. For attitudes of *vydvizhentsy*, see HP, #518 (XXVI), 63, #517 (XXVI), 56, #543 (XXVIII), 4, and the memoir of Benediktov, "O Staline."

79. *Geroini*, 162–63 (quote); *Istoriia sovetskogo kino* II, 173–84 (on *Member*).

80. Fitzpatrick, "Stalin and the Making of a New Elite," in *Cultural Front*; Archie Brown, *The Gorbachev Factor* (Oxford, 1996), 27–28.

81. *Izv.*, 4 October 1938, 3; *Pravda*, 30 April 1938, 3.

82. *Pravda*, 31 May 1938, 3; *Koms. pr.*, 17 December. 1937, 3.

83. Siegelbaum, *Stakhanovism*, 267–77.

84. The Russian is "*god ukhoda s proizvodstva ili ostavleniia sel'skogo khoziaistva.*" GARF, f. 5457, op. 22, ed. khr. 48, ll. 80–81 (Union of Knitting Workers, 1935: Lichnyi listok po uchetu kadrov).

85. TsGAIPD, f. 24, op. 2g, d. 48. ll. 197–201 (1937 letter); Robert A. McCutcheon, "The 1936–1937 Purge of Soviet Astronomers," *Slav. Rev.* 50:1 (1991), 104–11 (on a *vydvizhenets* from Tashkent).

86. *Trud*, 8 March 1936, 2.

87. *Koms. pr.*, 7 November 1937, 4. In this survey, N = 865. Note that this was years after the time of intensive "affirmative action" when workers could get into

rabfak or college almost on demand. These young workers were hoping to enter higher education via the general academic-competitive admissions process.

88. Barbara Alpern Engel and Anastasia Posadskaya-Vanderbeck, *A Revolution of their Own. Voices of Women in Soviet History* [henceforth Engel, *Revolution*] (Boulder, Colo., 1997), 44–45 (Dubova interview).

89. Cited by Kelly and Volkov, "Directed Desires," 207–08.

90. Angelina, *O samom glavnom*, 4–5.

Chapter 4

1. *Skatert'—samobranka*. See Maria Kravchenko, *The World of the Russian Fairy Tale* (Berne, 1987), 72.

2. See Leon Trotsky in his *The Revolution Betrayed* (London, 1967; 1st pub. 1937).

3. I have quoted the phrase in its sloganized form. Stalin's actual comment, in a speech to a meeting of leading male and female combine-drivers on 1 December 1935, was "Everybody now says that the material situation of the toilers has considerably improved, that life has become better, more cheerful." Stalin, *Soch.* I (XIV), 106.

4. For examples, see *Izv.*, 1 January 1936, 1; Lahusen, *How Life Writes the Book*, 52. The text of the song "Life's Getting Better" (1936), which uses the sloganized version as a refrain, is in van Geldern, *Mass Culture*, 237–38. For mimicry, see Chapter 7.

5. See N. S. Timasheff, *The Great Retreat. The Growth and Decline of Communism in Russia* (New York, 1946).

6. *Vech. Mosk.*, 4 October 1934, 2.

7. A. I. Mikoian, *Pishchevaia industriia Sovetskogo Soiuza* ([Moscow], 1939), 68, 80; *Gor'kovskaia kommuna*, 10 April 1938, 4.

8. *Kommuna*, 18 July 1936, 3–4. In August 1937, the "New Light" factory began production of champagne, using imported machinery, for a planned output of 10,000 to 12,000 bottles a day: *Krasnyi Krym*, 20 August 1937, 2.

9. On advertising, see Randi Barnes-Cox, "Soviet Commercial Advertising and the Creation of the Socialist Consumer, 1917–1941," in Christina Kiaer and Eric Naiman, eds., *Everyday Subjects: Formations of Identity in Early Soviet Culture*, forthcoming. On cultured trade, see Hessler, "Culture of Shortages," ch. 6.

10. Hessler, "Culture," 292, 294.

11. *Krasnaia gazeta* [henceforth *Kras. gaz.*], 27 June 1936, 4; *Ogonek*, 1936 no. 16, inside front cover.

12. *Ogonek*, 1936 no. 5, 19–21. The energetic marketing of perfume in the second half of the 1930s is generally attributed to the efforts of Molotov's wife, Polina Zhemchuzhina, who headed the Soviet cosmetics industry.

13. See advertisements for "Prekonsol'," described as "one of the best chemical means for preventing pregnancy," and "Vagilen" diaphragms (*shariki*) in *Krasnyi Krym*, 27 July 1937, 4; *Rab. put.*, 26 March 1937, 4; *Sovetskaia Sibir'* [henceforth *Sov. Sib.*], 4 September 1936, 1; and *Ogonek*, inside back cover of many issues in 1936. Thanks to Yuri Slezkine and his Moscow gynecologist friends for help on this question.

14. *Trud*, 4 May 1934, 4.

15. HP #1 (I), 15; 385 (XIX), 11–12; *Trud*, 2 July 1935, 1.

16. B. Glotov, "Bilet do Leningrada. Bol'shevik Zinaida Nemtsova, kak ona est'," *Ogonek* 1988 no. 27 (July), 7.

17. *Nash. dost.*, 1934 no. 6, 56, 60.

18. Quoted Khlevniuk, *1937-i*, 39, from *Baltimore Sun*, 18 November 1934.

The article was included in a summary of the foreign press distributed to party leaders.

19. See Iurii Elagin, *Ukroshchenie iskusstv* (New York, 1952), 178–82; *Vech. Mosk.*, 17 November 1934, 4.

20. See Stites, *Russian Popular Culture*, 88–93 (musicals); S. Frederick Starr, *Red and Hot. The Fate of Jazz in the Soviet Union* (New York: 1983), ch. 6 (jazz); *Trud*, 14 December 1935, 4 ("Soviet Hollywood"); *Zhenshchina—bol'shaia*, 75 (dance).

21. *Trud*, 3 January 1936, 4.

22. *Molot*, 23 June 1933, 4; *Izv.*, 9 January 1936, 1; *Rabochii*, 13 January 1934, 4.

23. On football, see Robert Edelman, *Serious Fun. A History of Spectator Sports in the U.S.S.R.* (New York, 1993).

24. See Karen Petrone, "Parading the Nation: Physical Culture Celebrations and the Construction of Soviet Identities in the 1930s," *Michigan Discussions in Anthropology*, XII (1996); *Agitatsiia za schast'e. Sovetskoe iskusstvo stalinskoi epokhi* (Düsseldorf-Bremen, 1994), 180–90; van Geldern, *Mass Culture*, 235–36. "*Fizkul't-ura-ura-ura!*" is a play on the words "*fizkul'tura*" (physical culture) and "hurrah" ("*ura*").

25. *Vech. Mosk.*, 30 November 1935, 4; Louis Fischer, *Soviet Journey*, 107–18; Marjory Fischer, *Palaces*, 67–73; Roland, *Caviar*, 55. See also Karl Schlögel, "Der 'Zentrale Gor'kij-Kultur-und Erholungspark' (CPKiO) in Moskau. Zur Frage des Öffentlichen Raums im Stalinismus," in Manfred Hildermeier and Elisabeth Müller-Luckner, eds., *Stalinismus vor dem Zweiten Weltkrieg. Neue Wege der Forschung = Stalinism before the Second World War. New Avenues of Research* (Munich, 1998).

26. Quoted in Rosalinde Sartorti, "Stalinism and Carnival," in Hans Günther, ed., *The Culture of the Stalin Period* (New York, 1990), 67. I have made a couple of small corrections to the translation.

27. *Vech. Mosk.*, 1 November 1935, 1. On the carnivals of the 1920s, see Shcheglov, *ZT*, 520–22.

28. *Vech. Mosk.*, 9 July 1935, 3; *Izv.*, 9 July 1935, 4; *Krok.*, 1936 no. 19, 3. A heavier-handed approach was reported from the mining town of Gorlovka, which advertised a costume ball in which "costumes must answer the following purposes: old and new [work] norms, the Italian-Abyssinian war, Japanese-German friendship, and victims of capitalism" (*Krok.*, 1936 no. 11, 15).

29. *Izv.*, 12 April 1935, 4. The composer Glière, the writer Boris Pilniak, the German theater director Erwin Piskator and the director of the Moscow Children's Theater, Natalia Sats, were among those involved in planning for the first night carnival, held in September 1935.

30. Roland, *Caviar*, 55.

31. Quoted Khlevniuk, *1937-i*, 41–42, from *Sotsialisticheskii vestnik* 1934 no. 19, 14. On the intelligentsia's privileges in the 1920s, see Fitzpatrick, *Education*, 79–86. On its fate during the Cultural Revolution, see idem, *Cultural Revolution*.

32. See *Izv.*, 27 Aug. 1934, 1, and Jeffrey Brooks, "Socialist Realism in Pravda: Read All about It!," *Slav. Rev.* 53:4 (1994), 976–81.

33. See above, p. 223.

34. See Elagin, *Ukroshchenie*, 143; HP #421 (XXI), 67 and #387 (XX), 56.

35. Bonner, *Mothers and Daughters*, 126; Osokina, *Ierarkhiia*, 63-65.

36. Gronskii, *Iz proshlogo*, 140. Gronskii takes credit for the artists' inclusion.

37. Hubbard, 82; Osokina, *Ierarkhiia*, 63–64; Bonner, *Mothers*, 251; HP, #385 (XIX), 47. GORT = *Gosudarstvennoe ob'edinenie roznichnoi torgovli*.

38. Osokina, *Ierarkhiia*, 71; *Ist. sots. ekon.* III, 454.

39. RTsKhIDNI, f. 78, op. 1, d. 549, ll. 76–77.

40. Tuominen, *Bells*, 205.

41. SA, WKP 355, 179.; RTsKhIDNI, f. 78, op. 1, d. 549, ll. 76–77; quoted in *Krok.*, 1936 no. 24, 14.

42. *Rab. put.*, 15 September 1937, 2.

43. Colton, *Moscow*, 168. For a less positive appraisal, see *Bells*, 89–90.

44. Colton, *Moscow*, 337 and 852 (note 174); Elagin, *Ukroshchenie*, 62–63; *Sov. iust.*, 1934 no. 8, 18, and 1935 no. 17, 24.

45. *Trud*, 14 Nov. 1933, 4; *Rabochii*, 28 March 1932, 1; Kotkin, *Magnetic*, 126–27 and plate 18; Scott, *Behind the Urals*, 86–89.

46. HP, #338 (XXXIII), 27, 8. "Domestic servants and day laborers" officially numbered 300,000 in 1935, and the 1939 census recorded over 500,000 domestic servants, virtually all of them women: *Trud v SSSR. Statisticheskii spravochnik* (Moscow, 1936); *Vsesoiuznaia perepis' naseleniia 1939 goda*, 111. Both figures are likely to be too low, since servants, alone among wage earners in the Soviet Union, were employed not by the state but by private persons (who did not always register them).

47. TsGAIPD, f. 24, op. 2v, d. 1748, ll. 167–68 (anonymous letter to Leningrad Soviet, 1 August 1936).

48. Scott, *Behind the Urals*, 130–33.

49. *Krok.*, 1937 no. 12, 13; 1939 no. 20, 6; 1940 no. 17, 5.

50. Although sanatoria were formally medical institutions, Soviet citizens often treated them as just another kind of vacation home (*doma otdykha*). From memoir evidence, it would appear that virtually all Soviet elite members in the 1930s (not to mention ordinary citizens) had chronic health problems for which a sanatorium regime (exercise, diet, and rest under medical supervision) was believed to be beneficial.

51. *Kras. Tat.*, 24 April 1937, 4; see also ibid., 21 April 1938, 4.

52. RTsKhIDNI, f. 17, op. 3, d. 995 (Politburo resolution of 9 Feb. 1938). On revocation, see Chapter 8.

53. D. L. Babichenko, *Pisateli i tsenzory. Sovetskaia literatura 1940-kh godov pod politicheskim kontrolem TsK* (Moscow, 1994), 11–13. Note that, as with all privileges in the Soviet Union, the privilege of "indefinite use" (*bessrochnoe pol'zovanie*) was abruptly withdrawn if the recipient became an "enemy of the people."

54. HP, #431 (XXI), 26–29. For a detailed account of dacha buying and selling, see Vaksberg, *Prosecutor*, 86–93.

55. Mandelshtam, *Vospominaniia*, 119–20; Sats, *Zhizn'*, 273.

56. Elagin, *Ukroshchenie*, 150–54; Fitzpatrick, *Education*, 78; Gronskii, *Iz proshlogo*, 140.

57. Ginzburg, *Into the Whirlwind*, 36–37; Bonner, *Mothers*, 168–72, 244–46, 259. On Artek, see *Nash. dost.*, 1932 no. 4, 94–95.

58. Sats, *Zhizn'*, 284.

59. *Pravda*, 19 May 1937, 4; *Za ind.*, 12 May 1937, 1; *Kras. gaz.*, 3 September 1936, 2.

60. RTsKhIDNI, f. 17, op. 3, d. 984, l. 70, and ibid., d. 1002 (Politburo resolutions on salary increases, 1937 and 1938); Khlevniuk, *1937-i*, 39 and 165; *Sov. iust.*, 1938 no. 19, 47.

61. Papernyi, *Kul'tura*, 176; *Izv.*, 29 July 1934, 2; *Kul'turnaia zhizn' v SSSR 1928–1941. Khronika* (Moscow, 1976), 418. On the workings of Litfond in the 1930s and 1940s, see Dietrich Beyrau, "Der organisierte Autor: Institutionen, Kontrolle, Fürsorge," in Gabriele Gorzka, ed., *Kultur im Stalinismus* (Bremen, 1994), 72–76.

62. For awards of M-1 cars to Stakhanovites, see *Pravda*, 19 May 1937, 4; *Za ind.*, 21 April 1937, 2; *Kr. pr.*, 30 Jun. 1936, 4; *Trud*, 21 September 1936, 4.

63. *Geroini*, 129, 71, 54–55.

64. Paraphrased from Magnitogorsk newspaper in Kotkin, *Magnetic*, 192 and 487, n. 179.

65. Cited Siegelbaum, *Stakhanovism*, 228 and 230.

66. *Geroini*, 129 (my emphasis). On the symbolic importance of acquiring a bed, see Vladimir Kontorovich's story in *Nash. dost.*, 1936 no. 3, 95.

67. *Trud*, 24 December 1935, 2.

68. See above, p. 95.

69. Pierre Bourdieu, *Language and Symbolic Power*, 151–53, 169–70, and passim.

70. "My borolis' za ideiu! Vospominaniia F. E. Treivas," in *Zhenskaia sud'ba v Rossii*, B. S. Ilizarova, ed. (Moscow, 1994), 90–91.

71. Bonner, *Mothers*, 109; *Kras. Tat.*, 21 April 1938, 4.

72. Fischer, *Soviet Journey*, 55 (my emphasis).

73. *Nash. dost.*, 1934 no. 6, 61.

74. "O proekte Konstitutsii Soiza SSR" (25 November 1936), in Stalin, *Soch.* I (XIV), 142, 145; Vera S. Dunham, *In Stalin's Time. Middleclass Values in Soviet Fiction* (Durham, 1990), 108 (quoted from V. Kochetov's 1952 novel, *Zhurbiny*).

75. Quotations from GARF, f. 1235, op. 141(2), d. 147, l. 8 (1932); ibid., f. 5446, op. 82, d. 42, ll. 75–77 (1935); RGAE, f. 7486s, op. 37, d. 237, l. 228 (1932).

76. *Sto sorok besed*, 410–11; RTsKhIDNI, f. 17, op. 3, d. 995.

77. Quotations from Inkeles, *Soviet Citizen*, 307; GARF, f. 5457, op. 22, d. 49, l. 28 (1935).

78. GARF, f. 5457, op. 22, d. 45, l. 9.

79. *Nash. dost.*, 1934 no. 6, 61.

80. Daniil Granin, "Leningradskii katalog," *Neva*, 1984 no. 9, 76–77; Paul Scheffer, *Seven Years in Soviet Russia* (New York, 1932), 47.

81. GARF, f. 3316, op. 2, d. 1529, ll. 4–5. See also Paperny, *Kul'tura*, 93–97.

82. The key works here are Timasheff, *Great Retreat*, and Trotsky, *Revolution Betrayed*.

83. *Izv.*, 11 Sep. 1935, 4; RTsKhIDNI, f. 17, op. 114, d. 822, l. 49 (letter to *Izv.*, n.d. [1936–37]).

84. Timasheff, *Great Retreat*, 319; Paperny, *Kul'tura*, 97.

85. Solov'ev, "Tetradi," loc. cit., 182–83.

86. Timasheff, *Great Retreat*, 319 and 448; Tucker, *Stalin in Power*, 323 and 648 (n. 68).

87. Fitzpatrick, *Education*, 219–20; *Sobranie zakonov i rasporiazhenii raboche-krest'ianskogo pravitel'stva SSSR* [henceforth *Sobr. zak.*] 1937 no. 21, art. 83.

88. *Sobr. uzak.*, 1926, no. 53, art. 412; *Izv.*, 8 September 1936, 1, cited in Kiril Tomoff, "People's Artist, Honored Figure: Official Identity and Divisions within the Soviet Music Profession. 1946–53," ms., 3. In Russian, the titles are *"Zasluzhennyi artist"* and *"Narodnyi artist."* The title of "Distinguished Master of Sport" was created in 1934; the titles "Distinguished Teacher" and "Distinguished Physician" were added in 1940: Tucker, *Stalin in Power*, 648 (n. 69); *Narodnoe obrazovanie v SSSR. Obshcheobrazovatel'naia shkola. Sbornik dokumentov 1917–1973 gg.* (Moscow, 1974), 474.

89. Tomoff, 5; *Kul'turnaia zhizn'*, 652.

90. *Sobranie postanovlenii i rasporiazhenii pravitel'stva SSSR* [henceforth *Sobr. post.*] 1940 no. 1, art. 6; ibid., 1940 no. 3, art. 89; Philomena Guillebaud, "The Role of Honorary Awards in the Soviet Economic System," *American Slavic and*

East European Review XII:4 (1953), 503; Paperny, *Kul'tura*, 276; *Sobr. post.* 1941, no. 11, art. 176.

91. *Sbornik vazhneishikh postanovlenii po trudu*, comp. Ia. L. Kiselev, S. E. Malkin (Moscow, 1938), 239–40, 241–45; Timasheff, *Great Retreat*, 319.

92. Trotsky, *Revolution Betrayed*, 156.

93. Shcheglov, *ZT*, 11 and 338.

94. *Protektsiia, pomogat', podderzhivat', vyruchat', sovet, pomoshch'*. Thanks to Yuri Slezkine and Alena Ledeneva for their advice on the language of patronage.

95. HP #385 (XIX), 30 (quotation); ibid., #415 (v. 20), 15; #432 (v. 21), 16; #524 (v. 27), 19. On Stakhanovites, see Siegelbaum, *Stakhanovism*, 67–71, 256; see also Angelina, *O samom glavnom*, 30. The patron's functions included setting the stage for the original record-breaking that earned the Stakhanovite title and selecting the client as a delegate to regional and national Stakhanovite conferences.

96. Mandelshtam, *Vospominaniia*, 119–20.

97. On Koltsov's and Babel's relationships to Ezhov, see *Mikhail Kol'tsov, kakim on byl* (Moscow, 1965), 69–76, and Shentalinskii, *Raby svobody*, 48–50.

98. Shentalinskii, *Raby*, 120.

99. For a more detailed discussion, see Sheila Fitzpatrick, "Intelligentsia and Power. Client-Patron Relations in Stalin's Russia," in Hildermeier, *Stalinismus*.

100. GARF, f. 5446, op. 82, d. 77, ll. 9–10; ibid., d. 56, l. 154. 1938 was a relatively propitious time for snapping up elite apartments: note the letter early in that year in which a housing official from Moscow Soviet reassures Molotov that the NKVD will soon be releasing for reallocation the apartments it has sealed up after arrests of "enemies of the people": GARF, f. 5446, op. 82, d. 72, l. 114.

101. GARF, f. 5446, op. 82, d. 51, l. 144; ibid., d. 53, l. 130; ibid. d. 70, l. 165.

102. Elagin, *Ukroshchenie*, 52–53; *Testimony. The Memoirs of Dmitri Shostakovich*, Solomon Volkov, ed., Antonina W. Bouis, trans. (New York, 1980), 98–99.

103. See, for example, GARF, f. 5446, op. 82, d. 53, ll. 82 and 102; d. 65, l. 207; d. 112, ll. 281–92; and P. L. Kapitsa, *Pis'ma o nauke 1930–1980* (Moscow, 1989), 151.

104. GARF, f. 5446, op. 81a, d. 337, ll. 76–78 (Fadeev, letter of January 1940); TSGAIPD, f. 24 op. 2v, d. 1515, ll. 64–65 (letter of 1935).

105. Kapitsa, *Pis'ma*, 174–75, 178–79; Paul Josephson, *Physics and Politics in Revolutionary Russia* (Berkeley, 1991), 316; Iurii Elagin, *Temnyi genii (Vsevolod Meierkhol'd)* (New York, 1955), 294–95.

106. Elagin, *Ukroshchenie*, 66–69.

107. Ibid., 48.

108. *Sto sorok*, 315; Gronskii, *Iz proshlogo*, 142–43; *O Valeriane Kuibysheve: Vospominaniia, ocherki, stat'i* (Moscow, 1983), 219–21.

109. *Sto sorok*, 315; Gronskii, *Iz proshlogo*, 143. Note, however, that despite this threatening preamble, Stalin was sympathetic to the artists when Gronskii described their situation and actively took up their cause, according to Gronskii's account.

110. HP #359 (XIX), 32.

Chapter 5

1. See E. H. Carr, *The Bolshevik Revolution, 1917–1923*, vol. 1 (Harmondsworth, Mx., 1966), 151–54; A. I. Dobkin, "Lishentsy," in *Zven'ia. Istoricheskii al'manakh*, vyp. 2 (Moscow–St. Petersburg, 1992), 601–03.

2. "Konstitutsiia (Osnovnoi zakon) Rossiiskoi Sotsialisticheskoi Federativnoi Sovetskoi Respubliki," resolution of V All-Russian Congress of Soviets, 10 July 1918, in *Dekrety sovetskoi vlasti* II (Moscow, 1959), 561.

3. The disfranchised were known as *lishentsy*, literally, deprived people. Alien ele-

ments = *chuzhdye elementy*; social aliens = *sotsial'no-chuzhie (-chuzhdye)*; former people = *byvshie*. Note the dehumanization implicit in the word *elementy*. This usage became so widespread that a respondent in the Harvard Project objected strongly when an interviewer used it to refer to things, not people, stating categorically that "the term 'element' ... applies only to people." HP, #387 (XX), 77.

4. Dobkin, "Lishentsy," 603–4; Elise Kimerling, "Civil Rights and Social Policy in Soviet Russia, 1918–1936," *Rus. Rev.* 41:1 (January 1982). 32 n. 20. The "loyalty" category was sometimes included, sometimes excluded, in the changing legislation of the 1920s.

5. See E. H. Carr, *Socialism in One Country, 1924–1926*, vol. 2 (London, 1959), 328–33; Alexopoulos, "Rights and Passage," ch. 2.

6. See Kimerling, "Civil Rights," 27–30, and Fitzpatrick, "Ascribing Class," 752–55.

7. See Fitzpatrick, "Ascribing," 756 and passim. Exceptions to the genealogical approach obviously had to be made for Bolshevik revolutionaries like Lenin himself, whose father had been a personal noble. According to the law, former landlords, capitalists, and priests became eligible to vote after engaging in "socially useful work" for five years, but this seems to have been honored in the breach rather than the observance.

8. On the expropriation of Nepmen, see Alan M. Ball, *Russia's Last Capitalists. The Nepmen, 1921–1929* (Berkeley, 1987), 72–82, 161–69. On collectivization, see R. W. Davies, *The Socialist Offensive. The Collectivisation of Soviet Agriculture, 1929–1930* (Cambridge, Mass., 1980). On Cultural Revolution, see Fitzpatrick, *Cultural Revolution.*

9. According to published figures, 8.6% of the adult population of the USSR was disfranchised in 1929, up from 7.7% in 1927 (Kimerling, "Civil Rights," 27: Table 1). Rates in the non-Russian republics tended to be higher: 11.8% disfranchised in the Ukraine and 13.7 percent in Uzbekistan, compared to 7.2 percent in the RSFSR. An archival source puts the number of disfranchised in the Russian Republic in 1930 at almost two and a half million, which suggests a figure of at least four million for the USSR as a whole. It is clear, however, that these figures are approximations at best. Most likely the authorities themselves did not know exactly how many people were disfranchised.

10. *Nasha gazeta* [henceforth *Nash. gaz.*], 22 August 1929, 3.

11. M. M. Prishvin, *Dnevniki* (Moscow, 1990), 165; *Nashi gaz.*, 15 October 1929, 4.

12. On opposition by Krupskaia, Lunacharsky, and the Ukrainian education commissar Mikola Skrypnik, see Fitzpatrick, *Education*, 122, 133, and 164, and note 15, below.

13. GARF, f. 5263, op. 1, d. 7 (1930).

14. GARF, f. 3316, op. 2, d. 918 (memo); *Koms. pr.*, 16 Mar. 1930, 4 (complaints).

15. GARF, f. 3316, op. 2, d. 909, l. 1.

16. For statements by Lunacharsky and Skrypnik against social purging of schools, see GARF, f. 5462, op. 11, d. 12, ll. 44–45, and ll. 11–12. For a secret Sovnarkom RSFSR decree of 27 April 1929 forbidding schools to expel children of the disfranchised, see GARF, f. 1235, op. 141(2), d. 308, l. 11.

17. Solovki was a notorious island prison in the North.

18. GARF, f. 1235, op. 141(2), d. 308, l. 9 (Kalmyk oblast soviet executive committee to VTsIK, 30 April 1929).

19. For more on the reintroduction of passports, see Fitzpatrick, *Stalin's Peasants*, 92–95.

20. *V tseliakh lichnogo ustroistva.*

21. GARF, f. 3316 s. ch., op. 2, d. 1227, ll. 1–69. The commission was chaired by Enukidze, secretary of TsIK, and included three prominent OGPU representatives: G. G. Iagoda, G. E. Prokof'ev, and Ia. Agranov.

22. GARF, f. 3316 s.ch., op. 2, d. 1227, l. 70.

23. GARF, f. 3316 s.ch., op. 2, d. 1227, l. 101. The source of this instruction was not identified, but it was probably TsIK or the corresponding institution for the Russian Republic, VTsIK.

24. GARF, f. 3316 s.ch., op. 2, d. 1227, l. 101.

25. All cases are from GARF, f. 3316 s.ch., op. 2, d. 1227, ll. 117–26.

26. Elagin, *Ukroshchenie*, 53–54.

27. Isaac Deutscher, *The Prophet Unarmed. Trotsky: 1921–1929* (Oxford, 1959), 390–94 (Trotsky); GARF, f. 3316, op. 2, d. 188 (counterrevolutionaries and former landlords, 1926–27) GARF, f. 3316, op. 16a, d. 430 (landlords, 1929).

28. Figure from V. N. Zemskov, "Sud'ba 'kulatskoi ssylki' (1930–1954)," *Otechestvennaia istoriia*, 1994 no. 1, 118. Note that this supersedes the 1991 figure from V. P. Danilov cited in Fitzpatrick, *Stalin's Peasants*, 83. Not included in this figure are the hundreds of thousands of kulaks who were classified either as more dangerous than the deportees, in which case they were sent to labor camps, or less dangerous, in which case they were simply expropriated and (in theory) resettled on inferior land in the same oblast. For a ballpark estimate of the numbers involved in the latter categories, see Sheila Fitzpatrick, "The Great Departure: Rural-Urban Migration in the Soviet Union, 1929–1933," in William G. Rosenberg and Lewis H. Siegelbaum, eds., *Social Dimensions of Soviet Industrialization* (Bloomington, 1993), 23–25.

29. For different approaches, see Moshe Lewin, *The Making of the Soviet System* (New York, 1985), 121–41; Lynne Viola, "The Second Coming: Class Enemies in the Soviet Countryside, 1927–1935," in Getty, *Stalinist Terror*; Fitzpatrick, *Stalin's Peasants*, 28–33.

30. On the process of dekulakization, see Fitzpatrick, *Stalin's Peasants*, 54–59. On the different administrative categories of kulaks and their punishments, see Davies, *Socialist Offensive*, 234–36.

31. GANO, f. 47, op. 1, d. 2005, l. 35 (letter to Eikhe from a raikom secretary, 25 January 1933, marked "personal").

32. For the deportees' distribution in terms of occupation, see Table 6, Zemskov, 127. At the beginning of 1935, 640,000 deported kulaks were working in industry: N. A. Ivnitskii, *Klassovaia bor'ba v derevne i likvidatsiia kulachestva kak klassa (1929–1932 gg.)* (Moscow, 1972), 326. The deportees' agricultural settlements became collective farms, and some of these "kulak kolkhozy" embarrassed the regime by quickly becoming much more prosperous than their non-kulak neighbors: see Zemskov, "Sud'ba," 125–26.

33. *Spetspereselentsy, trudposelentsy* (from 1934). In 1944, the term "*spetspereselentsy*" came back into official usage, being replaced in 1949 by "*spetsposelentsy*." Zemskov, "Sud'ba," 118.

34. GARF f. 3316, op. 2, d. 188 (OGPU memo, 1931). Of the 936,547 persons classified as "labor settlers" in 1941, 93 percent were deported kulaks: Zemskov, "Sud'ba," 129.

35. This applied to the basic contingent, but not to the smaller groups of "socially dangerous" persons sent into exile for 3–5 years after serving prison or camp terms. The distinction was relatively unimportant, however, since even the fixed-term exiles were released only haphazardly, if at all, when their terms expired. In 1936, Vyshinsky, always a stickler for legality, suggested to Stalin that they be allowed to

return home after serving their terms: GARF, f. 8131, op. 27, d. 72, ll. 168–69, 194 (memo of 23 July 1936).

36. *Sobr. zak.* 1934 no. 33, art. 257, law of 17 March 1934; SZ, 1935 no. 7, art. 57, law of 25 January 1935; GARF, f. 3316, op. 2, d. 1668, l. 1 (memo from Iagoda to Stalin, 17 January 1935, with Stalin's handwritten confirmation in the margin). For the hint of disagreement from Ia. Iakovlev, head of the Central Committee's agriculture department, see Fitzpatrick, *Stalin's Peasants*, 123-24, 240.

37. Zemskov, "Sud'ba," 128–45.

38. GARF, f. 9414, op. 1, d. 15, ll. 23–24, 79–80 (NKVD memo of 23 February 1938 summarizing laws governing *trudposelentsy;* Vyshinsky, memo to Ezhov, March 1938); GARF, f. 3316, op. 2, d. 1786, l. 1 ("Clarification" of February 1936); *Pravda*, 17 October 1937, 1.

39. GARF, f. 8131, op. 27, d. 72, ll. 168–69 (memo from Vyshinsky to Stalin, 23 July 1936); GANO, f. 47, op. 5, d. 214, l. 231 (Instruction of RSFSR Procuracy, 10 August 1936); GARF, f. 9414, op. 1, d. 15, ll. 23–24 (Zhukovskii memo, 23 February 1938); Zemskov, "Sud'ba," 128–29.

40. TSGAIPD, f. 24, op. 2v, d. 3548, ll. 81–82 (Leningrad NKVD report, 1939). For a pioneering, archive-based study of ethnic deportations in the 1930s, see Terry Martin, "The Origins of Soviet Ethnic Cleansing," *JMH*, 70(1998): 4..

41. TsGAIPD, f. 24, op. 2v, d. 1829, ll. 139–44 (special report of Leningrad NKVD, 1 February 1936). The 2,000 included 200 members of the Trotskyite and Zinovievite oppositions, 501 "antisoviet and counter revolutionary elements." and 809 social aliens.

42. Announcement in *Kr. pr*, 20 March 1935, 2. The rumor about the city directory, *Ves' Leningrad*, is repeated as fact in Mandelshtam, *Vospominaniia*, 330. It is even possible that there was some truth in it, given the enormous turnover of telephone subscribers between the 1934 and 1935 editions: see Sheila Fitzpatrick, "The Impact of the Great Purges on Soviet Elites: A Case Study from Moscow and Leningrad Telephone Directories of the 1930s," in Getty, *Stalinist Terror*, 259. Note that although Leningrad was the main site of "former people" deportations in early 1935, similar reports come from Moscow, the Ukraine, and elsewhere: Khlevniuk, *Politbiuro*, 144–45.

43. *Kr. pr.*, 24 March 1935, 3; GARF, f. 5446, op. 81a, d. 352, l. 55; *Sov. iust.*, 1935 no. 27, 14, and 1939 no. 10, 28; GARF, f. 3316, op. 2, d. 1658, l. 1.

44. TsGAIPD, f. 24, op. 2v, d. 2064, l. 7.

45. See David Shearer, "Policing the Soviet Frontier. Social Disorder and Repression in Western Siberia during the 1930s," papers presented at annual meeting of AAASS, Seattle, November 1997, and Paul M. Hagenloh, "'Socially Harmful Elements' and the Great Terror."

46. N. B. Lebina and M. V. Shkarovskii, *Prostitutsiia v Peterburge* (Moscow, 1994), 174.

47. For an example of the first, see *Krasnyi Krym*, 21 July 1937, 2; of the second, *Sov. iust.*, 1932 no. 10, back page. See also G. A. Bordiugov, "Sotsial'nyi parazitizm ili sotsial'nye anomalii (Iz istorii bor'by s alkogolizmom, nishchentsvom, prostitutsiei, brodiazhnichestvom v 20–30-e gody," *Istoriia SSSR*, 1989 no. 1.

48. Lebina, *Prostitutsiia*, 174–75; *Rapports secrets soviétiques. La société russe dans les documents confidentiels 1921–1991*, ed. Nicolas Werth and Gaël Moullec (Paris, 1994); Alaina M. Lemon, "Indic Diaspora, Soviet History, Russian Home: Political Performances and Sincere Ironies in Romani Culture," Ph.D. diss., University of Chicago, 1995, 129 and ch. 6.

49. GANO, f. 47, op. 5. d. 192, l. 1. For more detail on Siberian round-ups, see Shearer, "Policing."

50. The resolution, and the accompanying instruction from Ezhov, published for the first time in *Trud*, 4 June 1992, 1, are in J. Arch Getty, "In Word and in Deed. Repression and the Soviet Communist Party, 1932–1939," ms., 337–45.

51. *Trud*, 4 June 1992, 1.

52. N. Dugin, "Otkryvaia arkhivy," *Na boevom postu*, 27 December 1989, 3. The three categories of Gulag convicts were "socially harmful and socially dangerous" (285,831 on 1 January 1939), criminals (417,552) and counterrevolutionaries (503,166).

53. Engel, *Revolution*, 46, 165 (Dubova and Dolgikh interviews); *Izv.*, 24 February 1930, 5; GARF, f. 3316, op. 16a, d. 446, l. 17 (letter to TsIK, 1930). See also Geiger, *Family*, 140–41.

54. See, for example, *Diktatura truda*, 22 August 1929, 5; ibid., 7 September 1929, 6.

55. *Nash. gaz.*, 24 November 1929, 2.

56. TsGAIPD, f. 24, op. 2v, d. 2487, ll. 139–40 (1937 reports).

57. GARF, f. 1235, op. 2, d. 2021, l. 45 (1937 report); ibid., f. 5407, op., 1, d. 49, l. 14 (1930 document); ibid. f. 5407, op. 2, d. 348 (letters to League of Militant Godless, 1930).

58. GARF, f. 3316, op. 2, d. 918, ll. 11, 42–43 (petitions to VTsIK RSFSR).

59. GARF, f. 3316, op. 2, d. 918, ll. 47, 54–55.

60. Alexopoulos, "Rights and Passage," 366,395, 481, 488. The main source base for this work is a collection of over 100,000 such petitions to VTsIK discovered by Alexopoulos in a previously unknown archive in Ialutorovsk, a small town in Western Siberia. On the argument from misery, see Golfo Alexopoulos, "The Ritual Lament," *Russian History* [henceforth *Rus. hist.*], 1997 no. 1–2.

61. Alexopoulos, "Rights and Passage," 274, 436–48.

62. Rossiiskii gosudarstvennyi arkhiv ekonomiki (RGAE), f. 7486, op. 19, d. 259, l. 29 (letter of 1933).

63. GARF, f. 5446, op. 82, d. 51, l. 276 (letter of 1937). This may have been a disguised plea for a relative, though none was mentioned, but it was not written on behalf of Elagina herself, since she gave an address in central Moscow.

64. GARF, f. 3316 s. ch., op. 2, d. 922, ll. 35–37. This letter was taken seriously by TsIK, despite its doubtful provenance. The same file contains texts of several warnings TsIK issued against anti-Semitism in connection with the liquidation of NEP and chronicles this institution's energetic efforts on behalf of the disfranchised Jews.

65. See, for example, the handling of Stalin's "Son does not answer" remark (Fitzpatrick, *Stalin's Peasants*, 240), and the argument within judicial circles in 1935 about whether Stalin's new slogan that "Cadres decide everything" meant relaxation of repression against class enemies (GARF, f. 3316, op. 2, d. 1621, ll. 1–21).

66. *Koms. pr.*, 8 February 1935, 2.

67. *Koms. pr.*, 2 December 1935, 2.

68. *Sov. iust.*, 1936 no. 21, 8; ibid., 1936 no. 22, 15.

69. HP #416 (XXI), 16–17; ibid., #629 (XXIX), 21–22.

70. GARF, f. 3316, op. 64, d. 1610 (protocols of the meeting of the Constitutional Commission, 1935–36). The unexplained change, occuring suddenly after eight months of discussion, is on l. 161.

71. "Konstitutsiia (Osnovnoi zakon) Soiuza Sovetskikh Sotsialisticheskikh Respublik" (5 Dec. 1936), in *Istoriia sovetskoi konstitutsii. Sbornik dokumentov 1917–1957* (Moscow, 1957), 358; Stalin, *Soch.* I (XIV), 178–79.

72. GARF, f. 3316, op. 40, d. 14, ll. 33, 32 (letters to *Krest'ianskaia gazeta*, 1936, forwarded to Constitutional Commission).

73. RTsKhIDNI, f. 17, op. 3, d. 984, l. 25 (13 March 1937).

74. A cartoon by Boris Efimov in *Krok.*, 1936 no. 17, 6, even implied that the two categories were synonymous: "Before we were class enemies," one emigré says to another, "and now enemies of the people," implying that only the label has changed.

75. See SA, WKP 416 (Komsomol bureau, 1937–38), passim; and Roberta Manning, "The Great Purges in a Rural District: Belyi Raion Revisited," in Getty, *Stalinist Terror*, 191.

76. PANO, f. 3, op. 11, d. 542, l. 559.

77. TSGAIPD, f. 24, op. 2v, d. 3548, ll. 104–07. The schools department sent its protest to the Special Department of the Leningrad obkom.

78. Hryshko, in *Soviet Youth*, 98–99.

79. These themes are developed in Sheila Fitzpatrick, "Lives under Fire," and idem, "The Two Faces of Anastasia: Narratives and Counter-Narratives of Identity in Stalinist Everyday Life," in Kiaer, *Everyday Subjects*, and in somewhat different form in Jochen Hellbeck, "Fashioning the Stalinist Soul: The Diary of Stepan Podlubnyi (1931–1939), *Jahrbücher für Geschichte Osteuropas*, Bd. 44, Heft 3 (1996).

80. *Krok.*, 1935 no. 10, back page. The caption is "The Resumé (*anketa*) and Life. How One Should Sometimes Read the Resumé."

81. GARF, f. 3316, op. 16a, d. 446, ll. 248, 100 (letters to *Pravda*, 1930).

82. *Trud*, 14 July 1933, 4 (Oshkin trial) and 21 February 1936, 1; *Krok.*, 1935 no. 25, 10. On forgery of party cards, see J. Arch Getty, *Origins of the Great Purges. The Soviet Communist Party Reconsidered, 1933–1938* (Cambridge, 1985), 33–35.

83. HP, #167 (XXIII), 12–13; Geiger, *Family*, 142; Dubova interview, in Engel, *Revolution*, 46.

84. *Izv.*, 15 May 1935, 3.

85. See, for example, *Sov. iust.*, 1937 no. 4, 53–54; Fleisher interview in Engel, *Revolution*, 90.

86. SA, WKP 416, 37; HP, #301 (XV), 15; Dubova interview in Engel, *Revolution*, 31–2.

87. Ivan Tvardovskii, "Stranitsy perezhitogo," *Iunost'*, 1988 no. 3, 10–30; GANO, f. 47, op. 5, d. 179, l. 271 (Silaev case, 1932). After Silaev was picked up on black-market charges, the authorities recommended that "he should be exiled to the North together with his family as a typical representative of the rural bourgeoisie and a blatant class enemy of Soviet power."

88. Fleisher interview, in Engel, *Revolution*, 90–91.

89. *Kr. pr.*, 4 April 1935, 2.

90. Ibid., 11 April 1935, 2.

91. Dolgikh interview, in Engel, *Revolution*, 164–69.

92. Tsentral'nyi gosudarstvennyi arkhiv Oktiabr'skoi revoliutsii i sotsialisticheskogo stroitel'stva goroda Moskvy (TsGAOR g. Moskvy), f. 1474, op. 7, d. 72, ll. 119–21 (letter to Moscow Rabkrin, 1933); ibid., d. 79, ll. 86–87 (letter of 1933). On apartment denunciations, see Sheila Fitzpatrick, "Signals from Below: Soviet Letters of Denunciation of the 1930s," in Sheila Fitzpatrick and Robert Gellately, eds., *Accusatory Practices. Denunciation in Modern European History 1789–1989* (Chicago, 1997), 109–10.

93. PANO, f. 3, op. 11, d. 542, ll. 240–41 (1937 letter); Gosudarstvennyi arkhiv Novosibirskoi oblasti (GANO), f. 288, op. 2, d. 902, ll. 4–6 (letters to purge commission, 1930); *Trud*, 4 January 1936, 3.

94. *Rab. put.*, 29 March 1937, 2.

95. RTsKhIDNI, f. 475, op. 1, d. 2, l. 63 (Glavsevmorput', 1935).

96. HP, #358 (XIX), 18; #432 (XXI), 19; #87 (XXX), 3; #338 (XXIII), 3, 19–20; ibid., #359 (X), 31; #358 (XIX), 18; ibid., #527 (XXVII), 29.

97. Fleisher interview in Engel, *Revolution*, 93; HP, #407 (XX), 13; #359 (X), 31; ibid., #416 (XXI), 16–17.

98. HP, #167 (XIII), 12–13; Dolgikh interview in Engel, *Revolution*, 171–72; HP, #387 (XX), 44.

99. See above, pp. 4 (n. 9), 11, 13 (n. 35),and 19. No exact figures on administrative exiles are yet available: thanks to Arch Getty for guidance on the current state of investigation of this question: private communication, 7 September 1997.

100. Engel, *Revolution* (out of eight published life-history interviews, social stigmatization emerges as a central theme in four: Dubova, Fleisher, Berezhnaia, and Dolgikh). 477 (17.5%) of the Harvard Project's respondents were classified as "declassed non-manual" in social origin by the analysts: Inkeles, *Soviet Citizen*, 463.

101. *Sov. iust.*, 1934 no. 9, 2 (paraphrase by Krylenko).

102. RTsKhIDNI, f. 17, op. 85, d. 510, l. 186.

103. HP, #91 (VII), 11; Orlova, *Memoirs*, 12–13.

104. Jochen Hellbeck. ed., *Tagebuch aus Moskau 1931–1939* (Munich, 1996), 36–43, 147, and passim; *Soviet Youth*, 96.

Chapter 6

1. Quoted in Geiger, *Family*, 253.

2. Between 1928 and 1940, the number of women who were wage and salary earners grew from under three million (24 percent) to over thirteen million (39 percent). In the First Five-Year-Plan period alone (1929–32), the number of women in employment almost doubled: *Trud v SSSR. Statisticheskii sbornik* (Moscow, 1968), 73; *Trud v SSSR. Statisticheskii spravochnik* (Moscow, 1936), 25.

3. *Vsesoiuznaia perepis' naseleniia 1937 g. Kratkie itogi* (Moscow, 1991), 74–75, 82. The lower proportion of women presumably reflects demographic imbalance: there were twelve women in their 30s for every eleven men; and for the 40s age group the ratio was close to seven women for every six men. On comparative marriage patterns, see V. V. Paevskii, *Voprosy demograficheskoi i meditsinskoi statistiki* (Moscow, 1970), 344–46.

4. HP, #359 (XIX), 43; Inkeles, *Soviet Citizen*, 212–13.

5. Inkeles, 211–16.

6. Hellbeck, *Tagebuch*.

7. HP, #306 (CVI), 16.

8. Liubchenko, "Arbat," 32 and passim.

9. Liubchenko, 27–28.

10. Bonner, *Mothers and Daughters*, 15–17 and passim; Engel, *Revolution*, 67, 70. On the importance of babushkas in the urban family, see Geiger, *Family*, 176, 311–12.

11. See Fitzpatrick, *Commissariat*, 192, 196, 227–28; Wendy Z. Goldman, *Women, the State, and Revolution* (Cambridge, 1993), 60–63.

12. See Sheila Fitzpatrick, "Sex and Revolution," in Fitzpatrick, *Cultural Front*, 65–69.

13. See Charles Hachten, "Mutual Rights and Obligations: Law, Family, and Social Welfare in Soviet Russia, 1917–1945," unpublished paper (1996).

14. *Vsesoiuznaia perepis'* (1937), 82.

15. Timasheff, *Great Retreat*, esp. 192–203.

16. *2 sessiia Vserossiiskogo Tsentral'nogo Ispolnitel'nogo Komiteta XVI sozyva, 1-9 fevralia 1936 g. Stenograficheskii otchet* (Moscow, 1936), Bulletin 5, 10 (Artiukhina); *Rabotnitsa*, 1935 no. 13, 7 (Indykh). Note that the Russian term *alimenty* is often

translated as alimony or child support, but in fact it covers all types of support payments to family members, including aged parents. The most common form of *alimenty* was child support.

17. PANO, f. 3, op. 11, d. 41, ll. 172–73 (1937).

18. TsGAIPD, f. 24, op. 2g, d. 769, ll. 7–8 (1934).

19. *2 sessiia*, Bull. 5, 10.

20. PANO, f. 3, op. 9, d. 10, l. 100.

21. GANO, f. 47, op. 5, d. 206, l. 81 (1936 report).

22. TsGAIPD, f. 24, op. 2v, d. 1516, l. 74 (1935).

23. *Trud*, 23 June 1935, 2 (author E. Bodrin).

24. Ibid., 15 April 1936, 4 (Malodetkin); SA, WKP 385, 381. Polygamy = *mnogozhenstvo*.

25. *Gor'kovskaia Kommuna*, 10 July 1937, p. 4.

26. PANO, f. 3, op. 9, d. 10, ll. 648–57.

27. SA, WKP 386, 91–92 (letter to secretary of Western obkom, 1936).

28. *Kras. gaz.*, 23 May 1936, 4.

29. See Sheila Fitzpatrick, "Supplicants and Citizens. Public Letter-Writing in Soviet Russia in the 1930s," *Slav. Rev.* 55:1 (1996), 96 ("barefoot"); TsGAIPD, f. 24, op. 2g, d. 768, l. 117 (mascot); RTsKhIDNI, f. 5, op. 4, d. 1, ll. 14–15 (2 hunger cases).

30. GARF, f. 5446, op. 81a, d. 94, ll. 200–01.

31. This account is drawn from reports in *Trud*, 22 April 1935, 4; 23 April 1935, 4; 26 April 1935, 4; 6 May 1935, 4; 11 May 1935, 4; 10 July 1935, 4; and *Rabotnitsa*, 1935 no. 21, 14. There is some uncertainty about the child's name: some reports call her "Geta," others "Deta." Neither is a standard Russian name.

32. *Trud*, 22 April 1935, 4. It is unclear whether Vasil'eva or Marusia was the author of this note, but the malice towards Kashtanov suggests Vasil'eva.

33. *Trud*, 22 April 1935, 4.; 23 April 1935, 4; 26 April 1936, 4.

34. Court case reported in *Rabotnitsa*, 1935 no. 21, 14; *Trud*, 28 May 1936, 2; 10 Jul. 1935, 2.

35. *Kr. pr.*, 1 April 1935, 2.

36. On homeless children, see Ball, *And Now My Soul Is Hardened*.

37. *Za kommunisticheskoe prosveshchenie*, 12 July 1935, 3; *Rapports secrets*, 49.

38. "Deti Ariny. Vospominaniia M. K. Bel'skoi," in *Zhenskaia sud'ba*, 54–57; GARF, f. 7709, op. 8, d. 2, ll. 370–1; *Sov. Sib.*, 15 July 1936, 3.

39. *Sov. iust.*, 1935 no. 13, 4. It was raised to five years by the law of 7 April 1935. For hooliganism on the railroads, the NKVD was instructed in 1932 to make ten years the basic sentence, with execution available as a penalty in particularly egregious cases: GARF, f. 8131, op. 27, d. 72, l. 173.

40. *Stalinskoe Politbiuro*, 144. See also *Sov. iust.*, 1935 no. 14, 6, and Solomon, *Soviet Criminal Justice*, 197–208.

41. Solomon, *Soviet Criminal Justice*, 201; *Sov. iust.*, 1935 no. 13, 11. A secret instruction to prosecutors from the Politburo dated 20 April 1935 explained that this meant that adolescents could receive the death sentence (*Stalinskoe Politbiuro*, 144–45, n. 4), though according to Solomon (202) the archives show no examples of actual executions of adolescent hooligans.

42. *Kommunisticheskaia partiia Sovetskogo Soiuza v rezoliutsiiakh i resheniiakh s"ezdov, konferentsii i plenumov TsK* V (Moscow, 1971), 206–11.

43. RTsKhIDNI, f. 78, op. 1, d. 549, l. 45.

44. The draft law was published in *Pravda*, 26 May 1936, 1. Note the claim in the preamble that the draft law is "responding to the numerous statement from women toilers on the harmfulness of abortion."

45. *Trud*, 28 May 1936, 2; ibid., 26 May 1936, 1.

46. The tone of the rural debate was a little different, since peasant women suspected urban women of trying to get out of child-bearing. See Fitzpatrick, *Stalin's Peasants*, 223–24.

47. *Trud*, 28 May 1936, 2; ibid., 1 June 1936, 2; ibid., 2 June 1936, 2.

48. For example, *Trud*, 2 June 1936, 2, and *Kras. gaz.*, 7 June 1936, 3; *Trud*, 28 May 1936, 2, and 30 May 1936, 2; ibid., 27 May 1936, 2.

49. *Trud*, 27 May 1936, 2. See also *Rabotnitsa*, 1935 no. 17, 12.

50. *Trud*, 28 May 1936, 2. See also ibid., 27 May 1936, 2.

51. Ibid., 4 June 1936, 2; ibid., 27 May 1936, 2.

52. Ibid., 30 May 1936, 2.

53. *Kras. gaz.*, 7 June 1936, 3.

54. Against free marriage, see *Trud*, 28 May 1936, 2.

55. *Sobr. zak.*, 1936 no. 34, art. 309 (Law of 27 June 1936 "On the prohibition of abortions . . .").

56. On birth rates, see V. Ts. Urlanis, *Rozhdaemost' i prodolzhitel'nost' zhizni v SSSR* (Moscow, 1963), 65. On prosecutions for performing abortions, see *Pravda*, 1 July 1937, 6; *Krasnaia Bashkiriia*, 27 April 1938, 4; *Moskovskaia kolkhoznaia gazeta*, 14 October 1936, 4; *Sotsialisticheskii Donbass*, 9 October 1936, 4. On prosecution of women for having abortions, see Dubova interview in Engel, *Revolution*, 33–34, and *Moskovskaia krest'ianskaia gazeta*, 14 October 1936, 4.

57. *Trud*, 28 May 1936, 2.

58. *Moskovskaia krest'ianskaia gazeta*, 9 September 1936, 2.

59. GARF, f. 3316, op. 29, d. 312, ll. 87–9 and passim (letters on abortion law, 1936–38).

60. Queries in GARF, f. 3316, op. 29, d. 311, ll. 73, 235, 248. Vyshinsky's letter to Sovnarkom (March 1938) included the statement, crossed out by an unknown hand, that "Women with arrested husbands whose own records are clear should get benefits": GARF, f. 8131, op. 27, d. 165, l. 336.

61. GARF, f. 3316, op. 29, d. 312, l. 37.

62. *Obshch.*, 1939 no. 4, 25; O. G. Kotel'nikova, in Z. M. Rogachevskaia, ed., *Zhena inzhenera* (Moscow-Leningrad, 1936), 15. On contempt for housework, see Geiger, *Family*, 185.

63. N. P. Ivanova, in Rogachevskaia, *Zhena inzhenera*, 16–17. See also E. K. Rabinowitch, in ibid.

64. *Vsesoiuznoe soveshchanie zhen khoziaistvennikov i inzhenerno-tekhnicheskikh rabotnikov tiazheloi promyshlennosti. Stenograficheskii otchet* (Moscow, 1936); *Trud*, 27 May 1936, 4; *Kras. gaz.*, 14 May 1936, 1. On the origins of the movement, see V. Shveitser, A. Ul'rikh, *Zheny komandirov tiazheloi promyshlennosti* (Moscow-Leningrad, 1936), 17, and *Obshch*, 1936 no. 5, 7.

65. On Surovtseva's initiative, see Shveitser, *Zheny*, 17. On the range of activities, see instructions to wives in the Transport Ministry recorded in Shtange's diary, *Intimacy and Terror*, 171–72.

66. Kotkin, *Magnetic Mountain*, 186; *Obshch.*, 1937 no. 3, 13; Shveitser, *Zheny*, 30.

67. *Vsesoiuznoe soveshchanie*, 130 (Krupskaia's comment) and ibid., 130, 249 (rebuttals); *Obshch.*, 1938 no. 5, 5.

68. Kotkin, *Magnetic*, 127–28 (Magnitogorsk); TsGAIPD, f. 24, op. 2v, d. 2219, ll. 185–88 (Leningrad wives' addresses to Zhdanov, 1937); Shtange, in *Intimacy*, 190–91, 197; TsGA IPD, f. 24, op. 2g, d. 89, l. 74 ("Rabotnitsa" complaint, 1937).

69. Quotation from Rogachevskaia, *Zhena*, 64. On the organization of Stakhanovites' wives, see *Zhenshchina—bol'shaia sila*.

70. *Intimacy*, 175.

71. *Obshch.*, 1937 no. 1, 14 (Red Army wives' conference); ibid., 1939 no. 4, 19 (Iakunina).

72. Ibid., 1939 no. 6, 46.

73. Ibid., 1939 no. 9, 25–26.

74. Quoted Geiger, *Family*, 130. For the regime's "liberationist" approach to women, see G. N. Serebrennikov, *Zhenskii trud v SSSR* (Moscow-Leningrad, 1934) and P. M. Chirkov, *Reshenie zhenskogo voprosa v SSSR 1917–1937 gg.* (Moscow, 1978).

75. See ibid., 1937 no. 5, 7, no. 12, 16–17; ibid., 1936 no. 6 (October), front-page photo; ibid., 1937 no. 1, 14; ibid., 1936 no. 7–8. 43.

76. Ibid., 1939 no. 1(3), 17; 1937 no. 1, 14; 1936 no. 3, 31; *Intimacy and Terror*, 184; *Obshch.*, 1939 no. 6, 17.

77. *Obshch.*, 1939 no. 1, 22–23; ibid., 1938 no. 5, 4–6.

78. Ibid., 1936 no. 7–8, 8–9; ibid., 1939 no. 2, 15–16.

79. See *Zhenshchina—bol'shaia*, esp. 42.

80. *Zhenshchiny i deti v SSSR. Statisticheskii sbornik* (Moscow, 1969), 70–71 (1939 census figure for "Heads of enterprises, construction sites, state farms, administrative institutions, etc."); Ralph Talcott Fisher Jr., *Pattern for Soviet Youth* (New York, 1959), 202–3; Rigby, *Communist Party Membership*, 361.

Chapter 7

1. For a valuable comparative discussion of surveillance and opinion polling in the first half of the twentieth century, see Peter Holquist, "'Information is the Alpha and Omega of our Work:' Bolshevik Surveillance in its Pan-European Context," *JMH* 69:3 (1997).

2. The regular summaries of popular opinion (*svodki o nastroenii naseleniia*) are similar to the Stimmungsberichte regularly gathered by the Nazi regime in Germany: see Ian Kershaw, *Public Opinion and Political Dissent in the Third Reich* (Oxford, 1984), 7–8.

3. Jan. T. Gross, "A Note on the Nature of Soviet Totalitarianism," *Soviet Studies* 34 (July 1982), 3, and see Fitzpatrick, *Accusatory Practices*, 117.

4. On rural correspondents (*sel'kory*), see Steven Robert Coe, "Peasants, the State, and the Languages of NEP: The Rural Correspondents Movement in the Soviet Union, 1924–1928," Ph.D. diss., University of Michigan, 1993, and Fitzpatrick, *Stalin's Peasants*, 246–59; for Stalin's reply to Gorky, see Stalin, *Soch.* XII, 173–77.

5. TsGAIPD, f. 24, op. 2v, d. 1839, ll. 8–11, 24–26 (Leningrad NKVD report, 1936).

6. Ibid., d. 1841, l. 24, and d. 1839, l. 263 (1936).

7. One occasionally encounters the name of one of these informers in the archives, e.g., "L" (full name given in the file), identified as a "writer," working for the police under the codename "Philosopher" (RTsKhIDNI, f. 17, op. 125, d. 235, l. 10).

8. TsGAIPD, f. 24, op. 2v, d. 1839, ll. 286–88 (1936).

9. Ibid., ll. 272–3 (1936). Ethnics = *natsionaly*.

10. RTsKhIDNI, f. 17, op. 3, d. 975 (1936); ibid., d. 994 (1938); ibid., d. 994 (1937); ibid., d. 983 (1937); ibid., d. 995 (1938). The Politburo's decision turned out to be wise, since Goldshtein won fourth prize and Kozolupova fifth, with David Oistrakh taking 1st prize: *Kul'turnaia zhizn'*, 558.

11. RTsKhIDNI, f. 17, op. 3, d. 975 (1936), and d. 984, l. 18 (1937).

12. GARF, f. 3316, op. 2, d. 1300.

13. TsKhIDNI, f. 17, op. 3, d. 958, l. 33 (1935); ibid., d. 978, l. 13 (1936).

14. GARF, f. 3316, op. 16a, d. 446, ll. 36, 163, 166–67, 170.

15. Ibid., ll. 215–16; l. 6.

16. Ibid., l. 190.

17. RGAE, f. 7486, op. 37, d. 237, 224–3 (OGPU *svodki*, 1932).

18. TsGAIPD, f. 24, op. 2v, d. 3553, l. 62; GARF, f. 8131, op. 27, d. 165, l. 146. On reactions to the labor laws, see also Davies, *Popular Opinion*, 44–47, and Filtzer, *Soviet Workers*, 233–53.

19. RGVA, f. 9, op. 36, d. 4222, ll. 362–63; SA, WKP 415, 36, 22. On the "They Killed Kirov" *chastushki*, see also Fitzpatrick, *Stalin's Peasants*, 291–92, and Davies, *Popular Opinion*, 176–77.

20. See Lenoe, "Soviet Mass Journalism," 217–18.

21. TsGAIPD, f. 24, op. 2v, d. 1839, ll. 57–59; Davies, *Popular Opinion*, 96–97; TsGAIPD, f. 24, op. 2v, d. 1860, l. 267.

22. TsGAIPD, f. 24, op. 2v, d. 2064, ll. 41–46.

23. TsGAIPD, f. 24, op. 2v, d. 2064, ll. 41–46 (NKVD *svodki*, 1936); ibid., d. 1860, l. 184; GARF, f. 3316, op. 64, d. 1854, l. 210 (TsIK *svodki*, 1937).

24. TsGAIPD, f. 24, op. 2v, d. 772, ll. 1–16; ibid., d. 2486, ll. 182–83.

25. Ibid., d. 772, ll. 8, 4.

26. Ibid., d. 2064, ll. 24–28 (report of obkom's Osobyi otdel, 1936). To give the Leningrad NKVD due credit, Dudkin Jr. does not seem to have been punished for this game, but his father received a severe party reprimand for failure to discipline his son.

27. For statistics, see *Itogi desiatiletiia sovetskoi vlasti v tsifrakh 1917–1927* (Moscow, [1927]), 117; for the debate, see *Upadochnoe nastroenie sredi molodezhi: Eseninshchina* (Moscow, 1927); on Red Army suicides in the 1930s, see reports by the Army's political administration (PUR) "On political mood and amoral behavior in RKKA units," Rossiiskii gosudarstvennyi voennyi arkhiv (RGVA), f. 9, op. 36.

28. TsGAIPD, f. 24, op. 2v, d. 1852, ll. 180–84; ibid., d. 727, ll. 184–86; ibid., d. 1852, l. 184. Loss of reputation = *diskreditatsiia pered obshchestvennost'iu*; public shaming = *publichnoe oskorblenie*.

29. GARF, f. 8131, op. 27, d. 72, ll. 26–27.

30. *Krest'ianskaia gazeta*, 2 Apr. 1936; GANO, f. 47, op. 5, d. 192, ll. 2–3. For a "vice versa" case, see above, ch. 5.

31. Quotations from TsGAIPD, f. 24, op. 2v, d. 727, l. 184 (1936); RTsKhIDNI, f. 5, op. 4, d. 1, l. 34 (1937).

32. Solov'ev, "Tetradi," 160–61.

33. RGVA, f. 9, op. 29, d. 143, ll. 81–123 (1932 investigation).

34. *Pravda*, 2 Sep. 1937, 6; ibid., 1 June 1937, 6. See also Khlevniuk, *1937-i*, 196–207.

35. Quoted in Getty, "Afraid of Their Shadows," App. 10, in Hildermeier, *Stalinismus*, 185. On Furer, see also Khlevniuk, *1937-i*, 199–200.

36. See Fitzpatrick, "Supplicants and Citizens."

37. V. Markovich, in *Izv.*, 29 May 1934, 2. See also Lev Sosnovskii, in ibid., 5 May 1936, 4.

38. *Vech. Mosk.*, 20 November 1935, 1 (Kalinin); *Vopr. ist.*, 1995, no. 11–12, 6 (Khataevich); TsGAIPD, f. 24, op. 2g, d. 46, l. 13 (Zhdanov). Thanks to Terry Martin for drawing Khataevich's comment to my attention.

39. Osokina, "Krizis snabzheniia," 4.

40. J. Zawodny, "Twenty-Six Interviews," cited from Hoover Institution Archives in Stephen Kotkin, "Coercion and Identity: Workers' Lives in Stalin's Showcase City," in Siegelbaum, *Making Workers Soviet*, 308.

41. TsGAIPD, f. 24, op. 2v, d. 1554, ll. 226–39. Zhdanov received 199 collective letters in 1935.

42. GARF f. 5446, op. 82, d. 112, ll. 276–77 (1939); GARF, f. 5446, op. 82, d. 51, l. 276 (1936); TsGA IPD, f. 24, op. 2v, d. 1514, l. 37 (1935).

43. TsGAIPD, f. 24, op. 1b, d. 449, l. 68 (1932); ibid., op. 2v, d. 47, ll. 147–49 (1937); ibid., op. 2v, d. 48, ll. 219–20 (1937).

44. TsGAIPD, f. 24, op. 2v, d. 1839, l. 100 (1936).

45. TsGAIPD, f. 24, op. 2v, d. 727, ll. 255–57 (letter dated 4 December 1932; Stalin's comments dated 21 December 1932). Note that not all forwarding of private letters was motivated by fear, as was probably the case here. Sometimes individuals forwarded complaints about local abuses that they thought the authorities ought to know about: e.g., the letter from a rural teacher about kolkhoz abuses forwarded by the recipient, a former *sel'kor*, to the Western Siberian kraikom (PANO, f. 3, op. 9, d. 952, ll. 211–12). On perlustration, see V. S. Izmozik, *Glaza i ushi rezhima* (Saint Petersburg, 1995), and idem, "Voices from the Twenties: Private Correspondence Intercepted by the OGPU," *Rus. Rev.* 55:2 (1996).

46. TsGAIPD, f. 24, op. 2v, d. 1839, l. 100; ibid., d. 2487, l. 8; ibid., l. 89; ibid., l. 90. The intercepted letters are euphemistically referred to as *grazhdanskie dokumenty*.

47. J. Arch Getty, "State and Society under Stalin: Constitutions and Elections in the 1930s," *Slav. Rev.* 50:1 (1991), 18–35.

48. See, for example, GARF, f. 3316, op. 40, d. 14 (1936).

49. TsGAIPD, f. 24, op. 2v, d. 1857, l. 7 (Leningrad); *Neizvestnaia Rossiia* II (Moscow, 1992), 274 (Ivanovo).

50. GARF, f. 3316, op. 40, d. 14, ll. 32–33. On the strength of the pro-discrimination opinion, see Getty, "State and Society," 26–27, and Sarah Davies, *Popular Opinion*, 105.

51. GARF, f. 3316, op. 40, d. 14, l. 54. For rural efforts to reopen churches, see Fitzpatrick, *Stalin's Peasants*, 212–13; for urban petitions, see Davies, *Popular Opinion*, 78–79.

52. Davies, *Popular Opinion*, 46, 103–8; *Kr. pr.*, 6 September 1936, 3 (my emphasis).

53. "Konstitutsiia (Osnovnoi zakon) SSSR.," in *Istoriia sovetskoi konstitutsii*, 357.

54. TsGAIPD, f. 24, op. 2v, d. 1860, l. 8.

55. Ibid., ll. 5, 8; *Neizvestnaia Rossiia* II, 279. Art. 10 guaranteed "the right of private property of citizens" (*lichnoi sobstvennosti grazhdan*) with respect to their labor earnings and savings, their home (*zhiloi dom*) and subsidiary domestic plot, household objects, and objects of personal use and convenience, as well as the right of inheritance of such private property.

56. TSGAIPD, f. 24, op. 2v, d. 1860, l. 11; *Neizvestnaia Rossiia* II, 278 (my emphasis). Art. 12 of the Constitution states that it is "the obligation and honor of every citizen to work, on the principle 'He who does not work, does not eat'" ("Konstitutsiia," 346).

57. *Neizvestnaia Rossiia* II, 275. On expression of peasant grievances in the Constitution discussion, see Fitzpatrick, *Stalin's Peasants*, 148–51.

58. See recommendations in SA, WKP 191, 32 (1935). The national parliament was called TsIK up to 1937 and the Supreme Soviet thereafter.

59. *Intimacy*, 206.

60. GARF, f. 1235, op. 141, d. 147, ll. 1–4, 15 (1929).

61. Ibid., ll. 1–3, 8, 11.

62. *Intimacy and Terror*, 206 (Shtange). On the policy volte-face, see Getty, "State and Society," 31–32, and Fitzpatrick, *Stalin's Peasants*, 280–85.

63. GARF, f. 3316, op. 64, d. 1854, l. 220 (1937).

64. Ibid., l. 227. This was not the only "ethnic" objection reported. Komi voters also complained about being given a Russian candidate (l. 232).

65. Davies, *Popular Opinion*, 111–12.

66. On rumor, see Anand A. Yang, "A Conversation of Rumors: The Language of Popular Mentalités in 19th-Century Colonial India," *Journal of Social History* 21 (Spring 1987); Lynne Viola, "The Peasant Nightmare: Visions of Apocalypse in the Soviet Countryside," *JMH* 62:4 (1990); and Fitzpatrick, *Stalin's Peasants*, 45–47, 67–69, 75–76, 286–96. On the Kirov/rationing rumor, see Lesley A. Rimmell, "Another Kind of Fear: The Kirov Murder and the End of Bread Rationing in Leningrad," *Slav. Rev.* 56:3 (1997).

67. A. G. Man'kov, "Iz dnevnika riadovogo cheloveka (1933–1941)," *Zvezda*, 1994 no. 5, 151; HP, #518 (XXVI), 54; #524 (XXVII), 48; #517 (XXVI), 40.

68. Cf. Arlette Farge, *Subversive Words. Public Opinion in Eighteenth-Century France*, trans. Rosemary Morris (University Park, Pa., 1994).

69. W. H. Chamberlin, "The 'Anecdote': Unrationed Soviet Humor," *Rus. Rev.* 16:1 (1957), 33; Stites, *Mass Culture*, 213. On jokes (*anekdoty*), see also Robert W. Thurston, "Social Dimensions of Stalinist Rule: Humor and Terror in the USSR, 1935–1941," *Journal of Social History* 24:3 (1991).

70. Fitzpatrick, *Stalin's Peasants*, 69; Davies, *Popular Opinion*, 176; Man'kov, "Iz dnevnika riadovogo cheloveka," 151.

71. GARF, f. 5446, op. 81a, d. 336, ll. 28, 29, 56, 88 (list of excisions made by Glavlit, 10 May 1939); RTsKhIDNI, f. 17, op. 120, d. 106, l. 49 (1933).

72. SA, WKP 415, 36.

73. SA, WKP 415, 22 (1935); Kh. Kuromiia (H. Kuromiya), "Stalinskaia 'revoliutsiia sverkhu' i narod," *Svobodnaia mysl'*, 1992 no. 2, 95. On *chastushki*, see also Davies, *Popular Opinion*, 51–52, 175–77, and passim.

74. Inkeles, *Soviet Citizen*, 70 (paraphrase of joke told by Harvard Project respondent); Stites, *Mass Culture*, 284 (paraphrased) .

75. Iurii Borev, *Istoriia gosudarstva sovetskogo v predaniiakh i anekdotakh* (Moscow, 1995), 84. A variant of the first joke, assigned to the NEP period, is in van Geldern, *Mass Culture*, 120.

76. Chamberlin, "'Anecdote'," 33. For a classic Soviet joke on powerlessness, see p.218.

77. SA, WKP 320, 240 (NKVD report, 1937); TsGAIPD, f. 24, op. 2v, d. 2064, l. 6 (NKVD report, 1936). I am grateful to Vladimir A. Kozlov for drawing my attention to outbursts as a characteristic Soviet behavior: see V. A. Kozlov and S. V. Mironenko, eds., "Kramola: Inakomyslie v SSSR pri Khrushcheve i Brezhneve, 1953–1982 gg.," ms.

78. HP, #523 (XXVII), 13–14; GARF, f. 3316, op. 64, d. 1854, l. 244.

79. See Fitzpatrick, "Signals from Below," in Fitzpatrick, *Accusatory Practices*, 111.

80. Examples in TsGAIPD f. 24, op. 2v, d. 1518, ll. 1, 14 (1935); ibid., d. 727, l. 367 (1934); GANO, f. 47, op. 5, d. 206, l. 148 (1936).

81. GARF, f. 3316, op. 16a, d. 446, l. 216 (1930); TsGA IPD f. 24, op. 2v, d. 1518, l. 9 (1934); ibid., d. 7272 l. 367 (1934); ibid., d. 1518, l. 9 (1934); GARF, f. 3316, op. 16a, d. 446, l. 100 (1930).

82. RTsKhIDNI, f. 475, op. 1, d. 2, l. 79 (1935).

83. *Pervaia moskovskaia oblastnaia konferentsiia Vsesoiuznoi Kommunisticheskoi. Partii (bol'shevikov). Stenograficheskii otchet*, vyp. 1 (Moscow, 1929), 173–74 (read out by Molotov in his concluding remarks).

84. On peasant decoding, see Fitzpatrick, *Stalin's Peasants*, 287–96.

85. TsGAIPD, f. 24, op. 2v, d. 1829, l. 64 (1936); HP, #415 (XX), 42.

86. RGVA, f. 9, op. 36, d. 4222, ll. 362–3; SA, WKP 415, 4, 36.

87. *Krasnyi Krym*, 3 January 1935, 1 (reported denial by Communists that Op-positionists had murdered Kirov); RGVA, f. 9, op. 36, d. 4222, l. 607; Davies, *Popu-lar Opinion*, 116; SA, WKP 415, 36. See also Rimmell, "Another Kind of Fear."

88. Question 5 of the census questionnaire was "Religion," following "Sex," "Age," "Nationality," and "Native Language": *Vsesoiuznaia perepis' naseleniia v 1939 g. Perepisi naseleniia. Al'bom nagliadnykh posobii* (Moscow, 1938), 25. In the event, 57% of the population aged 16 and over identified themselves in terms of a religious confession and only 43% called themselves "non-believers": Poliakov, "Polveka molchaniia," 69.

89. TsGAIPD, f. 24, op. 2v, d. 2486, ll. 36–38 (1937).

90. The Piatakov trial began on 23 January, and on 1 February Piatakov and oth-ers were sentenced to death and shot (*Pravda*, 24 January 1937, 1; 2 February 1937, 2). The announcement of Ordzhonikidze's death was in *Pravda*, 19 February 1937, 1.

91. TsGAIPD, f. 24, op. 2v, d. 2487, ll. 141–46.

92. Ibid., ll. 141–460.

Chapter 8

1. RGAE, f. 396, op. 10, d. 66, l. 180 (as quoted by Elena Suslova in her com-plaint to *Krest'ianskaia gazeta* about the attempted rape [1938]).

2. Robert Gellately, "Denunciations in Twentieth-Century Germany: Aspects of Self-Policing in the Third Reich and the German Democratic Republic," in Fitzpatrick, *Accusatory Practices*, 214–15.

3. The severity of the 1937–38 terror against marginals—former kulaks, reli-gious sectarians, members of diaspora nationalities, and so on—has only recently be-come known: see Khlevniuk, *Politbiuro*, 191–93; Getty, "In Word and In Deed," 336–46; Shearer, "Policing," 39–49; Hagenloh, "Socially Harmful Elements", 7–9, 25–28; Martin, "Affirmative Action Empire," ch. 8.

4. RTsKhIDNI, f. 17, op. 2, d. 561, ll. 130, 155. The speaker was E. G. Evdokimov from the Northern Caucasus.

5. See memo from Malenkov to Stalin early in 1937, cited in Khlevniuk, *1937-i*, 82–83; speech by Eikhe at February-March plenum 1937, RTsKhIDNI, f. 17, op. 2, d. 612, l. 16.

6. Papernyi, *Kul'tura*, 169; Hellbeck, "Fashioning," 350–55.

7. *Report of Court Proceedings* (1937), 4, 475, 480–81, 496.

8. The proceedings of the February-March plenum have been published in *Vopr. ist.*, beginning 1992 no. 4–5.

9. Stalin, *Soch.* I (XIV), 254.

10. *Zvezda*, 3 August 1937, 2.

11. *Pravda*, 9 February 1937, 1 (editorial); ibid., 30 May 1937, 2 (Postyshev); *Za ind.*, 8 Apr. 1937, 2 (Gvakhariia).

12. *Kras. Tat.*, 21 April 1938, 4; see also ibid., 24 April 1937, 4, and *Partiinoe stroitel'stvo*, 1937 no. 15, 41–42.

13. *Pravda*, 25 August 1937, 3.

14. Memo from A. I. Angarov and V. Ia Kirpotin (cultural department of the Central Committee) to CC secretaries Kaganovich, Andreev, and Ezhov, 29 August 1936, in *"Literaturnyi front.' Istoriia politicheskoi tsenzury 1932–1946 gg. Sbornik dokumentov*, comp. D. L. Babichenko (Moscow, 1994), pp. 16–20.

15. For vilification of Averbakh, see *Literaturnaia gazeta*, 20 April 1937, 1 (editorial); *Pravda*, 23 April 1937, 2, and 17 May 1937, 4; *Molot* (Rostov), 28 May

1937, 2, etc. On Kirshon, see *Pravda*, 15 May 1937, 4.

16. *Literaturnaia gazeta*, 5 Mar. 1937, 2; *Pravda*, 17 March 1937, 1; *Za ind.*, 21 May 1937, 4, and 22 May 1937; *Pravda*, 30 June 1937, 6.

17. *Pravda*, 11 Apr. 1937, 1; I. V. Stalin, "'Nevol'niki v rukakh germanskogo reikhswera' (Rech' I. V. Stalina v Narkomate oborony), *Istochnik*, 1994 no. 3, 73–74.

18. *Pravda*, 18 June 1937, 6.

19. Anna Larina, *This I Cannot Forget. The Memoirs of Nikolai Bukharin's Widow*, trans. Gary Kern (New York, 1993), 43–4; Sats, *Zhizn'*, 306–13.

20. For that, see Robert Conquest, *The Great Terror* (Harmondsworth, Mx., 1971); Khlevniuk, *Politbiuro*.

21. For a broader view of Stalinist self-criticism within the collective, see Kharkhordin, "Collective," ch. 4.

22. On these meetings, see *Trud*, 21 March 1937, 2; *Pravda*, 22 April 1937, 2; *Za ind.*, 21 August 1937, 1; Fitzpatrick, "Workers against Bosses: the Impact of the Great Purges on Labor-Management Relations," in Siegelbaum, *Making Workers Soviet*, 315–20; Victor Kravchenko, *I Chose Freedom* (London, 1949), 216–26. On the anti-management theme in the Stakhanov movement in 1936, see Francesco Benvenuti, *Fuoco sui Sabotatori! Stachanovismo e organizzazione industriale in URSS 1934–1938* (Rome, 1988), 307–27, and Robert Maier, *Die Stachanow-Bewegung 1935–1938* (Stuttgart, 1990), 379–85.

23. *Pravda*, 10 May 1937, 3.

24. The elections were reported in *Za ind.*, 8 April 1937, 2; 10 April 1937, 2; 15 April 1937, 2; 22 April 1937, 4. See ibid., 18 May 1937, 2, for Gvakhariia's identification as a "wrecker," and Roy Medvedev, *Let History Judge. The Origins and Consequences of Stalinism* (New York, 1989, revised ed.), 398, for Zykov's fate.

25. The story of this election is told in Fitzpatrick, "Lives under Fire."

26. *Za ind.*, 20 July 1937, 2; ibid., 1 August 1937, 3; *Tikh. zv.*, 3 November 1937, 2; *Pravda*, 16 June 1937, 4; *Tikh. zv.*, 9 May 1937, 3, and 16 October 1937, 3.

27. The Far East case is a partial exception: Khavkin's patron, Vareikis, succeeded in preventing his expulsion from the party for some months, but then Vareikis was himself disgraced (for other reasons), and both were arrested. See Robert Weinberg, "Purge and Politics in the Periphery: Birobidzhan in 1937," *Slav. Rev.* 52: 1 (1993), 22.

28. *Neizvestnaia Rossiia* IV, 192, and see attacks on Nosov in *Pravda*, 13 May 1937, 2, and 4 July 1937, 2. Nosov, whose death date is given as 1937 in *Stalinskoe Politbiuro*, 297, was almost certainly a Purge victim.

29. Adzhubei, *Te desiat' let*, 185–88 (*Izv.*, 15 June 1937).

30. *Sev. rab.*, 10–12 July, 4–6 August, and 22–23 September 1937; *Rab. put.*, 22 July 1937; B. G. Men'shagin, *Vospominaniia: Smolensk . . . Khatyn . . . Vladimirskaia t'iurma* (Paris, 1988), 31–33; *Kommuna*, 23 November 1937, 3, and 24 November 1937, 3. On the general phenomenon, see Sheila Fitzpatrick, "How the Mice Buried the Cat: Scenes from the Great Purges of 1937 in the Russian Provinces," *Rus. Rev.* 52 (1993), 299–320.

31. A documentary on the Bukharin trial, entitled *The sentence of the court is the sentence of the people*, was showing in Kazan a month later in a double bill with another documentary, *Strana sovetov*: *Kr. Tat.*, 28 April 1938, 4.

32. See above, ch. 3, on the reclamation of thieves.

33. On Sheinin's part in the show trials, see Vaksberg, *Prosecutor*, 66, 74–75, and *Za ind.*, 30 August 1937, 1. On his play, see *Molot*, 8 May 1937, 3 (review of Rostov production by G. Kats); Scott, *Behind the Urals*, 197–203.

34. L. Sheinin and Tur brothers, *Ochnaia stavka* (Moscow-Leningrad, 1938), 44, 79.

35. See above, ch. 5.

36. Fitzpatrick, *Stalin's Peasants*, 201; *Za ind.*, 21 August 1937, 1; GARF, f. 5446, op. 81a, d. 93, l. 88; *Sov. iust.*, 1937 no. 4, 53–54; *Koms. pr.*, 5 October 1937, 2.

37. GARF, f. 5446, op. 81a, d. 250, ll. 2, 6; d. 340, l. 107.

38. TsGAIPD, f. 24, op. 2v, d. 1570, l. 49.RTsKhIDNI, f. 17, op. 114, d. 822, l. 62; ibid., f. 475, op. 1, d. 16, l. 36; ibid., d. 9, l. 259. These examples come from denunciations sent to various authorities, 1936–38.

39. PANO, f. 3, op. 11, d. 542; SA, WKP 111, 22.

40. SA, WKP 392, 66, 91–94.

41. Reports on the cases of the "Saratov Nine" and the "Saratov Twenty" (my labels, based on the number of defendants on a single docket), heard by the Saratov oblast NKVD troika on 29 November and 31 December 1937, were requested by Vyshinsky after he received petitions from relatives of some of the accused; they are together with the petitions in GARF, f. 5446, op. 81a, d. 348, l. 141; and d. 353, ll. 59–61.

42. GARF, f. 1235, op. 141, d. 1859, l. 1.

43. See above, p. 198.

44. Robert A. McCutcheon, "The 1936–1937 Purge of Soviet Astronomers," *Slav. Rev.* 50:1 (1991).

45. RTsKhIDNI, f. 17, op. 2, d. 639, ll. 13–14, 20. See also Khlevniuk, *Politbiuro*, 216–28.

46. *Intimacy and Terror*, 142.

47. GARF, f. 5446, op. 82, d. 56, ll. 331 and 243–44; ibid., d. 51, ll. 213–23.

48. *Istochnik*, 1994 no. 3, 75: *Gor'kovskaia kommuna*, 27 July 1937, 3; *Sovetskoe studenchestvo*, 1939 no. 1, 16–17.

49. *Zvezda*, 1 August 1937, 3. The young Elena Bonner encountered another child spy-catcher from Belorussia at the Artek children's camp in the Crimea: Bonner, *Mothers*, 245.

50. GARF, f. 5446, op. 81a, d. 335, ll. 29–45 (1939).

51. *Krok.*, 1939 no. 11, 8–9. Note that these "denunciation" jokes are in connection with an official campaign against "false denunciations"; generally, this was a taboo subject.

52. RTsKhIDNI, f. 475, op. 1, d. 10, l. 138 and ibid., d. 16, l. 36 (celebrities); GARF, f. 5446, op. 82, d. 56, ll. 315–16, and ibid., ll. 261–3 (politicians); ibid., f. 5446, op. 81a, d. 339, l. 64; ibid., d. 348, l. 52; ibid., d. 349, ll. 129–35 (photographer, artist, leather worker).

53. For examples of bureaucratic and professional denunciation, see GARF, f. 5446, op. 82, d. 65, l. 53; ibid., op. 81a, d. 154, l. 2; GARF, f. 5446, op. 82, d. 65, l. 207; and TsGAIPD, f. 24, op. 2g, d. 226, l. 1. For evidence of RAPP's and Averbakh's unpopularity in the provinces, see *Molot*, 28 May 1937, 2, and *Rab. put.*, 20 May 1937, 3–4, and 3 June 1937, 3.

54. HP, #338 (XXXIII), 19–20.

55. RTsKhIDNI, f. 17, op. 2, d. 639, ll. 7–8 (cited in Malenkov's report to the January 1938 Central Committee plenum).

56. *Kras. Tat.*, 12 June 1938, 2; GARF, f. 5446, op. 81a, d. 94, ll. 99–100 (NKVD report on suicide investigation).

57. *Ural'skii rabochii*, 2 February 1938, 2. Khrushchev drew similar conclusions about Postyshev's accuser, Nikolaenko: *Khrushchev Remembers. The Glasnost Tapes*, trans. Jerrold L. Schecter with Vyacheslav V. Luchkov (Boston, 1990), 34–35.

58. GARF, f. 5446, op. 81a, d. 93, ll. 321–23.

59. Ol'ga Adamova-Sliozberg, "Put'," in *Dodnes' tiagoteet*, vyp. 1: *Zapiski vashei sovremennitsy* (Moscow, 1989), 12.

60. F. E. Treivas, "My borolis' za ideiu," in *Zhenskaia sud'ba*, 91–92.

61. Bonner, *Mothers*, 207. This actually turned out to be a false alarm—only an interrogation about her parents, not an arrest.

62. Ibid., 265.

63. Iurii Trifonov, *Dom na naberezhnoi*, in his *Moskovskie povesti* (Moscow, 1988); I. A. Shikheeva (Gaister), "Semeinaia khronika vremen kul'ta lichnosti (1925–1953 gg.)," ms., 41, 43, 52; Bonner, *Mothers*, 261, 285–86.

64. Lydia Chukovskaya, *Sofia Petrovna*, trans. by Aline Worth and revised by Eliza Kellogg Klose (Evanston, 1988), 71–72. Sofia Petrovna is a fictional character, but Chukovskaia knew this scene from life, since her own husband was a victim of the Great Purges.

65. Shikheeva, "Semeinaia khronika," 42.

66. Bonner, *Mothers*, 324–25.

67. Latvijas valsts arhiva social-politisko dokumenta nodala (LVA SPDN), f. 101, op. 15, d. 122, ll. 108–9 (woman lawyer's statement to investigator, 1952).

68. Shikheeva, "Semeinaia khronika," 40–41.

69. Aleksandr I. Solzhenitsyn, *The Gulag Archipelago* I–II, trans. Thomas P. Whitney (New York, 1974), 160–61.

70. Nina Kosterina, *The Diary of Nina Kosterina*, trans. Mirra Ginsburg (New York, 1968), 128.

71. Iuliia Piatnitskaia, *Dnevnik zheny bol'shevika* (Benson, Vt., 1987), 39, 47–48, 53–54.

72. Orlova, *Memoirs*, 61; Lidiia Libedinskaia, *Zelenaia lampa. Vospominaniia* (Moscow, 1966), 82–88.

73. Hellbeck, *Tagebuch*, 240 (entry for 18 December 1937). For other assertions of parents' innocence, see Kosterina, *Diary*, 85; Shikheeva, "Semeinaia khronika," 37; Khlevniuk, *1937-i*, 216.

74. Bonner, 317 (my emphasis).

75. TsGAIPD, f. 24, op. 2v, d. 2487, ll. 141–46; Sheila Fitzpatrick, "Workers against Bosses: The Impact of the Great Purges on Labor-Management Relations," in Siegelbaum, *Making Workers Soviet*, 330–36; Davies, *Popular Opinion*, 130–33.

76. N. Khvalynsky, in *Soviet Youth*, 123.

77. HP, #395 (XX), 40, and #87 (XXX), 14; SA, WKP 415: 142 (1937 letter); *Krest. pr.*, 2 August 1937, 2.

78. *Neizvestnaia Rossiia* IV, 192 (entry for 19 April 1937). For his conversations with Krupskaia and Krylenko, see ibid., 192–93.

79. *Intimacy and Terror*, 141–42, 162.

80. *Intimacy*, 350–51.

81. M. A. Svanidze, "Dnevniki," in *Iosif Stalin*, 186–87, 188, 192–93, 193–94, n. 1.

82. GARF, f. 5446, op. 81a, d. 348, l. 4; ibid., f. 3316, op. 64, d. 1854, l. 238.

83. RTsKhIDNI, f. 17, op. 2, d. 639, ll. 708.

84. G. A. Chigrinov, "Pochemi Stalin, a ne drugie?" *Voprosy istorii KPSS*, 1990 no. 6, 92.

85. The quantitative question remains a matter of dispute, even though we are now very much better informed as a result of the opening of Soviet archives. Archival data collected by Arch Getty and associates show almost 700,000 executed and a similar number sentenced to camps and prison terms in the years 1937–38, as well as a much smaller number (around 20,000) sentenced to exile. The same source gives a

figure of 1.4 million arrests for "counterrevolutionary crimes" and almost 300,000 arrests for "anti-Soviet agitation" in these years (Getty, "Word and in Deed," 425: Appendix 1).

Conclusion

1. Paraphrased from Chamberlin, "'Anecdote'," 31. Another version of the joke is in Borev, *Istoriia*, 40.

2. Kornai, *Economics* vol. B, 567; idem, *The Socialist System. The Political Economy of Communism* (Princeton, 1992), 56; HP, #357 (XIX), 6; #394 (XX), 11; #399 (XX), 12.

3. Engel, *Revolution*, 46; HP, #511 (XXVI), 6; #420 (XXI), 10; #4 (I), 36. Note that the complaint about being deprived of the possibility of living "normally" was heard once again in the 1980s when it was linked to the perception that the Soviet Union was not a "civilized" country. In its *perestroika* incarnation, the substance of the complaint was that educated professionals were unable to secure a Western lifestyle and living standards.

4. HP #92 (VII), 39 (my emphasis).

5. L. Sigel'baum [Siegelbaum] and A. Sokolov, eds., "1930-e gody: Obshchestvo i vlast'. Povestvovanie v dokumentakh," ms., 199; HP, #531 (XXVII), 14 and 28–29; Harvard Project respondent, quoted Geiger, *Family*, 172.

6. The peasant diarist is Fyodor Shirnov in *Intimacy and Terror*.

7. Hellbeck, *Tagebuch*; diaries of Shtange, and Shaporina in *Intimacy and Terror*; A. G. Man'kov, "Iz dnevnika riadovogo cheloveka (1933–1934 gg.)," *Zvezda*, 1994 no. 5, and "Iz dnevnika 1938–1941 gg.," ibid., 1995 no. 11; Kosterina, *Diary*.

8. David L. Ransel, "Summer Nurseries under the Soviets as Device for Mobilizing Peasant Women and Diminishing Infant Mortality," paper delivered to First Midwest Russian History Workshop, Ann Arbor, March 1991, and private communications to the author, 14 and 23 January 1998. See also responses in Engel, *Revolution*, using revolution, collectivization, and war as markers: e.g. 83, 114, 128–29, 173.

9. See, for example, HP, #3 (I), 11; #4 (I), 9; #8 (I), 9.

10. Berliner, *"Blat,"* 31.

11. The Russian terms are *po planu, planomernost', planovoe nachalo, planovoe raspredelenie; stikhiinost'* (spontaneity) and *sluchainost'* (accident), both antonyms of *zakonomernost'; sluchainye elementy.*

12. "This too will pass" = *Proidet.* On the Soviet positive hero, see Clark, *Soviet Novel*, 167–71 and passim.

13. I. Il'f and E. Petrov, *Dvenadtsat' stul'ev* (1918) and *Zolotoi telenok* (1930–31); Harlow Robinson, *Sergei Prokofiev* (New York, 1988), 277; (*Kizhe*); Aleksandr Tvardovskii, *Vasilii Terkin* (1941–45). Note that the equally popular samizdat sequel of the post-Stalin period, *Terkin na tom svete* (1954–63) [in Aleksandr Tvardovskii, *Vasilii Terkin* (Moscow, 1995)] was an explicit mockery of Soviet bureaucracy.

14. See Jerry F. Hough, *Democratization and Revolution in the USSR, 1985–1991* (Washington, D.C., 1997), 52.

15. For an interesting discussion, see Sarah Davies, "'Us Against Them': Social Identities in Soviet Russia, 1934–41," *Russian Review* 56:1 (1997).

16. GARF, f. 3316, op. 40, d. 14, l. 80 (1936); TsGAIPD, f. 24, op. 2v, d. 1518, l. 32 (letter signed "Workers of the Kirov plant," 1935); worker's comment (1934), quoted in Davies, *Popular Opinion*, 139.

17. Inkeles, *Soviet Citizen*, 300–301.

18. Quoted in Lenoe, "Soviet Mass Journalism," 313.

19. Adam B. Ulam, *Stalin* (New York, 1973) (ch. 8: "The War against the Na-

tion"). On renewal of elites, see Fitzpatrick, *Education*, ch. 9.

20. Although passivity was the rule, there were exceptions: see Jeffrey J. Rossman, "The Teikovo Cotton Workers' Strike of April 1932: Class, Gender and Identity Politics in Stalin's Russia," *Russian Review* 56:1 (1997).

21. Solzhenitsyn, *Gulag*, 160; Geiger, *Family*, 300; Engel, *Revolution*, 97.

22. On labor in the 1930s, see Siegelbaum, *Making Workers Soviet*, and the excellent summary of the current state of knowledge in Ronald Grigor Suny, *The Soviet Experiment* (New York, 1998), 240-49. For the exploitation position, see Filtzer, *Soviet Workers*, 8-9; on resistance, see Rossman, "Teikovo."

23. Hellbeck, "Fashioning," 365; see also Kotkin, *Magnetic Mountain*, 225–30.

24. The rural population is another matter for, as I argued in *Stalin's Peasants*, the trauma of collectivization left the peasantry angry and alienated throughout the decade. For census data, see Poliakov, "Polveka molchaniia," 65–66.

25. See above, ch. 4, and Timasheff, *Great Retreat*.

26. Kornai, *Socialist System*, 315, 56. On the allocative function of the state, see Verdery, *National Ideology*, 74–83. "Dependent" = *izhdivencheskii*.

Bibliography

Archives

GANO — *Gosudarstvennyi arkhiv Novosibirskoi oblasti*

GARF — *Gosudarstvennyi arkhiv Rossiiskoi Federatsii* (formerly *Tsentral'nyi gosudarstvennyi arkhiv Oktiabr'skoi revoliutsii i sotsialisticheskogo stroitel'stva SSSR*, TsGAOR)

GASO — *Gosudarstvennyi arkhiv Sverdlovskoi oblasti*

HP — Russian Research Center, Harvard University, "Project on the Soviet Social System. Interview Records. 'A' Schedule Protocols," ("Harvard Project")

LVA SPDN — *Latvijas valsts arhiva social-politisko dokumenta nodala*

PANO — *Partiinyi arkhiv Novosibirskoi oblasti*

RGAE — *Rossiiskii gosudarstvennyi arkhiv ekonomiki* (formerly *Tsentral'nyi gosudarstvennyi arkhiv narodnogo khoziaistva SSSR*, TsGANKh)

RGVA — *Rossiiskii gosudarstvennyi voennyi arkhiv*

RTsKhIDNI — *Rossiiskii tsentr khraneniia i izucheniia dokumentov noveishei istorii* (former *Tsentral'nyi partiinyi arkhiv Instituta marksizma-leninizma*, TsPA IM-L)

SA — Smolensk Archive

TsGAIPD — *Tsentral'nyi gosudarstvennyi arkhiv istoriko-politicheskoi dokumentatsii Sankt-Peterburga* (formerly *Leningradskii partiinyi arkhiv*, LPA)

TsGAOR g. Moskvy — *Tsentral'nyi gosudarstvennyi arkhiv Oktiabr'skoi revoliutsii i sotsialisticheskogo stroitel'stva goroda Moskvy*

Newspapers and Journals

Abbreviations in brackets after title

(A) Newspapers and Journals of the 1930s
Biulleten' Narodnogo Komissariata Snabzheniia SSSR, Moscow
Diktatura truda, Stalino
Gor'kovskaia kommuna, Gorky
Groznenskii rabochii, Groznyi
Izvestiia, Moscow [*Izv.*]
Kommuna, Voronezh
Kommunist, Saratov
Komsomol'skaia pravda, Moscow [*Koms. pr.*]
Krasnaia Bashkiriia, Ufa
Krasnaia gazeta, Leningrad [*Kras. gaz.*]
Krasnaia Tatariia, Kazan [*Kras. Tat.*]
Krasnyi Krym, Simferopol
Krest'ianskaia gazeta, Moscow
Krest'ianskaia pravda, Leningrad [*Kr. pr.*]
Krokodil, Moscow [*Krok.*]
Leningradskaia pravda, Leningrad
Literaturnaia gazeta, Moscow
Molodaia gvardiia, Moscow
Molot, Rostov on Don
Moskovskaia kolkhoznaia gazeta, Moscow
Moskovskaia krest'ianskaia gazeta, Moscow
Nasha gazeta, Moscow [*Nash. gaz.*]

Nashi dostizheniia, Moscow [*Nash. dost.*]
Obshchestvennitsa, Moscow [*Obshch.*]
Ogonek, Moscow
Partiinoe stroitel'stvo, Moscow
Pravda, Moscow
Puti industrializatsii, Moscow
Rabochii, Minsk
Rabochii krai, Ivanovo
Rabochii put', Smolensk [*Rab. put.*]
Rabotnitsa, Moscow
Severnyi rabochii, Iaroslavl [*Sev. rab.*]
Sotsialisticheskii vestnik, Berlin etc
Sotsialisticheskii Donbass, Stalino
Sovetskaia iustitsiia, Moscow [*Sov. iust.*]
Sovetskaia Sibir', Novosibirsk [*Sov. Sib.*]
Sovetskii sport, Moscow
Sovetskoe gosudarstvo, Moscow
Sovetskoe studenchestvo, Moscow
Tikhookeanskaia zvezda, Khabarovsk [*Tikh. zv.*]
Trud, Moscow
Ural'skii rabochii, Sverdlovsk
Vecherniaia Moskva, Moscow [*Vech. Mosk.*]
Vecherniaia krasnaia gazeta, Leningrad
Za industrializatsiiu, Moscow [*Za ind.*]
Za kommunisticheskoe prosveshchenie, Moscow
Zvezda, Dnepropetrovsk

(B) Scholarly Journals
Istoriia SSSR/Otechestvennaia istoriia
Istochnik
Journal of Modern History [*JMH*]
Kommunist/Svobodnaia mysl'
Rodina
Russian History [*Rus. Hist.*]
Russian Review [*Rus. Rev.*]
Slavic Review [*Slav. Rev*]
Sotsiologicheskie issledovaniia
Soviet Studies/Europe-Asia Studies
Voprosy istorii [*Vopr. ist.*]
Voprosy istorii KPSS/Kentavr

Books, Articles, Dissertations, and Unpublished Papers Cited

Abbreviations in brackets after title

Adamova-Sliozberg, Ol'ga. "Put'," in *Dodnes' tiagoteet*, vyp. 1: *Zapiski vashei sovremennitsy* (Moscow, 1989).
Adzhubei, A. *Te desiat' let* (Moscow, 1989).
Agitatsiia za shchast'e. Sovetskoe iskusstvo stalinskoi epokhi (Dusseldorf-Bremen, 1994).
Alexopoulos, Golfo. "Rights and Passage: Marking Outcasts and Making Citizens in Soviet Russia, 1926–1936," Ph.D. diss., University of Chicago, 1996.
—— "Portrait of a Con Artist as a Soviet Man," *Slavic Review*, forthcoming.
—— "The Ritual Lament," *Russian History*, 24(1997): 1–2.

Alfavitno-predmetnyi ukazatel' k prikazam i rasporiazheniiam NKTP [Narodnogo Komissariata Tiazheloi Promyshlennosti SSSR] za 1935 g. (Moscow, 1936).

Andrle, Vladimir. *Workers in Stalin's Russia. Industrialization and Social Change in a Planned Economy* (New York, 1988).

Angelina, Pasha. *Liudi kolkhoznykh polei* ([Moscow, 1948).

———. *O samom glavnom* (Moscow, 1948).

Ariès, Philippe. *Centuries of Childhood: A Social History of Family Life*, trans. Robert Baldick (New York, 1962).

Babichenko, D. L. *Pisateli i tsenzory. Sovetskaia literatura 1940-kh godov pod politicheskim kontrolem TsK* (Moscow, 1994).

Bailes, Kendall E. *Technology and Society under Lenin and Stalin. Origins of the Soviet Technical Intelligentsia, 1917–1941* (Princeton, 1978).

Ball, Alan M. *And Now My Soul is Hardened. Abandoned Children in Soviet Russia, 1918–1930* (Berkeley, 1994).

———. *Russia's Last Capitalists. The Nepmen, 1921–1929* (Berkeley, 1987).

Barber, John. "Stalin's Letter to the Editors of *Proletarskaya revolyutsiya*," *Soviet Studies* 28:1 (1976).

Bauer, Raymond A. *The New Man in Soviet Psychology* (Cambridge, 1952).

Belomorsko-Baltiiskii kanal imeni Stalina: Istoriia stroitel'stva (Moscow, 1934).

Benediktov, I. A. "O Staline i Khrushcheve," *Molodaia gvardiia*, 1989 no. 4.

Benvenuti, Francesco. *Fuoco sui Sabotatori! Stachanovismo e organizzazione industriale in URSS 1934–1938* (Rome, 1988).

Berg, Raissa L. *Memoirs of a Geneticist from the Soviet Union*, trans. David Lowe (New York, 1988).

Berliner, Joseph. "Blat is Higher than Stalin," *Problems of Communism* 3:1 (1954).

———. *Factory and Manager in the Soviet Union* (Cambridge, Mass., 1957).

Beyrau, Dietrich. "Die organisierte Autor: Institutionen, Kontrolle, Fürsorge," in Gabriele Gorzka ed., *Kultur im Stalinismus* (Bremen, 1994).

Bone, Jonathan. "Soviet Controls on the Circulation of information," paper presented at conference on "Assessing the New Soviet Archival Sources," New Haven, May 16–18, 1997.

Bonner, Elena. *Mothers and Daughters*, trans. Antonina W. Bouis (New York, 1993).

Bordiugov, G. A. "Sotsial'nyi parazitizm ili sotsial'nye anomalii (Iz istorii bor'by s alkogolizmom, nishchenstvom, prostitutsiei, brodiazhnichestvom v 20–30-e gody," *Istoriia SSSR*, 1989 no. 1.

Borev, Iurii. *Istoriia gosudarstva sovetskogo v predaniiakh i anekdotakh* (Moscow, 1995).

Bourdieu, Pierre. *Language and Symbolic Power*, trans. Gino Raymond and Matthew Adamson (Cambridge, Mass., 1991).

Boym, Svetlana. *Common Places. Mythologies of Everyday Life in Russia* (Cambridge, Mass., 1994).

Brooks, Jeffrey. "Socialist Realism in Pravda: Read All About It!," *Slavic Review* 53:4 (Winter, 1994).

———. *When Russia Learned to Read. Literacy and Popular Literature, 1861–1917* (Princeton, 1985).

Brown, Archie. *The Gorbachev Factor* (Oxford, 1996).

Bulgakova, Elena. *Dnevnik Eleny Bulgakovoi* (Moscow, 1990).

Busygin, A. *Zhizn' moia i moikh druzei* (Moscow, 1939).

Carr, E. H. *The Bolshevik Revolution, 1917–1923*, vol. 1 (Harmondsworth, Mx., 1966).

———. *Foundations of a Planned Economy, 1926–1929*, vol. 2 (London, 1971).

———. *Socialism in One Country*, 1924–1926, vol. 2 (London, 1959).

Carr, E. H. and R. W. Davies. *Foundations of a Planned Economy, 1926–1929*, vol. 1 (London, 1969).

Carswell, John. *The Exile: A Life of Ivy Litvinov* (London, 1983).

Chamberlin, W. H. "The 'Anecdote': Unrationed Soviet Humor," *Russian Review* 16:1 (1957).

Chaadaeva, O. N., ed., *Rabotnitsa na sotsialisticheskoi stroike: Sbornik avtobiografii rabotnits* (Moscow, 1930).

Chamkina, M. *Khodozhestvennaia otkrytka* (Moscow, 1993).

Chigrinov, G. A. "Pochemu Stalin, a ne drugie?" *Voprosy istorii KPSS*, 1990 no. 6.

Chirkov, P. M. *Reshenie zhenskogo voprosa v SSSR 1917–1937 gg.* (Moscow, 1978).

Chukhin, I. *Kanalarmeitsy. Istoriia stroitel'stva Belmorkanala v dokumentakh, tsifrakh, faktakh, fotografiiakh, svidetel'stvakh uchastnikov i ochevidtsev* (Petrozavodsk, 1990).

Chukovskaya, Lydia. *Sofia Petrovna*, trans. by Aline Worth, revised by Eliza Kellogg Klose (Evanston, 1988).

Clark, Katerina. *Petersburg. Crucible of Cultural Revolution* (Cambridge, Mass., 1995).

———. *The Soviet Novel. History as Ritual* (Chicago, 1985).

Coe, Steven Robert. "Peasants, the State, and the Languages of NEP: The Rural Correspondents Movement in the Soviet Union, 1924–1928," Ph.D. diss., University of Michigan, 1993.

Cohen, Stephen F. *Bukharin and the Bolshevik Revolution* (New York, 1973).

Colton, Timothy J. *Moscow. Governing the Socialist Metropolis* (Cambridge, Mass., 1995).

Conquest, Robert. *The Great Terror* (Harmondsworth, Mx., 1971).

Crankshaw, Edward. *Khrushchev's Russia* (Harmondsworth, Mx., 1959).

David-Fox, Michael. *Revolution of the Mind. Higher Learning among the Bolsheviks, 1918–1929* (Ithaca, 1997).

Davies, R. W. *The Socialist Offensive. The Collectivisation of Soviet Agriculture, 1929–1930* (Cambridge, Mass., 1980).

Davies, Sarah. "The 'Cult' of the Vozhd': Representations in Letters from 1934–1941," *Russian History*, 1997 no. 1–2.

———. *Popular Opinion in Stalin's Russia. Terror, Propaganda and Dissent, 1934–1941* (Cambridge, 1997).

———. "'Us Against Them': Social Identities in Soviet Russia, 1934–41," *Russian Review* 56:1 (1997).

De Certeau, Michel. *The Practice of Everyday Life*, trans. Steven F. Rendall (Berkeley, 1984).

Dekrety sovetskoi vlasti, vol. 2 (Moscow, 1959).

Deutscher, Isaac. *The Prophet Unarmed. Trotsky: 1921–1929* (Oxford, 1959).

Dobkin, A. I. "Lishentsy," in *Zven'ia. Istoricheskii al'manakh*, vyp. 2 (Moscow–St. Petersburg, 1992).

Druzhnikov, Iurii. *Voznesenie Pavlika Morozova* (London, 1988).

Dugin, N. "Otkryvaia arkhivy," *Na boevom postu*, 27 December 1989.

Dunham, Vera S. *In Stalin's Time. Middleclass Values in Soviet Fiction*, enlarged and updated edition (Durham, 1990).

Edelman, Robert. *Serious Fun. A History of Spectator Sports in the U.S.S.R.* (New York, 1993).

Elagin, Iurii. *Temnyi genii (Vsevolod Meierkhol'd)* (New York, 1955).

———. *Ukroshchenie iskusstv* (New York, 1952.)

Engel, Barbara Alpern, and Anastasia Posadskaya-Vanderbeck. *A Revolution of their Own. Voices of Women in Soviet History* (Boulder, Colo., 1997) [Engel, *Revolution*].

Fainsod, Merle. *Smolensk under Soviet Rule* (London, 1958).

Farge, Arlette. *Subversive Words. Public Opinion in Eighteenth-Century France*, trans. Rosemary Morris (University Park, Pa.., 1995).

Feuchtwanger, Lion. *Moscow, 1937. My Visit Described for my Friends*, trans. Irene Josephy (New York, 1937).

Filtzer, Donald. *Soviet Workers and Stalinist Industrialization. The Formation of Modern Soviet Production Relations, 1928–1941* (Armonk, N.Y., 1986).

Fischer, Louis. *Soviet Journey* (New York, 1935).

Fischer, Marjorie. *Palaces on Monday* (Harmondsworth, Mx, 1944).

Fisher, Ralph Talcott Jr. *Pattern for Soviet Youth. A Study of the Congresses of the Komsomol, 1918–1954* (New York, 1959).

Fitzpatrick, Sheila. "After NEP: The Fate of NEP Entrepreneurs, Small Traders, and Artisans in the 'Socialist Russia' of the 1930s," *Russian History* 13: 2–3 (1986).

———. "Ascribing Class: The Construction of Social Identity in Soviet Russia," *Journal of Modern History* 65:4 (1993).

———. *The Commissariat of Enlightenment. Soviet Organization of Education and the Arts under Lunacharsky, October 1917– 1921* (Cambridge, 1970).

———. *The Cultural Front. Power and Culture in Revolutionary Russia* (Ithaca, 1992).

———. *Education and Social Mobility in the Soviet Union, 1921–1934* (Cambridge, 1979)

———. "How the Mice Buried the Cat: Scenes from the Great Purges of 1937 in the Russian Provinces," *Russian Review* 52 (1993).

———. "Lives under Fire. Autobiographical Narratives and their Challenges in Stalin's Russia," in *De Russie et d'ailleurs. Mélanges Marc Ferro* (Paris, 1995).

———. *Stalin's Peasants. Resistance and Survival in the Russian Village after Collectivization* (New York, 1994).

———. "Supplicants and Citizens. Public Letter-writing in Soviet Russia in the 1930s," *Slavic Review* 55:1 (1996).

Fitzpatrick, Sheila, ed. *Cultural Revolution in Russia, 1928–1931* (Bloomington, 1978).

Fitzpatrick, Sheila, and Robert Gellately, eds. *Accusatory Practices. Denunciation in Modern European History 1789–1989* (Chicago, 1997).

Gambrell, Jamey. "The Wonder of the Soviet World," *New York Review of Books*, 22 December 1994, 30–35.

Geiger, H. Kent. *The Family in Soviet Russia* (Cambridge, Mass., 1968).

Geroini sotsialisticheskogo truda (Moscow, 1936).

Getty, J. Arch. "In Word and In Deed. Repression and the Soviet Communist Party, 1932–1939," ms.

———. *Origins of the Great Purges. The Soviet Communist Party Reconsidered, 1933–1938* (Cambridge, 1985).

———. "State and Society under Stalin: Constitutions and Elections in the 1930s," *Slavic Review* 50:1 (1991).

Getty, J. Arch and Roberta T. Manning, eds. *Stalinist Terror. New Perspectives* (Cambridge, 1993).

Getty, J. Arch, Gabor T. Rittersporn, and V. N. Zemskov. "Victims of the Soviet Penal System in the Pre-war Years: A First Approach on the Basis of Archival Evidence," *American Historical Review* 98:4 (1993).

Giliarovskii, Vl. *Moskva i moskvichi* (Moscow, 1979; 1st pub. 1926).

Gill, Graeme. *The Origins of the Stalinist Political System* (Cambridge, 1990).

Ginzburg, Eugenia. *Into the Whirlwind*, trans. Paul Stevenson and Manya Harari (Harmondsworth, Mx., 1968).

Glotov, B. "Bilet do Leningrada. Bol'shevik Zinaida Nemtsova, kak ona est'," *Ogonek* 1988 no. 27 (July).

Goldman, Wendy. *Women, the State and Revolution. Soviet Family Policy and Social Life, 1917–1936* (Cambridge, 1993).

Gor'kii, M. *Sobranie sochinenii v tridtsati tomakh* (Moscow, 1949–55).

Gorzka, Gabriele, ed. *Kultur im Stalinismus* (Bremen, 1994).

Granin, Daniil. "Leningradskii katalog," *Neva*, 1984 no. 9.

Gromyko, A. A. *Pamiatnoe*, book 1 (Moscow, 1988).

Gronskii, Ivan. *Iz proshlogo... Vospominaniia* (Moscow, 1991).

Gross, Jan T. "A Note on the Nature of Soviet Totalitarianism," *Soviet Studies* 34 (July 1982).

Guillebaud, Philomena. "The Role of Honorary Awards in the Soviet Economic System," *American Slavic and East European Review* XII:4 (1953).

Günther, Hans, ed. *The Culture of the Stalin Period* (New York, 1990).

Hagenloh, Paul M. "'Socially Harmful Elements' and the Great Terror," paper presented at annual meeting of AAASS, Seattle, November 1997.

Harris, James R. "The Great Urals: Regional Interests and the Evolution of the Soviet System, 1917–1937," Ph.D. diss., University of Chicago, 1996.

Hatchen, Charles. "Mutual Rights and Obligations: Law, Family, and Social Welfare in Soviet Russia, 1917–1945," unpublished paper (1996).

Hellbeck, Jochen. "Fashioning the Stalinist Soul: The Diary of Stepan Podlubnyi (1931–1939), *Jahrbücher für Geschichte Osteuropas*, Bd. 44, Heft 3 (1996).

Hellbeck, Jochen, ed. *Tagebuch aus Moskau 1931–1939*, (Munich, 1996).

Hessler, Julie. "Culture of Shortages. A Social History of Soviet Trade, 1917–1953," Ph.D dissertation, University of Chicago, September 1996.

Hildermeier, Manfred with Elisabeth Müller-Luckner, ed. *Stalinismus vor dem Zweiten Weltkrieg. Neue Wege der Forschung / Stalinism before the Second World War. New Avenues of Research* (Munich, 1998).

Hoffman, David L. *Peasant Metropolis. Social Identities in Moscow, 1928–1941* (Ithaca, 1994).

Holquist, Peter. "'Information is the Alpha and Omega of our Work:' Bolshevik Surveillance in its Pan-European Context," *Journal of Modern History* 69:3 (1997).

Hough, Jerry F. *Russia and the West. Gorbachev and his Politics of Reform* (New York, 1988).

Hough, Jerry F., and Merle Fainsod, *How the Soviet Union in Governed* (Cambridge, 1979).

Hubbard, Leonard E. *Soviet Trade and Distribution* (London, 1938).

Il'f, I. and E. Petrov. *Zolotoi telenok* (1st pub. 1928) and *Dvenadtsat' stul'ev* (1931)— see below: Shcheglov, Iu. K.

Inkeles, Alex, and Raymond Bauer. *The Soviet Citizen. Daily Life in a Totalitarian Society* (New York, 1968).

Intimacy and Terror. Soviet Diaries of the 1930s, ed. Véronique Garros, Natalia Korenevskaya, and Thomas Lahusen (New York, 1995).

Iosif Stalin v ob"iatiiakh sem'i. Iz lichnogo arkhiva (Moscow, 1993).

Isaev, V. I. "Formirovanie gorodskogo obraza zhizni rabochikh Sibiri v period sotsialisticheskoi rekonstruktsii narodnogo khoziaistva," in *Urbanizatsiia sovetskoi Sibiri*, ed. V. V. Alekseev (Novosibirsk, 1987).

Istoriia sotsialisticheskoi ekonomiki SSSR v semi tomakh, chief ed. I. A. Gladkov, vols. 3 and 4 (Moscow, 1977–78 [*Ist. sots. ek.*].

Istoriia sovetskogo kino, vol. 2: *1931–1941* (Moscow, 1973).

Istoriia sovetskoi konstitutsii. Sbornik dokumentov 1917–1957 (Moscow, 1957).

Itogi desilatiletiia sovetskoi vlasti v tsifrakh 1917–1927 (Moscow, [1927]).

Ivnitskii, N. A. *Klassovaia bor'ba v derevne i likvidatsiia kulachestva kak klassa (1929–1932 gg.)* (Moscow, 1972).

Izmeneniia sotsial'noi struktury sovetskogo obshchestve 1921-seredina 30-kh godov (Moscow, 1979).

Izmozik, V. S. *Glaza i ushi rezhima. Gosudarstvennyi politicheskii kontrol' za naseleniem sovetskoi Rossii v 1918–1928 godakh* (Saint Petersburg, 1995).

———. "Voices from the Twenties: Private Correspondence Intercepted by the OGPU," *Russian Review* 55:2 (1996).

Kapitsa, P. L. *Pis'ma o nauke, 1930–1980* (Moscow, 1989).

Kershaw, Ian. *Public Opinion and Political Dissent in the Third Reich. Bavaria 1933–1945* (Oxford, 1984).

Kharkhordin, Oleg V. "The Collective and the Individual in Soviet Russia: A Study of Background Practices," Ph.D. diss., Berkeley, 1996.

Khlevniuk, O. V. *Politbiuro. Mekhanizmy politicheskoi vlasti v 1930-e gody* (Moscow, 1996).

———. *Stalin i Ordzhonikidze. Konflikty v Politbiuro v 30-e gody* (Moscow, 1993).

———. *1937-i: Stalin, NKVD i sovetskoe obshchestvo* (Moscow, 1992).

Khrushchev Remembers, ed. Strobe Talbott (Boston, 1970).

Khrushchev Remembers. The Glasnost Tapes, trans. Jerrold L. Schecter with Vyacheslav V. Luchkov (Boston, 1990).

Kiaer, Christina and Eric Naiman, eds. *Everyday Subjects: Formations of Identity in Early Soviet Culture* (Cornell University Press, forthcoming).

Kimerling, Elise. "Civil Rights and Social Policy in Soviet Russia, 1918–1936," *Russian Review* 41:1 (January, 1982).

Kingsley, Charles. *The Water-Babies. A Fairy Tale for a Land Baby* (London, 1903; 1st ed. 1863).

Klein, Joachim. "Belomorkanal. Literatur und Propaganda in der Stalinzeit," *Zeitschrift für slavische Philologie* 55:1 (1995/6).

Kommunistcheskaia partiia Sovetskogo Soiuza v rezoliutsiiakh i resheniiakh s"ezdov, konferentsii i plenumov TsK, vol. 5 (1931–1941) (Moscow, 1971).

Kopelev, Lev. *The Education of a True Believer*, trans. Gary Kern (New York, 1980).

Kornai, Janos. *Economics of Shortage* (Amsterdam, 1980: *Contributions to Economic Analysis* #131), 2 vols.

———. *The Socialist System: The Political Economy of Communism* (Princeton, 1992)

Korzhikhina, T. P. "Bor'ba s alkogolizmom v 1920-e–nachale 1930-kh godov," *Voprosy istorii*, 1985 no. 9.

Kosterina, Nina. *Dnevnik Niny Kosterinoi* (Moscow, 1964).

Kotkin, Stephen. *Magnetic Mountain. Stalinism as a Civilization* (Berkeley, 1995).

Kozlov, V. A. and S. V. Mironenko, ed., with E. Iu. Zavadskaia and O. V. Edel'man. "Kramola: Inakomyslie v SSSR pri Khrushcheve i Brezhneve, 1953–1982 gg.," ms.

Kravchenko, Maria. *The World of the Russian Fairy Tale* (Berne, 1987).

Kravchenko, Victor. *I Chose Freedom. The Personal and Political Life of a Soviet Official* (London, 1949).

Kritsman, L. *Geroicheskii period velikoi russkoi revoliutsii* (2nd ed., Moscow-Leningrad, 1926).

Kul'turnaia zhizn' v SSSR 1928–1941. Khronika (Moscow, 1976).

Kul'turnoe stroitel'stvo SSSR. Statisicheskii sbornik (Moscow- Leningrad, 1940).

Kuromiya, Hiroaki. *Stalin's Industrial Revolution. Politics and Workers, 1928–1932* (Cambridge, 1988).

———. (Kh. Kuromiia), "Stalinskaia 'revoliutsiia sverkhu' i narod," *Svobodnaia mysl'*, 1992 no. 2, 93–96.

Josephson, Paul. *Physics and Politics in Revolutionary Russia* (Berkeley and Los Angeles, 1991).

Jowitt, Ken. *New World Disorder. The Leninist Extinction* (Berkeley, 1992).

Lahusen, Thomas. *How Life Writes the Book, Real Socialism and Socialist Realism in Stalin's Russia* (Ithaca, 1997).

Larina, Anna. *This I Cannot Forget. The Memoirs of Nikolai Bukharin's Widow*, trans. Gary Kern (New York, 1988).

Lebina, N. B., and M. V. Shkarovskii. *Prostitutsiia v Peterburge* (Moscow, 1994).

Ledeneva, Alena. *Russia's Economy of Favours: Blat, Networking and Informal Exchanges* (Cambridge, 1998).

Lemon, Alaina M. "Indic Diaspora, Soviet History, Russian Home: Political Performances and Sincere Ironies in Romani Culture," Ph.D. diss., University of Chicago, 1995.

Lenoe, Matthew E. "Soviet Mass Journalism and the Transformation of Soviet Newspapers, 1926–1932," Ph.D. diss., University of Chicago, 1997.

———. "Unmasking, Show Trials, and the Manipulation of Popular Moods," ms.

"The Letter as a Work of Art," publication by S. Fitzpatrick, *Russian History* 1997 no. 1–2.

Lewin, Moshe. *The Making of the Soviet System. Essays in the Social History of Interwar Russia* (New York, 1985).

Leyda, Jay. *Kino. A History of the Russian and Soviet Film* (London, 1973).

Libedinskaia, Lidiia. *Zelenaia lampa. Vospominaniia* (Moscow, 1966).

"Literaturnyi front." Istoriia politicheskoi tsenzury 1932– 1946 gg. Sbornik dokumentov, comp. D. L. Babichenko (Moscow, 1994).

Littlepage, John D., with Demaree Bess. *In Search of Soviet Gold* (New York, 1938)

Liubchenko, N. "Arbat, 30, Kvartira 58," *Istochnik*, 1993 no. 5–6.

Lüdtke, Alf, ed. *The History of Everyday Life. Reconstructing Historical Experiences and Ways of Life*, trans. William Templer (Princeton, 1995).

Maclean, Fitzroy. *Eastern Approaches* (London, 1949).

Maier, Robert. *Die Stachanow-Bewegung 1935–1938* (Stuttgart, 1990).

Makarenko, A. S. *Learning to Live (Flags on the Battlements)*, trans. Ralph Parker (Moscow, 1953).

———. *The Road to Life (An Epic of Education)*, in 3 parts, trans. Ivy and Tatiana Litvinov (Moscow, 1951).

———. *Sochineniia v semi tomakh* (Moscow, 1957–58).

Malafeev, A. N. *Istoriia tsenoobrazovaniia v SSSR (1917–1963 gg.)* (Moscow, 1964).

Mandelshtam, Nadezhda. *Hope Abandoned*, trans. Max Hayward (New York, 1974).

———. *Vospominaniia* (New York, 1970).

Man'kov, A. G. "Iz dnevnika riadovogo cheloveka (1933–1934 gg.), *Zvezda*, 1994 no. 5.

———. "Iz dnevnika 1938–1941 gg.," *Zvezda*, 1995 no. 11.

Martin, Terry D. "An Affirmative Action Empire: Ethnicity and the Soviet State, 1921–1938," Ph. D. diss., University of Chicago, 1996.

———. "Origins of Soviet Ethnic Cleansing," *Journal of Modern History*, 70:4 (1998).

"Materialy fevral'sko-martovskogo plenuma TsK VKP(b) 1937 goda," *Voprosy istorii*, 1992 no. 4–5.

McCannon, John. "Positive Heroes at the Pole: Celebrity Status, Socialist-Realist Ideals, and the Soviet Myth of the Arctic, 1932–39," *Russian Review* 56:3 (July 1997).

———. *Red Arctic: Polar Exploration and the Myth of the North in the Soviet Union, 1932–1939* (New York, 1998).

McCutcheon, Robert A. "The 1936–1937 Purge of Soviet Astronomers," *Slavic Review* 50:1 (1991).

Melkaia promyshlennost' SSSR. Po dannym perepisi 1929 g., vyp. 1 (Moscow, 1933).

Men'shagin, B. G. *Vospominaniia: Smolensk . . . Khatyn . . . Vladimirskaia t'iurma* (Paris, 1988).

Medvedev, Roy. *Let History Judge. The Origins and Consequences of Stalinism*, ed. and trans. George Shriver (New York, 1989, revised ed.).

Messana, Paola. *Kommunalka. Une histoire de l'Union soviétique à travers les appartements communautaires* (Paris, 1995).

Mikhail Kol'tsov, kakim on byl (Moscow, 1965).

Mikoyan, A. I. *Pishchevaia industriia Sovetskogo Soiuza* ([Moscow], 1939).

Miller, Frank J. *Folklore for Stalin. Russian Folklore and Pseudofolklore of the Stalin Era* (Armonk, N.Y., 1990).

The Moscow Theatre for Children (Moscow, 1934).

Muggeridge, Malcolm. *Winter in Moscow* (London, 1934).

Narodnoe khoziaistvo Pskovskoi oblasti. Statisticheskii sbornik ([Leningrad], 1968).

Narodnoe obrazovanie, nauka i kul'tura v SSSR. Statisticheskii sbornik (Moscow, 1971).

Narodnoe obrazovanie v SSSR. Obshcheobrazovatel'naia shkola. Sbornik dokumentov 1917–1953 gg. (Moscow, 1974).

Neiman, G. Ia. *Vnutrenniaia torgovlia SSSR* (Moscow, 1935).

Neizvestnaia Rossiia. XX vek, vols. 1–4 (Moscow, 1992–93).

Neuberger, Joan. *Hooliganism. Crime, Culture, and Power in St. Petersburg, 1900–1914* (Berkeley, 1993).

Nove, Alec. *An Economic History of the U.S.S.R.* (Harmondsworth, Mx., 1972).

O Valeriane Kuibysheve: Vospominaniia, ocherki, stat'i (Moscow, 1983).

Ocherki istorii sovetskogo kino, vols. 1 and 2, ed. Iu. S. Kalashnikov et al. (Moscow, 1956, 1959).

Orlova, Raisa. *Memoirs*, trans. by Samuel Cioran (New York, 1983).

Osokina, E. A. *Ierarkhiia potrebleniia. O zhizni liudei v usloviiakh stalinskogo snabzheniia 1928–1935 gg.* (Moscow, 1993).

———. "Krizis snabzheniia 1939–1941 gg. v pis'makh sovetskikh liudei," *Voprosy istorii*, 1996 no. 1.

———. "Liudi i vlast' v usloviiakh krizisa snabzheniia 1939–1941 gody," *Otechestvennaia istoriia*, 1995 no. 3.

———. "Za zerkal'noi dver'iu Torgsina," *Otechestvennaia istoriia*, 1995 no. 2.

Paevskii, V. V. *Voprosy demograficheskoi i meditsinskoi statistiki* (Moscow, 1970).

Papernyi, Vladimir. *Kul'tura 'dva'* (Ann Arbor, 1985).

Party, State, and Society in the Russian Civil War. Explorations in Social History, eds. Diane P. Koenker, William G. Rosenberg, and Ronald Grigor Suny (Indiana, 1989).

Payne, Matthew J. "Turksib: The Building of the Turkestano-Siberian Railroad and the Politics of Production during the Cultural Revolution, 1926–1931," Ph. D. diss., University of Chicago, 1994.

Penzenskaia oblast' za 50 let sovetskoi vlasti. Statisticheskii sbornik (Saratov-Penza, 1967).

Perepis' naseleniia. Al'bom nagliadnykh posobii (Moscow, 1938).

Perrot, Michelle, ed. *A History of Private Life*, vol. 4. *From the Fires of Revolution to the Great War*, trans. Arthur Goldhammer (Cambridge, 1990).

Pervaia moskovskaia oblastnaia konferentsiia Vsesoiuznoi Kommunisticheskoi Partii (bol'shevikov). Stenograficheskii otchet, vyp. 1 (Moscow: 1928).

Petrone, Karen. "Parading the Nation: Physical Culture Celebrations and the Construction of Soviet Identities in the 1930s," *Michigan Discussions in Anthropology* XII (1996).

Peukert, Detlev J. K. *Inside Nazi Germany. Conformity, Opposition, and Racism in Everyday Life*, trans. Richard Deveson (New Haven, 1987).

Piatnitskaia, Iuliia. *Dnevnik zheny bol'shevika* (Benson, Vt., 1987).

Pipes, Richard. "The Russian Military Colonies, 1810–1831," *Journal of Modern History* 22:3 (September, 1950).

Poliakov, Iu. A., V. B. Ziromskaia, I. N. Kiselev, "Polveka molchaniia (Vsesoiuznaia perepis' naseleniia 1937 g.)," *Sotsiologicheskie issledovaniia*, 1990 no. 7.

Pramnek, E. *Otchetnyi doklad V Gor'kovskoi oblastnoi partiinoi konferentsii o rabote obkoma VKP(b)* (Gorky, 1937).

Pospelov, E. M. *Imena gorodov: vchera i segodnia. Toponomicheskii slovar'* (Moscow, 1993).

Prishvin, Mikhail. *Dnevniki* (Moscow, 1990).

Raeff, Marc. *Origins of the Russian Intelligentsia. The Eighteenth-Century Nobility* (New York, 1966).

Ransel, David L. "Summer Nurseries under the Soviets as Device for Mobilizing Peasant Women and Diminishing Infant Mortality," paper presented at First Midwest Russian History Workshop, Ann Arbor, March 1991.

Rapports secrets soviétiques. La société russe dans les documents confidentiels 1921–1991, eds. Nicolas Werth and Gaël Moullec (Paris, 1994).

Reese, Roger R. *Stalin's Reluctant Soldiers. A Social History of the Red Army, 1925–1941* (Lawrence, Kans., 1996).

Report of the Court Proceedings in the Case of the Anti-Soviet Trotskyite Centre, Heard before the Military Collegium of the Supreme Court of the U.S.S.R. Moscow, January 23–30, 1937 (Moscow, 1937).

Report of the Court Proceedings in the Case of the Anti-Soviet "Bloc of Rights and Trotskyites" heard before the Military Collegium of the Supreme Court of the U.S.S.R. Moscow, March 2–13, 1938 (Moscow, 1938).

Resheniia partii i pravitel'stva po khoziaistvennym voprosam (1917–1967 gg.), vol. 2 (Moscow, 1967).

Revelations from the Russian Archives. Documents in English Translation, Diane P. Koenker and Ronald D. Bachman, eds. (Washington DC, 1997).

Richmond, Steven D. "Ideologically Firm: Soviet Theater Censorship, 1921–1928," Ph.D. diss., University of Chicago, 1996.

Rigby, T. H. *Communist Party Membership in the U.S.S.R. 1917– 1967* (Princeton, 1968).

———. *Political Elites in the USSR. Central Leaders and Local Cadres from Lenin to Gorbachev* (Aldershot, 1990).

Rimmel, Lesley A. "Another Kind of Fear: The Kirov Murder and the End of Bread Rationing in Leningrad," *Slavic Review* 56:3 (1997).

Rogachevskaia, Z. M., ed. *Zhena inzhenera* (Moscow-Leningrad, 1936).

Roland, Betty. *Caviar for Breakfast* (Sydney, 1989).

Rosenberg, Harry. *The Leica and Other Stories* ([Canberra], 1994).

Rosenberg, William G. and Lewis H. Siegelbaum, eds. *Social Dimensions of Soviet Industrialization* (Bloomington, 1993).

Rossman, Jeffrey J. "The Teikovo Cotton Workers' Strike of April 1932: Class, Gender and Identity Politics in Stalin's Russia," *Russian Review* 56:1 (1997).

Rukeyser, W. A. *Working for the Soviets: An American Engineer in Russia* (New York, 1932).

Russia in the Era of NEP. Explorations in Soviet Society and Culture, ed. Sheila Fitzpatrick, Alexander Rabinowitch, and Richard Stites (Bloomington, 1991).

Rybakov, Anatoli. *Children of the Arbat*, trans. Harold Shukman (Boston, 1988).

———. *Fear*, trans. Antonina W. Bouis (Boston, 1992).

Sats, Nataliia. *Zhizn' — iavlenie polosatoe* (Moscow, 1991).

Sbornik vazhneishikh postanovlenii po trudu, comp. Ia. L. Kiselev and S. E. Malkin (Moscow, 1938).

Scheffer, Paul. *Seven Years in Soviet Russia* (New York, 1932).

Schlesinger, Rudolf. *Changing Attitudes in Soviet Russia. The Family. Documents and Readings* (London, 1949).

Schwarz, Solomon M. *Labor in the Soviet Union* (New York, 1951).

Scott, James C. *The Weapons of the Weak. Everyday Forms of Peasant Resistance* (New Haven, 1985).

Scott, John. *Behind the Urals. An American Worker in Russia's City of Steel* (Bloomington, 1973; original ed. 1942).

Serebrennikov, G. N. *Zhenskii trud v SSSR* (Moscow-Leningrad, 1934).

Serge, Victor. *Memoirs of a Revolutionary 1901–1941*, trans. Peter Sedgwick (London, 1963).

Shcheglov, Iu. K. "Kommentarii k romanu 'Dvenadtsat' stul'ev'," in I. Ilf and E. Petrov, *Dvenadtsat' stul'ev. Roman* (Moscow, 1995) [Shcheglov, *DS*].

———. "Kommentarii k romanu 'Zolotoi telenok'," in I. Il'f and E. Petrov, *Zolotoi telenok. Roman* (Moscow, 1995) [Shcheglov, *ZT*].

Shearer, David R. "Policing the Soviet Frontier. Social Disorder and Repression in Western Siberia during the 1930s," paper presented at annual meeting of AAASS, Seattle, November 1997.

Sheinin, Lev. *Zapiski sledovatelia* (Moscow, 1965).

Sheinin, Lev and Tur brothers. *Ochnaia stavka* (Moscow-Leningrad, 1938).

Shentalinskii, Vitalii. *Raby svobody. V literaturnykh arkhivakh KGB* ([Moscow], 1995).

6-aia Vsekazakskaia konferentsiia RKP(b) 15–23 noiabria 1927 goda. Stenograficheskii otchet (Kzyl-Orda, 1927).

Shikheeva (Gaister), I. A. "Semeinaia khronika vremen kul'ta lichnosti (1925–1953 gg.)," ms.

Shveitser, V., and A. Ul'rikh. *Zheny komandirov tiazheloi promyshlennosti* (Moscow-Leningrad, 1936).

Siegelbaum, Lewis H. "Dear Comrade, You Ask What We Need:' Soviet Rural 'Notables' and the Politics of Distribution in the Mid-1930s," *Slavic Review*, 57:1(1998).

———. *Stakhanovism and the Politics of Productivity in the USSR, 1935–1941* (Cambridge, 1988).

Siegelbaum, Lewis H. and Ronald Grigor Suny, eds. *Making Workers Soviet. Power, Class, and Identity* (Ithaca, 1994).

Sigel'baum [Siegelbaum], L. and A. Sokolov, eds. "1930-e gody. Obshchestvo i vlast'. Povestvovanie v dokumentakh," ms. [English title: "Stalinism as a Way of Life: A Documentary Narrative"].

Simonov, N. S. "'Strengthen the Defence of the Land of the Soviets': The 1927 'War Alarm' and its Consequences," *Europe-Asia Studies* 48:8 (December, 1996).

Slezkine, Yuri. *Arctic Mirrors. Russia and the Small Peoples of the North* (Ithaca, 1994)

———. "From Savages to Citizens: The Cultural Revolution in the Soviet Far North, 1928–1939," *Slavic Review* 51:1 (1992).

Sobranie postanovlenii i rasporiazhenii pravitel'stva SSSR [*Sobr. post.*].

Sobranie uzakonenii i rasporiazhenii rabochego i krest'ianskogo pravitel'stva RSFSR [*Sobr. uzak.*].

Sobranie zakonov i rasporiazhenii raboche-krest'ianskogo pravitel'stva SSSR [*Sobr. zak.*].

Solomon, Peter H. Jr. *Soviet Criminal Justice under Stalin* (Cambridge, 1996).

Solov'ev, A. G. "Tetradi krasnogo professora, 1912–1941 gg." in *Neizvestnaia Rossiia. XX vek*, vol. 4 (Moscow, 1993).

Solzhenitsyn, Aleksandr I. *The Gulag Archipelago*, vols. 1–2, trans. Thomas P. Whitney (New York, 1974).

Sotsialisticheskoe stroitel'stvo Soiuza SSR (1937–1938 gg.). Statisticheskii sbornik (Moscow, 1939) [*Sots.stroi.*, 1939].

Sotsialisticheskoe stroitel'stvo SSSR. Statisticheskii ezhegodnik (Moscow, 1934) [*Sots.stroi.*, 1934].

Soviet Youth. Twelve Komsomol Histories, Nikolai K. Novak-Deker, ed. (Munich, 1959); Institut zur Erforschung der UdSSR, Series 1, no. 51.

Stalin, I. V. *Sochineniia* (13 vols.) (Moscow) and *Sochineniia*, 3 vols. (XIV–XVI), Robert H. McNeal, ed. (Stanford, 1967) [Stalin, *Soch.*].

———. "'Nevol'niki v rukakh germanskogo reikhswera' (Rech' I. V. Stalina v Narkomate oborony), *Istochnik*, 1994 no. 3.

Stalinskoe Politbiuro v 30-e gody. Sbornik dokumentov (Moscow, 1995).

Stalin's Letters to Molotov, ed. Lars T. Lih, Oleg V. Naumov, and Oleg V. Khlevniuk (New Haven, 1995).

Starkov, B. "Kak Moskva chut' ne stala Stalinodarom," *Izvestiia TsK KPSS*, 1990 no. 12.

Starr, S. Frederick. *Red and Hot. The Fate of Jazz in the Soviet Union* (New York, 1983).

Statisticheskii sbornik po Severnomu kraiu za 1929–1933 gody (Arkhangelsk, 1934).

Stites, Richard. *Russian Popular Culture, Entertainment and Society since 1900* (Cambridge, 1992).

Sto sorok besed s Molotovym. Iz dnevnika F. Chueva (Moscow, 1991).

Suny, Ronald Grigor. *The Soviet Experiment. Russia, the USSR, and the Successor States* (New York, 1998).

Sytin, P. B. *Iz istorii moskovskikh ulits (ocherki)* (Moscow, 1958).

Testimony. The Memoirs of Dmitri Shostakovich, ed. Solomon Volkov, and trans. Antonina W. Bouis (New York, 1980).

Thurston, Robert W. *Life and Terror in Stalin's Russia, 1934– 1941* (New Haven, 1996).

———. "Social Dimensions of Stalinist Rule: Humor and Terror in the USSR, 1935–1941," *Journal of Social History* 24:3 (1991).

Tikhomirov, V. A. *Promkooperatsiia na sovremennom etape* (Moscow, 1931).

Timasheff, N. S. *The Great Retreat. The Growth and Decline of Communism in Russia* (New York, 1946).

Tolkovyi slovar' russkogo iazyka, ed. D. N. Ushakov, 4 vols. (Moscow, 1935–40).

Tomoff, Kiril. "People's Artist, Honored Figure: Official Identity and Divisions within the Soviet Music Profession. 1946–53," unpublished paper.

Trifonov, Iurii. *Dom na naberezhnoi*, in his *Moskovskie povesti* (Moscow, 1988).

Trinadtsatyi syezd RKP(b). Mai 1924 goda. Stenograficheskii otchet (Moscow, 1963).

Trotsky, Leon. *The Revolution Betrayed* (London, 1967; 1st pub. 1937).

Trud v SSSR. Statisticheskii spravochnik (Moscow, 1936).

Trud v SSSR. Statisticheskii spravochnik (Moscow, 1968).

Tucker, Robert C. *Stalin in Power. The Revolution from Above, 1928–1941* (New York, 1990).

Tucker, Robert C., and Stephen F. Cohen, eds. *The Great Purge Trial* (New York, 1965).

Tuominen, Arvo. *The Bells of the Kremlin. An Experience in Communism*, ed. Piltti Heiskanen, trans. Lily Leino (Hanover and London, 1983).

Tvardovskii, Aleksandr. *Vasilii Terkin, poema. Terkin na tom svete, poema. Stikhi raznykh let* (Moscow, 1995).

Tvardovskii, Ivan. "Stranitsy perezhitogo," *Iunost'*, 1988 no. 3.

Ulam, Adam B. *Stalin. The Man and his Era* (New York, 1973).

Upadochnoe nastroenie sredi molodezhi: Eseninshchina (Moscow, 1927).

Urlanis, V. Ts. *Rozhdaemost' i prodolzhitel'nost' zhizni v SSSR* (Moscow, 1963).

Urussowa, Janina. "'Seht die Stadt, die leuchtet': zur Evolution der Stadtgestalt in den sowjetischen Filmen der 20er und 30er Jahre," paper delivered at University of Tübingen, 6 May 1997.

Vaksberg, Arkadi. *Hotel Lux. Les partis frères au service de l'Internationale communiste*, trans. Olivier Simon (Paris, 1993).

———. *The Prosecutor and the Prey. Vyshinsky and the 1930s Moscow Show Trials*, trans. Jan Butler (London, 1990).

Van Geldern, James. "The Centre and Periphery: Cultural and Social Geography in the Mass Culture of the 1930s." in Stephen White, ed., *New Directions in Soviet History* (Cambridge, 1992).

Van Geldern, James and Richard Stites, eds. *Mass Culture in Soviet Russia. Tales, Poems, Songs, Movies, Plays and Folklore 1917–1953* (Bloomington, 1995).

Verdery, Katherine. *National Ideology under Socialism. Identity and Cultural Politics in Ceausescu's Romania* (Berkeley, 1991).

Verner, Andrew M. "What's in a Name? Of Dog-Killers, Jews and Rasputin," *Slavic Review* 53:4 (1994).

Viola, Lynne. "The Peasant Nightmare: Visions of Apocalypse in the Soviet Countryside," *Journal of Modern History* 62:4 (1990).

———. *Peasant Rebels under Stalin. Collectivization and the Culture of Peasant Resistance* (New York, 1996).

Vodolagin, M. A. *Ocherki istorii Volgograda 1589–1967* (Moscow, 1968).

Volkogonov, Dmitri *Stalin. Triumph and Tragedy*, trans. Harold Shukman (Rocklin, CA, 1992).

Volkov, A. *A. M. Gor'kii i literaturnoe dvizhenie sovetskoi epokhi* (Moscow, 1958).

Voslensky, Michael. *Nomenklatura. The Soviet Ruling Class*, trans. Eric Mosbacher (New York, 1984).

Vsesoiuznaia perepis' naseleniia 1937 g. Kratkie itogi (Moscow, 1991).

Vsesoiuznaia perepis' naseleniia 1939 g. Osnovnye itogi (Moscow, 1992).

Vsesoiuznoe soveshchanie zhen khoziaistvennikov i inzhenerno- tekhnicheskikh rabotnikov tiazheloi promyshlennosti. Stenograficheskii otchet (Moscow, 1936).

Vtoraia sessiia Vserossiiskogo Tsentral'nogo Ispolnitel'nogo Komiteta XVI sozyva, 1–9 fevralia 1936 g. Stenograficheskii otchet (Moscow, 1936).

XVII syezd V. K. P. (b). 20 ianv. — 10 fev. 1934 g. Stenograficheskii otchet (Moscow, 1934).

Weinberg, Robert. "Purge and Politics in the Periphery: Birobidzhan in 1937," *Slavic Review* 52: 1 (1993).

Werth, Nicolas. *Etre communiste en URSS* (Paris, 1981).

Widdis, Emma. "Decentring Cultural Revolution in the Cinema of the First Five-Year Plan," paper presented at annual meeting of AAASS, Seattle, November 1997.

Witkin, Zara. *An American Engineer in Stalin's Russia. The Memoirs of Zara Witkin, 1932–1934*, ed. Michael Gelb (Berkeley, 1991).

Yang, Anand A. "A Conversation of Rumors: The Language of Popular Mentalités in 19th-Century Colonial India," *Journal of Social History* 21 (Spring 1987).

Zemskov, V. N. "Sud'ba 'kulatskoi ssylki' (1930–1954), *Otechestvennaia istoriia*, 1994 no. 1.

Zhenshchina—bol'shaia sila. Severnoe kraevoe soveshchanie zhen stakhanovtsev, Arkhangel'sk 1936 (Arkhangelsk, 1936).

Zhenshchiny i deti v SSSR. Statisticheskii sbornik (Moscow, 1969).

Zhenskaia sud'ba v Rossii. Dokumenty i vospominaniia, ed. B. S. Ilizarova with preface by T. M. Goriaeva (Moscow, 1994).

Zinoviev, Aleksandr. *Homo Sovieticus*, trans. Charles Janson (Boston, 1985).

———. *The Radiant Future*, trans. Gordon Clough (New York, 1980).

Zoshchenko, Mikh. *Rasskazy, fel'etony, povesti* (Moscow, 1958).

Index